T0406527

Black British Postcolonial Feminist Ways of Seeing Human Rights

Pamela Odih

Black British Postcolonial Feminist Ways of Seeing Human Rights

palgrave
macmillan

Pamela Odih
Department of Sociology
Goldsmiths University of London
London, UK

ISBN 978-3-031-71876-2   ISBN 978-3-031-71877-9   (eBook)
https://doi.org/10.1007/978-3-031-71877-9

© The Editor(s) (if applicable) and The Author(s), under exclusive license to Springer Nature Switzerland AG 2024

This work is subject to copyright. All rights are solely and exclusively licensed by the Publisher, whether the whole or part of the material is concerned, specifically the rights of translation, reprinting, reuse of illustrations, recitation, broadcasting, reproduction on microfilms or in any other physical way, and transmission or information storage and retrieval, electronic adaptation, computer software, or by similar or dissimilar methodology now known or hereafter developed.
The use of general descriptive names, registered names, trademarks, service marks, etc. in this publication does not imply, even in the absence of a specific statement, that such names are exempt from the relevant protective laws and regulations and therefore free for general use. The publisher, the authors and the editors are safe to assume that the advice and information in this book are believed to be true and accurate at the date of publication. Neither the publisher nor the authors or the editors give a warranty, expressed or implied, with respect to the material contained herein or for any errors or omissions that may have been made. The publisher remains neutral with regard to jurisdictional claims in published maps and institutional affiliations.

Cover credit © caia image / Alamy Stock Photo

This Palgrave Macmillan imprint is published by the registered company Springer Nature Switzerland AG.
The registered company address is: Gewerbestrasse 11, 6330 Cham, Switzerland

If disposing of this product, please recycle the paper.

This book is dedicated, in loving memory, to the LGBT human rights and social justice advocate, James Pitt (2002–2023).

Preface

Fig. 1 O2 Academy Brixton, Stockwell Road, London SW9 9SL, December 2023 © Pamela Odih

O2 Academy Brixton is the official trading name of Academy Music Group (AMG) Limited, which is registered in England and Wales. AMG Ltd, operates in partnership with the United Kingdom subsidary of the O2 telecommunications brand. Built in 1929 as part of the Astoria Group's series of opulent variety theatres, the Brixton Academy venue is acclaimed for its architecturally enchanting Art Deco exterior design—majestic in its situation at 211 Stockwell Road London. The Astoria, with its Italian Renaissance style exterior alongside an impressionistic Italian garden auditorium, ceilinged with decorative twinkling stars, encased by "the grand half-cupola that domes the exterior entrance to the proscenium arch … that frames the stage" intended to be experienced as the "Mediterranean Night" in London; it was considered as "the jewel in the crown" of the capital city's theatre landscape (Parkes and Rafaeli 2014: 41). The Brixton Academy venue retains the Astoria splendour, its arena-style interior is resplendent, with a superb entrance hall and panoramic double stairway in the foyer, radiating visually through interconnecting strands of iconic Art Deco architecture. The central auditorium houses, "Europe's largest fixed stage", which is "framed by an elaborate proscenium arch" premised in its design on the Rialto Bridge, in Venice (AMG 2024). In conjunction with its resplendent 140 ft dome uniquely distinguishes O2 Academy Brixton. Visuality was an ostentatious feature of the Brixton Astoria as so it is with O2 Brixton Academy. Consequently, a focus on visibility in respect to this entertainment venue is not unusual. Less usual is its featuring in an empirical study of human rights, the night-time economy and the communicative action of Black music cultures. This book is an empirical examination of the West African diaspora, focussing on the applicability of the feminist antecedents of Afrobeat to the critical investigation of digitally policing human rights in Black British urban communities.

I was born in London, and spent my infant years, in the recently highly gentrified, Ferndale Road, Clapham. Consequently, my proximity to Brixton is sedimented, embodied and embolden into my habitus. Indeed, Brixton and its West African immigrant community never ceases to intrigue my Nigerian cultural heritage and its sensibility. Thus, news media and press releases relaying that a tragic incident had happened during the 15th December 2022 concert of the Nigerian Afrobeat artist, Asake at London's O2 Academy Brixton, was an occasion of genuine astonishment and concern.

PREFACE   ix

Initially, my intellectual response to the incident was incredulity and disappointment at the mass-media's rehash of monochrome folk devils and racialised moral panics. Some indication of the latter is evident in the following selection of the news media headlines: "Horror at O2 Academy Brixton as Victim Trampled in Crush 'Thought She Was Dead'" (Mirror 2022); "Asake 'devastated' after woman dies in crowd crush outside" (Evening Standard 2022). Usually a few innovatively crafted, expressive posts from my social media ameliorates my consternation at new media use of racialised clickbait headlines; but this time my intrigue abruptly evolved into scholastic curiosity. Such were the conditions that led to the following research question: Why do Black people pay more for their music? Why is the human right to security so inexpensively minimalised in Black music cultures? These questions provide the basis for a case study, in which the O2 Academy Brixton 15th December 2022 critical incident provides the aperture for a retrospective forensic sociological investigation into the significance of race and colonial digital capitalism in respect to the conditions that led up to the tragedy. In so doing the case study is arranged with regard to three principal areas of my conception of capitalistic digital colonialism. Firstly, my theoretical framing of the book's Black British postcolonial feminist lens through its interpolation with three traditions of Black feminist human rights activism. Secondly, the deployment of capitalistic digital media in the spectacular cultural commodification, image making of Black people and licencing of Black music entertainment. Thirdly, the integration of Smart City analytics, into the digital policing of the Black entertainment industry and the impact of this for existing racialised inequities in the actuarial calculations of insurance risk alongside the algorithmic capitalisation of the surveillance industry. Suffice to say, this book is about the cultural politics of a music venue, its Black music cultures of Afrobeat and the West African diaspora. But ultimately this book is about: How are we to be Black British London born, children from the African diaspora in a country that once colonised our maternal ancestors?

London, UK

Pamela Odih

REFERENCES

Academy Music Group (2024); *Venue Information, O2 Academy Brixton, Academy Music Group.* Available at: https://www.academymusicgroup.com/companyo2academybrixton/

Evening Standard (2022); *Asake 'Devastated' After Woman Dies in Crowd Crush Outside*, Evening Standard 17 December 2022. Available at: https://www.standard.co.uk/culture/music/o2-academy-brixton-metropolitan-police-sadiq-khan-asake-london-b1047945.html

Mirror (2022); *Horror at O2 Academy Brixton as Victim Trampled in Crush 'Thought She Was Dead'*, Mirror. Available at: https://www.mirror.co.uk/news/uk-news/horror-o2-academy-brixton-victim-28747444

Parkes, S., and Rafaeli, S. J., (2014); *Live at the Brixton Academy; A Riotous Life in the Music Business*, London: Serpent's Tail.

ACKNOWLEDGEMENTS

I would like to express a heartfelt thank you to my PhD supervisor Professor David Knights who continues to inspire my academic development. Professor Barbara Adam's prolific contribution to the study of time and society has been inspirational, and I would like to pay tribute to her work. Appreciation to the commissioner of this book, Nina Guttapalle *Editor* Gender Studies Palgrave Macmillan (an imprint of Springer Nature). My colleagues at Department of Sociology, Goldsmiths University of London have been supportive: Dr. Brian Alleyne, Prof. Vikki Bell, Prof. Vic Seidler and Prof. Bev Skeggs. Big thank you to my friends Andrea Reay and Ivalee Harris. Special heartfelt thank you to my friend and inspirational scholar Andy, with whom I share an enchantment for cultural delights. Genuine appreciation to Dame Prof. Mary Beard for being very kind. Heartfelt thank you to Professor Rosemary O'Kane, who after a long day's teaching filled my heart with joy, as she reminded me that I achieved, as an undergraduate, "impressive" grades in both Political Sociology and African Studies. Love and best wishes to my mother.

ABOUT THE BOOK

Communicative action is a human right as per the portents of the United Nations in its 1948 declaration, which recognises the human right to communication. Borne from the cultural political struggles against persistent coloniality in post-independence Nigeria, Afrobeat is communicative action. Afrobeat is the music of Nigerian dissent, that has become the music of an African diaspora. This book traces the feminine soul of Afrobeat from tumultuous colonial (her)stories through to the vibrant heterotopias of the urban spaces and times of Black British youths of African racial heritage. Unique in its way of seeing intergenerational decolonial diaspora studies through the refracted prism of Nigerian Afrobeat, this book's extensive empirical and theoretical basis is directed towards the question: How to be Black British born in a country that colonised our maternal ancestors?

CONTENTS

1 Introduction: Black British Postcolonial Feminist Diaspora Studies   1

2 Feminine Soul of Afrobeat   39

3 Anticolonial Feminist Human Rights   59

4 Communicative Human Rights and Colonial Digital Capitalism   121

5 Decolonial Feminism, Civil Rights Refutation of "Colonial Mentality"   153

6 Decolonial Intermediation in Crisis Heterotopic Space   181

7 Post-colonial Feminist, Interpolation   215

8 Post-colonial Challenges to the Spectacle of Black Music Culture   271

9 Conclusion: Feminine Soul of Black Critical Theory 299

References 311

Index 339

About the Author

Pamela Odih, BSoc.Sc., PhD is a widely admired academic and leading scholar. Her research specialises in Black British postcolonial diaspora studies of technologically mediated civic justice and human rights communicative action. Pamela's innovative interdisciplinary approach brings together her Keele University awarded BSoc.Sc in Sociology and Politics (with subsidiaries in Physics and American Studies) and her PhD in Management Studies awarded by Manchester University (Institute of Science and Technology). Proudly achieving teaching excellence Peake Award as a university lecturer, Pamela has been for over 20 years a dedicated and committed academic within the Sociology Department at Goldsmiths University of London.

Dr. Pamela Odih at the Royal Academy, Summer Exhibition Preview Party, Burlington House, Wednesday 12th June 2024, Photograph by ©Matt Chung.

CHAPTER 1

Introduction: Black British Postcolonial Feminist Diaspora Studies

"Not only will I stare. I want my look to change reality"—(bell hooks 1992:116). Reflecting upon such exquisite pronouncement calls forth a level of unbridled introjection. Memoirs visualising the spectacular accomplishments of African-American civil rights are plentiful in their exigency. In the spring of 2020, amidst the ravages of a global pandemic, Black American civil rights engendered Black Lives Matter (BLM), setting forth a resilient global protestation. For decades, conspicuous transatlantic civil rights movements had unwittingly preponderated the progression of their Black British counterparts. Consequently, the BLM promenade cascading through British cities, town centres, recreational public spaces were an intriguing inevitability. Witnessing, the BLM carnivalesque dais in Trafalgar Square and its arcadian corollary in London's Hyde Park provided empirical averment of a mirror effect esurient for an independent self-identity. One's thoughts, tentatively addle at a photographic scene, in which I capture a young protestor poignantly staring forefront a BLM gathering in Hyde Park, amidst the few lawfully conceded enclaves of the spring 2020 marches. Clenching aloft a studiously handcrafted placard featuring the iconic male portrait emblem of the transatlantic BLM, the young British born protestor also signified an imperative towards divergence. The cries of "No justice no peace" were emanating from an ethnically diverse generation eliding against the existence of a Britishness, persistently defined in terms of Whiteness. Indeed, it is the principal

© The Author(s), under exclusive license to Springer Nature Switzerland AG 2024
P. Odih, *Black British Postcolonial Feminist Ways of Seeing Human Rights*, https://doi.org/10.1007/978-3-031-71877-9_1

1

assertion of this book that the British BLM movement amplified a frustrating disenchantment with the status quo of identity politics and cultural representations of racialised, gendered ethnicity. Integral here is the positionality of the Black male, i.e., the refracted British born Other of White patriarchy straining in its broken spectacle. Why was this rainbow alliance of BLM protestors prepared to risk their own health amidst a virulent respiratory afflicting pandemic, to vociferate the name of a dead African-American man? Why were they so disassociated with Black British civil rights movements? Why had the Metropolitan Police Service become a source of such embitterment?

Several years later …

In the early hours of 16th December 2022 (04.57hrs), the Metropolitan Police published onto its News website a report of a critical incident at O2 Academy Brixton, London. The Metropolitan Police were called on Thursday 15th December 2022 at 21:35hrs to the O2 Academy Brixton, following information "that a large number of people were attempting to force entry to the venue" and that "Officers, London Ambulance Service (LAS) and London Fire Brigade attended and found a number of people with injuries believed to have been caused by crushing", furthermore "Eight people were taken by ambulance to hospital, four of whom remain in a critical condition. LAS treated two other less seriously injured people at the scene" (Metropolitan Police 2022). The situation was quickly apprehended as a critical incident and within 24hrs of its occurrence its severity was progressed into "urgent investigation" directed by detectives from Specialist Crime; with cordons remaining in place at the location as officers forensically investigated at the scene. The 16th December notice stated that "Nobody has been arrested". Notably in an update statement provided by Chief Superintendent Colin Wingrove, about the O2 Brixton Academy incident, attention was drawn to the avalanche of imagery that was circulating on social media. Specifically, it was stated:

> We are working incredibly closely with our partners and community members and would like to thank them for their support so far in the investigation and for people coming forward with information. We mentioned some of the images being circulated on social media. I can confirm that an incident involving one of our officers apparently seen to push a member of the public is currently under review by our Directorate of Professional Standards and another incident where a member of the public was seen to assault an officer has led to the arrest

of that member of the public. I can also confirm that there were no police dogs or dog handlers at the scene last night. I'd like to just make the point that London has a number of concerts and events that take place every day, every single week and every single year. These are run by event organisers and a police presence is not usual. We were called to the scene last night and we are working with our partners to establish the cause of the incident. We have set up an online page for the submission of photos and videos. There were 4,000 potential witnesses present at the time of this incident and we want to urge any members of the public with information to come forward. We need your information as we try to establish what happened as quickly as we can. (Metropolitan Police Service 2022a—16 December [16:46hrs GMT])

Digital image production, aggregation and circulation have been ascribed increasing significance to policing and particularly in respect to the data informational schema of digital policing adopted by the Metropolitan Police. Thus, it is unsurprising that digitally informationalised data would feature so integrally to the policing investigation of the 15th December 2022 O2 Academy Brixton tragedy. What is remarkable is the extent to which the digital policing strategy was increasingly undermined in its attempts to reach out into the local community; and this was glaringly obvious because, to my observation, it was based on a "pseudo-Gemeinschaft" as Goldman (1983: 97) describes in terms of commercialised leisure, the resurrection of "a sense of community by manufacturing an artificial commonality of interests around commercialized spectacles". While effective in terms of framing theoretically the extension of the commodity-form into leisure, Goldman's insufficient recognition of gender racialised structures in the amplification of the making of spectacular leisure communities, limits its application to my case study. Conversely, in my analysis of the 15th December 2022 O2 Academy Brixton tragedy, pseudo-Gemeinschaft conceptually refers to a commercially contrived simulacra of the "feminine soul" of the Afrobeat music community.

Communicative action is human dignity, it is a human right, as per the portents of the United Nations in its 1948 declaration, which recognises the human right to communication. Borne from the cultural political struggles against neocolonialism in post-independence Nigeria, Afrobeat is communicative action. Afrobeat is the music of Nigerian dissent, that has become the music of an African diaspora. This book traces the feminine soul of Afrobeat from tumultuous colonial (her)stories through to the vibrant heterotopias of the urban spaces and times of Black British youths of African racial heritage. In this respect this book is also about colonial digital capitalism as seen through the refracted prism of a Black British postcolonial feminist framework in respect to its ethics of social justice in human rights. Colonial digital capitalism refers to a conjuncture of digital primitive accumulation and colonialism motivated by a logic of capitalist accumulation, directed at the exploitative expropriation of black bodies, cultural identity and history. Original in its contribution to critical theory, in respect to my consistent refusal to anthropomorphise (e.g., Casalini 2021) and deterministically essentialise digital technology (e.g., Jefferson 2020) as being inherently racist. Colonial digital capitalism is a conjuncture of disciplinary sign-technologies (Odih 2010) eliding with digital primitive accumulation, in coexistence with the colonial expropriating logic of accumulation of digital capitalism. Unique in its way of seeing intergenerational decolonial diaspora studies through the refracted prism of Nigerian Afrobeat, this book's extensive empirical and theoretical basis is directed towards the question: *To what extent does pseudo-Gemeinschaft best explain the contribution of the culture industry to the disintegration of the feminine soul of Afrobeat?* And the sub-question: *How to be a Black London born, British citizen in a country that once colonised our maternal ancestors?* This book is an empirical examination of the West African diaspora, focussing on the culture industry, its commodification of the feminist ethics of justice antecedents of Afrobeat and its reappropriation as a basis for securing human rights and social justice for Black British urban communities.

Theoretical Framework—Post-colonial Feminist Critical Theory on Digital Capitalism

The theoretical framework is unusual in that it is a confluence of three (her)stories affirming their trajectories in the Nigerian derivation of Afrobeat. Anticolonial feminist protestations against the gender racialised impact of a regionally distinct period of colonisation feature alongside feminist resistant praxis directed at the obstinate legacy of colonialisation. Long before my interviews with these Nigerian feminist traditions, I was profoundly aware of the environmental crisis consequent of the oil industry in Nigeria. Habitus inculcates one's predisposition to capital of a cultural form; thus, explains how my childhood listening to stories of rivers in Nigeria that had catastrophically been contaminated by toxic agrochemical pollutants and oil extractive chemicals, became transposed into my Marxist ecofeminism and translated into my empirically based writing on water ecology and London's River Thames (Odih 2014). Additionally, my childhood wonderment of how it was that my maternal grandmother's red clay, built home in an Igbo community situated in Nigeria's Delta State, made solely from earth was more resilient, environmentally sustainable and ergonomic than the shiny new buildings in the city of Lagos. As these thoughts sedimented into my habitus through childhood stories of collapsing city dwelling and the chorus of protestors that braved to challenge the architects of such sites, it was evident that I subconsciously transposed this witnessing into my studies of London's urban ecology (2019a, 2019b). Indeed, in my study of colonial digital capitalism and aesthetic gentrification in the district of Shoreditch London, I explored Brick Lane and Fashion Street as aligned in respect to the financing of their initial establishment as having derived historically from the violent expropriation of Red Gold (copper) from West Africa. In my empirical study of the 2017 Grenfell Tower London fire tragedy my capital of a cultural form transposed through my habitus as a Black British born first-generation daughter of the Nigerian Biafra diaspora informed my unique conception of adsensory urban ecology. For in the still smouldering ruins and acrid smoke infused air of the Grenfell Tower carcass that I visited soon after the 14th June 2017 blaze, I could see the ruinous consequences of an exasperated intersecting disordering of urban ecology, ethnic diaspora displacements and capitalistic investment in propertied urban planning. Primarily informed by these empirical pursuits, I define my post-colonial feminism as a praxis borne from an intellectual resistance to the gender racialised colonial discrimination that continues to vitiate the life experiences of people from the Black British Nigerian diaspora. The Black British born, West African heritage post-coloniality of my perspective coupled with an integral focus on digital technologies mediating communicative human rights activism distinctively sets my perspectives of Black British feminism apart from salient predecessors e.g., Dadzie (2020) and Mirza (1997).

Integral to my Black British post-colonial feminist framework is a critical race theory borne from a close reading of *Grundrisse* in respect to communication and the costs of circulation. For, it is here that Karl Marx (1857/1973) details a direct correspondence between an increase in the extent to which capitalist production comes to depend on exchange value, hence on capital exchange, and a multiplication in the consequence of the physical conditions of exchange, the mechanism of transport and communication, in terms of the costs of circulation. Thus, in the creation and in the advancement of the physical conditions of exchange, "the annihilation of space by time – becomes as extraordinary necessity for it" (ibid.: 449). All labour required to propel the finished artefact into circulation—it is in economic circulation singularly when extant on the market—is from the viewpoint of the capitalist a barrier to be conquered. To the extent that circulation time is a downward moderation to labour ("an increase in necessary labour time = a decrease in surplus labour time = a decrease in surplus value") it is an impediment to the realisation of capital (ibid.: 464). Consequently,

> while capital must on one side strive to tear down every spatial barrier to intercourse, i.e., to exchange, and conquer the whole earth for its market, it strives on the other side to annihilate this space with time, i.e., to reduce to a minimum the time spent in motion from one place to another. (ibid.)

Historically capitalism has sought to overcome circulation time as an impediment to the productivity of labour through its creation of colonies for primary accumulative extraction. In its more advanced form capitalism, and its colonial variants, seeks extraordinarily extensive markets across which it circulates, "which forms the spatial orbit of its circulation"; thus, requiring a vaster "annihilation of space by time" (ibid.). It is this impetus that makes the drive towards "the production of cheap means of communication and transport a condition for production based on capital, and promoted by it for that reason" (ibid.: 449). In its rapacious pursuit of inexpensive communication to transport capital in acutely time and space compressed condition, capitalism intensifies its exploitative primary accumulative extraction through colonialisation and colonial pursuits. Indeed, Marx recognised this when he writes about conditions impacting on the exchange-value of gold in the 1800, "when paper quite displaced gold in England" (ibid.: 794). In Capital Vol.1, Marx describes further how "the cheapness of the articles produced by machinery and the revolution in the means of transport and communication provide the weapons for the conquest of foreign markets" (ibid.: 579). Indeed, just as "the colonial system and the extension of the world market, both of which form part of the general conditions for the existence of the manufacturing period" so it is that capitalism's necessity for cheap communication and transportation systems so as to "annihilate" ever more the friction of space by time, relies again on the expansion of colonialism (ibid.: 474). Accepting this, it is my contention that cultural political campaigns within West Africa's copper rich "red gold coast" and across the West African diaspora, for communicative action to be recognised as a human right, constitute an attempt to reclaim this resource from a legacy of colonial capitalist exploitation. It is in this respect that this book identifies anticolonial, decolonial and postcolonial feminist antecedents to Afrobeat and explores their efficacy when mobilised in the affirmation of communicative action as a human right.

METHODOLOGICAL REFLECTIONS ON CLOSE CRITICAL READING

Cultural Studies 1983 is an edited volume of lectures delivered by Stuart Hall during the summer of 1983 at the University of Illinois at Urbana-Champaign in contribution to the teaching institute called "Marxism and the Interpretation of Culture: Limits, Frontiers, Boundaries" (Hall 2016). The lecture entitled, "The Formation of Cultural Studies" provides methodological insights relevant to approaching "as a political project" the analysis of contemporary capitalist culture. Particularly interesting is Hall's application of F.R. Leavis's methodologically informed technique of "close critical reading". In its intent on cultivating rigorous technical procedure in the analytic review of textual documents, close critical reading prescribes "that one cannot make interpretations or judgements about texts in vague and imprecise ways" (ibid.: 12). Meticulous consideration of meaning and value prerequisite, probing into "the language, the structure, or the thematic of the particular text" (ibid.). The making of general statements of meaning is antithetical to close critical reading, for the latter requires contextualising themes in respect to their local meaning within the text. One, is encouraged "to localise the qualities in the particular literary work as your critical judgement moves from one localised instance to another" (ibid.). Structuration operates here through a focus on how the text rationalises its objectives through its composition in language and configuration of factual material. In this sense, one ascribes a "mixture of close attention to the text and broad sensitivity to the ways language and feeling worked" (ibid.). In so doing, the analysis gains an effective position "to make judgements about the culture as a whole, and not just about a particular text" (ibid.: 12–13).

Advertising and Its Ideology, a book review by Stuart Hall, provides a close critical reading analysis of a text that in its interpellation of advertising ideology is imbricated in advertising ideology. In the Guardian newspaper review of Fred Inglis's *The Imagery of Power: A Critique of*

Advertising, Hall (1972) applies the literary criticism practice of F.R. Leavis, so as to achieve a close reading of the latter's indebtedness to the advertising ideology that is the focus of the book's critique. Guided by the close critical reading praxis, Hall eschews equivocal and doubtful review, favouring instead an evaluation within the language and thematic framework of the text. In so doing, Leavis's critique is deciphered in terms of its language composition, its cultural context and rationale of structure in its configuration of "advertising as a portent of the cultural decline and standardisation characteristic of mass culture" (ibid.). Localising the qualities of this characterisation of advertising, compels Hall to recognise Leavis's analysis, as having a pre-emptive self-awareness of advertising's "manipulative strategies" and in so doing encourage the author to steer a critical distance from advertising assigning "it to its position in the decay of standards implicit in industrial civilisation" (ibid.). Contiguous with this mode of review, Hall (ibid.) attempts "to localise the qualities in the particular literary work" as the "critical judgement moves from one localised instance to another" so as "to make judgements about the culture as a whole, and not just about a particular text" (Hall 2016: 12–13). Consequently, Hall (1972) appreciates Inglis's departure from a tradition of writing; away from a notion of cultural chaos amplified by advertising and towards a promotional confluence of cultural homogeneity: "In modern capitalist consumer economies. Its function is to enlarge consumption and maintain the system" (ibid.).

Close reading is contextual and Stuart Hall employs this to explore reflexivity in Inglis's account of critical distance in observing the continuous manipulative functions of advertising. For, as Hall observes "it performs a sort of ceaseless symbolic work on behalf of the system, linking, by means of its imagery and rhetoric 'the objects and services advertised with key social and personal values and symbols'". In the close reading of the structural composition of the book Hall discerns Inglis's reflexivity in recognising their cultural production as, with advertising, having a "relatively autonomous rhetoric and imagery" (ibid.). Hall in close reading situates the text within its economic context; and so evaluates the extent to which, Inglis reconciles the economics of advertising with the economics of writing about advertising ideology. Indeed, Hall observes Inglis's use of a language of "insistence" as a mechanism to interpolate the writing about and living within advertising ideology. Evidence of this proposition is provided in the following quotation extract of Hall's book review:

This insistence on the way advertising is 'locked into' the socio-economic system marks a decisive departure from the previous body of critical literature and turns a rather unsituated and a-historical 'cultural criticism' toward: a more charged area – the analysis of ideology – and of public legitimations. (ibid.)

Integral to the manufacture of public legitimation is the equation of advertising with economic progress. Thus, Hall in close reading explores critically the extent to which Inglis advances an evaluation of their academic text, outside of the economics of advertising text. Whereby, the latter can be constructed as e.g., the economics of a newspaper advertising classified. Evidence of this aspect of the close reading of the language of the text in respect to its similarity to advertising text is relatively apparent in the following extract: "The most original parts of the book, then are the chapter which attempts to unpack the ideology of the advertising industry including its treacherous rationalisation that advertising equals economic progress" (ibid.). Retaining a structuration in close reading Hall progresses from a localised emphasis into a wider synergistic connection of the cultural identity of the text to a broader focus on citizenship, nationalism and Britishness; and in so doing one gains a sense of reflexive interrelation between the authors and their writing of the text(s) within the context of an superstructural advertising ideology invoked to reproduce British capitalist nationalism. Evidence of this supposition derived from Hall's close reading is thus: "the second part of the chapter on 'The Economics of Advertising' where Mr Inglis makes a bold attempt to place his critique at the heart of an analysis of the British as a whole" (ibid.). Appreciating that, "This is no easy task, but it is a necessary one" stating further, "Mr Inglis admirably succeeds at least in 'marking out its main features'". Thus, provoking Hall to state: "Just here, cultural criticism as an 'innocent' practice ends, and the 'politics' of culture begins" (ibid.).

Axiomatic with close critical reading is the recognition of positionality; as is evident in postcolonial application of this technique. Arising as part consequence of recent intellectual developments in the close reading genre, postcolonial perspective renders integral the broader cultural interaction between text and context. This culturally sensitive reflexive writing practice, introduces into the formalist technical processes of close reading, the "discursive transgressiveness of strategies of critical reading" (McCaw 2011: 32). In this book's case study of the O2 Brixton Academy tragedy of 15th December 2022 the close reading's structuration is informed by decolonial diaspora studies. Issues of migration cultivate resonances between the text, its context and the journalistic writing. This is done through the interrogation of how the memory of the event is cultivated, shaped, archived and transmitted across government agencies as the situation enters into the *law-and-order-society*. By, tracing the texts' circulation through government agencies, and night-time economy regulation it is intended to highlight inconsistencies in the State's political economy of licencing regulation. Elsewhere, Maedza (2019) similarly applied close reading in the study of the "sometimes contradictory dynamics" evident in the total anti-apartheid cultural movement's attempt to isolate the South African government in all areas of international cooperation and in respect to "the use of art as a weapon for the struggle" (ibid.: 235). Maedza's application of close reading also contrasts in respect to its focus on Judith Butler's framework of performativity. It is through the empirical analysis of "performative discourse" that Maedza's work observes how the South African state constituted cultural production, and exercised "oversight over who had the right to engage in cultural production, where such production could occur and for whom such cultural production could be staged for and how" (ibid.: 252–253). Conversely a focus on close reading in respect to race relations within a racial equality enshrined in law thus requires an analysis, not of the phenomenology of a performativity of racial inequality, but rather a focus on social structure and as with this case study, a focus on racial inequality as materialising through contradiction in legislative regulation.

Decolonial diaspora studies perspective presupposes a direction of analysis with respect to agency and cultural identity. In the following case study analysis of the O2 Brixton Academy tragedy of December 2022, subjectivity in respect to cultural identity relates to my shared diaspora with that of the Nigerian Afrobeat music artist that was the headline performance. The complexity arising in this respect is merely one of sustaining investigatory critical distance with regard to cultural identity. The Nigerian writer Chigozie Obioma (2018) provides insights, in their close reading of two scribes involved in the translation into English of literatures written in diverse African languages. Obioma identifies strategies adopted by the scribes, so as to reconcile their ethnicity and cultural identity with the task of English translation. A first methodology is where the translator assumes the role of "witness" and ascribes the responsibility of conveying "exactly what was seen and heard with accurate precision; any addition or subtraction could violate the very place of a witness, and render him a collaborator" (ibid.: 246). The second methodology ascribes the translator with a collaborative role creatively interpretating sequences and scenes with the substitution of "sublime equivalences in English for untranslatable words" (ibid.). Obioma prefers the latter, as is evident in the following extract:

> Readers who can only read Fagunwa in English through the binoculars of Soyinka's translation will flow with the momentum that the author, then the translator creates. But readers who can read both the original and the translated text must decide to what extent their reading is helped – and to what degree it is hindered – by what is produced when writers translate writers. (ibid.)

With regard to my case study of the O2 Brixton Academy 2022 tragedy the possibilities of translation relate to diaspora and the cultural identity of the Afrobeat performance of the music artist Asake. In the absence of having ever been in proximity or present during this time, it is my Nigerian diaspora intuition that provides a prism through which the factual and the subjectively meaningful reports of the tragedy are deciphered, decoded and deduced.

Close reading is guided by a depth of analysis of language, its vocabulary, syntax structure and detailing through visualisation and or rhetorical devices, which contribute to the excavation of layers of meaning construction throughout the text (McConn 2018: 67). Close reading involves discovering the layers of salient meaning by meticulously attending to patterning through literary techniques such as "irony, metaphor, paradox and symbolism" (Hinchman and Moore 2013: 443). The text is ascribed a primacy in its analysis, whereby "The emphasis is on diligent attention to the text and nothing but the text as a self-contained entity; readers interpret meaning within the confines of what the text offers" (ibid.). In the proceeding case study of the O2 Brixton Academy December 2022 tragedy, the technique of close reading employed is partially informed by the following how-to-advice provided by Hinchman and Moore (ibid.: 444). Firstly, "Read and reread – Read for different purposes (gain an impression of the text's contents and location of information, analyze the text's message) and at different rates (fast, medium, slow)". Text-dependent close reading takes time to deliberate, probe and contemplate the meaning of individual words in their denotative display; alongside deciphering the connotations of words unfolding and developing into sentences, phrases and arguments. Secondly, "Annotate – Be an active reader. Take notes about remarkable passage elements, key factual information, and significant ideas in the text. Identify the most important words, phrases, sentences, or paragraphs" (ibid.). This feature of method requires attentiveness to performance of the text in respect to its public reception. Consideration is applied to rhetoric in respect to proportionality in the styling of individuals mentioned and discussed within the text—rhetorical figuration. Thirdly, "Summarize – Retell the passage according to its structure" (ibid.). Responsiveness here is ascribed to tracing also an interrelation of segments of the text across the complete text; i.e., a hermetic intrinsic analysis. Fourthly, "Self-explain – Figure out how ideas and information relate to one another. Ask and answer questions about the text" (ibid.). In this prescription, one may encounter a limitation of applying close reading in its literary formalist practice of intrinsic reading in isolation of extrinsic context. Conversely, in determining the relation of ideas and information in non-fiction, factual text one gains enhanced appreciation when focussing also on the interrelatedness of the text with respect to its formal communication with other texts e.g., licensing documents, interrelating with licensing law. Fifthly, "Determine the significance of what you notice – Figure out why certain ideas and information attract your attention" (ibid.). Subjectivity is integral to this technical feature of the close reading practice. Whereby, one is urged to recognise that the choices between themes, passages and words are mediated by a sentient being living in the world and to some extent cognitively constructed through the syntax and language of the text.

In an effort to theoretically triangulate (Denzin 1970) my developing methodological presupposition, I have explored tensions and fissures in the hermeticism of the close reading genre. Of initial interest are New Critical perspective and its shifts towards postmodernism; the synergistic critical approach and collaborative close reading practices. According to Lockett's (2010: 399) modernist perspective, close reading is a process that "enables an exploration of nuance and detail and their relations with functionality: from the surface textures, like choices of materials or diction, to the structure's large, interwoven connective aspects, stairwells or metaphors, that take us from one level to the next, literally or figuratively". It is Lockett's (ibid.) observation that the relativism, positionality and denial of truth that arise in the culture of postmodernism have directly impacted on "the practical benefits of close reading" (ibid.). In response they attempt to formulate and delineate "New Critical close reading techniques to support a claim for the synergistic approach" (ibid.: 400). With regard to the latter, New Critical approach in response to a perceived threat from a solipsistic postmodernism advances the pursuit of "organic unity within a text" and in so doing presents an inverse to the vogue, "of contemporary pedagogies that seek (or try to generate) connections between literature and a student's private life" (ibid.). Recognising the limitations of neglecting the co-dependence of the modernist and postmodernist close reading genres: "Modernist critical techniques can explore a work's soul; postmodernism can relate and share that soul with the diverse world outside the work" (ibid.: 402). Consequently, Lockett argues that the modernist and postmodernist genre of close reading are most relevant to contemporary analyses when they are brought together in "synergy". Whereby synergistic assembly "is a conception that echoes the human condition: our souls, though fostered within, are meaningless if we fail to share them with the world outside" (ibid.). In further response to the consequences of close reading in respect to a crisis of representation, consequent of the postmodernist paradigm, writers have also explored collaborative close reading, by which is meant a process of reading in collaboration with the text, line by line, in order to enable conflictual and questioning feedback as part of bringing the reader "into contact with powerful metaphors, intriguing ambiguities and nuances and questions" (ibid.), that sufficiently inform the complexity and toleration of a known, unknown. Suffice to say, this New Critical approach to close reading recognises text to be socio-culturally produced and inherently contextual. The single-mindedness of formalist process, in its determination to bracket-off social structural relations, is by necessity reductive in its pursuit. For, "Attempting to bracket off readers' (and the authors') thoughts, experiences, and lives is not only impossible ... but also brackets off the potentials of reading and writing, its complete definition, and its purpose" (Eppley 2019: 343).

Postcolonial close reading is using modernist paradigmatic universalising struggles to cohere the postmodern positionality which fragments and scatters (her/his)torical self-definition, dispersing personal identity into infinite multiples and contextualities. Postmodernist anti-essentialism casts aside decolonial diaspora studies for its essentialist Africanness and disrupts the Afrocentrists "heroic epic of cultural transmutation" (Van Binsbergen 2005: 29). Such austerity can seem a befitting response to unanimous Afrocentric writings pursing grand historicism in their autodidatic scholarship. But, in its vehement disregard of essentialism postmodern critique dismisses important testable truths of the Afrocentricism proposition. For it is a verifiable historical and contemporary truth that the African continent is integral to Western capitalism, its science, economics and civilisation. Few African scholars would be inclined to deny these affirmations of Afrocentricist social scientific perspective. Conversely, the distinctiveness of a universal African culture is a point of scholarly contention. The dilemma of appealing to a grand narrative purveying African identity, is its anti-historicism, for, it is necessary to appreciate that African ethnicity is traditionally tribal and its universalism owes more to the colonial language of race, rather than to the lived reality of fragmentation in and through local collective representations of Africanness (ibid.). Born in London, a child of first-generation Nigerian immigrants, I am the daughter of their Black British Biafra diaspora. Complexity of cultural identity is therefore integral to my heritage; and I delight in a positionality of being, which interpolates a far-reaching African ethnicity with the contextual lived experience of Black Britishness. Accepting this, the political culture of my postcolonial close reading exceeds beyond "ethnocentric textual comments produced in order to keep [the] North-South hegemony in place" (ibid.: 60); for, its structuration is critical in its analysis of "the parochial struggle over meaning and resources which make up the smaller, local universe, turning it into vital locality" (ibid.).

METHODOLOGICAL REFLECTIONS ON VISUALITY; INTRODUCING THE CASE STUDY ANALYSIS

In the early hours of 16th December 2022 (04.57hrs), the Metropolitan Police published onto its News website a report of the O2 Academy Brixton incident and featuring Commander Ade Adelekan (Met Police Gold Commander). Commencing with compassionate due diligence in the detailing of the critical incident, we are informed that the Metropolitan Police were called on Thursday, 15th December 2022, at 21:35hrs to the O2 Academy Brixton, following information "that a large number of people were attempting to force entry to the venue" and that "Officers, London Ambulance Service (LAS) and London Fire Brigade attended and found a number of people with injuries believed to have been caused by crushing", furthermore "Eight people were taken by ambulance to hospital, four of whom remain in a critical condition. LAS treated two other less seriously injured people at the scene" (Metropolitan Police Service 2022b). The situation was quickly apprehended as a critical incident and within 24hrs of its occurrence its severity enervated an "urgent investigation" directed by detectives from Specialist Crime, with cordons remaining in place at the location as officers forensically worked at the scene. And, it was stated that "Nobody has been arrested" (ibid.). In an update statement provided by Chief Superintendent Colin Wingrove on O2 Brixton Academy incident, attention was drawn to the avalanche of imagery of the critical incident scene that was circulating on social media. Specifically, it was stated:

> Firstly, I'd like to extend my thoughts to all those that have been affected by last night's incident and those that have been injured. Having seen some of the really upsetting images on social media our thoughts are with them ... We are also aware of a vast amount of footage on social media and of course this will be examined as part of the investigation along with the body worn video that officers have as well. (Metropolitan Police Service 2022a—16 December [16:46 GMT])

Digital image production, aggregation and circulation have been ascribed increasing significance to policing and particularly in respect to the data informational schema of digital policing adopted by the Metropolitan Police. In this analysis of Black music entertainment, risk and financialisation the visual image is conceived as an integral feature of the processes in which Black people pay more for their music. The following section provides indication of the logic that informs the structure of the analysis of the government documents, Metropolitan Police and other official documents examined as of the case study's forensic sociological investigation.

Visuality and Forensic Sociological Criminological Investigation

Visuality and the making visual are prominent features of the Metropolitan Police, in respect to the "digital policing" of the O2 Academy Brixton critical incident. According to mainstream visual studies, the term "visible" refers to that which is incidentally and/or prominently evident. As Wagner (2006: 55) states, "visible refers to physical-optical attributes of phenomena or materials, regardless of how interesting or meaningful they are to researchers or research subjects". Its relation to the term visual, in this theory, refers to the process of focussing on that which is visible, noticing and assessing. Thus, "visual, on the other hand, refers to an attribute, dimension or mode of sense perception, not to objects per se" (ibid.). Contiguous with this formulation of "visible data" is the concept of "visualised theory". Where, the latter refers to the systematic application of visual analysis technique so as to render knowable that which is being visualised. Accepting this, "the term 'visualise' or 'visualised' refers to neither objects nor direct perceptions, but to a mode, process or dimension of understanding, a strategy of comprehension or conceptualisation" (ibid.). The merit of distinguishing these three concepts is particularly evident when visualising the strategies of rendering the witness footage of the critical incident at the O2 Academy Brixton as evidence of a crime scene. Furthermore, the concept of visualisation is adept at directing attention to the framework of analysis that is applied, in this case study, to the digital policing blue print, broadcast media investigation and social media communications that were mobilised prior to and in the immediate aftermath of the 15th December 2022 critical incident. For it is my contention that the apparitions of the capitalist spectacle are rife throughout commercialised Black music cultures and this sets in place the preconditions for inscriptive advertising technologies to sensationalise the prospects of the artists in excess of material realities. It is the principal proposition of this case study that the capitalist spectacle was a precondition to the tragic incident; it was a ubiquitous feature of the promotional advertising for the Asake concert and perilously contributed to the condition in which the oversubscribed concert was inundated with ticket holding clients in excess of its hosting capacity. Thus, the concept of the "spectacle" provides for a boundary logic and rationale for the selection and collation of case studies artefacts.

The conception of the "spectacle" that guides the structure of this case study analysis is derived from Guy Debord's *La Société du Spectacle*, which was originally published 1967, and it is the translation by Ken Knabb (published in 2014) that is the foremost version read and referred to in this case study. Whereby, Debord (ibid.: 2) describes the spectacle as thus: "In societies where modern conditions of production prevail, life is presented as an immense accumulation of *spectacles*. Everything that was directly lived has receded into a representation". Guy Debord's *Comments on the Society of the Spectacle* was first published in 1988, and it is the translation by Malcom Imrie (published in 2014) which informs the principal features of the spectacle that direct the structuring of this case study. Of particular significance to the critical assemblage of investigatory materials is Debord's proposition: XXVIII detailed in *Comments on the Society of the Spectacle*, which commences as thus: "Networks of promotion/control slide imperceptibly into networks of surveillance/disinformation" (ibid.: 74). In this statement can be extrapolated contemporary features of advertising technology. For, the vitality of the spectacle relies upon subjects conspiring to invest professional practice into maintaining the "wellbeing" of the spectacle; advertising ingenuity encompasses aspects of professional life hitherto unconnected with publicising the "variously calculated future projections" of the capitalist regime of accumulation (ibid.). In proposition XXIX Debord provides insights into the networks of surveillance that emerge from these non-traditional sights of advertising presentation.

Whereby, as "A GENERAL working rule of the integrated spectacle, at least for those who manage its affairs, is that in this framework, everything which can be done, must be done" (ibid.: 79). Thus, surveillance technological innovation in its advertising guise is achieving unprecedented capital investment, such that, if the panoptic inveigle of the surveillance technology increased exponentiality with the glossal investment in its development, it would have devastating consequences for freedom and liberty.

Circumventing, the descent into a technological panoptic dystopia is the self-limiting ambition for conclusive control. In proposition XXX Debord argues that an obstruction to the intention of absolute surveillance is an inherent incapability of achieving a corresponding absolute comprehension of the corpus of data. As Debord expresses it, "The quantity of data demands constant summarising: much of it will be lost, and what remains is still too long to be read. Management of surveillance and manipulation is uncoordinated" (ibid.: 81). These limitations are compounded by the tendency for an extension of surveillance advertising into state and parastate echelons alongside the fervent struggles of existing private sector companies trading also in securing and investigation. As more areas of social life are subject to invasive surveillance and informationalised security activities the question becomes "Who is observing whom?". In the myriad of proliferating, automated surveillance interfaces the ultimate influence remains obscure; indeed, in the spectacle of surveillance technology "the ultimate aims can barely be suspected and almost never understood" (ibid.: 83). Attempting to resolve these problems with more advanced surveillance merely multiplies the information data point outlets, overwhelming an already indecipherable avalanche of data and escalating the propensity for system destabilising incomprehension. Thus, as Debord expresses it, "The reasonably well known fact that all information on whatever subject under observation may well be entirely imaginary, or seriously falsified, or very inadequately interpreted, complicates and undermines to a great degree the calculations of the inquisitors" (ibid.: 83–84). These conceptual insights when applied to my case study provide a means of structuring the literary analytics applied to the assemblage of surveillance technologies advertised by the Metropolitan Police, so as to enable the general public to provide witness statements and data; whereby, the conceptual analytics utilised are critically informed by a realisation of the fallibility of surveillance technology, as a consequence of their incessant inconceivable proliferation. Actors and networks of advertising surveillance technologies are mapped in terms of the structuration of the capitalist securities market economy, and both are conceived in terms of "domination's falling rate of profit" (ibid.: 84); by which is meant, a proliferation of personnel, labour and means so as to mirror the expansive demand for surveillance; the resulting situation, is one where "each means aspires, and labours, to become an end", consequently: "Surveillance spies on itself, and plots against itself" (ibid.).

There is a strong consensus in Debord's writing that in conjunction with the incessant proliferation of surveillance is occurring a loss of objective (mission creep) precipitated by a loss of focus as to whom the surveillance is directed. For if surveillance is an apparatus of the state mobilised to sustain the normative order against insurgence from oppositional ideologies the disaggregation of critical perspectives has disorientated the focus of surveillance. In this situation surveillance becomes obsessed with anticipating a decentralised potentially dissident present. As Debord expresses it, "Surveillance and intervention are thus rightly led by the present exigencies determining their terms of engagement to operate on the very terrain of this threat in order to combat it *in advance*" (ibid.). In this case study, the analysis is structured around the mobilisation of surveillance in respect to Black music cultures and the use of the spectacular surveillance data output to affirm discriminatory and prejudicial assumption, which sought to blame the Black community for an inadequate circumstance that was largely out of their control. Suffice, to say, "This is why surveillance has an interest in organising poles of negation itself, which it can instruct with more than the discredited means of the spectacle, so as to manipulate, not terrorists this time, but theories" (ibid.: 84–85). It is my contention that the theory to which the surveillance spectacle is increasingly obsessed with discrediting is that of the blameless, unmarked Black body. So as to advance this supposition, I have here and elsewhere developed the concept of adsensory inscriptive technologies. Whereby, adsensory refers to the body as subject and object of advertising inscriptive technologies integral to a biopolitics of marketised financialisation of health and wellbeing. Axiomatic to the study of the O2 Academy Brixton incident of 15th December 2022, is a critical examination into the colonial digital capitalism of the deployment of inscriptive technologies directed at discrediting the positive affirmation of the human rights of the public presentation of the Black body as innocuously ordinary.

Outline of Book Chapters

This book identifies the anticolonial, decolonial and post-colonial feminist antecedents of the West African music genre Afrobeat and examines the cultural political efficacy of mobilising these antecedents into campaigning for the communicative action of Afrobeat as a human right. Chapter 2 is entitled *Feminine Soul of Afrobeat*. This chapter provides a descriptive account of Fela Anikulapo-Kuti's pioneering of Afrobeat and his concert performances at the Brixton Academy London during the 1980s and provides some initial comparative insights with the performance of the Afrobeat artist Asake at the O2 Academy Brixton London in December 2022. Heteronormative hegemonic masculinity is challenged in the analysis. Indeed, an official news Update issued, on December 20th 2022 at 11:15 GMT, by the Metropolitan Police referred specifically to the fatality of Gaby Hutchinson using an indecorously irregular mistitle as thus "Man injured in O2 Brixton Academy incident dies" (MPS 2022b).

In January 2023 the British Broadcasting Corporation (BBC) newscast its File on 4 documentary entitled *Catastrophe at the Academy*. This chapter formulates an original post-colonial conception of astonishing spectacular news broadcasting in respect to a way of seeing the BBC Radio 4 programme's depiction of the 15th December 2022 crowd crush tragedy at the Asake Nigerian Afrobeat concert at the O2 Academy Brixton London, in which mother-of-two, 33-year-old Rebecca Ikumelo and security guard 23-year-old Gaby Hutchinson lost their lives.

Chapter 3 is entitled *Anticolonial Feminist Human Rights*. This chapter explores anticolonial feminism as one of the three feminist frameworks relevant to the antecedent communicative action of Afrobeat. Anticolonial feminism seeks to disconcert and apprehend gender-based manifestations of coloniality. It interrogates the power knowledge configurations and historical specificity of gender coloniality in operation as part of the production and validation of colonial governance (Álvarez 2022). As private selves in public spaces, its direct-action activism "directly confronts the state through public space and challenges it through anticolonial resistance" (ibid.: 182). Chapter 3 explores the antecedents of the human rights activism of Fela Anikulapo-Kuti's pioneering Afrobeat as manifest in the anticolonial activism of Olufunmilayo Ransome-Kuti. Principal to the critical aspects of anticolonial feminism explored include the development of activist praxis of direct intervention and disruption of colonial oppression and its gender dimensions. The chapter details the past and present of anticolonial in respect to the vehicle of Afrobeat and the feminist antecedent influences on its communicative action. Anticolonial feminism, counterpropositions in public space, and does so by interrupting the ideological (mis)tellings of entitlement to colonised land. Mobilising native activities, deployed to counter-position colonised public space e.g., art and music festival situationism, these feminists generate "hacks of masculinist, hegemonic and colonial modernity" (Engelmann 2022: 34). Integral to this approach is a disquiet with the combined effect of the rationalisation of colonial power through Eurocentric Western colonial systems of knowledge, immersed and productive of universal truth claims and dichotomous oppositional antinomies, which eternally position Africa as the lesser aspect of the simplistic binary. Colonial binary approximations of culture and society are used to rationalise the enactment of economic practices and institutions that reproduce racialised gendered inequitable relationships as and between colonised people. These practices include the use of taxation to segregate along axes of ethnic and gender dimensions the control and exploitation of the colonised. Similar practices include the privatisation of land and the enforcement of copyright law, a colonial logic "that has been implemented by (settler) colonial governments around the world to appropriate Indigenous lands" (Emard and Nelson 2021: 1048). Anticolonial feminists criticise these practices for operating through the reinforced ascription of patriarchy in terms of gender-based racialised hierarchies of differentiation. Chapter 3 concludes by exploring these features of anticolonial feminism in its application to a critical theory analysis of *Fela!* the musical. It does so in conjunction with an application of W.E.B. Du Bois's (1903) *Souls of Black Folk* chapter XIV entitled "Of the Sorrow Songs". Although writing primarily about African-American experience, there is potential in applying Du Bois's writing on American folk music to the native music traditions that have inspired West African Afrobeat. In a chapter entitled "Of One Spiritual Strivings" Du Bois describes the Black "son" (sic) as "born with a veil and gifted with second-sight in this American world, a world which yields him no true self-consciousness, but only lets him see himself through the revelation of the other world" (ibid.: 2). The veil signifies a blind, in converse to a privation of vision, it embroiders a visibility of one's Otherness in a world pervaded by hegemonic White ideology. The veil is a sense of seeing the world in respect to the distorted motivations of a dominant White ideological optic. It is a focal point of a common Black consciousness of the limits of meritocracy, expressed as thus " … and above all, from the sight of the Veil that hung between us and

Opportunity" (ibid.: 41). Evident in this conception is the realisation of one's being, in respect to hegemonic White ideology, as implied by, "the Veil of Race". Ascribed with agency the experiential existence of the veil, is at times as having been precipitated by cultural productions and education; but oftentimes as a result of "double consciousness". With regard to the former, he writes about creative inspiration emerging from describing defiance and lamenting in sorrow. As Du Bois (1903: 109) expresses it,

> Within and without the sombre veil of color vast social forces have been at work, – efforts for human betterment, movements toward disintegration and despair, tragedies and comedies in social and economic life, and a swaying and lifting and sinking of human hearts which have made this land a land of mingled sorrow and joy, of change and excitement and unrest.

While bestowed with the potentialities of transformational agency there are structural limitations to the ability of creative arts, music and education to enable the Black subject to transcend the barrier of the veil. As is expressed in the observation that, "The worlds within and without the Veil of Color are changing and changing rapidly, but not at the same rate, not in the same way; and this must produce a peculiar wrenching of the soul, a peculiar sense of doubt and bewilderment" (ibid.: 122). The resulting impact on Black subjectivity is defined in respect to a "double consciousness" in which there is a "sense of always looking at one's self through the eyes of others, of measuring one's soul by the tape of a world that looks on in amused contempt and pity" (ibid.: 2). Everyday existence for the African-American is described in Du Bois's erudite prose as beset by a "two-ness", in which they are, "an American a Negro; two souls, two thoughts, two unreconciled strivings, two warring ideals in one dark body, whose dogged strength alone keeps it from being torn asunder" (ibid.). The issue of transformative agency is quite obviously integral to the account Of Our Spiritual Strivings; and elsewhere in the chapter titled The Sorrow Songs. Indeed, in the latter Du Bois details a praxis of non-violent resistance articulated in the historically expressive African-American music traditions rooted in slavery. In developing this, he opens with the eloquent statement that, "the Negro folk-song – the rhythmic cry of the slave – stands to-day not simply as the sole American music, but as the most beautiful expression of human experience born this side the seas" (ibid.: 156). Cognisant of the potentiality for this music genre to present a challenge to race relations it is suggested that this has led to its neglect, misunderstanding and attempts at its depoliticisation through cultural

22   P. ODIH

appropriation. Du Bois was clearly dismayed by the use of imitation and the caricature of Black folk music, and he criticised these practices as having the conscious intention to belittle and suppress its political effectivity by polluting "the air with many debased melodies which vulgar ears scarce know from the real" (ibid.: 157). Nevertheless, despite these cynical colonising impediments the music thrives, "the true Negro folk song still lives in the hearts of those who have heard them truly sung and in the hearts of the Negro people" (ibid.). Developing the notion of thriving and the legacy of African-American music, the chapter titled The Sorrow Song identifies three stages through which the music has progressed while encountering formidable limits. The first represents cultural articulations of African music crafted with nostalgic melancholy and yet inspiriting reminiscence of a forcefully transported African diaspora. The second genre is described as Afro-American in respect to its stylistic content as a unique expression of the experiences of a community transitioning from racial segregation into civil rights. The third and a fourth genre refers to hybridity and the cross pollination of Black-American music with White American influences. It is Du Bois's observation that, "In these songs ... the slave spoke to the world. Such a message is naturally veiled and half articulate. Words and music have lost each other and new and cant phrases of a dimly understood theology have displaced the older sentiment" (ibid.: 159). Significantly, it is a recurring feature of The Sorrow Songs, that these "Negro folk" musical articulation although they may invariably be melancholy can through their consciousness raising and in respect to their critical lyrics, provide for conditions of transformative resistance and changes to conditions of racialised discrimination. This optimising in the "Negro folk" genre is expressed as thus,

> Through all the sorrow of the Sorrow Songs there breathes a hope – a faith in the ultimate justice of things. The minor cadences of despair change often to triumph and calm confidence. Sometimes it is faith in life, sometimes a faith in death, sometimes assurance of boundless justice in some fair world beyond. But whichever it is, the meaning is always clear: that sometime, somewhere, men will judge men by their souls and not by their skins. Is such a hope justified? Do the Sorrow Songs sing true? Du Bois (1903: 162)

It is my contention that the application of Du Bois's analysis of The Sorrow Songs has relevance to an anticolonial feminist account of Afrobeat as human rights-based communicative action. Firstly, the notion of double consciousness resonates with the experiences of people from the West African diaspora generation hence from British colonial rule and its corresponding legacy of "two-ness". In many respects, the historical basis of Afrobeat in terms of its anticolonial struggles, speaks truth to the contradictions of colonialism, and ascribes validity to being "gifted with second-sight" imbuing a counter-positionality to the distorted self-consciousness that is present to a Black indigenous people whose sense of belonging is defined in opposition to colonial Whiteness. Secondly, the analysis of the political engagement of Afrobeat with regard to the cultural-economy of British colonialism is further enlightened in respect to the genre's optimism in its ability to decipher the propagation of injustice and thus raise consciousness necessary for mobilising transformative resistance. In this respect the "Negro folk" music of Du Bois's analysis although rooted in African-American heritage and thus dissimilar from the folk traditions of British colonial Africa, nevertheless shares an antimodernist, anti-Western epistemologically incantation of optimism, which can be epitomised as thus, "If somewhere in this whirl and chaos of things there dwells Eternal Good, pitiful yet masterful, then anon in His good time America shall rend the Veil and the prisoned shall go free" (ibid.: 163). The freedom to which Du Bois refers while foremost and ultimately pertaining to liberation from the inhumanity of slavery also opines to the quest for the liberation of the enslaved soul, so that it can be free in its metaphysical spirit. "Free, free as the sunshine trickling down the morning into these high windows of mine, free as yonder fresh young voices welling up to me from the caverns of brick and mortar below – swelling with song, instinct with life, tremulous treble and darkening bass" (ibid.). Threading together anticolonial antecedents of Afrobeat and its commercial representation in *Fela!* the musical through the critical theory of W.E.B. Du Bois provides a basis of innovative and creative reflections on Afrobeat's present history.

Chapter 4 is entitled *Communicative Human Rights and Colonial Digital Capitalism*. Generally recognised in feminist culture and communication critical studies is the innovative contribution of the political scientist Jodi Dean. It is notable that the culture and communication feminism of Jodi Dean, in their pioneering formulation of "communicative capitalism", deprioritises and renders as largely irrespective the advertising medium of the communicative message. Such that the circulation of communication digitally and the circulation of messages through analogue channels are considered and treated as interchangeable features of communicative capitalism. Dean recognises that messages, in communicative capitalism "are contributions to circulating content – not actions to elicit responses" (ibid.: 58). Nevertheless, discounting the medium of the message within dot.com media communication is a consistent feature of Dean's *Communicative Capitalism: Circulation and the Foreclosure of Politics.* The unmitigated parturition of the message from its medium is disputed and in so doing bringing into question the assertion that, "Uncoupled from contexts of action and application – as on the Web or in print and broadcast media – the message is simply part of a circulating data stream" (ibid.). It is my contention that Dean's work has some anticolonial feminist application in terms of a challenge to the colonising features of digital communication. As is evident in the following expression which can be reframed as exhibiting anticolonial concern, "The value of any particular contribution is likewise inversely proportionate to the openness, inclusivity or extent of a circulating data stream – the more options or comments that are out there, the less of an impact any one given one might make" (ibid.). Chapter 4 develops the notion of communicative capitalism so as to formulate an anticolonial feminist conception of colonial digital capitalism. It is evident that Black female represent a disproportionally high cohort of users of social media, and it is plausible that they use these platforms as a basis of communicative discourse and activism. The principal objective of Chap. 4 is to critically interrogate the venture capitalist exploitation of the disproportionately high numbers of Black female users of social media. The latter claim is verified by Statista (2024) which documents that:

> As of 2022, the share of female internet users worldwide was 63 percent, six percent less than that of men. Gender disparity in internet usage was bigger in the Arab States and Africa, with around a ten percent difference Worldwide regions, like the Commonwealth of independent States and Europe showed a smaller gender gap.

One needs to overlayer this observation with recognition of the demographic profile of users distributed across social media. According to a recent Pew Research Center (2024) report titled, Americans' Social Media Use: (1) Adults under the age of 30 are more likely to use online social media platforms; (2) across social media platforms women outnumber men, except for Twitter (X); and (3) people of the racial category "Black" have a slightly higher usage rate of social media except Facebook, but more so for Twitter (X). A disconcerting feature of similar user profile analyses is the finding that Black females experience excessive levels of online abuse. Amnesty International's (2018) *Toxic Twitter* report on research carried out in 2018 looking into abuse perpetuated against female politicians and journalists on Twitter revealed that: "black women were disproportionately targeted, being 84% more likely than White women to be mentioned in abusive or problematic tweets" (Amnesty International 2020). Suffice to say, if one accepts the theory that the hyper-circulation of data-flows online are less about dialogue and more about para-social data-flows, then it is also evident that the capitalistic mass extraction of these involve the surveying, collection and processing of communications disproportionately by women, about women and often promoting harm to women. These issues of vulnerability to harm as a consequence of communicative action are addressed in Chap. 4. The overall aim of the chapter is to explore, through the use of anticolonial feminist frames, the extent to which the inflation and excessive supply of tickets for the case studied 15th December 2022 Asake concert at the O2 Academy Brixton was attributable to covetous and avaricious capitalistic promotional advertising exploitation of a largely Black female populated community of social media users.

Chapter 5 is entitled *Decolonial Feminism, Civil Rights Refutation of "Colonial Mentality"*. In my previous empirical studies of aesthetic gentrification and the 14th June 2017 Grenfell Tower fire tragedy my embodied cultural capital transposed through my habitus as a Black British London born first-generation daughter of the Nigerian Biafra diaspora informed my unique conception of *Adsensory Urban Ecology*. Whereby, in the smouldering ruins and acrid smoke infused air of the Grenfell Tower carcass that I visited soon after the 14th June 2017 blaze, I could see the ruinous consequences of the exasperated intersecting disordering of the urban ecology, ethnic diaspora displacements and capitalistic investment in propertied urban planning. Through these primary observations, intellectual pursuits and conversations with Nigerian feminist allies such as the legendry Afrobeat artist Sandra Izsadore I formulated a definition of decolonial feminism. Whereby, I define decolonial feminism as a praxis borne from resistance to the continued pervasion of gender racialised colonial discrimination in a regional context that has long since dismantled the perpetrating architecture of colonialism. Françoise Vergès (2021: 10) expresses poignantly what it means to be a decolonial feminist stating that it is an embodied experiential praxis, dissuaded by nihilistic "empty ideologies" because it is to affirm the fidelity of the material and cultural conditions of struggle of the women in the Global South who have preceded us in their fortitude and resistance. In this respect, decolonial feminism "means recognizing that the offensive against women that is now openly justified and acknowledged by state leaders is not simply an expression of a brazen, masculine dominance, but a manifestation of the destructive violence generated by capitalism" (ibid.). Consequently, decolonial feminism calls for the building of alliances across colonial difference; and in Black music cultures such vivacity nourished and inspirited the feminine soul of Afrobeat enabling its revolutionary mobilisation, by Fela Anikulapo-Kuti. This chapter identifies and explores four main areas of mobilisation which are specific pertinent to aspect of my wider case studied theme, in respect to an analysis of decolonial feminist influence on Afrobeat.

Chapter 6 is entitled *Decolonial Intermediation in Crisis Heterotopic Space.*

In November 2023 Brixton BID Team members (Managing Director and Cultural Manager) attended an inauguration of the Women's Night Safety Charter Summit, supported by Safer Business Network. The summit congregated together organisations across sectors proactive in their concern to protect the safety of women in the night-time economy. The initiative was original in its praxis of inviting members to the "men panel 'Manel'" intended to "open up the conversation between men around Violence Against Women & Girls" (VAWG) (Brixton BID 2024). It was reported that, "The panellists all agreed that men need to get involved in the conversation, get comfortable with feeling uncomfortable and support women and girls in ending violence". It is further reported that members resolved to speak up, "about the importance of education, behaviour change and calling out unacceptable behaviour from other men". Members were invited to join the Greater London Authority's (GLA) Women's Night Safety Charter (WNSC) Steering Group, to develop further the premises of the charter. Brixton BID are signatories of the charter and actively encourage colleagues and its BID members to also become signatories. Brixton BID's press releases on the subject of VAWG are informative of practice and immensely facilitative of an attempt to map together the scope of the institutional networks in London dedicated to VAWG. As an outcome of my mapping exercise, it is evident that the Brixton BID as signatories to WNSC are obligated to abide by the charter's pledges, which include a commitment to "design your public spaces and work places to make them safer for women at night". Writing in 2024, post a Mayoral election for London in which the incumbent retained their position and a UK general election in which Labour was also successful, one can safely assume that the over £100,000 invested in WNSC for the development of training events, the Good Night Out Campaign co-produced toolkit and knowledge exchange will achieve continued support (London Assembly 2023). While I am immensely in praise of the initiative, I think that its objectives would be more precise in terms of scope and application with the inclusion of a post-colonial insight into the intersectionality of diaspora, gender and the structuration of heterotopic space.

The Black British post-colonial feminist, West African diaspora perspective articulated thus far is in advocacy of decolonial strategy in respect to an inherent scepticism of liberal ideology pertaining to protect women's safety within the night-time economy, in respect to its promulgation of a "colour-blindness". Kimberlé Crenshaw (1988: 1282) identifies how "colourblind" antiracist agenda "tend to focus only on single issues. They are thus incapable of developing solutions to the compound marginalization of Black women victims, who yet again fall into the void between concerns about women's issues and concerns about racism". Furthermore, these mainstream analytical frameworks are often premised on the insistence of a post-racial society—as espoused by neoconservative scholars— which presumptively professes that "the extension of formal equality to all Americans regardless of color – has already been achieved" or when articulated by Critical Legal Studies (CLS) a question is postulated as to whether "civil rights struggle represents a long, steady march toward social transformation" (Crenshaw 1988: 1334). When considering the Women's Night Safety Charter (WNSC) by the London Assembly one perceives that there is a cognisance of the significance of commercial interests to the legal ideology and hegemony of liberal antiracist reform discourse. Nevertheless, there is a reticence to respond to what Crenshaw identifies as "the relationship of racism to hegemony" (ibid.). Decolonial feminist perspective is astute in its response, for it insists that the legacy of colonial racism is at the root of the disproportionate violence perpetrated against Black women. Consequently, the decolonial feminist analytical framework when applied to the critical analysis of the London Assembly's WNCS would result in the insistence that—as with the other colourblind legal ideology of similar charters, "must include race consciousness if the accepted objective is to transcend oppressive belief systems" (ibid.: 1336). Furthermore, there is a definitional contradiction evident in WNCS, which is frequently evident also in the critical legal scholar scripting of antidiscrimination goal "which attempts to distinguish equality as process from equality as result" (ibid.). In specific respect to WNCS the contradiction translates as thus: Is the goal to eradicate violence against women or is the goal to eradicate the conditions of the subjugation of women? It is clear to me that both critical legal scholarly questions pertain to a recognition of specifically pertinent intersections in respect to diaspora, racialised gender and space and their consequence in regard to protecting against VAWG. Crenshaw's (1991: 1296) conception of "intersectionality" defines "a way of framing the various interactions of race and gender in the context of violence against women of color". An often misconception of intersectionality is to proport the mapping of multiple intersecting axes each of similar weighting; the resulting effect of this excessive postmodern application is so unlimited in its multiplicities, that it depletes the transformative agency of political effectivity. Conversely, and more accurately Crenshaw is in actuality presenting "intersectionality as a way of mediating the tension between assertions of multiple identity and the ongoing necessity of group politics" (ibid.). Preeminent to the latter proposition is the emphasis on analysing the way in which power circulates and concentrates "around certain categories and is exercised against others" (ibid.). Intersectionality thus refers to the compounded intersecting axes of structured inequalities. Such an intellectual practice seeks to reveal the powerful relations through which groups are subordinated and others privileged by social structural configurations of power and inequality. The exercise's most compelling problem is not the mapping of intersections per se, "but rather the particular values attached to them and the way those values foster and create social hierarchies" (ibid.: 1297). In so doing it becomes apparent the way that the intersections of diaspora, race, gender and class come together in respect to the experiences of Black women and provides comprehensive coherence so as not to undermine the possibilities of organising communities of resistance around these intersections. Consequently, I concur with the assertion that "recognizing that identity politics takes place at the site where categories intersect thus seems more fruitful than challenging the possibility of talking about categories at all" (ibid.: 1299).

Davis (2003) as part of their exposé question "Are Prisons Obsolete?" provides insights relevant to the application of a decolonial feminist analysis of local community policing in respect to the human rights of Black women to have security in public recreational leisure spaces. The plenteously detailed insights about the gendering of capitalistic policing services, elucidated in Chap. 5 of this book, renders further luminosity to the extent to which policing directed at protecting the security of women in public space is perforated by oppressive patriarchal ideologies and practices perpetuating the gendering of recreational space. In August 2023 as part of its response to a Freedom of Information request for information pertaining to "Homicides/Murder Data from June 2022 to June 2023", the Metropolitan Police Service (2023i) posted a table entitled: "Count of Homicide Victims by Gender and Ethnicity Crime Recorded Between 01/06/2022 and 30/06/2023". Reading from the table it states: a grand total of 28 homicide victims were female, of which 10 White, 1 other, 7 Black, 9 Asian and 1 Not recorded/Unknown. It is conceivable that, given the timeframe, at least two of these homicide victims, by female gender, were as a result of the case studied tragedy at the O2 Academy Brixton. Local communities are understandably concerned about these rates of homicide, and policing services are duly responding to these concerns. However, it is evident, as detailed in Chap. 6, that the pervasive entrance into the local community policing complex of digital surveillance media linking local government, BIDs and commercial recreation is mutually symbiotic in their rendering of women of colour as objects and subjects of the hyper-technologically mediated "ethico-synoptic" (Odih 2019a) surveillance of their digital presence in cyberspace and their urban recreational leisure spaces. Ethico-synoptics amplify and exaggerate the scope for the criminalisation of an electronically mediated gaze, in which the many are watching the many. The transformation, through "ethico-synoptic" surveillance of citizens in public space, into surveillance capitalising sources of profit is an egregious form of human rights abnegating, morbidly inquisitive experimentation on civilian populations. Extensive corporate capitalist and local community investment in "ethico-synoptic" surveillance technology has significantly exaggerated the stakes for human rights activists such as Amnesty International and Big Brother Watch. This means that in an era in which biometrics are routinely producing false-positive results for the cohort Black female activists they must pose critical questions to their local communities as to the ethics and efficacy of actively participating as subjects and objects of the digital policing industry. Further dimensions of this observation pertain to the need to theorise racialised discrimination and regulation through the digital policing of Black music cultures. Some indication of the complexity of the problem is detailed in Chap. 6 in regard to social media content and the interventions of the Metropolitan Police Service. So as to avoid the reductive applications of panoptic surveillance, Chap. 6 advances the supposition that social media spaces are "heterotopic" and proceeds from this perspective to examine the actions of the Metropolitan Police Services in respect to its digital policing of Black music cultures in social media. Furthermore, the heterotopic prescience of social media digital space provides expansive scope for the application of colonial digital capitalist surveillance directed at the regulation of Black music cultures. In 2022 the Metropolitan Police Service posted its response to a FOI pertaining to Drill Music. In their published response, they admit to pre-empting the extraction from social media digital fields of communication, material pertaining to the Black music genre described as Drill Music. Whereby they state,

> The MPS has been monitoring violent content online, including videos on YouTube since September 2015. Calling out rival gangs online takes place regularly and social media provides the ability for gangs to maintain disputes and tensions, which can result in homicides, serious assaults involving knives and firearms ... Where officers believe online content will incite gang violence based on a range of information available to the police, we will refer that material to a social media company or streaming site seeking its removal for breaching the company's community guidelines. (Metropolitan Police Service 2022c)

In 2024, the Metropolitan Police Service (MPS) having received a Freedom of Information (FOI), replied to my request for access to information pertaining to: Number of Drill music videos, rap and its sub-genre music, Afrobeat and other Black music referred to other music platforms for removal/and number of removals granted 1st April 2019 to 31st March 2024 (broken down by year). Among the six social media platforms sampled, Twitter was surprisingly low with 7 referred and 0 removed; TikTok was second highest with 73 referred and 61 removed; and Instagram was highest with 92 referred and 66 removed. Indeed, for TikTok and Instagram the referred/removed trajectory is increasingly high, whereby in 2023-24 (April-March) the latter received 27 referred and 12 removed and the former 43 referred and 31 removed. The MPS reply stated that the referred/removed data was of "unique items of content". Additionally, it was detailed that,

> [MPS] do not record whether the content is specifically from the genre of drill music as this is a subjective description. However, all musical content referred/removed would likely be considered as being from the genres of drill/rap/hip-hop and other similar genres and sub-genres of music.

In this research correspondence with me, it was insisted that "The MPS does not request the removal of content from online platforms, the MPS refers breaches of community guidelines to the platforms and the platforms make a decision on whether the content is removed" (Metropolitan

Police Service 2024c). However, it is my contention that the MPS's focus on "unique items of content" somewhat distorts the huge amounts of referred/removed that actually are taking place, as is inferred by their statement that: "[it] may be lower than previously published figures which included details of multiple referrals for the same item of content" (ibid.). Technoculturists identify the propensity of the digital culture of social media to create unique content that proliferates into memes through a digitally emboldened amplification "fecundity and copy fidelity" (Shifman 2014:17). Given the sui generis of the digital culture of black music and the metamorphic diffusion through memetic repurposing of its memes, the removal of an item of unique content will in actuality involve hundreds of its propagated memes; and unquantifiable multitudes of simulacra. The problematic is therefore, is this actually take down? Later in 2024 I received a response to another of my FOIs in which I asked specifically about police decision-making to ban/remove from online streaming services, Afrobeat music songs. In response it was stated:

> The MPS do not ban or remove musical content from online streaming services, however if the content of a particular track was deemed to breach a platform's terms of service and might incite real world violence a referral would be made to the platform for their consideration for further action such as removal. We have made no referrals in regards to Afrobeat/Afrobeats to date. (Metropolitan Police Service 2024e)

The issue of concern is therefore more sophisticated than one conceptualised in terms of an erasure; rather it appears that a more complex disciplinary sign-technology is in operation. Whereby, black music cultures are particularly susceptible to a colonial digital capitalism online digital harvesting and are disproportionately an object of surveillance and punitive forms of intervention in terms of policing regulation. This makes it all the more curious why, as stated by the Metropolitan Police Service, there have been "no referrals" to date "in regards to Afrobeat/Afrobeats". Which makes me wonder what really is actually going on here; to what extent is this colonial digital capitalism working in terms of regulation or to what extent is it actually working in terms of commercial capitalism? Indeed, it is my contention that too often such actions by policing services are defined one-dimensionally in terms of the unidirectional surveillance by a digital policing panopticon. Conversely when discerning social media as a heterotopic space one gains insights into the contested interplay of disciplinary sign-technologies that are brought to bear in the colonial digital capitalist surveillance of Black music cultures. Such contemplations are pertinent when international circuits of capital accumulation within the live music industry present as a local incident of tragedy as was evident on 15th December 2022 when O2 Brixton Academy hosted a live music concert for the Nigerian Afrobeat artist, Asake.

Chapter 7 is entitled *Post-colonial Feminist Interpolation*. Bill Ashcroft's (2001) *Post-colonial Transformation* critically engages with Althusser's concept of interpellation in respect to limitations in the latter's formulation of agency. Principal to this critique is the notion that: "The colonial subject may engage imperial culture by using it as a communicative medium or consuming it as cultural capital" (ibid.: 45). Irrespective of the process of utilisation it is argued that engagement with imperial culture is intensely involved with consumption and production; the magnitude and force of this implication is such as to present the potentiality of transformation in the hegemony of the dominant culture itself. Analysing these happenings of autonomous agency has proved a complex endeavour for post-colonial feminism. As Ashcroft interjects, "The most contentious problems in post-colonial theory continue to be those hinging on the capacity of the colonized subject to intervene in colonial discourse to contest it, change it or generally make the voice of the colonized heard" (ibid.). For, post-colonial feminist, an epistemological jeopardy inherent in anticolonial and decolonial discourse theory is the formulation of "absolutes" and their depiction as an impervious hegemony accomplished in its totality effect of silencing resistance to colonialist delineation. Whereby, colonial theory in its perpetuation of absolutes presents the colonial discourse as capable of devouring, systematically unravelling and dismantling anticolonialist intransigence. Ironically if such a totality were to exist it would have subverted the flourishing of postcolonialism as an area of literary studies. Conversely Ashcroft enlists the following post-colonial supposition: "Gayatri Spivak's now notorious question – Can the subaltern speak?" (ibid.). In his envisaging of a porous hegemony, through its continuous embattlement with itself and Others, there emerges aspects of an appreciation that, "In practice, the cultures apparently 'silenced' by this process nevertheless continue to exist, and not only develop their own operations and revisions but develop coherent strategies of self-determination with the new discursive tools at their disposal" (ibid.). Chapter 7 presents an interview with Fela Anikulapo-Kuti and the later to be known as Prof. Emerita Jane Bryce, journalist and feminist of post-colonial theory. Principal objective of this chapter is to formulate Ashcroft's concept of "interpolation" as a counterpoint to Althusser's conception of "interpellation" and in so doing advance post-colonial feminist praxis as an efficacious interventionist strategy for securing the human right to communicative action. The chapter defines the principal distinction of post-colonial feminist activism as directed at challenging the singularity of the notion of black consciousness that is purported by decolonial praxis. Post-colonial feminism provocatively questions the resolute essentialism evident in the decolonial (her)story. Neither is post-colonialism a form of solipsism relativism, indeed the chapter advocates for its use as a transgressive and transformative feminist praxis.

Chapter 8 is entitled *Post-colonial Challenges to the Spectacle of Black Music Culture*. The appeal to the spectacle in respect to Black music cultures and its implications for the construction of risk evaluation requires an additionally nuanced appreciation of agency, subjectivity and identity. *Why, given our popular knowledge of algorithmic capitalism and the commercialisation of petitions would individuals invest their human capital in the production of capitalistic metrics for the survey industry?* Such insights are axiomatic to the methodological logic of the unstructured interview and hence I conducted qualitative interviews with several campaigners involved in the community-led online campaign entitled Save Brixton Academy. Central objective of the qualitative interviews was to focus on agency and so doing ascertain the subjective meaning making that motivated campaigning activities directed at reinstituting the O2 Academy Brixton as a music venue.

Chapters 3, 5 and 7 are all respectively dedicated to exploring empirically the feminist antecedents of Afrobeat by focusing on anticolonial, decolonial and post-colonial feminist human rights influences on the pioneering communicative justice of Fela Anikulapo-Kuti. Generational differences aside, anticolonial, decolonial and post-colonial feminism compare favourably with the human rights activist expression of Fela Anikulapo-Kuti at the zenith of the artist's 1980s international Afrobeat appeal. Celebrated for advancing post-independence, Black consciousness, in Nigeria and Africa as a whole, by the 1980s he was using his revolutionary imprint, to articulate the incredibility of the fiscal policy and neocolonial acquiescence made by the political regimes in his native country. In an atmosphere of political intimidation, injustice and oppression he became a rallying vocal point for disaffected Nigerians, especially the youth who were particularly affected by the dire economic outcome of the Structural Adjustment Programme (SAP) imposed in 1986 by the government of General Ibrahim Babangida. Nigeria had been a bona fide member of The

International Monetary Fund (IMF) a year after achieving independence from Britain in 1960. It was at this time rapidly transitioning from an agro-petrol economy into an oil-based economy with crude oil extraction constituting 80% of the Federal Government income and approximately 95% of its foreign exchange earnings (Isiani et al. 2021: 6). The economic crisis of the early 1980s, precipitated by a fall in the price of oil, had dramatically blighted the Nigerian economy. Accepting the IMF's SAP measures required the devaluation of the Naira, the liberalisation of imports, privatisation initiated by a large-scale retrenchment of the state from the public sector and the deregulation of public utilities, removal of agricultural subsidies, rationalisation of the civil service and extension of market-based capitalism to Nigeria's fiscal management. In return Nigeria qualified for the structurally adjusted loans that were required to service the outstanding loans which in their repayment were consuming a vast proportion of the country's foreign exchange earnings from the export of goods and services. Indeed, an immediately evident consequence of subsidy removal was the compounding of the existing incapacities of petroleum-led manufacturing and transportation. The government's inability to track wage rises against epidemic inflation rendered the civil service and public sector vulnerable to inexcusable corruption and bribery. Observing these crippling conditions of IMF imposed neoliberal marketisation, Fela Anikulapo-Kuti used Afrobeat to articulate resistance to the neocolonial conditions that were causing impoverishment and precipitating civil unrest protests. This book is original, firstly in its identification of anticolonial, decolonial and post-colonial human rights feminist antecedents to Fela Anikulapo-Kuti's pioneering of Afrobeat communicative justice. Uniquely informed by archive data in respect to the anticolonial feminism of Funmilayo Ransome-Kuti, primary sourced interviews with the decolonial Afrobeat feminist Sandra Izsadore and post-colonial African-Caribbean feminist Prof. Emerita Jane Bryce this book explores Afrobeat's communicative action as a human right. In many respects Chaps. 3, 5 and 7 are daringly transgressive in their supposition that core antecedents of Afrobeat are feminist. This book is original, secondly in respect to Chaps. 4, 6, 8 and 9 which variously examine the efficacy of mobilising the feminist human rights antecedents of Afrobeat to campaign for its communicative action as a human right. The originality here resides with an empirically informed case study of the O2 Brixton Academy tragedy that happened in December 2022, which led to the closure of the venue and precipitated a tremendous campaign in a bid to recognise a claim by the local community for the venue to be reopened as a human right!

REFERENCES

Álvarez, M., (2022); Monumentality and Anticolonial Resistance: Feminist Graffiti in Mexico, *Public Art Dialogue*, 12:2, 178–194, https://doi.org/10.1080/21502552.2022.2112349

Amnesty International (2018); *Toxic Twitter – A Toxic Place for Women*, Amnesty International. Available at: https://www.amnesty.org/en/latest/research/2018/03/online-violence-against-women-chapter-1-1/

Amnesty International (2020); *UK: Online Abuse Against Black Women MPs 'Chilling'*, Amnesty International. Available at: https://www.amnesty.org.uk/press-releases/uk-online-abuse-against-black-women-mps-chilling

Ashcroft, B., (2001); *Post-Colonial Transformation*, London: Routledge.

Binsbergen, W., Van (2005); 'An incomprehensible miracle' – Central African clerical intellectualism versus African historic religion: A close reading of Valentin Mudimbe's *Tales of Faith, Journal of African Cultural Studies*, 17:1, 11–65, DOI: https://doi.org/10.1080/0090988052000344638

Brixton BID (2024); *Women's Night Safety Summit; Safe Day and Night*, 01/09/24. Available at: https://brixtonbid.co.uk/womens-night-safety-summit/

Crenshaw, K. (1988). Race, Reform, and Retrenchment: Transformation and Legitimation in Antidiscrimination Law. *Harvard Law Review, 101*(7), 1331–1387. https://doi.org/10.2307/1341398

Crenshaw, K. (1991). Mapping the Margins: Intersectionality, Identity Politics, and Violence against Women of Color. *Stanford Law Review, 43*(6), 1241–1299. https://doi.org/10.2307/1229039

Casalini, G., (2021); Trans Ecologies of Resistance in Digital (after)Lives: **micha cárdenas'** *Sin Sol/No Sun, Media-N, The Journal of the New Media Caucus*, Fall 2021, volume 17, Issue 2, Pages 8-26.

Dadzie, S., (2020); *A Kick in the Belly, Women, Slavery and Resistance*, London and New York: Verso.

Davis, A., (2003); *Are Prisons Obsolete?* New York: Seven Stories Press

Debord, G., (1967/2014); *The Society of the Spectacle*, Trans. Knabb, K., Berkeley: Bureau of Public Secrets.

Debord, G., (1988/1990); *Comments on the Society of the Spectacle*, Trans. Imrie, M., London: Verso.

Denzin, N., (1970); *Research Act. A Theoretical Introduction to Sociological Methods*, New Brunswick and London: Aldine Transaction.

Du Bois, W. E. B., (1903/1994); *The Souls of Black Folk*, [unabridged text as first published by A.C. McClurg and Co., Chicago in 1903], USA: Dover Publications.

Emard, K., & Nelson, L. (2021). Geographies of global lifestyle migration: Towards an anticolonial approach. *Progress in Human Geography, 45*(5), 1040–1060. https://doi.org/10.1177/0309132520957723

Engelmann, S. (2022); Pollution is Colonialism; Feminist Queer Anticolonial Propositions for Hacking the Anthropocene: Archive and Feminist Queer. *The AAG Review of Books, 10*(4), 33–35. https://doi.org/10.1080/2325548X.2022.2114761

Eppley, K., (2019) Close reading: What is reading for?, *Curriculum Inquiry*, 49:3, 338–355, DOI: https://doi.org/10.1080/03626784.2019.1631701

Goldman, R. (1983). "We Make Weekends": Leisure and the Commodity Form. *Social Text, 8*, 84–103. https://doi.org/10.2307/466324

Hall, S., (1972); *Advertising and its Ideology*, Book Review: The Imagery of Power; a Critique of Advertising by Fried Inglis, The Guardian (London, Greater London, England), Thursday, July 20th, 1972. Available at: https://theguardian.newspapers.com/image/259859352

Hall, S., (2016); *Cultural Studies 1983*, Durham and London: Duke University Press.

Hinchman, K. A., and Moore, W. D., (2013); Close Reading: A Cautionary Interpretation. *Journal of Adolescent and Adult Literacy* 56 (6): 441–450. DOI: https://doi.org/10.1002/JAAL.163

Hooks, B., (1992); *Black Looks; Race and Representation*, Boston, MA: South End Press.

Isiani, M. C., Anthonia Obi-Ani, N., Obi-Ani, P., Chidume, C. G., & Okoye-Ugwu, S. (2021). Interrogating the International Monetary Fund (IMF) Policies in Nigeria, 1986–2018. *Cogent Arts & Humanities, 8*(1). https://doi.org/10.1080/23311983.2021.1932283

Jefferson, B., (2020); *Digitize and Punish; Racial Criminalization in the Digital Age*, London and Minneapolis: University of Minnesota Press.

Lockett, M. (2010). Close Reading: A Synergistic Approach to the (Post)Modern Divide. *Changing English, 17*(4), 399–409. https://doi.org/10.1080/1358684X.2010.528874

London Assembly (2023); More Needed to Keep Londoners Safe on Nights Out, London Assembly, London Assembly Press Release. Available at: https://www.london.gov.uk/who-we-are/what-london-assembly-does/london-assembly-press-releases/more-needed-keep-londoners-safe-nights-out

Maedza, P. (2019). *Sarafina!*: The children's revolution from Soweto to Broadway. *South African Theatre Journal, 32*(3), 235–256. https://doi.org/10.1080/10137548.2018.1544503

Marx, K., (1857/1973); *Grundrisse; Foundations of the Critique of Political Economy*, Trans. Nicolaus, M., London: Penguin Books in Association with New Left Reviews.

McConn, M., (2018) Close Reading of Literary Nonfiction: The Three-column Journal, The Clearing House: *A Journal of Educational Strategies*, Issues and Ideas, 91:2, 66–71, https://doi.org/10.1080/00098655.2017.1386001

Metropolitan Police (2022); *Four People Critical Following Incident in Brixton*, Metropolitan Police, News – 16 December 2022 [04:57 GMT]. Available at: Four_people_critical_following_incident_in_Brixton.pdf

Metropolitan Police (2022d); Privacy Notice, Metropolitan Police. Available at: https://www.met.police.uk/hyg/fpnm/privacy/

Metropolitan Police (2023); [Metropolitan Police] Statement of Witness, 14th April 2023. Available at: https://planning.lambeth.gov.uk/online-applications/licencingApplicationDetails.do?activeTab=documents&key Val=RT9HVVBO0BN00

Metropolitan Police Service (2022a); UPDATE: Statement from Chief Superintendent Colin Wingrove on O2 Brixton Academy Incident, Metropolitan Police, News - 16 December 2022 [16:46hrs GMT]). Available at: UPDATE__Statement_from_Chief_Superintendent_Colin_Wingrove_on_O2_Brixton_Academy_incident.pdf

Metropolitan Police Service (2022b); *Man Injured in O2 Brixton Academy Incident Dies in Hospital*, Update, December 20, 2022 11:15 GMT, Metropolitan Police. Available at: Man_injured_in_O2_Brixton_Academy_incident_dies_in_hospital.pdf

Metropolitan Police Service (2022c); Definitions of Terms of 'Drill Rap Music' Banned/Removed Online, 01 May 2022, Freedom of information request reference no: 01.FOI.22.023585, Metropolitan Police Service. Available at: https://www.met.police.uk/foi-ai/metropolitan-police/d/april-2022/definitions-of-terms-of-drill-rap-music-bannedremoved-online/

Metropolitan Police Service (2023i); Homicides/Murder Data from June 2022 to June 2023 – Att 1, Freedom of information request reference no: 01. FOI.23.031100, Metropolitan Police Service. Available at: https://www.met.police.uk/foi-ai/metropolitan-police/disclosure-2023/august-2023/homicides-murder-data-june2022-june2023/

Metropolitan Police Service (2024c); *Number of Drill music videos, rap and its sub-genre music, Afrobeat, and other Black music referred to other music platforms for removal/ and number of removals granted April 2019 to March 2024 (broken down by year)*, Freedom of Information Request Reference No: 01/FOI/24/039803/U, Metropolitan Police Service (MPS) response 12/09/2024.

Metropolitan Police Service (2024e); "I want to know how the police decide what Afrobeat music songs and videos should be banned/removed from online streaming services", 19/10/2024, Your ref: FOI-20105-24-0100-000; Our ref: 01/FOI/24/039772/E

McCaw, N., (2011) Close Reading, Writing and Culture, *New Writing*, 8:1, 25–34, DOI: https://doi.org/10.1080/14790726.2010.527349

Mirza, H., (1997); *Black British Feminism*, London and New York: Routledge.

Obioma, C., (2018); Teeth Marks: a Close Reading of the Translator's Dilemma, *Journal of the African literature Association*, 12:3, 241–249.

Odih, P., (2010); *Advertising and Cultural Politics in Global Times.* Farnham: Ashgate. ISBN 978-0-7546-7711-6

Odih, P., (2014): *Watersheds in Marxist Ecofeminism.* Newcastle upon Tyne: Cambridge Scholars Publishing. ISBN 978-1-4438-6602-6

Odih, P., (2019a); Adsensory Urban Ecology (Volume One). Newcastle upon Tyne: Cambridge Scholars Publishing. ISBN 9781527523173

Odih, P., (2019b); Adsensory Urban Ecology (Volume Two). Newcastle upon Tyne: Cambridge Scholars Publishing. ISBN 9781527524682

PEW (2024); Americans' Use of Social Media PEW Research Center. Available at: https://www.pewresearch.org/internet/2024/01/31/americans-social-media-use/

Shifman, L., (2014); *Memes in Digital Culture*, Cambridge, Massachusetts.

Statista (2024); Worldwide Internet User Demographics, (ed) Petrosyan, A., World Digital Population 2024, *Statista.* Available at: https://www.statista.com/statistics/617136/digital-population-worldwide/

Vergès, F., (2021); *A Decolonial Feminism*, Trans. Bohrer, A., London: Pluto Press.

Wagner, J., (2006) Visible materials, visualised theory and images of social research, *Visual Studies*, 21:01, 55–69, https://doi.org/10.1080/14725860600613238

CHAPTER 2

Feminine Soul of Afrobeat

O2 Academy Brixton, 211 Stockwell Road, London, SW9 9SL. © Photographer, Pamela Odih, December 2023

© The Author(s), under exclusive license to Springer Nature Switzerland AG 2024
P. Odih, *Black British Postcolonial Feminist Ways of Seeing Human Rights*, https://doi.org/10.1007/978-3-031-71877-9_2

40   P. ODIH

Nigeria's Fela Anikulapo-Kuti, pan-Africanist and humanitarian emperor of Afrobeat, on 24th April 1986, was granted freedom when Nigerian authorities ordered his release from conviction in 1984 to five years' imprisonment. The musician was detained by police authorities at Murtala Muhammed international airport in Lagos on 4th September 1984. Ominous in its theatrical enactment this arrest preceded a campaign of police harassment involving the siege of Kalakuta Republic studio residence; disqualification from candidacy in his country's presidential election and the traumatic death of his mother. Signposted, as events, in the evolution of his music from mainstream highlife to an Afrobeat's infusion of jazz into African Yoruba musicality, the troubled circumstances that preceded the arrest in 1984 witnessed the need of African peoples to undergo liberation from "colonial mentality". He was suspected of attempting to leave the country in possession of undeclared sterling withdrawn legitimately from his British bank account and according to the defendant he declared the currency to the authorities at the point of departure. On 7th September 1984, Fela Anikulapo-Kuti was charged by the Federal High Court with two counts of unlawfully exporting foreign currency (Amnesty International 1985). On 20th September 1984 his trial commenced before the Port Harcourt Zone of the Exchange Control (Anti-Sabotage) Tribunal. Suspicions concerning the veracity of the court's impartiality were compounded by the prominence of military assessors. The special tribunal judge, as is the order of the special tribunal, was assisted by military assessors appointed by the government of Major General Muhammadu Buhari to hear cases against those accused of contravening Nigeria's foreign exchange control regulations. The issue of contention being that there was insufficient explanation as to why the case had been transferred from the Federal High Court to the military assisted tribunal (ibid.). On 8th November 1984 the special tribunal convicted the musician for unlawfully exporting foreign currency—drawn from his own British bank account; sentencing him to five years' imprisonment. The circumstances surrounding Fela Anikulapo-Kuti's detention and conviction insinuated an underlying political motivation; prompting Amnesty International to initiate an investigation in the case. In January 1985, the human rights organisation published for general distribution its *Nigeria: The Case of Fela Anikulapo Kuti*. Amnesty International expressed immense concern about the reports circulating at the time that the trial was legally corrupt and morally unfair. Of particular concern was that the right to appeal had not been permitted; furthermore "the proceedings may have been prejudiced by statements alleged to have been made by government authorities, and defence witnesses were apparently detained in order to prevent them from giving evidence" (ibid.). These circumstances precipitated Amnesty International to question whether the prosecution had been efficacious in proving, incontrovertibly, that the defendant was guilty as charged. Furthermore, the irregularities of the case coupled with the prominence of the military's political bias against the musician led to Amnesty International declaring its concern that Fela Anikulapo-Kuti, "may be a prisoner of conscience imprisoned for his nonviolent political behaviour rather than for any criminal offence" (ibid.). Consequently, in January 1985 Amnesty International called upon the Nigerian government "either to ensure Fela Anikulapo-Kuti be re-tried within a reasonable time by a court which is in accordance with internationally accepted standards of fairness or that he be released" (ibid.).

Amnesty International in conjunction with the "Free Fela" campaign (led by Herbie Hancock etc.) aided in persuading the Nigerian authorities to release Fela Anikulapo-Kuti. On 24th April 1986 he was released from prison. It has been documented that the artist's release from incarceration was trailed by a statement from the presiding judge admitting to having conceded to pressure from the Nigerian regime to issue a disproportionately severe punishment (Felakuti.com 2024). Shortly, after being released the artist holds a press conference at the Shrine, here he declares an intention to resurrect the Movement of the People (MOP) political party and campaign for election as president of Nigeria. Promptly after the media storm, Fela Anikulapo-Kuti and Egypt 80 perform a revival concert in Lagos and then make tracks to embark on a tour of the United States (USA). In a spirit of appreciation, the artist participates in Amnesty International's 1986 *Conspiracy of Hope* concert tour of the USA. The music concert's 15th June 1986 setlist of artists performing live in Giants Stadium, East Rutherford New Jersey, is poignant for Fela Anikulapo-Kuti featuring alongside iconic music dignitaries like Carlos Santana and Miles Davis in conjunction with the internationally renowned feminist musicians Joni Mitchell, Joan Baez, the Black British LGBT feminist musician Joan Armatrading, with a cameo role ascribed to the actress and civil rights campaigner Pam Grier. The *Conspiracy of Hope* concert tour was a celebration of the 25th Anniversary of Amnesty International. Fela Anikulapo-Kuti being party to the commemoration introduced innumerable Americans to his human rights activism and crusade.

42 P. ODIH

Significant to this post-prison renascence chronology was the release in 1986 of albums bringing into prominence an edification for critically informed erudition. In the Wally Badarou produced studio album *Teacher Don't Teach Me Nonsense*, the gritty Yoruba infused highlife arrangements that give way to a pioneering Anglo-Nigerian Afrobeat in its elusively sympathetic use of "lush, almost orchestral, multi-layered horns and keyboards arrangements" (Felakuti.com 2024). Released on the independent American music label Knitting Factory Records, *Teacher Don't Teach Me Nonsense* provides for a poignant meticulous affiliation of transatlantic, African-American and Anglo-Nigerian ideological allies evident in the anti-colonial, decolonial and postcolonial trajectories of his oeuvre. Accordingly, one might ascertain, as an unsurprisingly logical development, the advent of Fela Anikulapo-Kuti at London's Brixton Academy in the winter of 1986. Indeed, in contrast to the "cultural circus" that reigned over him, the performance, "apart from a few references to 'animals in human skin'" was a "benign" and contemplative expression of a distinctly Anglo-Nigerian Afrobeat; with fewer "signs of anger and bitterness" (Fielder 1986). Unflinching, tenacious melodic syncopations appear to have been momentarily superseded by "moderately paced, meandering between gently insidious rhythms and surges of bright horn passes or anthem-like choruses" (ibid.). Also evident was, self-disciplined ensemble, requiring limited "circus rolling"; for "The atmosphere was relaxed and easy going with no one rushing to be heard", but also, "with none of the numbers clocking in under half an hour, stamina was as important as skills" (ibid.). The concert was wholly without the heightened Afrobeat verve; for "If the show lacked the kind of high-powered intensity that other Nigerian superstars achieve, it certainly had its moments" (ibid.). Poignant similarities connected this 1986 orchestration of Afrobeat with the 1983 preceding debut at Brixton Academy. Whereby music meejas corresponded anxiously about their concerns "that it was too slow-moving, too long, too laidback, too casual" and although not dissimilar from "the effervescent mixture of funk, jazz and Nigerian elements" that had pronounced Fela Anikulapo-Kuti's distinct Afrobeat sound, it was eerily conspicuous in its absence of racialised provocations suggesting "'racism is not sexualism'", that had irked feminist sensibilities (ibid.). Indeed, in an after-show interview when questioned about intersections of oppression in terms of gender and race, it is reported that the artist replied, "For me sex is between the individual. Racism is more of a new thing in the world, it's caused by slavery, colonialism. Racism has no place at all in this world for me" (ibid.). When the same journalist dared to antagonise the artist by conveying their disappointment in the 1983 Brixton Academy concert, averring that "It was too slow moving" that they "liked the records a lot better" the artist's response was emblematic of a deeper problematic and limitation in the White Western positionality on Black African human right and gender justice. Fela Anikulapo-Kuti is quoted to have replied, "Oh, I see. Anyway, that's cool ... because Europeans think that African music must be *fast*" (ibid.). Similar misapprehensions are evident in regard to the 1986 Brixton Academy concert and its music correspondences. Whereby, the delivery is described as "reliable rather than predictable" and the contribution of the female arts is occidentalised as thus, "So we got that delicious, beat accentuated slowness that is Fela's trademark with breakouts from the nine strong brass with Fela's deep vocals embellished and punctuated by the women singers. 'Confusion Breaks Bonds' is a mesh of plucked guitar and brass, the incessant song carried by the women" (Owen 1986). Also highlighting the slower pace of the 1986 Brixton Academy concert, the artist lead is described as thus, "Fela's role was to keep the circus rolling and he did it without having to crack the whip. If the show lacked the kind of high-powered intensity that other Nigerian superstars achieve, it certainly had its moments" (Fielder 1986). One such preforming trice appears to have been "the time he [Fela] decided to play a percussion solo while the rhythm guitarist had a quick work-out ... and the four girl singers got down on all fours and shimmied their bums at the audience" (ibid.). Why was this a moment? Surely it is apparent to observers of its distinct naissance, that Fela Anikulapo-Kuti's pioneering Afrobeat involved mobilising Nigerian femaleness so as to momentarily reconcile in music contentious antinomies that taunt the British settled Nigerian diaspora; How are we to be Black, British gendered subjects in a country that once colonised our Nigerian maternal ancestors?

CASE STUDY

We are shocked and saddened by the devastating incident in Brixton on Thursday night, and we are working to support our communities in the wake of this tragedy. The council is also fully playing its role in the investigations that are now underway. We are determined that answers must be found as to why these awful events occurred. (Lambeth.gov.uk 2022a)

On Thursday 15th December 2022 the O2 Academy Brixton, an iconic entertainment venue at 211 Stockwell Road, London SW9 9SL (Brixton North), hosted a live music concert by the Nigerian Afrobeat artist known as "Asake". The ticketed event "was known in advance to be sold out" (Lambeth.gov.uk 2022b). Early into the start of the event, at 21:04hrs, the Metropolitan Police were called to the venue "in response to reports of serious disorder presenting a clear threat to public safety" (ibid.). Reportedly, upon arrival, the police officers were immediately aware that crowd control outside the entrance doors was in disarray and "Crowds had forcibly breached the doors of the venue and were seen in large numbers to be forcing their way into the event"; the venue's on-duty security staff had apparently "completely lost control of the situation with regards to crowd control" (ibid.). Metropolitan Police evidence to Lambeth Council's Licensing Sub-Committee on Thursday 22nd December 2022 stated categorically that their "Officers witnessed scenes of large scale disorder while present at the venue" (ibid.). Surging crowds forcibly breaching the concert venue's entrance doors and precipitated an inevitable crush, as the ordinary interdependence of a crowd gave way to frenetic fear and chaotic disorderly behaviour. Individuals colliding against each other, fearfully pushing, descended rapidly into crowd crushes. The sheer force of people resulted in "numerous people being injured (many via crushing injuries) and 4 members of the public were taken to hospital in a critical condition. Subsequently, two people have since lost their life with one remaining in a critical condition" (ibid.). It is widely reported that the Rebecca Ikumelo (concert attendee) and Gaby Hutchinson (venue security operative) were the two initial fatalities. The Metropolitan Police announced soon after the 15th December 2022 incident its intention to launch a process of review of the O2 Academy Brixton's premises licence. To which the Lambeth Council responded in accordance with the 2003 Licensing Act, "We are asking for the interim step of immediate suspension of the licence while police conduct the initial stages of the investigation, in order to establish what failings have taken place and identify what needs to be done to prevent recurrence" (Lambeth.gov.uk 2022b).

Contextualising the Case Study—O2 Academy Brixton, Critical Incident 15th December 2022

In the early hours of 16th December 2022 (04.57hrs), the Metropolitan Police published onto its News website a report of the O2 Academy Brixton incident featuring Commander Ade Adelekan (Met Police Gold Commander). Commencing with compassionate due diligence in the detailing of the critical incident, we are informed that the Metropolitan Police were called on Thursday 15th December 2022 at 21:35hrs to the O2 Academy Brixton, following information "that a large number of people were attempting to force entry to the venue" and that "Officers, London Ambulance Service (LAS) and London Fire Brigade attended and found a number of people with injuries believed to have been caused by crushing", furthermore "Eight people were taken by ambulance to hospital, four of whom remain in a critical condition. LAS treated two other less seriously injured people at the scene" (Metropolitan Police 2022). The situation was quickly apprehended as a critical incident and within 24hrs of its occurrence its severity enervated an "urgent investigation" directed by detectives from Specialist Crime; with cordons remaining in place at the location as officers forensically worked at the scene. And, it was stated that "Nobody has been arrested" (ibid.). In an updated statement provided by Chief Superintendent Colin Wingrove on O2 Brixton Academy incident, attention was drawn to the avalanche of imagery of the critical incident scene that was circulating on social media. Specifically, it was stated:

> We are working incredibly closely with our partners and community members and would like to thank them for their support so far in the investigation and for people coming forward with information. We mentioned some of the images being circulated on social media. I can confirm that an incident involving one of our officers apparently seen to push a member of the public is currently under review by our Directorate of Professional Standards and another incident where a member of the public was seen to assault an officer has led to the arrest of that member of the public. I can also confirm that there were no police dogs or dog handlers at the scene last night. I'd like to just make the point that London has a number of concerts and events that take place every day, every single week and every single year. These are run by event organisers and a police presence is not usual. We were called to the scene last night and we are working with our partners to establish

the cause of the incident. We have set up an online page for the submission of photos and videos. There were 4,000 potential witnesses present at the time of this incident and we want to urge any members of the public with information to come forward. We need your information as we try to establish what happened as quickly as we can. (Metropolitan Police Service 2022a—16 December [16:46GMT])

In *Society of the Spectacle*, Guy Debord identifies the extension of the commodity-form into "The entire life of societies", as a modern precondition of the reign of capitalist production. In Western consumer capitalism this "announces itself as an immense accumulation of *spectacles*" into which "Everything that was directly lived has moved away into a representation" (1967/2014: 2). Detached from the longue durée of collective social solidarities these fragmenting images depicting in granular exactitude the medium of their representation coalesce into live streams of reformulated pseudo-worlds that are accessed via escalating commercial exchange. Consequently, "The specialization of images of the world has culminated in a world of autonomized images where even the deceivers are deceived" (ibid.). It is in this sense that the spectacle is defined as "a concrete inversion of life, an autonomous movement of the non-living" (ibid.). The spectacle presents simultaneously in these two opposing forms; for its centripetal inducement towards a unifying focal perspective "of all vision and all consciousness" is consequentially delineating every aspect of life so as to bring it together "into a new unity as a *separate pseudo-world*"—which is denoted in the "official language of universal separation" (ibid.). Accepting this, one might plausibly advance the proposition that these features of Western capitalist spectacle making are evident also in public sector, government funded broadcast media. I shall now explore this proposition in respect to the British Broadcasting Corporation (BBC) radio documentary investigation of the O2 Academy Brixton critical incident that is the focus of this case study.

BBC File on 4 Documentary on O2 Academy Brixton—Spectacle of Licencing Risk

On 18th January 2023, the day after its BBC Radio 4—File on 4 documentary, the BBC (2023a) published a lead article on the tragedy entitled: O2 Brixton Academy: *Crush Victim's Family Call For Answers.* The article commences with a tribute to the pleas for "answers" being made by the family of Ms. Ikumelo—one of the two fatally injured casualties of the 15th December 2022 critical incident at the O2 Academy Brixton Afrobeat Asake concert. Evidently, the article's main purpose is to provide a visual postscript to the series of remarkable disclosures, presented by the BBC File on 4 (2023b), in the radio documentary released on 17th January 2023. In this respect the article has relevance as part of the evolving criminal investigation role of the British Broadcasting Corporation (BBC) in amplifying the incident as a spectacle and the relation of the latter to the Metropolitan Police's use of broadcast news media in its digital policing strategy. Thus, it is significant that the article discloses the BBC as having accessed documents from Academy Music Group (AMG) detailing its management of security at its trading name venue, O2 Academy Brixton. In its evaluation of the documents the BBC reporters provide a categorical adjudication pertaining to their inferred discrepancy between AMG documented security management and its actual resourcing of security guards at its venues; for according to the BBC in the AMG documents it obtained, music events of the scale of the Asake concert require "up to 200+" security guards, but AMG had allegedly informed the BBC that "there were only 157 security staff" (BBC 2023a). Further detail about these security management documents is provided, whereby we are informed that their original purpose in 2021 was that of risk management; for they provide a risk assessment at AMG music events. As part of the risk assessment strategy "five risk levels" were formulated to manage the building entrance. Recognising that it is not my objective to discredit the veracity of the BBC documentary journalism elements of spectacle making feature prominently. For, "The spectacle is not a collection of images; it is a social relation between people that is mediated by images" (Debord 1967/2014: 2). While surfeit with imagery the spectacle is neither entirely image or "a mere visual excess produced by mass-media technologies" (ibid.).

Commercial mass-media aligns with the spectacle, but its production exceeds the confines of the advertising-led business modelling of privately owned media, as its endeavour to produce a "worldview" also overarches the objective reality of non-commercial media. Whereby, "In all of its particular manifestations – news, propaganda, advertising, entertainment – the spectacle is the model of the prevailing way of life" (ibid.: 3). Existing within the sphere of capitalist production, non-commercial media is incredible in other purposes than to be the omnipresent affirmation of the condition and ambitions of the existing system of capitalist production. Axiomatic to this is integration of non-commercial media into the

48   P. ODIH

"constant presence" of the spectacle is the mirroring of its sign-making with a political economy of the sign. In so doing, it assumes the linguistic cadence of spectacular sign-making, as Debord (ibid.) expresses it, "The language of the spectacle consists of signs of the dominant system of production – signs which are at the same time the ultimate end – products of that system". Indeed, the concept of the spectacle interrelates seemingly oppositional aspects of the BBC Radio 4—File on 4 documentary on the 15th December tragedy at O2 Academy Brixton. Whereby objectivity and factual enquiry anchor the BBC to a Charter of impartiality; but reconciled in versus with commercial media the BBC's role to independently map the historical moment translates as an exchange-market for the trading of moral indignation. Integrated as it is, within the core of spectacle sign-making apparatus the BBC Radio 4—File on 4 documentary presented spectacularly, "itself as a vast inaccessibly reality that can never be questioned". Its sole message is: "What appears is good; what is good appears" (ibid.: 4). As Britain's primary government-funded broadcast media, "The passive acceptance it demands is already effectively imposed by its monopoly of appearances, its manner of appearing without allowing any reply" (ibid.).

Axiomatic with the BBC's spectacular monopoly is its ascendency as the utmost raconteur of British history and the foremost broadcast media chronicler British national identity. In its development of the World Service, the chronological depiction of British cultural and ethnic diversity, broadcasted internationally has defined the charter and ambitions of the BBC. Universal histories of diverse nations and community involve the acceptance of the globally unified time of the capitalist economy; amenable to its spectacular abstraction; a "time cut up into equal abstract fragments" (ibid.: 79). According to Debord, "This unified irreversible time is the time of the global market, and thus also the time of the global spectacle" (ibid.: 79–80). It is my contention that it is the unified time of the capitalist spectacle, rather than nuanced contextual social time(s), that permeates and directs the BBC's conception of risk in respect to its BBC Radio 4—File on 4 documentary on the 15th December tragedy at O2 Academy Brixton. For, as Debord recognises, "The irreversible time of production is first of all the measure of commodities" (ibid.: 80). In the following analysis of several aspects of the BBC's documentary, I contend that the linear time of risk investigation that pervades the documentary, coupled a predilection towards clickbait journalism, contributes in the constitution of the tragedy as a spectacle. And, furthermore, this spectacular depiction of Black music has self-fulling consequences in terms of the actuarial risk calculation of its entertainment venues. For, as Debord recognises, "The time officially recognized throughout the world as the general time of society actually only reflects the specialized interests that constitute it, and thus is merely one particular type of time" (ibid.) i.e., in respect to the BBC documentary's risk assessment of the event, the time of global insurance markets.

Indeed, in its article entitled, *O2 Brixton Academy: Crush Victim Family Call for Answers*, the BBC make prominent their access to what they describe as: "The AMG risk document". The revelations consequent of the BBC's investigation of the document consistently infer a construction of risk and security premised on the linear time of global insurance markets. As it is evident in the following statement: "The document seen by the BBC, dating from 2021, appears to be AMG's risk assessment for music events at the Academy. It details five risk levels associated with entry to the building" (ibid.). Of particular significance is the BBC's verification, that in AMG's risk assessment of Black music events, rates these situations at a higher risk level, as according to the BBC: "Afrobeats and Dancehall gigs are classed as level five, the highest risk" (ibid.). Accompanying this risk level is a requirement for a higher calibre of security, which the BBC (ibid.) transcribe as thus from the AMG risk document: "the need for '40-80 high-caliber [sic] security' at level five events – although it doesn't make clear if this would be in addition to the 'up to 200+' guards" (ibid.). As obtained by the BBC, according to the AMG risk assessment document, characteristic features of an event deemed "level five" risk, include: "Fraudulent tickets – plus 'late arriving' and 'noncompliant' audiences" all of which "are listed as potential issues at level five events" which the document states "should be 'hard tickets' only" (ibid.). Evidence of a breach in this, and several other aspects of the AMG risk management strategy were revealed through the BBC's interviews with, "whistleblowers".

Issues of reliability and validity pertaining to this form of information source are blithely overlooked in the BBC's article; and thus, we as audience are presented with a series of anecdotal evidence of misconduct with regard to the security company and its staff. For example, the BBC article states: "BBC Radio 4 programme File on 4 which has been investigating the night of the crush, also spoke to a whistleblower – a security guard – who said there had not been enough security for the Asake show … Rohan, not his real name, was working on 15 December. He said there

50   P. ODIH

were only 110 staff on duty, when there should have been 190" (ibid.). This anecdotal and largely unsubstantiated statements are interlaced with more grounded factual evidence based on the reporters' direct communications with AMG, as in the following statement seeking to verify the whistleblower's statement: "AMG has told the BBC that 157 contracted security staff worked that night – but did not respond when asked about the risk document" (ibid.).

The BBC's investigation also revealed allegations of extortion in respect to the security staff operating at the entrance of the O2 Academy Brixton. According to a whistleblower reporting to the BBC (ibid.), "some security guards at the Brixton Academy – employed by the company he works for, AP Security – regularly took bribes to let in people without tickets, including on the night of the Asake show". According to the BBC's reporters the AP Security whistleblower disclosed that "members of his team would each allow 'a couple of hundred' extra people into venues in exchange for money. 'Some staff made £1,000 cash'" (ibid.). The BBC's article clearly revels in the subterfuge of the extortion as evident in the following transcription extracts derived from the reporters' interviews with the whistleblower:

> He described what happened on the night of the crush: 'when you let a few people in, they would text their friends, and they'll text their friends' … 'And the bouncers started being greedy, and it got out of hand. And people wanted to come in anyway, without a ticket' … 'You can train someone to the max, but when that happens in front of you, you actually stop … you freeze'. (ibid.)

In a rather sensational part of the BBC's reporting there includes declaration that the whistleblower "said he had also seen bribes being taken at a number of other venues, stadiums and festivals. The amount of money handed over depended on who was playing" (ibid.). A further, although less surprising, discovery by the BBC is pertaining to the circulation of counterfeit tickets. As the BBC describe in now customary sensational words: "The BBC has also spoken to someone who got into a gig with a fake ticket at the Brixton Academy earlier in December" (ibid.). It is a recurring disconcerting feature of the BBC's reporting that this accusation seems to be based on a disproportionately small self-selected individuals, but this flaw in the validity and reliability of the witnesses is insufficiently accounted for in the publication. Rather, it is evident that in the presentation of this finding in particular there is an attempt to visually exaggerate the extent to which the testament is representative; for example, in the bold large typeface of the sub-section entitled: "'We got in without real tickets'". Elsewhere, the sensational scope seems to be based on one customer's experience in which, he after arriving at O2 Academy Brixton with the intention of buying legitimate tickets to watch DJ Fred Again, according to the BBC reporters that interviewed him: "He said he asked a doorman where he would be able to buy a ticket and was told to go across the street to a cash machine, where someone selling tickets would meet him … After some haggling, and despite not trusting the tout" the interviewee said that he "handed over cash and was sent tickets on WhatsApp" (ibid.). According to the BBC reporter's account of the interview there was suggestion that the door security was complicit in ticket subterfuge and fraud in respect to the unauthorised selling of the counterfeit duplicate tickets.

These astonishing revelations were foremost in the BBC's investigatory role and focal to the making of the O2 Academy Brixton critical incident into a media spectacle. Whereby, it clearly yielded currency in terms of directing and attracting audience listening to the on-demand File on 4 programme and with the apparent intention of widening the audience for its current affairs documentary series hosted on its digital platforms. One might anticipate from this review of BBC's report that an answer to my case study research question as pertaining to the cost of security management in respect to Black music events i.e., Black people pay more for their music because of an expectation that Black music cultures require higher volume and calibre of security guard presence. While this is plausible, it is my assertation that the situation is more complex.

On 8th February 2023 the London Assembly published a press release entitled: "More needed to keep Londoners safe on nights out". The publication commences with some key findings of the BBC's File on 4 documentary. Significantly, the BBC's findings are presented uncritically as is evident in the following extract: "Following the Brixton Academy crowd crush on 15 December 2022, it was reported that some security guards regularly took bribes to let people in without tickets and that there were not enough security guards in place on the night of the tragedy" (London Assembly 2023). In its near verbatim acceptance of the BBC report, there is presumed legitimate evidence for the London Assembly to implore: "that the Mayor and London Boroughs should do more to make sure licensing conditions for night-time venues in London are enforced" (ibid.). Consequently, while recognising that "the Mayor is not the decision maker in licensing applications", the London Assembly insists in the press release that "given the convening role the Mayor can play, the Mayor should collaborate with London Boroughs and the existing work they are doing to keep an up-to-date register of all night-time venues, their capacities and licensing conditions" (ibid.). The inference that such measures were not ongoing is of lesser significance compared here to a focus on the extent to which the BBC's File on 4 documentary influenced the London Assembly's strategic response to the O2 Academy Brixton. For example, in its call for the Mayor of London to instruct London's Night Czar to coordinate a meeting, at City Hall, with all municipal stakeholders including the Metropolitan Police, local authorities and security, there is included direct reference to the BBC's bribery accusations. For it is stated that the purpose of the across agency conference meeting is "to discuss bribery allegations and what can be done to combat overcrowding in night-time venues" (ibid.).

In a contribution by Shaun Bailey (conservative member of the Assembly and unsuccessful in the 2021 Mayoral campaign) and immediately following the BBC's report references, it is stated that, "I am pleased that the London Assembly has approved my motion to call on her [the Night Czar] and the Mayor to work with all relevant parties to ensure best practice is followed, and to improve data sharing with boroughs so that licensing conditions can be more closely tracked" (ibid.). It is my contention that while not direct in its determination of the London Assembly's response, the BBC's documentary was so frequently cited that it can plausibly be identified as an informational basis for governmental decision-making. It is also my contention that the BBC's news media investigation and spectacular reporting of the O2 Academy Brixton critical incident beneficially, succeeded in spotlighting crucial health and safety inadequacies. Some support for this disputation is provided in Lambeth Council's 6th April 2023 news posting entitled, *Lambeth: Health and safety review into O2 Academy Brixton*. Whereby, Lambeth Council provided notice that it had instigated action under Regulation 3 and Schedule 1 of the Health and Safety (Enforcing Authority) Regulations 1998. One might question why the local authority had not instigated earlier the investigation, using its legal entitlement, as the enforcing authority, for health and safety in the O2 Academy Brixton premises. Could it have been that the BBC documentary's audience capture had elicited the public assurance, the local authority coveted so as to investigate a venue that is so integral to the minority ethnic communities of Brixton? The following statement, by Bayo Dosunmu (Lambeth Council's Chief Executive), provides insight into the plausibility of the afore stated conjecture: "I appreciate that the O2 Academy Brixton is an iconic and much-loved venue and the impact of the current closure will be felt keenly by many people in Brixton and further afield. However, we are acutely aware of our fundamental health and safety responsibility and that this consideration overrides all others" (ibid.).

TIMELY REFLECTIONS

On 17th April 2023, the Metropolitan Police submitted, to Lambeth Council, an Application for the Review of a Premises Licence or Club Premises Certificate under the Licensing Act 2003. The premises licence subject to review, was cited as Brixton Academy, located at: 211 Stockwell Road, London SW9 9SL. The Metropolitan Police acted as applicant in accordance with their statutory role as a responsible authority. The application of summary review related to the following principal licensing objectives: The prevention of crime and disorder; Public safety. The formally stated grounds for the review of licence are detailed as follows: "The MPS [Metropolitan Police Service] has lost confidence in the Premises Licence Holder. Regrettably, the agreed 'variation solution' suggested to the sub-committee at the review hearing on 16 January has not been successful in identifying the remedial measures which need to be in place before the Academy can safely re-open" (Metropolitan Police 2023). To appreciate the extraordinary precedence that had been established and the ramifications of these actions, it is necessary to briefly outline the aspects of the Licensing Act 2003 that were being enacted.

Section 52 of the Licensing Act 2003 makes provision for the "Determination of application for review", premised on the Section 51 "Application for review of premise licence" (Legislation Gov.UK 2003). Whereby the latter establishes requirements where a premises licence operates, for the relevant licensing authority, having received from a responsible authority, application for a review of the licence, must undertake procedures that invite representation and advertise the application.

So as to be clear as to the operational costs of an interim suspension of an entertainment venue's licence it is necessary to apprehend what a licence entails. The Licensing Act 2003 is an act approved by the Parliament of the United Kingdom. The act institutes an integrated scheme of regulation for licensing premises in respect to their provision of the sale and supply of alcohol, the provision of entertainment and late-night refreshment; and "about offences relating to alcohol and for connected purposes" (Legislation Gov.UK 2003). Thus, O2 Academy Brixton's premises licence authorises the venue to sell regulated alcohol, night-time refreshments and provide entertainment (including live music concerts and recorded music entertainment). O2 Academy Brixton had been issued its premises licence by London Borough of Lambeth, which acted as the relevant licensing authority for the purposes of the Summary Review proceedings. It is noted that: "Since 7 April 2010 the premises licence holder has been Academy Music Group Limited. Mr E.J. Hassan became the Designated Premises Supervisor on 14 April 2022" (Lambeth.gov.uk 2022c).

In accordance with the Licensing Act 2003, Section 53A, sub-section 2 London Borough of Lambeth, Lambeth Council as the principal Licensing Authority, on receipt of a Summary Review application is dutybound to hold a hearing within 48hrs, so as to ascertain the veracity of the complaint of alleged infringement of the Act's licensing objectives, which include "the prevention of crime and disorder" and to consider this in conjunction with "the licensing Authority's own statement of licensing" (Lambeth.gov.uk 2022d). The Licensing Authority's Sub-Committee meeting, instigated within 48hrs of the receipt of the Summary Review application, also decides whether interim measures should be put in place, pending the determination of the Summary Review of the premises licence. In further accordance with the Licensing Act 2003, Section 53A, sub-section 2 the licensing authority within 28 days of receipt of an application for Summary Review, must review the licence and make a determination as an outcome of that review.

The Metropolitan Police officers, having witnessed the conditions of the critical incident of 15th December 2022, it was perceived as a basis of their Summary Review application, made by the relevant responsible policing authority, that the O2 Academy Brixton is a premises "associated with serious crime or serious disorder (or both)" (ibid.). Requesting a Summary Review is formal process, which can only be instigated by the police when a premise is directly "associated with serious crime or serious disorder or both" (ibid.). It is stipulated under "notes for guidance" on the *Form for Applying for a Summary Licence Review*, that serious crime is defined in accordance with section 81 of the Regulation of Investigatory Powers Act 2000 and is taken to mean: "conduct that amounts to one or more criminal offences for which a person who has attained the age of eighteen and has no previous convictions could reasonably be expected to be sentenced to imprisonment for a term of three years or more; or conduct that amounts to one or more criminal offences and involves use of violence" (Lambeth.gov.uk 2022b). It is conceivable that because serious disorder is less defined in legislation it has been necessary to seek a senior officer's visual witness and opinion "that the premises in question are associated with serious crime, serious disorder or both" (ibid.). Thus, the Metropolitan Police's Summary Licence Review application (under section 53A of the Licensing Act 2003) was accompanied with "a certificate signed on 19 December 2022 by Superintendent Daniel Ivey in which he expressed his opinion that the premises is associated with serious crime and serious disorder" (Lambeth.gov.uk 2022c).

Stipulated in the 2003 Act, under sections 53A–53D of the Act, is the provision of interim measures that can be applied to a venue while it is under Summary Review; and allows interim conditions to be swiftly attached "to a premises licence, or order its interim suspension, pending the main review hearing which is fast-tracked and must take place within a prescribed 28 day timeframe" (ibid.). It was announced quickly that: "The main review hearing will take place on 16 January 2023" (ibid.). In the interim, the O2 Academy Brixton venue remained closed, while interim measures were put in place for suspending the licence, facilitating an in-depth review of the legal conditions necessitated to ensure that the venue meet public safety arrangements and other licensing objectives.

In conclusion, within my account of broadcast media and its representation of Black music cultures, I have explored the role of the British broadcast media in the making visual of the O2 Academy Brixton critical incident, as a spectacle; and the consequences of this for the venue's licence review and the insurantial evaluation of its risk assessment. Situating these processes macroscopically there is very limited contemporary precedence in identifying music with "a caring social order" directed toward human rights in respect to achieving a "communicative justice" via "experiential learning of caring togetherness" (Hamelink 2023:141). While the latter focus on *Communication and Human Rights* premises a devotedness to the inseparability of communicative justice it neglects the historic estrangement of women from the public/private dualism and the masculine objectivist rationalities through which the universal declarations of human rights is constructed. In the absence of a feminist ethics of justice mainstream accounts of communicative action insufficiently account for the specificity of human rights inequity precipitating from an intersectionality of race, gender class and colonialism. Conversely, the principal objective of the following chapters is to identify the anticolonial, decolonial and post-colonial feminist antecedents of Afrobeat and in so doing construct a feminist theoretical framework for the evaluation of Black music culture in terms of a human right to communicative action.

REFERENCES

Amnesty International (1985); *Nigeria: The Case of Fela Anikulapo Kuti*, Amnesty International, January 1, 1985, Index Number: AFR 44/002/1985. Available at: https://www.amnesty.org/en/documents/afr44/002/1985/en/

Amnesty International (1986); Conspiracy of Hope. 1986. Art for Amnesty. Available at: https://web.archive.org/web/20070928153159/http://www.artforamnesty.com/view_event.php?id=3

BBC (2023a); Brixton Academy Crush Victims' Families Still Seek Justice, BBC News. Available at: https://www.bbc.co.uk/news/uk-england-london-65900715

BBC (2023b); *Catastrophe at the Academy*, File on 4, BBC Radio 4. Available at: https://www.bbc.co.uk/programmes/m001h49y

Debord, G., (1967/2014); *Society of the Spectacle*, Trans. Knabb, K., Berkeley: Bureau of Public Secrets.

Felakuti.com (2024); Story:1986. Available at: https://felakuti.com/gb/story/1986

Fielder, H. (1986) "Fela Kuti: Brixton Academy, London". *Sounds*. Fela Kuti. Retrieved February 3, 2024, from http://www.rocksbackpages.com/Library/Article/fela-kuti-brixton-academy-london-2

Hamelink, C. (2023); *Communication and Human Rights; Towards Communicative Justice*, Cambridge: Polity Press.

Lambeth.gov.uk (2022a); *Statement: Brixton Academy O2 Incident and Review.* Lambeth News; News from Lambeth Council. Available at: https://love.lambeth.gov.uk/statement-brixton-academy-o2-incident-and-review/

Lambeth.gov.uk (2022b); Licensing Sub-Committee; Thursday 22 December 2022; Annex A, Protective Marking, Metropolitan Police, Total Policing; *Form for Applying for a Summary Licence Review Application for the Review of a Premises Licence Under Section 53A of the Licensing Act 2003.*

Lambeth.gov.uk (2022c); *Licensing Sub-Committee, Thursday 22 December 2022 at 10.00am*, Lambeth Council.

Lambeth.gov.uk (2022d); *Licensing Sub-Committee 22 December 2022; Item No:3a. Report title: Licensing Act 2003: Section 53A Expedited Review – Interim Steps Hearing – O2 Academy Brixton, 211 Stockwell Road London SW9 9SL.* Available at: https://moderngov.lambeth.gov.uk/documents/s142574/O2%20Academy%20Brixton%20211%20Stockwell%20Road%20London%20SW9%209SL.pdf

Legislation.Gov.UK (2003); *Licensing Act 2003, 2003.* Available at: https://www.legislation.gov.uk/ukpga/2003/17/contents

London Assembly (2023); More Needed to Keep Londoners Safe on Nights Out, London Assembly, London Assembly Press Release. Available at: https://www.london.gov.uk/who-we-are/what-london-assembly-does/london-assembly-press-releases/more-needed-keep-londoners-safe-nights-out

Metropolitan Police (2022); *Four People Critical Following Incident in Brixton*, Metropolitan Police, News – 16 December 2022 [04:57 GMT]. Available at: Four_people_critical_following_incident_in_Brixton.pdf

Metropolitan Police (2023); *Renewed Appeal for Witnesses and Footage of the Brixton Academy Fatal Crush Incident*, Metropolitan Police News. Available at: https://news.met.police.uk/news/renewed-appeal-for-witnesses-and-footage-of-the-brixton-academy-fatal-crush-incident-463706

Metropolitan Police Service (2022a); UPDATE: Statement from Chief Superintendent Colin Wingrove on O2 Brixton Academy Incident, Metropolitan Police, News - 16 December 2022 [16:46hrs GMT]). Available at: A - UPDATE__Statement_from_Chief_Superintendent_Colin_Wingrove_ on_O2_Brixton_Academy_incident.pdf

Metropolitan Police Service (2022b); *Man Injured in O2 Brixton Academy Incident Dies in Hospital*, Update, December 20, 2022 11:15 GMT, Metropolitan Police. Available at: Man_injured_in_O2_Brixton_Academy_ incident_dies_in_hospital.pdf

Owen, F. (1986) "Fela Kuti: Brixton Academy, London". *Melody Maker*. Fela Kuti. Retrieved February 4, 2024, from http://www.rocksbackpages.com/ Library/Article/fela-kuti-brixton-academy-london

CHAPTER 3

Anticolonial Feminist Human Rights

© The Author(s), under exclusive license to Springer Nature
Switzerland AG 2024
P. Odih, *Black British Postcolonial Feminist Ways of Seeing Human
Rights*, https://doi.org/10.1007/978-3-031-71877-9_3

59

National Theatre, *Fela*! © Monique Carboni Photographer, Licensed by National Theatre Archive, London

It is an unquestionable verity that the cultural political Afrobeat of Fela Anikulapo-Kuti constitutes an indispensable aspect of the Nigerian post-colonial imagination. Writers have variously described the lyrical content of the music as a praxis of oppositional post-coloniality. Pan-Africanism is the pronounced aegis into which the artist's Afrobeat is politically positioned. Although somewhat vague and inconsistent the ideological posture of anti-establishment, in the musical form of dissidence, stands out as a principal motivating force in the artist's insistence on exposing the political and cultural context of post-colonial Nigeria as repressive. Less evident, but similarly important to his oeuvre was the political influence of formidable Black feminist activists; foremost of which was his mother, Olufunmilayo Ransome-Kuti (1900–1978). She was an astounding feminist advocate for women's suffrage and an anti-imperialist activist for human rights. In this analysis of African feminism and the cultivation of the feminine soul of Afrobeat, her activism is defined as Nigerian "anticolonial" feminism. Whereby, she is acknowledged as challenging the gender-specific inequalities and disadvantages incipient of the British colonial governance in Nigeria. In accordance with the anticolonial tradition her feminist praxis centred the intersectionality of patriarchy with the contiguity between the racialised female body and colonised land. Opposition to her women's movement protestation and activism against the gender disproportionality of colonial municipal laws was tantamount to "assaults on their bodily integrity" (Castledine 2008: 61). Anticolonial feminism is justified not by incorporeal intellectualised deduction but by the corporeal veracities of the everyday existence of racialised gender difference (Vasudevan et al. 2023). Such body-land realities are transformative praxis repudiating the Western colonial bifurcations which deny the body's basis as "both a site and source of memory, knowledge, healing, and resistance, connected to humans and nonhumans through scales of connectivity" and in so doing disrupting "colonial logics" (ibid.: 1738). This disordering of the sovereign body encounters and disputes the linear epistemological and enlightened mediations of racial-colonial modernity. In so doing, anticolonial feminists bring to mind the violent actuality of colonial conquest in respect to the harms and violation perpetrated against women. As Ramírez and Adzich (2023: 1089) detail in their analysis of "anticolonial disruptions" in the situation of colonial commemoration, unchallenged racial-colonial modernity "not only erase or elide the violent histories of settler colonialism and racial capitalism, but also the ways that indigenous and Black women's bodies bear the violence of conquest". The following

62   P. ODIH

discussion brings together original documents from the National Archives with secondary sourced materials and feminist historians so as to explore the contemporary cultural political ramifications of the feminist anticolonial antecedents of Afrobeat.

Theorising the Musicality of Feminist Anticolonial Human Rights

In their bringing to light how racial-colonial modernist histories recount and reproduce imperialist fictions, anticolonial feminists cultivate space for "conceptions of the world [that] offer meaningful nonsovereign positions – which challenge modernity's assertion of sovereignty as land, nation, and state" (Walcott 2015: 189). With the transatlantic slave trade "as the beacon of the Enlightenment's dark excess"; imperialism and colonialism as "forged out of modernity's brutality" anticolonial feminism had a surfeit of examples to "constantly remind us of both the limits of European humanism and possibilities of living a human life" (ibid.: 194). Their voice as female activists in the Pan-Africanist civic sphere encountered the oppositional forces of patriarchy and the colonial exploitation of Africans. In their politics of racial-welfare focussing on the enactment of European-style legislation to improve the healthcare, utilities and educational amenities in the African colonies, anticolonial feminists resisted the limiting cultural traditions of patriarchy and worked towards the underlying nationalist imperative of independence. In so doing, anticolonial feminists ameliorated Pan-African intellectual elites who advanced the need "to forge new public spheres and networks of social welfare programs through social politics and other variants of the liberal democratic tradition" (Adejumobi 2003: 34). The colonial governance of Nigeria was predominantly concerned with securing and enforcing control. Negligible interest was bestowed to progressing public welfare reforms, relying instead on the "self-regulating markets" of compassionate philanthropy (ibid.). The presentiment of a racialised domination enforced through institutional segregation tracing the histographies of the entrenched tribal antipathies meant that "complex relationships forged with colonial administrators often engendered increased competition for resources and power" (ibid.). Negotiating between the institutional segregation of tribal communities and the patriarchal dimensions enacting claims to women's bodies, property and personhood, anticolonial feminism defended the political rights of women to universal suffrage. In so doing, they bring to prominence intersectionality in respect to the private life of public politics. Anticolonial feminists in their praxis acutely interrogate, challenge and encounter "patriarchal power in their daily negotiation and transformation of political space" (Moore 2020: 1306). Of particular focus has been a privation of women's status and power under the British colonial system's predilection for governing through "a bifurcation between civil and customary law" (Zambakari 2020: 866).

Presented with the fearsome power of the colonial municipality the colonised resourcefully mobilised a retort in customary law. Indeed, it has been observed that, "It was through customary law that the colonial state mediated its relationship with the mass of the local populace and provided a medium which allowed a conquered people to represent themselves to the state" (ibid.). Indeed, nationalist projects mobilising customary law, in reposit to the colonial municipality, intertwined into the traditional musicality of cultural display of female performance practices derived from precolonial histories, so as to "position women as bearers of tradition during colonial rule" (Hornabrook 2019: 193). In a cultural political "aesthetic that was responsive to colonialism" the festival traditions of cultural display centred the female as customarily empowered "music and dance custodians" of precolonial (his)tographies (ibid.: 206). Elsewhere, similarly eliding cultural-economy anticolonial feminist writers identify gender discrimination in the structures and systems of colonial governance. For instance, British colonial indirect rule in West Africa assembled a local governance via the monetised co-option and corroboration of native authority structures which unremorsefully replicated the gendered equites of traditional patrilineal gender hierarchies. Referring to their study of West African anticolonial feminism titled, *For Women and the Nation*, Cheryl Johnson-Odim and Nina Mba (1997: 68) describe how colonialism determinately altered, "the character of women's traditional offices and access to power". Social status and political regard that existed in precolonial traditions were undermined as women were rendered "invisible" by the structuring of in-direct rule, thus challenging, their decision-making role in street market trading and the capitalistic cash crop agricultural economy. Visual representations of these contested publics retrace the gender and class axis of the economic precarity of colonised female (re)productive labour. Whereby, in societies where nationalist ideologies of anticolonialism are concurrent with traditional patriarchal values, the ethnicised and "racialised Self-Other dynamics" of the subjective identity of the colonised are uniform and unambiguous in their resistance to the Whiteness and Europeanness of British coloniality (Baker 2020: 354).

Anticolonial feminism seeks to disconcert and apprehend gender-based manifestations of coloniality. It interrogates the power knowledge configurations and historical specificity of gender coloniality in operation as part of the production and validation of colonial governance (Álvarez 2022). As private selves in public spaces, its direct-action activism "directly confronts the state through public space and challenges it through anticolonial resistance" (ibid.: 182). Its counterpropositions in public space interrupt the ideological (mis)tellings of entitlement to colonised land. Mobilising native activities, deployed to counter-position colonised publics space e.g., art and music festival situationism, these feminists generate "hacks of masculinist, hegemonic and colonial modernity" (Engelmann 2022: 34).

Consequently, this analysis of anticolonial feminism explores "the material workings of colonial power" and is directed in its focus on the manifestation of "gendered and racialized social hierarchies and labor relations that have endured into the present" (Emard and Nelson 2021: 1048). Integral to this approach is a disquiet with the combined effect of the rationalisation of colonial power through Eurocentric Western colonial systems of knowledge; immersed and productive of universal truth claims and dichotomous oppositional antinomies, which eternally position Africa as the lesser aspect of the simplistic binary. Colonial binary approximations of culture and society are used to rationalise the enactment of economic practices and institutions that reproduce racialised gendered inequitable relationships as and between colonised people. These practices include the use of taxation to segregate along axes of ethnic and gender dimensions the control and exploitation of the colonised. Similar practices include the privatisation of land and the enforcement of copyright law; a colonial logic "that has been implemented by (settler) colonial governments around the world to appropriate Indigenous lands" (ibid.). Anticolonial feminists criticise these practices for operating through the reinforced ascription of patriarchy in terms of gender-based racialised hierarchies of differentiation.

Additionally, in discussing the feminist praxis of Olufunmilayo Ransome-Kuti, emphasis is ascribed to the extent to which her activism precipitated contemplations on the privation of rights during the colonial period. There exists within human rights studies, paradigms of perspectives that interrogate the extent to which anticolonial movements in their preoccupation with collective liberation were in actuality philosophically antithetical to the humanist concerns for restraining the excesses of state power over the individual. Ibhawoh (2014) in their *Linking Anticolonialism Self-determination* has identified three principal postulates used in academic writings against corresponding anticolonialism with human rights. Firstly, proponents of the scholarly tradition that proports "anticolonialism as non-human rights" presuppose the existence of "a hard distinction between the principle of self-determination and the human rights idea at that historical moment" often citing empirical evidence of limited and inconsistent invocations of human rights in the Charters of anticolonial liberation movements (ibid.: 844). Secondly, it is evident that where anticolonialism is conjoined with a reticence towards human rights, this has involved ascribing the latter with a narrow definition pertaining to an "individual rights" counterpoised against a nationalist steadfast determination "to liberate collective national entities from the grip of imperial arms"; rather than a devout resolution to curtail the power of the state over the individual (ibid.). Consequently, the determination of "the collective freedom of colonised people" galvanises the undertakings of the liberation movement to such a zero-sum pursuit that, "for colonial states at the threshold of independence, self-determination took precedence over a notion of universal human rights" (ibid.: 845). Similarly, anticolonial reticence concerning "justiciable individual rights" was premised on the belief that these hindered "the extent to which individual interests can be overridden by collective goals and communitarian values such as Ubuntu" (Cachalia 2018: 383). According to Ibhawoh (2014: 845), a third premise structuring the association between human rights and anticolonial movements is "the human-rights-as-political-strategy" approach in which human rights discourse is mobilised only in respect to achieving national sovereignty; that is to say human rights discourse "was borne out of sheer political expediency rather than deep ideological commitment". Conversely, as is applicable to all three precepts, is the observation that, anticolonial nationalist resistance to British colonial rule in Africa, "was concerned not only with independence from the metropolitan colonial power but also with questions of justice and injustice posed by 'internalised' colonial relations of domination and subordination" (Cachalia 2018: 390).

Evidence shows that anticolonial activism embattled localised excesses of colonial state sanctioned violence perpetuated in violation of the health, wellbeing and security professed by individual rights to liberty. In so doing, these activists expanded the contextual frontiers for the application of human rights; "by highlighting its contradictions and questioning its universalist assumptions" (Ibhawoh 2014: 855). The insistence that anticolonialism developed in tandem with the declaration of universal human rights in Western discourse is a conceivable proposition. Particularly, in consideration of the concept of "vernacularisation" which refers to the interpolation into existing traditions of native rights or universal human rights. More specifically, "vernacularisation ... mean[s] the complex process by which external impulses were appropriated and intersected into local ideas and situations to produce hybridised understandings of human rights" (ibid.). Sufficient evidence exists to sustain the conjecture that, "Colonised people not only draw on universal human rights in their struggled against imperialism, they also shaped the global meaning of human rights" (ibid.). Appreciating the intersecting trajectories of anticolonial mêlées within its own movement and against imperialist repressive violations of the liberty of the individual, provides a basis for examining anticolonial feminist praxis that centres on human rights.

Axiomatic to an anticolonial feminist consideration of human rights is the affirmation that native rights existed in the histories and culture of indigenous people prior to colonialism. Histories of the negotiation of rights during colonialism bear witness to the inviable truth, "whether human or citizen rights, are shaped not only by Europeans and Americans but also by those thinkers and activists who were subjects, but not citizens in Europe's colonial empires" (Bijl 2017: 249). It has been suggested, conversely that anticolonialism is antithetical to human rights; because its focus on absolute standpoints and its self-determination as a national liberation movement rendered it to be mutually exclusive from individual rights. The assumption being that, "Its central concern is the community, not the individual; absolutist ideologies think in collectivities and mass movements" and not the attention to protecting the civil liberties and rights bestowed onto the individual by virtue of their being human (ibid.: 261). In absolutist nationalist liberation ideology, the individual has rights only in its duties to surrender its individuality so as to service the needs of the community. Against an absolutist anticolonial liberation movement is positioned, "the spirit of pedagogical humanism" and its enthusiasm for critically informed, self-reflexive cultural texts that propagate the humanist merits of analytical introjection and personal consciousness (ibid.: 262). This contemplation of the generative authority of human rights discourse resists a tendency to disclaim the indigenous heritage of native rights, intervening, therefore, in the individualistic logic of knowledge production engrained within "colonial mentality" (Kuti 1984).

Olufunmilayo Ransome-Kuti, in marriage to a fellow school teacher and having been educated in a Nigerian grammar school and then in England, gained credence for boundary-crossing intellectual work that coheres a consanguinity overriding the fissures maintained by colonial domination. In this respect, critically engaged humanism foregrounded her anticolonial feminist ideal of human rights and wrongs. Thus, in my analysis of British colonial education training and her imperative attributed to the negotiation of culture and economy in seeking reprobation for the experience of market-women in low-income communities; the emphasis is on the pursuit of individual rights. In accordance with the praxis of pedagogical humanism, it "has to be humanist in the moral sense of the word and therefore it had to be dynamic, its projects and workings constantly reflected upon" (Bijl 2017: 262). Ultimately, my aim in recounting famous episodes in her activism is to demonstrate a legacy of humanist anticolonial feminism as having been shaped by human rights discourse and reciprocally shaping human rights for the achievement of feminist political and ideological objectives. Theorising the transference of influence of Fela Anikulapo-Kuti's mother on the cultural politics of Afrobeat focusses on her formulation of an anticolonial feminist human rights praxis, in tune with the rhythms and negotiations of nationalist self-determination. Ultimately, it will be argued that anticolonial feminism economics was central to his advocacy for communicative human rights and social justice.

Feminine Soul of Afrobeat Human Rights— Olufunmilayo Ransome-Kuti

The Afrobeat pioneer, Fela Anikulapo-Kuti, was born Olufela Olusegun Oludotun Ransome-Kuti in 1938 in Abeokuta, Ogun State Nigeria. He was raised in an educated, relatively prosperous middle-class and profoundly anticolonial family. Christianity featured appreciably in his formative years. Reverend Israel Ransome-Kuti, as the Principal of Abeokuta Grammar School nurtured his family into Pan-Africanist ideals, while negotiating this conservativism with his wife's intent to cultivate in their children an ethics of nationalist pride in their Yoruba cultural heritage.

68 P. ODIH

Both parents allied to be founding members of the Nigerian Union of Teachers. Reverend Israel Ransome-Kuti was appointed president from its establishment in 1931 until the year of his death in 1955 (Johnson-Odim 2009: 54).

Anticolonial Feminism, Human Right to Education

Fela Anikulapo-Kuti's childhood household gives the impression of being elaborately multicultural in its confluence of European education, Western Christian conservativism and ethnonationalism. It is evident that activism was an imperative component of Fela's family history; especially with regard to his mother, Olufunmilayo Ransome-Kuti, born in 1900 in Abeokuta, which was at that time the Southern Nigeria, British Colonial Protectorate. Her parents were forerunners as Yoruba converts to the Anglican Christian religion (Johnson-Odim 2009). Having received their own education in Christian missionary schools, her parents were fervent supporters of girls' education. She was among the first female students at the Abeokuta Grammar school, returning there to become a kindergarten teacher, after furthering her education in England. Later as a married woman of four children, Fela Anikulapo-Kuti being the most famous, she became vehemently engaged as an educationalist, anticolonial feminist and foremost a human rights activist. In a correspondence titled *The Plight of Nigerian Women*, written in 1947–1948, for the British protectorate governors she traces links between slavery and colonialism in respect to the subjugation of female life chances in respect to education and an undermining of their traditional position in the native hierarchies of power, as is evident in the following extract of the above stated correspondence – derived from an undigitized National Archives document.

> **Before saying anything about the present condition of women in Nigeria, it will be necessary to give a brief description of their condition before the British advent. The life then was mainly agricultural, and there was division of labour between men and women. The man cultivated the land, sowed and it was chiefly the duty of women to reap. Women also owned property and traded with men and exercised considerable political and social influence in the society and were responsible for crowning the Kings on Coronation days. Whatever disabilities there were then, were endured both by men and women alike.**
>
> **...**

In the days of yore, women took a prominent part in the administration of this country, and according to custom tradition and usages, certain state ceremonies were performed by them. But now, the country is de facto and de jure ruled by the British Government, through their agents, the so-called Natural Rulers who are in most cases not only 'an integral part of the machinery of the Government', but are nominees of the British Government and are created 'Sole Native Authorities' which system is neither British nor Indigenous. By this despotic innovation, those Native Authorities, are in most cases, the oppressors of their people [...].

The women of Nigeria are poverty-stricken, disease ridden, superstitious and badly nourished; they are the main productive machinery of the country's economies. They make palm-oil, kernel, ground-nut oil; pottery; they spin and weave clothing; they haul rice, prepare cocoa and coffee beans and so on. The men sow and hoe, and women have to do the rest of the work; but in spite of all their hard work and toil they hardly realise an appreciable income commensurate with the dignity of their manual labour. Funmilayo Ransome-Kuti (1947–1948)

Olufunmilayo Ransome-Kuti was a verdant anticolonial educationalist and Nigerian feminist renowned in her lifetime for contending determinedly to advance women's access to education and political representation in a traditionally patriarchal society. Intent on forging unity between similarly educated elite women and less prosperous labouring women, she abandoned her English Christian names (Frances and Abigail) and adopted the abbreviated Nigerian Christian name, Funmilayo. Through outreach programmes she worked hard to advance the educational opportunities of the mostly illiterate market women in Abeokuta. Indeed, in an article titled *A Talk About Women*, published in c.1949, she scripted passionately her aspirations and hopes for equality of opportunity for males and females. In so doing she took on directly the need for a subjugated people to negotiate between the colonial intent of the British rulers and the suspicions of the patriarchal native traditionalists fearful of their loss of power consequent of delimiting the gender barriers to the scope of schooling. Elementary education at the time was preserved for sons often to the neglect of daughters; a situation adumbrated by the British colonialists transposing their pre-existing patriarchal values onto their facile stereotypical tropes, both of which patronised the cultural traditions of the colonised. Thus, an attempt to enable equality of gender and education, would require seizing any redeemable features bestowed by the British patronage of patriarchal colonialism; and this would most benefit rural women. Funmilayo witnessed these intersections of British colonial patriarchy and Nigerian native tradition. She was extremely concerned with the consequent devaluing of the perceived monetary reward ascribed to educating females; expressing the outcome of this as thus, "A wife is never a companion but a slave. As there is no country that can rise above her womenfolk. I am therefore appealing to the parents in this little article to give their daughters equal opportunity with their sons" (Ransome-Kuti 1949). As hope springs eternal, she appealed to the system of patriarchy to "rally round and cooperate with women to redeem them from their present status". Of particular significance is her belief in the role of teachers to inspire and motivate others to seek to better themselves through education. To which she infers as thus, "But the women too should strive to acquire knowledge in anything from everywhere and anybody. They should try to take the best from all that comes their way". Teachers are presented here as motivations for women to become learners as well as providing knowledge and understanding through their teaching practices. There is a sense of expediency evident in her writing, such that the urgency of the situation overrode one's questioning of the pedagogy and epistemology of knowledge; in such a situation of urgency there was little time to question the marginalisation of an African cultural identity in terms of the curriculum content of British colonial education. Rather the imperative was to raise consciousness and build alliances between women. Thus, she concludes the article stating, "There is such a lot of work before us, before we can take our place efficiently side by side with other women of the world, socially educationally, economically and so on, and pleased God, we shall" (ibid.). Her belief in the value of education irrespective of the system of education, was clearly a position born of necessity. But in the neocolonial, political authoritarianism aftermath of Nigerian's independence, an indiscriminate devotion to the British colonial curriculum was deemed by many to be insufficiently expedient in provisioning reparation for the demonisation of Nigerian traditional cultural identity and values. Advances in this direction are evident in the anticolonial human rights antecedents to the critical pedagogical approach articulated in the lyrics and interviews of Fela Anikulapo-Kuti.

Anticolonial Feminist Antecedents Afrobeat, Human Right to Education – "Teacher Don't Teach Me Nonsense" (Fela Anikulapo-Kuti)

The Nigerian nationalist, consciousness raising intent of his mother's educational activism impacted tremendously on Fela Ransome-Kuti's formative years; and in his developing discourse in respect to decolonialising education from its British colonial legacy. He is renowned for being disillusioned with his early schooling experience, because of the predominance of an acculturation into an English culture as the main cultural identity of school teaching during the British colonial governance of Nigeria's social, cultural and educational institutions. Although largely positive about the experience; living and studying in England awakened a poignant insight into the conflictual and contradictory identity endowed by the British era of colonial Nigeria. Whereby the hegemony of Englishness to the Nigerian curriculum displaced and belittled African identity; it was African racial identity that displaced and belittled their sense of belonging in England. In June 1984 with his 20-piece music assemblage Egypt 80, Fela Anikulapo-Kuti played top billing at the Glastonbury mid-summer Festival, this set along with interview extracts, was recorded and archived by the BBC under the title, *Fela Kuti at Glastonbury 1984.* Available in the British Broadcasting Corporation (BBC) Arena programme archives, are extracts of exclusive testimony by Fela Anikulapo-Kuti, drawn upon for *Fela Kuti at Glastonbury 1984,* and revealing the anticolonial antecedents that influenced his human rights postulation on decolonising "colonial mentality". In 2024, in communication with the British Broadcasting Corporation, it was agreed that an extract of the programme is available to quote providing I adhere to Fair Dealing stipulation and quote the extracts as thus: Kuti, F., (1984); *Fela Kuti, Arena: Teacher Don't Teach Me Nonsense* (Television Documentary, 30 November 1984).

Fela Anikulapo-Kuti's commitment to Afrobeat as a cultural political intervention is pronounced throughout the Arena programme's exclusive extracts; illustrated in statements such as, "It is very difficult for me not to have music that is not politics; even if it is not politics it will have to be music that is very culturally aware for people to see the beauty of the African concept. That is the whole think about me" (ibid.). Featured in this recording is a thought-provoking recounting by Fela about his subjective experience of diaspora and Otherness, as encountered while studying in London. As he expresses it, "Everything was European background;

the upbringing; teaching in school". The sense of estrangement was made even more despondent by the preponderance of English; and the subjugation of Nigeria's rich tapestry of native languages. Listening to his words and articulation in relaying a visceral distain for the impediment of the hegemony of English to the curriculum schooling in Nigeria is disconcerting as one has the sense of a sublimation of early years frustration. A situation in which, as is described, "Everything had to be English. We were not; We were not even allowed to speak our country's languages in schools. And they called the language; they called our own languages vernacular. So English was the real language you had to speak in school". Language teaching is integral to one's racialised cultural identity. Consequently, to be forced to be schooled in a foreign language is an impediment to one's conscious awareness of one's racial identity. As he expresses it, "So, everything was English. With what we were taught in school nobody was thinking of whether to be African or not, we just accepted that we were English and everybody that went to England was told it was the master. Everybody wants to go to England and come back home to the master".

Fela Anikulapo-Kuti in 1958 lived in England, while studying arts at Trinity College of Music, London. "I never thought about it", Fela recounts of this time, "being African as such; so, it didn't mean anything to me. Until much later in my life. Whilst in England I started to feel the awareness of having to be an African because for the first time I came to England I started to feel: 'Oh wow; so, this white people don't like, like us too much'". The brutal realities of the domestication of racism became immediately concerning when he, as with other foreign national students sought "rooms" for residence. Whereby, he describes his experience in renting rooms in terms of the domestication of racism in the popular press news media. Stating, "this is my experience from having to rent rooms you know; I had so much, at that time you read the newspapers in England: 'House for rent; no coloureds, no dogs'. That annoyed me a lot … And my student days in England I started to be aware of having to be an African; but we had nothing to offer as Africans because we were always taught English". Fela, transposed into music this incongruity between the lived and taught English curriculum experienced by Nigerians in British (post)colonial Africa. Describing the inherent contradictions in this process as thus,

> One of the latest songs I am singing now, I said 'teacher don't teach me nonsense' right… I was trying to make my people see. Because in Africa

3 ANTICOLONIAL FEMINIST HUMAN RIGHTS 73

people respect teachers; you know, teachers, because they teach English and they teach their pupils. Respect teachers and pastors in Africa. So okay, now I saw that I should now use teacher as my focus. So, I titled the song, *Teacher Don't Teach Me Nonsense.* I wove the song to let the people see that white men have taught us everything we know.

But therein resides the inimitable impediment, because as Fela goes on to argue the imposition of British cultural political ideas onto the language and practice of politics in Nigeria will inevitably be interrupted by the inherent contradictions of "colonial mentality". As Fela expresses it, "I made people see; one important thing they taught us was politics. Because I wove into the song the elections in Nigeria. Because it was a farce". For if it is not inherently contradictory to do so,

> if it is not crazy [to impose democracy] why doesn't Africa as time goes forward, things [are] getting worse ... Poor man de cry, rich man de mess ... Democracy, crazy demo; demonstration of craze... Then I ended up ... to f*** the minds of the colonialists, I said: if good teacher teach something; if a good teacher teaches something and a student make mistake, teacher must tell him that he is making mistake.

In these lyrics there flourishes a dynamic and poignant exposition of an educational ideology operating to sustain the hegemony of a British colonial mentality devoid of the critical intellectuality necessary to the cultivation of an affirmative post-colonial consciousness. His belief and commitment to an Afrocentric critical pedagogy was pronounced triumphantly during the Glastonbury 1984 headline performance, when introducing *Teacher Don't Teach Me* Nonsense to the mostly White audience. Scanning through the BBC's footage of the audience reaction, the facial expressions of astonishment are evocative of the revolutionary effect of Fela's deviation from the docile deference of "colonial mentality", as is evident in the following extract of Fela's address to the Glastonbury audience in 1984.

The song I'm gonna sing now is mine one of my explanations of why Africa is low today. We all know that the Europeans taught the Africans what they know today. What we use for our governmental processes. We all know about democracy. I condemn democracy now. Because it's more democracy. I write a tune about democracy. And I called the tune TDTMN. Teacher Don't Teach Me Nonsense. Fela Anikulapo-Kuti, Glastonbury Mid-Summer Festival June 1984

It has been written elsewhere that Funmilayo Ransome-Kuti's anticolonial educational praxis is borne from her predisposition as a "moral exemplar", i.e., "admired and praised for living up to moral ideals and standards, including promoting social justice and fighting injustice" (Obiagu 2023: 253). In the decolonised moral education advocated by her son, there is some continuity of respect for moral exemplars, but this continuation of approach is largely displaced by a robust contention against the veracity and integrity of the British colonial tradition, which is redefined as perpetuated by "(neo)colonizers who destroy the psychology of the colonized" (ibid.). Conversely, in the afore discussed lyrics there is some advocacy for what is described as "moral disruptors" evident in the incorporation into the lyrics numerous "anticolonial questions of African spirituality and humaneness" (ibid.: 254). Such sentiment is evident in the following extract from the song *Teacher Don't Teach Me Nonsense*: "Let's get down, to the underground spiritual game. We all sing together, play music together in happiness. All you have to do is sing what I play on my horn. Now let's go down". Pride in a consciousness of African identity is a prominent feature of these lyrics. As is evident in the following extract: "Let us face ourselves for Afrika. Na de matter of Afrika. This part-ee of my song. Na all the problems of this world. In we dey carry, for Afrika". However, as one progresses through the song lyrics it is evident that there is a vehement disregard for the level of critical awareness that is bestowed by the British colonial curriculum and teaching praxis. As one can discern from the following extract, "When Shagari finish him elections. Wey dem no tell am, say him make mistake-ee. Say this yo, no be democracy. Oyinbo dem no tell army self. Na for England-ee, I me no fit take over. I come think about this demo-crazy".

Teacher Don't Teach Me Nonsense is corroborated with a critical pedagogy that stands in dialectical opposition to the uncritical and disengaging pedagogic practice of the British colonial curriculum tradition. Thus, the lyrics emphasise critically informed engagement with the curriculum as a basis for raising consciousness in the dignity and resilience of African identity. Where his mother's anticolonialism proficiently navigated through the British colonial system, discerning the long-term goal of achieving an education; her son's visceral disillusionment with the neocolonial context in Nigeria integrates anticolonialism into a broader decolonial agenda directed by postcolonial critique of the stupefying British colonial educational ideology and curriculum practice. Indiscriminate compliance was deemed to be irreconcilable with the moral and political development of Nigerian society; as is evident in the following extract from *Teacher Don't Teach Me Nonsense*, "Teacher, teacher-o na the lecturer be your name. Teacher, teacher-o na the lecture be the same. Make-ee no teach-ee me again oh. As soon teaching finish yes, da thing-ee it gon die it dey-o …". The inference to mortality speaks to an incredulity and disdain levied at the tempest of social problems that were allied to the neocolonial context of post-independent Nigeria. Thus, it is my contention that here and elsewhere the artist combines the human right to education with the right to cultural participation. Specifically, with regard to letter, the United Nations Declaration of Human Rights (UNDHR) states that: "Everyone has the right freely to participate in the cultural life of the community, to enjoy the arts and to share in scientific advancements and its benefits" (United Nations 1948).

African feminists have long since identified the social problems that have beset the neocolonial context as, "contrary to Pan-African goals and Ubuntu and communalism principles which are values that are common across African countries" (Obiagu 2023: 237). Such discordance with the order of education and culture is inferred in the lyrics of the afore song in which the artist responding to their rhetorical question "Who be teacher" describes a cycle of knowledge transfer that is embedded in Nigerian native culture and tradition. As is evident in the following verse to the afore discussed lyrics, "Who be teacher? I go let you know. When we be pikin (fatha mama be teacher); When we dey for school (teacher be teacher); Now dey University (lecturer be teacher); When we start to work; (government be teacher); Who be government teacher? (cu-ulture and tradition); Cu-ulture and tradition". In these strands of the lyrics to *Teacher Don't Teach Me Nonsense*, there is contended the imperative to integrate throughout the cycle of moral education insights from the distinctly traditional histories of the indigenous culture and society. The integrity of the British to cultivate an Afrocentric "cu-ulture and tradition" is cynically questioned given the decontextualised nature of the Eurocentric modernist tradition of the teaching of morals. Such suspicions and scepticism are evident in the strands of lyrics dedicated to decolonising the Eurocentric association of democracy with a linear modernist progressive educational advancement. As expressed in the following extract: "Na dem-o-cr-azy be the deal. Who don teach us ee demo-o-cr-azy? Bo-ptch! Oyinbo teach-ee us. Yuh-ngh! Oyinbo for Europe-oh". Whereby the expressed inference in the detournement of democracy is that the uncritical application of its Eurocentric modernity, to the governance of African nations, inherently destabilises its modernist rationalistic sanity. Hence, the lyric's continuous ridicule of an uncritical pedagogy, "If it no be craze (Demo-crazy); Why for Afrika? (Demo-crazy); As time dey go (Demo-crazy); Things just dey bad (Demo-crazy); They bad more and more (Demo-crazy); Poor man

76 P. ODIH

dey cry (Demo-crazy); Rich man dey mess (Demo-crazy)". The lyric's interruption into the Eurocentric modernist convention of progressive moral education is effective in its anticolonial detournement. Indeed, its decolonial education praxis meritoriously deploys anticolonial "pedagogical practices of moral education for social justice" also evident in the "moral exemplar" of Funmilayo Ransome-Kuti's "promoting social justice and fighting injustice" (Obiagu 2023: 253).

Anticolonial Feminism, Human Right to Work and Favourable Conditions of Work

In the early 1930s, Funmilayo Ransome-Kuti facilitated establishment of the Abeokuta Ladies' Club (ALC) which, although initially directed towards cultivating the transferable skills relevant to middle-class cultural life, developed into a formidable advocacy for furthering the educational opportunities and political representation of working-class women; in so doing, recognising as a human right, the entitlement of women alongside men to an education. Indeed, as part of its inaugural 1944 presentation of "Rules and Regulations" ALC lists as central to its aims, "to help in raising the standard of womanhood in Abeokuta … to help in encouraging learning … thereby wipe out illiteracy" (cited in Johnson-Odim 2009: 54). By the mid-1940s ALC expanded to take up the unfair trading conditions of market trading women. The British colonial government was designating and implementing policies that were ill-disposed to the securities of the predominantly poorly educated market trading women. At this time of Funmilayo being made aware of the ill-treatment of these women, she was hearing accounts of the gender discriminatory injustices of the British colonial system consequent of the actions of the traditional ruler of Abeokuta, the Alake Ademola. In response the ALC was renamed the Abeokuta Women's Union (AWU) in 1946, with Funmilayo as president the initiative progressed in its transformation from a focus on charitable concerns into a political campaign: protecting and preserving the political rights of women; advancing women's educational opportunities; demanding that the British government cease its controls over market trading; petitions for improved water supply and sanitation; and an active support for Nigerian independence. In all these purposes the AWU made a considerable number of accomplishments. Most notably, in the 1947–1949 female-led protest, which is recognised in more recent times to have been, "a legendary historical tax protest against the British imperial and traditional powers" (Salawu 2019: 10). During its time, the protest directly challenged the gendered irregularities of the British colonial taxation regime. Due to British colonial indirect rule, the collection of taxes, in the administrative southern Nigerian province Abeokuta was subcontracted to the inhabitant traditional authorities such as the time-honoured role of chiefs who were renumerated for the undertaking.

A consequence of monetising the role of the traditional leaders was that, "the local, indigenous authorities as much as the European representatives of the colonial government" were sometimes "deemed to be enemies of the people, especially the Alake, viewed as closest to British authorities" (Johnson-Odim 2009: 55). In conjunction with converting their traditional powers into transactional facets of the British colonial state, the in-direct administrative rule of the provinces by a system of Sole Native Authority (SNA) removed the traditional powers of the chiefs and this impacted particularly on the financial welfare of women, who also lost representation via the native system of female chiefs and priestess (Johnson-Odim and Mba 1997). Funmilayo wrote an elegiac commentary denouncing these structures of British colonial rule. Published in the British Communist Party newspaper, Daily Worker, in 1947, the title of her article is, *We Had Equality Till Britain Came*. In the article Nigeria prior to British rule is depicted as an agricultural economy in which males and females shared equally tasks necessary to the cultivation of the land. With limited obstructions impeding their opportunities, "Women owned property, traded and exercised considerable political and social influence in society" (Ransome-Kuti 1947: 545). Women achieved formal status in respect to the traditional native rulers; "they were responsible for crowning the Kings on Coronation days". Much of this prestige, power and influence ceased with the establishment of British colonial rule. Indeed, as Funmilayo expresses it, "With the advent of British rule, slavery was abolished, and Christianity introduced into many parts of the country, but instead of the women being educated and assisted to live like human beings their condition deteriorated". Notable areas of diminution of women's status related to education with an estimated "not more than one percent of the women in Nigeria" having adequate levels of literacy. Sanitation and medical provision fared worse, with virtually no free services for women and children; medical officers demanded fees to be paid before administering to the sick. Additionally, the female traders were experiencing disadvantage by the imposition to prioritise their purchase of imported goods at inflated prices.

Most firms in West Africa, and Nigeria in particular, are out to oppress and exploit the people in order to be able to declare fabulous profits at the expense of the already poverty stricken people. They dictate the selling-price of their own imported goods which are very prohibitive for the average man and woman in Nigeria, as well as the buying prices of the people's products, so that the people of Nigeria have no bargaining power in the sale of their commodities. Right now a system of conditional sale is in vogue, where the unsaleable goods are forced on the African traders at exorbitant cost and have to be sold at a loss and thereby wipe away any gain they might have made on the actual goods they willingly bought. Funmilayo Ransome-Kuti (1947–1948)

Given these conditions it is unsurprising that the imposition of an unjust gender discriminatory system of taxation was irately rejected. The AWU called into contention egregious sex-based discrimination in the collection of taxes. It had already transpired in the 1917 imposition of a poll tax, that women in the Abeokuta province were among the first females in Nigeria to be subjected to a British colonial system of taxation. The situation is described in detailed anticolonial prose by Funmilayo Ransome-Kuti (ibid.) as thus:

Taxation of women is unknown in the Colony and Protectorate of Nigeria with the single exception of the Abeokuta and Ijebu Provinces of Western Nigeria, where poll tax are forcible demanded of the women. Quite apart from the fact that payment of Poll and Income taxes by poor women is oppressive, the brutal and unbecoming method of exaction leave much to be desired. The method of collecting and assessing taxes is abominable. Young girls are sometimes stripped naked in the streets by the men officially designated collectors, in order to ascertain whether they are mature enough to pay tax or not. Women are more often than not prevented from going to sell their goods in the market and detained for hours on and in unbearable rays of the tropical sun because they do not pay tax in time. Funmilayo Ransome-Kuti (1947–1948)

From its onset there was pronounced disquiet about the flat-rate system of taxation, which taxed wives separately from their spouse regardless of whether they had an independent income. The AWU submitted letters of protest to the SNA council, challenging the "double taxation" burden by the women of Abeokuta. It has been observed that, "In addition to paying income and water rate taxes, market women were required to pay the salaries of the traditional parakoyis or market supervisors" (Johnson-Odim 2009: 78). By the mid-1940s the AWU became more resilient in the voicing of resistance to the paid puppet king of the colonial government, highlighting his part in facilitating the imposition of a tax regime which was relying upon intrusive practices to administer a system in which girls were taxed younger than boys; and women were struggling more to afford the flat tax rate, while supporting their husbands to pay the fees imposed by the local government.

These conditions set the backdrop for an international focus and direction for the AWU. In 1947 Funmilayo accompanied a delegation of the nationalist party, the National Council of Nigeria and the Cameroons (NCNC), to England (Johnson-Odim 2009). Unilaterally, she made contact with the British Broadcasting Corporation (BBC). It is also reported that she visited several daycare centres and dedicated time to visit the National Council for Maternity and Child Welfare (ibid.). Funmilayo as the only woman in a NCNC delegation took it upon herself to represent the situation of Nigerian women. While in London she published an article in the communist newspaper, *The Daily Worker*. In the publication she verdantly argued that British colonialism had marginalised Nigerian women from the civic sphere, while debilitating their welfare through the imposition of arbitrary taxes. She castigated the impropriety of the gender racialised intrusive strategy of tax collection and in so doing highlighted the anticolonial denouncement of colonialism's abusive treatment of the Black female body.

The AWU tax revolt is heralded as a moment in Nigerian colonial history in which women came together to protest and challenge their economic subjugation and political marginalisation under colonialism. "No taxation without representation" led the cry of the taxation revolt against exclusion of women from political decision-making and the right to vote. After three years of sustained petitioning to the British colonial government, mass demonstration, civil disobedience and market boycotts, the protest against unjust taxation steered by the AWU achieved concessions by the colonial government, allowing women to participate in local elections; the removal of the flat tax, dismantling the façade of a dutiful native authority traditional king leading to their abdication in 1949. Although the colonial state inevitably reneged on these concessions, the female led protest group, with Funmilayo's at its helm was able to temporarily reset the agenda of gender discriminatory taxation set by the colonial state.

80 P. ODIH

Indeed, it is evident that although their protest grew out of local issues, conditions and grievances it spoke to a dawning new era in Nigerian political economic history. For, the protestors aligned with the demands of unions elsewhere in Nigeria which had "called on capital and the state to assume a greater part of the cost of social reproduction" (Byfield 2003: 272). Thus, while other unions, "called for a family wage, the AWU demanded greater educational opportunities and maternal health care for women" (ibid.).

Funmilayo Ransome-Kuti established the AWU in conjunction with Eniola Soyinka, the mother of Fela's first cousin Wole Soyinka, later a Nobel Prize-winning writer. In his poignant memoir *Aké; The Years of Childhood*, Wole Soyinka provides an affecting narration of patriarchy and colonialism as the antecedent foundation for the AWU's tax revolt; "The Great Upheaval". Soyinka in prosaic prose depicts the impact on domestic life of the sanitation fines that local officials had imposed in the Abeokuta region so as to raise revenue; and the exasperation of the over layering of these court fines with the Colonial Office imposed direct taxation in the region initiated in 1917. Nigeria's patriarchally structured domestic division of labour led to women bearing the brunt of the sanitation fines imposed harshly for the most minor of infringements of the capriciously designated sanitation rules. Soyinka captures exceedingly well the indignation and the frustration voiced by women whose livelihood and freedom were being curtailed by the arbitrary increases in British colonial taxes. In one poignant scene a female protagonist screeches with fury at the situation fines, thus, "What you are all saying in so many words, is that the women of Egbaland are no longer free to walk the streets of their own land, or pursue their living from farm to home and farm to market without being molested by these bloodsuckers – am I right?" (Soyinka 1983: 183). The theme of defiance against the collusion of patriarchy and colonialism in the capitalisation of women's finance is also evident as thus, "Tax! Tax on what? What is left after the woman has fed children, put school uniform on his back and paid his school fees? Just what are they taxing?" queries a female market-trader in a scene from Soyinka's memoire. The approbation that was bestowed to Funmilayo's AWU campaigning against the colonial government's arbitrary taxation empowered her, "to give notice of a demand for the abolition of tax for women, both to the District Officer and the Alake of Abeokuta and his Council of Chiefs" (ibid.: 184). Indeed, her strength of conviction and ability to rally thousands, cultivated a

3 ANTICOLONIAL FEMINIST HUMAN RIGHTS 81

fearless and powerful reputation; aided by an astoundingly astute aptitude for self-publicity.

As part of, "the Great Upheaval that ended in Aké", Funmilayo assisted in the creation and served as president of the Nigerian Women's Union, which was dedicated to the enfranchisement of women throughout the country. It was later renamed the Federation of Nigerian Women's Society, in 1953 and became heavily involved in the Nigerian suffragette movement. After Nigeria achieved its independence in 1960 the adult universal suffrage was extended for men and women. In the early 1970s, she again used her name to indicate a direction in her political activism. In this instance it was to assume the newly affirmed surname of her son Fela as she also became Anikulapo-Kuti. It is often deliberated as to whether this was an indication of shared identification with Pan-Africanism; but such nationalist commitment was not new to her politics as was evident in the 1947–1948 deputation to the British colonial government. For the open letter titled *The Plight of Nigerian Women* emphasises the following in respect to the "fallacious propaganda" that had been propagated in the British colonial controlled Nigerian press and mainland British press accusing Funmilayo and her allies of being anti-British.

Before I conclude I would very much like to correct some misleading and fallacious propaganda which has been appearing in some British and Nigerian Press quite recently, 'That we are anti-British and that we would like to drive the white man, especially the English away from Nigeria'. I would like to make it abundantly clear that we are neither anti-British nor do we desire to drive away the British from our country. But we are definitely anti-oppression and anti-exploitation. Finally, may I appeal to Members of Parliament who have paid official, semi-official and private visits of inspection to the West African Colonies and particularly Nigeria in recent months, including Mrs Creech Jones who have actually seen our plight to come over to Macedonia to help us. Our women and young girls could be trained to become useful members of society. We have the materials at our disposal; all we need is the opportunity. Funmilayo Ransome-Kuti (1947–1948)

It is evident from this extract that the protestations regarding the levying of taxation without granting representation, coupled with the arbitrary increases and intrusive procedures of tax collection, meant that the British system of colonial administration was inflicting multiple layers of

82   P. ODIH

harmful gender discrimination onto Nigeria's subjugated cultural identity. A situation best described by Funmilayo in her own words.

> The women of Abeokuta Province do not necessarily oppose the imposition of income tax, provided this is in consonant with the conditions obtaining in other parts of the civilised world, and provided income tax is demanded from those who can afford it. But to extort money from women who find it difficult to maintain life with children to feed, clothe and shelter when the men folk are unemployed is not only cruel and tyrannical, but is repugnant to natural justice. In the year 1946, 106,259 women paid tax in Abeokuta, and this had been going on for some considerable number of years past; yet the women have no voice in the management of the administration of the country. Is taxation compatible with no representation in the twentieth century? Funmilayo Ransome-Kuti (1947–1948)

The taxation system purposely imposed British ideals of monogamous marriage so as to tether, the financial income of women, as part of compelling the dependence of the traditional homestead "on the cash sectors of the [capitalist] economy" (Byfield 2003: 270). Accepting this, there is a growing consensus among feminist economists that, "women were central to the expansion of capitalism in Yorubaland" (ibid.). So as to examine further this supposition, in April 2024, I visited the National Archives, in London and read through the National Council of Nigeria and the Cameroons: Activities of Mrs Ransome-Kuti which is a collection of handwritten and typed original correspondences, written to and from the Colonial Office and Commonwealth Offices, dated 1947–1948. In a correspondence by what appears to be the British Colonial Office, the following justification was given for the blatant sex-based discrimination in the taxing of women from the Abeokuta province of Nigeria.

> We know that in the Abeokuta and Ijebu Province, alone of the Provinces of Nigeria, a flat rate of tax is levied on all adult females, (the rate being 3/- as compared with 7/- tax on men in the same area). It is understood that the reason for this tax ie, that in these Provinces women carry on a great deal of trade independently … We have however in Nigeria Political Summary for December, an account of the demonstrations which occurred from the 8th to 10th December. From this it appears that the trouble started when seven were being prosecuted in the Native Court for not paying their tax. A crowd of about

300 women assembled at the Court, and after the defaulters had been convicted, this crowd, led by Mrs Ransome Kuti, marched to the Alake's palace. On the following two days the crowd grew to about 8,000, and there was some stone-throwing and other disorder. On the 10th December, however, certain peaceable persons paid the fine of the seven women who had been arrested, and this fact, together with the arrival of police reinforcements from Lagos caused the demonstrations to subside … Colonial Office (1947–1948)

Towards the end of the Colonial Office statement, it is admitted that despite the protests against the flat rate tax levied against women, the system will be retained until and unless a method for making up for the loss of revenue consequent of the abolition of women's taxation was developed. It is clear here and elsewhere that the taxation of the income generation of women within the Eastern Province of Nigeria was an integral feature of the spread of capitalism during British colonial rule. As is also evident in the following sentence derived from the end of the Colonial Office statement: "If it did dispense with it, it would involve wholesome retrenchment and a great reduction in the various amenities provided by the Native Authority". This statement makes apparent that the British colonial power structures had subjected, to commodity capitalism, the precolonial amenities of the native population; and having done so, forced women's taxation as an income stream to provision these amenities.

Anticolonial Feminist Antecedents Afrobeat, Human Right to Work and Favourable Conditions of Work

It is an often-written supposition that Fela Kuti cultivated an anticolonial commitment as direct consequence of travelling to the USA in 1969 and being introduced to the civil rights politics of the Black Panthers. Saheed Adejumobi's (2003) account of African Intellectual History surmises that it was upon Fela Anikulapo-Kuti's return from the USA that Afrobeat was created from a fusion of "African highlife, jazz, funk and traditional Yoruba music" (ibid.: 51). It is claimed that the artist later rejected Afrobeat due to its association with commodified music. Furthermore, the complex lengthy compositions of the artist resisted the culture industry's disaggregating commodification and the "technologization of music" (ibid.). While it is consistently evident that Afrobeat resisted and challenged the commodified processes of the popular music industry, it is more probable that the critical theory disputation with the capitalist processes of the culture industry was propagated by the artist's appreciation of his mother's forbearance against the discriminatory systems of taxation levied by the British colonial rulers.

Echoes of his mother's stance against exorbitant financial exploitation reverberate through the anti-capitalist direct action undertaken by Fela Anikulapo-Kuti in 1978. For, in addition to the notorious spectacle of defying the British colonial principle of monogamy by marrying 27 women in unison, 1978 was momentous for the fact that Fela, and his entourage, in a dispute over unpaid royalties, occupied the Lagos offices of the record label Decca. In video footage, filmed in situ during the protracted squat at Decca West Africa limited recording studio he speaks provocatively about the political role of Afrobeat. Expediency in a situation of continued exploitation is described by Fela as a distinguishing imperative of their music, as is evident from the following extract of Fela's address to media during the situation of occupying the offices of the record label Decca in West Africa.

> If you are England music can be an instrument of enjoyment; you can sing about love; can sing about whom you're going to bed with next. But in my own environment, my society is under developing because of an alien system on our people. So, there is no musical enjoyment there is nothing like love. There is something like a struggle for people's existence. So as an artist politically, artistically, the whole idea about your environment must be represented in the music, in the arts. Art is what is happening at a particular time of a people's development or underdevelopment. So, I think as far as Africa is concerned music cannot be for enjoyment. Music has to be for revolution. Working with the people, enlighten the people and we need your duty as a citizen. Playing music and act, do something about the system. If you feel bad about it; do something about it. I see African's today, what we do is just we suffer and smile… We smile because we are good people, but you see people don't have to smile in bad condition. That is making the matters worse; that is going to slavery. You see because our condition is not a condition of smiling. So, I write a tune called *Shuffering and Shmiling* you see. And it is been very; I think it is one of my biggest hits now since, for years … It uses this religious thing to go an attack the ills of our society. To see why things happen, why this way police brutality, I mean army oppression [at this point he plays music using his saxophone]. Fela Anikulapo-Kuti (1978/2011)

It is an interesting feature of the afore extract of verbatim speech that Fela refers to citizenship in terms of politically engaged local activism set within the context of the international forces of colonialism. Similarly, his mother Funmilayo Ransome-Kuti's political activism also encompassed the international significance of the local, as was evident in respect to her focus on environmental issues, in conjunction with her protestations concerning the irregular and sex-based discriminatory taxation burden that the local market women experienced. Thus, when in 1952 the colonial governing council decided to invalidate the AWU's hard-fought for 1948 exemption of women from paying the water rate tax, she and several other women took direct action and ceased payment. The action received stern rebuke from the regulatory authorities; Funmilayo capitalised on the impediment and through communication with her allies in Britain heartened Oliver Lyttleton, the secretary of state for the colonies, to in April 1953 address the issue in the House of Commons (Johnson-Odim and Mba 1997: 92). Into 1959 the AWU were consistently protesting against the water rates; Funmilayo's dexterity in letter writing directly to the Western Regional Government secured and amplified the profile of the situation. Thus, when in the same year she was detained for "inciting women to not pay the tax on water" the charges discarded and in the year of Nigeria's independence from British colonial rule in 1960, the water rates imposed on women were abolished (ibid.).

Anticolonial Feminism, Human Right to Motherhood and Childhood as Entitled to Special Care and Assistance

As consummate professional and ambassador for non-violent anticolonial feminist praxis, her manner of address here is consistently with prioritising her noble cause, consciously reaching out to British women to assist in the liberation of Nigerian women from the situation of colonial slavery and disenfranchisement. According to Funmilayo this was the basis of the situation that led to "the people of Nigeria and the Cameroons" sending, "a delegation of protest to Britain under the auspices of their National Council". Her self-perceived role as the sole female in the delegation is expressed as thus.

> The people of Nigeria and the Cameroons, fed up to the teeth with the un-British treatment they have for decades received at the hands of Civil Servants of the country (European Civil Servants) supported by

some African Quislings and Aunt Jennys, whose sole aim is personal aggrandisement for what officialdom can do for them, regardless of the interest of the greatest good of the majority, have sent a delegation to England under the auspices of the National Council of Nigeria and the Cameroons to protest to the British people, and as the only female delegate on the deputation, I have been charged with this duty. 'To appeal fervently to the women of Great Britain, in the name of the women of Nigeria and the Cameroons under British Mandate to use all the available resources at your disposal to help free us from slavery, political, social and economic in order that we may be able to take our rightful place amidst the Commonwealth of Nations'. Funmilayo Ransome-Kuti (1947–1948)

The above extract from *The Plight of Nigerian Women* provides further indication of anticolonial feminist formulation of absolutes in their making or rejection of political allies. For it is evident that Funmilayo's consideration of allying with British women is premised on a negotiation of absolutes i.e., "White British women" versus "Black British colonised Nigerian women". It is my contention that this tendency towards essentialised absolutes encourages the ascription of essentialised maternalistic universal appellations to anticolonial feminists. Examples include "mother of Africa", which while befitted the anticolonial feminist conscious opposition to an absolute protagonist in White British patriarchy, these constructs are vulnerable to deconstructive critique by post-colonial praxis. But in respect to examining a typography of anticolonial feminist they are useful. For, Funmilayo Ransome-Kuti's activism led her to being bestowed the title, doyen of female rights in Nigeria as well as earning the title "The mother of Africa". Writers have since sought to theorise the applicability of role as mother in respect to her African feminist politics. Judith Byfield (2012) in an article entitled, *Gender, Justice and the Environment*, empathetically examines Funmilayo's politics as a feminism of maternal thinking and "human security". It is evidence of the international scope of Funmilayo's feminism that she was able to interweave connections between family, community, Nigerian nationalism and food security with an international focus on environmental suitability. Integral to her dexterity of union is a particular feminist practice of situating motherhood as a platform and dais from which to instigate dialogue. According to Byfield, it was Funmilayo's belief that motherhood provided a strategic basis and preparation for politics. Firstly, it is probably that Funmilayo, "believed that mothers established the values through which good citizens were nurtured, including those of kindliness, selflessness, and a willingness to contribute to progress" (ibid.: 4). Secondly, the management of the household and the domestic sphere have direct impact on the homestead and local community. Consequently, the contribution of mothers to the provisioning of a household nourishes also the immediate community and facilitates the integration of its members as responsible citizens. Byfield expresses the latter issue thus, "Furthermore, women who were good managers of their home displayed 'a full fledged life as a citizen in your country'. For her, citizenship meant not only being born in a certain location, but also contributing to one's community, and motherhood in particular invested in women the qualities that make good politicians" (ibid.).

Anticolonial Feminist Antecedents Afrobeat, Human Right to Motherhood and Childhood as Entitled to Special Care and Assistance

As a result of her activism Funmilayo was of interest to the various Nigerian regimes of government; considered by 1977 as a radical political activist that was challenging the legitimacy of the Nigerian state. In retribution, for her impeccable human rights campaigning, it was in 1977 that around one thousand soldiers raided Fela Anikulapo-Kuti's residential and recording studio compound Kalakuta Republic. During the raid, they critically injured his mother by literally throwing her from the window of her family home; and in so doing critically injuring her, such that Funmilayo Ransome-Kuti, died from her injuries in 1978. Her accolades include the Lenin Peace Prize. On the anniversary of the death, Funmilayo's three sons, alongside hundreds of sympathisers, devotedly staged a convoy in commemoration of her life and politics. Reportedly, "They carried a mock coffin that they deposited at the 14A Agege Motor Road property (*Sunday Observer*, Apr. 15, 1979)" (Johnson-Odim and Mba 1997: 171). In this instance and numerous other occasions, it is possible to discern an immense insight into the impact his mother had on the cultural political contribution of Fela's Afrobeat. Indeed, it has been determined that substantial areas of crossover exist uniting their respective politics. Stephanie Shonekan's (2009) close study of *The Revolutionary Songs of Funmilayo Ransome-Kuti* identifies distinct bridges between Fela and his mother, first and foremost, the neocolonial propensities towards corruption and bribery that blighted successive political regimes in the decades post

Nigeria's hard-fought independence from British colonial rule. His mother's trail blazing protestations and cultural political activism clearly sedimented an alert consciousness of the colonial governance as operating through the institutional administration of local governance; and the long-term negative effects of a disregard for native cultural traditions. Of particular pertinence is the disregard by British officials of the status positions that Nigerian women held within their local native communities, in respect to tribal politics and ceremonies, whereby, pre-existing sex-based discrimination held by the British colonial administrators were conferred onto the structures of indirect rule with little appreciation of their destructive impact on the rectitude "of women's traditional offices and access to power" (Johnson-Odim and Mba 1997: 68). The assumption here being that Funmilayo Ransome-Kuti's political intentions to reinscribe cultural-political value to the role of the mother in respect to the responsibilities of the citizen was a counteraction to the sedimentation in Nigeria's administrative system of a neocolonial capitalistic culture of bribery and corruption.

Translating Anticolonial Feminism into Contemporary Iconography of Afrobeat

It's Lagos, Nigeria. It's the late 1970s. The hottest musician in Africa is Fela Kuti. His club he calls the Shrine. But it's no ordinary club, and he's no ordinary musician. He created a new kind of music, Afrobeat – pounding eclectic rhythms (drawn from music traditions around the globe) mixed with incendiary lyrics to openly attack the corrupt and repressive military dictatorships that rule Nigeria and much of Africa. And now his music is rocking not only Africa, but the world. National Theatre Archive (2010)

Fela! (Everybody Say Yeah Yeah) provides for a pertinent axiom of translation enfolding the anticolonial feminist human rights legacy of Funmilayo Ransome-Kuti and the contemporary Afrobeat music scene. The music theatre production was an epic acclaimed success in its debut on Broadway, where it performed to sold-out auditoriums in the USA from autumn 2009 to early 2011 (Felakuti.com 2023). Its success was welcomed across the music press; and even Afrobeat aficionados exalted praise at *Fela!* variously describing it as "an authentic, impressive experience which was the next best thing to being at the real like Afrika Shrine" (ibid.). A preeminent online gateway to information about the artist Fela

Anikulapo-Kuti attributes the music theatre production's ingenuity to the aptitude of the author/producer Stephen Hendel and the multi-award-winning African-American choreographer Bill T Jones (ibid.). The pair in unison with the author Jim Lewis, spent several years creatively developing *Fela!* which, centres around the indisputably awfully, dreadful politically motivated military police raid of 1977 when 1000 soldiers stormed Kalakuta Republic, vandalising, beating and brutalising its inhabitants. *Fela!* quickly garnered approval from the Black culture industry's USA elite; receiving endorsement from the billionaire American rapper and record producer Shawn "Jay-Z" Carter and the award-winning director Spike Lee. *Fela!* performed its world premiere in New York at 37 Arts, Off-Broadway, in September 2008, prior to opening on Broadway on 23rd November 2009 in a theatre named after the American playwriter of *The Emperor Jones.*

During its highly acclaimed Broadway run, *Fela!* achieved three Tony Awards and the soundtrack album competed successfully to be nominated for a Grammy. The music theatre production subsequently transferred to Lagos Nigeria where its highly acclaimed cast and performance was received favourably. Opening at the Olivier Theatre on 16 November 2010, *Fela!* achieved an astounding sold-out run at London's South Bank National Theatre (NT) and then successfully rolled-out across the NT's repertoire of theatre productions. The National Theatre Live, broadcasted *Fela!* via a simulcast internationally in 2011. I attended one of the National Theatre, London South Bank, sell-out sessions of *Fela!*, which was performed in the Oliver Theatre, during its 11/06/2010–01/23/2011 sell-out season of 53 performances. It was a delightful and enchanting extravaganza in its hybrid fusion of dynamic dance, exhilarating music and mesmeric theatre—intensified by the immersive effect of being there in-person. The cast was a vibrant ensemble; Sahr Ngaujah was an enchanting enigmatic in his portrayal of Fela Anikulapo-Kuti and Melanie Marshall was graceful in her rendering of the artist's mother, Funmilayo Ransome-Kuti. Indeed, the musical theatre production, *Fela!* was in my opinion, immensely worthy of the Olivier nomination for Best New Musical, that it achieved (National Theatre Archive 2010).

Poignantly, I recall initially feeling trepidation about the musical retaining integrity in its depiction; for, I have been nurtured on the narrative of Fela Anikulapo-Kuti and cultivated into a singular appreciation of his pioneering Afrobeat which had become sedimented into the DNA of my habitus. Furthermore, my sceptical scrutiny was invigorated by the thought-provoking critical theory that I was reading and lecturing to undergraduates within the Sociology department at Goldsmiths University of London, specifically, the writers of the Frankfurt School, which refers to a group of mainly German intellectuals that were affiliated during the 1930s to the Institute for Social Research within the University of Frankfurt. This ensemble of Marxist writers have affinities with anticolonial praxis in that these mostly Jewish academics were forced to migrate away from Germany with the rise of the Nazi imperialist Third Reich, in 1933. It is the Frankfurt School's provocative writings on the culture industry which particularly fuelled my trepidation about the extent to which the musical *Fela!* could be an authentic depiction of the artist's political conviction and the anticolonial activism of his mother, Funmilayo Ransome-Kuti. Prior to pronouncing my verdict on the artistic veracity of *Fela!* the musical and its effectivity in translating the politics of Afrobeat into contemporary popular culture, it is necessary to outline the critical theory of the Frankfurt School and to do so through a primary source reading of its leading contributor Theodor Adorno.

In several key respects *Fela!* the musical corresponds with principal concerns expressed by Adorno about the products and processes of mass popular culture. Firstly, as with all aspects of the culture industry the commodity-form determines most aspects of the manufacturing and production of the musical. Critical theory inherently challenges the following narrative suggesting *Fela!* the musical arose spontaneously from the masses:

> Producer Stephen Hendel, a New York commodities trader, discovered Afrobeat when on an impulse he bought a copy of the CD compilation The Best Of Fela. The album changed Hendel's world. He became obsessed with creating a show telling Fela's story and passed his enthusiasm on to the multi-award-winning African-American choreographer and artistic director Bill T Jones. (ibid.)

In contrast, critical theory identifies content inspiration and the manufacturing of culturally creative products to arise through the capitalistic standardised ordering of the structures and processes of culture industry. Thus, it is of no surprise that the musical generated a cornucopia of merchandise including CD compilations, marketed with a chimera of individuality. For, it is a central contention of the Frankfurt School that mass produced standardisation is obscured intentionally so as to seduce the consumer into the misconstrued desire for infinitesimally small difference between product offerings. As exemplified in the statement: "memories can be kept alive with

Knitting Factory Records' CD *Fela! Original Broadway Cast Recording*" (ibid.). Similar critical reflections can be directed at the technical rationalities of the www.ntlive.com National Theatre Live, *Fela!* offering of 2011, whereby these contemporary technical capabilities enable a convergence of economic and administrative fields enabling frictionless continuity in the culture industry's top-down schema of powerful apparatuses of control, which intentionally integrate consumers into commodity capitalism. The National Theatre Live, Fela! offering while credible in its algorithmic deciphering of the conscious and unconscious needs of a diversified prospective audience, the mass will always be secondary to the imperative of capital accumulation. "The masses are not the measure but the ideology of the culture industry, even though the culture industry itself could scarcely exist without adapting to the masses" (Adorno 2001: 99).

Remaining with critical theory as a means to reconsider the musical theatre extravaganza *Fela!* Given that cultural commodities within the industry are directed by the capitalist commodity-form, realising value is less inclined towards artistic integrity of the content and more the pursuit of the profit maxim. The primary practice of the industrial production of culture is to pursue the imperative of capital accumulation, thus transferring the profit motivation onto its cultural forms. Ever since the Afrobeat form first initiated an earning yield sufficient to achieve self-sustenance in the market-place the genre already possessed elements of the profit motive. But in the twilight dawning of Afrobeat, the artists, according to myth and legend, sought financial gain secondarily to the replenishment of their everyday needs. Propelled into the culture industry by the meteoric success of its pioneer, the musical theatre *Fela!* inevitably enticed the undisguised primacy of calculably profitable returns on investment. The latter include the venture capitalists that discharge directives as well as the powerful elites that wield control in the arts and creative industries. "In economic terms they are or were in search of new opportunities for the realization of capital in the most economically developed countries" (ibid.). In specific regard to the musical theatre *Fela!* a similar schema of practice was evident, despite it being a music genre emerging from a country previously colonised by Britain. As has been described earlier within this chapter Afrobeat was borne in critical response to the impoverishment of neocolonialism and brutality of the militarisation of the political hegemony of the post-independence governance in Nigeria. The vibrant fusion of native Yoruba, with jazz and Ghanaian highlife presented new exciting opportunities to a Black music industry that in contemporary times appears bereft of originality. The music genre Afrobeat was sufficiently uncapitalised for it to retain the semblance of authentic cultural display. "Culture, in the true sense, did not simply accommodate itself to human beings; but it always simultaneously raised a protest against the petrified relations under which they lived, thereby honouring them" (ibid.: 100). Ultimately, it is as soon as the cultural artefact enters into the circuits of capitalistic cultural production that it too becomes defined as a value yielding commodity.

An intriguing feature pertaining to the billionaire music director, Jay Z, from whom the creative team of *Fela!* gained funding, is the extent to which his monetary input was communicated in philanthropic tropes. It is though, as Adorno (ibid.) observed more generally about the culture industry, its ideology of capitalist commodity culture extends everywhere. Such that the act of patronage is now so imbued with capitalistic benevolence the industry has transformed altruism into a venture capitalist business. An eloquent exposition of this process is as thus, "The culture industry turns into public relations, the manufacturing of 'goodwill' per se, without regard for particular firms or saleable objects" (ibid.). Ultimately, the culture industry is a capital generating mechanism for the production of capital; which exists as a valuable currency in its material and immaterial form. The multi-millionaire endowment entourage that facilitated the parturition of *Fela!* were rewarded for their "goodwill" both monetarily and immaterially through their enhanced positioning in respect to the reproduction of cultural capital. Each magnificently ostentatious patronage contributing to the start-up financing of *Fela!* like every, production "of the culture industry becomes its own advertisement" (ibid.). It is therefore, of little surprise that the published list of "Production in association with ..." reads like a who's who of the Black creative arts, music and cultural elite of the first quarter of the twenty-first century as it includes, Shawn "Jay-Z" Carter, Will and Jada Pinkett Smith, in collaboration with the industrial giant Sony Pictures Entertainment and the international music producer Knitting Factory Entertainment.

The creative direction of *Fela!* provides a trajectory of reconsideration regarding the extent to which the notion of industry refers to the actual standardisation of the musical theatre genre itself and to the rationalisation of its techniques of distribution, but not specifically to the creative production process. In April 2024, I requested from the Archive Studio of the National Theatre London its digital research pack for *Fela!* (2010) in which is detailed the creatives that featured prominently in the artistic aspects of the musical's innovation. The book that is alleged as the narrative basis was written by Jim Lewis and Bill T. Jones. Music and lyrics are the inspiration of Fela Anikulapo-Kuti, with additional lyrics attributed to the Jim Lewis and its arrangements by Aaaron Johnson and Jordan McLean. Conceived by, is accredited to Bill T. Jones, Jim Lewis and Stephen Hendel. The setting of the narrative is more prominently described in respect to the matriarch, as is evident in the following entry, "Setting: Fela's final concert at the Shrine in Lagos, Nigeria. The Summer of 1978, six months after the death of Funmilayo, Fela's mother". The National Theatre provided sessions for the creatives to talk about their craft, Bill T. Jones is listed to have provided, in the Olivier theatre, a discussion of "his visionary production, featuring his own Tony-award-winning choreography". Here and elsewhere, it was clear that, although the production process of *Fela!* resembles the application of technological rationality to standardise the technical modes of operation so as to coordinate the division of labour, individual forms of creative production were catalysts to innovative expression. But this is not to assume that individual creativity is entirely exposed or hermetically sealed from the capitalist production of culture.

Adorno (2001: 101) observes that the notion of an individual creative innovation can also stem from capitalistic ideology. More specifically, "individuality itself serves to reinforce ideology, in so far as the illusion is conjured up that the completely reified and mediated is a sanctuary from immediacy and life". Techniques that the culture industry deploys for the escape into illusion include, "the star system, borrowed from individualistic art and its commercial exploitation" (ibid.). The star system is operation in many aspects of the information provided about *Fela!* the musical. For example, within the programme is an account of Stephen Hendel and Bill T Jones's creative journey. Titled, *Fela!* the musical the piece is organised around a narrative structure that resembles the linear chronological journey to stardom that is formulated in Hollywood *rags to riches* storying, which is replicated in its Nigerian equivalent, Nollywood. Basic to most European and Anglo-American narrative framework structure is a chronological temporal sequencing that recapitulates past experience by corresponding a verbal sequence of passages with the sequence of events that occurred in reality. Narratives are not, merely, "syntactic embedding" (Labov and Waletzky 1967: 20), because each passage in the story sequence is interconnected in a journey towards a resolution, rather than existing independently as an endpoint. The programme brochure to *Fela!* includes extracts from the sleeve notes for the CD of *Fela!* the musical.

94   P. ODIH

Close reading of this enables the elicitation of a Western narrative schema that construes the programme into a characteristically culture industry production.

The text to the theatre programme pamphlet for *Fela!* commences with an "orientation" (Labov and Waletzky 1967: 32), which as is the nature of Western narratives, has a referential function designed to situate the reader in respect to time, place and situation. We are informed in the programme brochure that features a sleeve note for the CD of *Fela!* the musical that in 2001 Stephen Hendel purchased a copy of *The Best Best of Fela*, (a CD compilation) and that this initiated an obsession with the idea of creating a musical theatre piece "embodying the life and music of Fela Kuti". As is a characteristic feature of the Western narrative form the account of the birth of the idea is depicted as a single point in time, a model of the eureka moment of the sole (White) male pioneer. The orientation is performed by phrases and lexical items situating the text within its culture industry context; and thus, rhetorical devices are included that refer to other areas of the commercial industry that surrounds the Afrobeat pioneered. For example, the compilation CD that was important to catalysing the interest of Stephen Hendel is described as "the Best Best of Fela, a compilation double CD containing 13 of Fela's most accessible tracks". The main body of the narrative formulation of the programme brochure's sleeve notes feature a sequencing of events described using informal semantic criteria, so as to establish in the simplest of terms what happened to inspire the idea of *Fela!* and what happened next after this eureka moment. Such detailing is known as the "complication or complicating action" (ibid.: 32) phase of the narrative, which comprises a series of descriptions of events detailing what actually happened to move the narrative forward. In the sleeve notes featured in the programme brochure this complication phase is formulated as thus: The director Stephen Hendel having spent months seeking the rights to develop the musical theatre play receives a telephone call from his lawyer, during which the choreographer of Bill T Jones was proposed as a prospective collaborator in the project. This complication phase is evolved in the following text of the narrative: "That client was Bill T Jones, African-American multi-award-winning artistic director, choreographer and dancer. They met, and within a short space of time, Steve Hendel passed his passion for the project to Bill T Jones". The semantic detailing in respect to passing on to another the passion for the musical is evidence of the narrative device of complicated action initiating a state of resolution to the beginning of the sequence of events. This is because as William Labov and Joshua Waletzky (1967) identify "a narrative which contains an orientation, complicating action and result is not a complete narrative" (ibid.: 33). Rather as is the case with the brochure, the story thus far is constructed to respond to the external stimuli of a desire for a beginning to the musical's conception. But as has been observed, "Beyond such immediate stimulus, we find that most narratives are so designed as to emphasize the strange and unusual character of the situation – there is an appeal to the element of mystery in most narratives" (ibid.: 34). The elements of intrigue and enchantment are evident in the programme brochure's account of "the challenging task of trying to turn Fela's unique style of music (Afrobeat) into a dramatic theatre piece". At this point one discerns the narrative entering into an "evaluation" phase (ibid.: 37) in which the narrator begins to openly collaborate with or assume a contrary position to the content of their story, whereby the narrator becomes more obviously discerning in the plotting and introduction of elements into the narrative.

Thus, for example, the narrator of the brochure sleeve notes mid-way through the content switches positionality from neutral description to a more politically inspired instructor. As is evident in the following extract: "The goal was to develop a 'show' that would capture the feel and energy of a live concert with all the passion and politics that made Fela a worldwide sensation". Having revealed their predilection the narrator using the Western chronology of narrative structure, then proceeds into a "resolution" phase in which their evaluative preferences are resolved into the overall objective of the narrative. In the brochure this involves an attempt to convince the reader that the direction of the protagonists is more widely received and part of a community that shares the vision of a musical theatre portrayal of the artist Fela Anikulapo-Kuti. Such a resolution is evident in the following extract from the programme brochure article "And over the course of the next four years, Bill and Jim developed the material 'on its feet' in a series of short developmental workshops that brought together an ever-growing number of talented collaborators and the musicians of Antibalas (one of the world's best Afrobeat bands, who happen to be based in Brooklyn)". Towards the end of the article, the narrator introduces a further technique characteristic of the Western narrative structuring of a conclusion that brings the story into the present, i.e., the use of a "coda", in which operates "a functional device for returning the verbal perspective to the present moment" (ibid.: 39). The sleeve notes' coda operates most effectively in the final section which writes about the summer of 2008 as a period of intense working on the design of the musical,

96   P. ODIH

which along with the technicians is described as, having "literally transformed 37 Arts, a new theatre complex at 37th Street and 10th Avenue, into Fela's fabled club in Lagos, Nigeria ('The Shrine')". While the coda does not actually structure the content elements so as to extend into the present, it does effectively use "the linguistic category that points to a referent instead of naming it explicitly: in this case, it has the effect of standing at the present moment of time; and pointing to the end of the narrative, identifying it as a remote point in the past" (ibid.: 40); and in so doing making the past relevant to the present. This deployment of the coda is evident in the following final sentence, "In September, Fela! the musical began performances Off Broadway", the reader gains from the narrative sequences an inspirited illusion that this enchanting ensemble could in the September of any number of years magic again into being the Off-Broadway production of *Fela!* the musical, whereby the formulaic interchangeability of the elements of the creative and productive process is mechanically reproducible so as to make exact mimetics of the original. Similar procedures of Western narrative structure are evident in the programme in all aspects of its depiction of female characters in the musical theatre performance. As is evident in the following extract,

> No two nights are ever the same. There's always plenty of 'Fela music', but also a seemingly random mix of consciousness-raising lectures, gyrating female dancers, pamphleteering, Yoruban rites and idiosyncratic rituals aimed at connecting to the spirit world – all a part of Fela's personal search for a 'true African style'. And after each number (which can easily run more than half an hour) Fela 'yabis' his audience. He actively engages in a humorous, often caustic give and take, poking fun at his audience and a wide variety of topics – first and foremost, the corrupt Nigerian generals and the large multi-nationals and oil companies that keep them in power. So it's not uncommon that before dawn, when the 'concert' finally starts to wind down, the Army might show up to harass Fela, his Queens, band and audience, or depending on what's been said and done, haul them off to jail to be beaten and tortured. National Theatre Archive (2010)

Close reading of the programme brochure for *Fela!* provides insights into the narrative structuring of musical theatre production's commodity-form. In relating the sequence of narrative elements to the popularly known sequencing of actual events that led to the creation of *Fela!* there is performed a recapitulation of the past into a Western linear chronological schema. Even a cursory appreciation of Nigerian ethnocultural distinction provides some basis in the suspicion that the programme brochure, sleeve note feature contains a facile and simplistic cultural display of creative inspiration. The Igbo and Yoruba story telling traditions to which I am acculturated into are nonlinear in their sequencing because they express the historical presence as a community of storytelling embedded in and through relational aura of embodied temporality. Conversely, the narrative structure of promotional technique and production of *Fela!* reflects the physiognomy of gender within the culture industry which is often an amalgam of typicality in photographable precision and confected sentimental, rationally disposed romanticism. Adorno (2001: 102) adapts Walter Benjamin's idea of aura i.e., the accumulated sense of being imbued in a work of art. According to Adorno the culture industry, in its pursuit of capitalist commodification "does not strictly counterpose another principle to that of aura" but rather it sustains "the decaying aura as a foggy mist" (ibid.). In response to writers that present the opaque descending hue of the world seen through the lens of the culture industry, as a functional means of inculcating orientating standards on populations, critical theorist purports a dialectical materialist opposition. As a riposte to defenders of musical theatre biopics, of anticolonial political activism, critical theorists admonish the technical and creative processes that reduce cultural history into esculent *byte-sized* platitudes. Detailed reading of Adorno provides some respite from a mostly pessimistic judgement. Adorno refers to a "deep unconscious mistrust" as a defensive residue into which the discerning can disentangle confected art from the subject's grounding in empirical reality (ibid.: 105). Cognisance of the difference between representation and reality, it is argued, constitutes "the spiritual make-up of the masses" and provides some explanation as to why human beings "have not, to a person, long since perceived and accepted the world as it is constructed for them by the culture industry" (ibid.). In summing up his argument Adorno (ibid.: 106) refers to the view of an "American interviewee who was of the opinion that the dilemmas of the contemporary epoch would end if people would simply follow the lead of prominent personalities". Such an encounter is interpreted as mere confirmation of Adorno's existing position, espoused with Horkheimer in *Dialectic of Enlightenment*, insisting that the ideology of the culture industry is anti-Enlightenment, whereby Enlightenment's notion of a progression towards the advancement of civilisation through the application of technical rationality is upended by the culture industry in which technological advancement is dissuading developments towards autonomous independent thinking. Indeed, Adorno (2001: 106) contends,

> If the masses have been unjustly reviled from above as masses, the culture industry is not among the least responsible for making them into masses and then despising them, while obstructing the emancipation for which human beings are as ripe as the productive forces of the epoch permit.

Adorno is unrelenting in dismissing popular music as prefabricated in its standardising pseudo-individualization. In so doing Adorno provides limited critical space for self-reflection regarding the power and privilege ascribed to the cultural capital of classical music. There is also limited critically informed conceptualising of music borne from inequality, deprivation and disadvantage as presenting an oppositional counter discourse to the hegemony of capitalist ideology. Conversely, in W.E.B. Du Bois's (1903) *The Souls of Black Folk* we are encouraged to discern Black music productions as seeing beyond the "veil" that obscures and refracts the "true self-consciousness" of Black people. It is my contention that the application of Du Bois's analysis of "The Sorrow Songs" has relevance to an anticolonial feminist account of Afrobeat as human rights-based communicative action. For, the notion of double consciousness resonates with the experiences of people from the West African diaspora generation hence from British colonial rule and its corresponding sense of "two-ness". In many respects, the historical basis of Afrobeat in terms of its anticolonial struggles, speaks truth to the contradictions of colonialism, and ascribes validity to being "gifted with second-sight" imbuing a counter-positionality to the distorted self-consciousness that is present to a Black indigenous people whose sense of belonging is defined in opposition to colonial Whiteness. In the following discussion, I discern how in the creative productions of contemporary Afrobeat artists we can distinguish anticolonial feminist mechanisms and strategies for rendering bridges across the "two-ness" of a West African identity generations hence from British colonialism and for that matter a Black British identity reconciling the legacy of colonialism that manifests locally in our everyday lives internationally manufactured racism.

ANTICOLONIAL DIGITAL CULTURES; RESISTING THE APPROPRIATION OF THE FEMININE ANTECEDENTS OF AFROBEAT

Such dystopian cynicism about the jazz genre and for that matter the derivative that is Afrobeat is difficult to accept, knowing as I do the politics and (her)story of the Afrobeat of Nigerian women. In the process of collecting qualitative data for this research I spoke with creatives within the Nigeria-based Afrobeat music scene. In one such discussion, with a Nigeria-based creative, that was tutored at the University of Ibadan, I asked about the cultural political relevance of Funmilayo Ransome-Kuti. My interviewee described the anticolonial feminist politics icon in the following context and as thus.

Interviewer: **Pamela Odih:** *You mentioned his [Fela Anikulapo-Kuti's] mother [Funmilayo Ransome-Kuti]. So, what was the influence of feminism in relation to Fela's music?*

Interviewee: **Afrobeat Music Creative:** *Yeah, yeah, I think. We can't talk about Fela's, mother, without actually talking about the tribe she comes from. Yeah, in Nigeria, the Yoruba tribe. Which Fela and his people came from or comes from there. They are, they are very, very liberal people. Even before the Western people came, so there is this history, whereas in a part of the Yorubaland around Ogun State, the present Ogun State, the colonial masters were taxing the locales too much. And it became so unbearable that the women came together and form an alignment and like a group and in which the group became so fierce and like somehow, they were able to like change the status quo and that then and from then, I can say; one of the most solid feminism movement started around then, in which, they protested the tax and everything. And they were able to, like, overcome what the colonial masters were doing then. So with that, the locals, everyone, even colonial masters, and the local chiefs and everyone; then there was like able to feel the presence of the women; that these women can actually, like change things on their own. Even what the men were afraid to do. So, women were very part of politics from that point onward, even at the other side of the ... So, women in politics are vocal in Nigeria right from time. So that actually helped Fela coming from one of those women. So, it gave him a lot of audacity that: this is my mom. That, I can even do more.* (Afrobeat Music Creative: Semi-structured qualitative interview, 19th January 2024)

The narrative sequencing of my interviewee's description of Funmilayo Ransome-Kuti is distinct in its form and function. Jazz temporality has been described as "chaotic" in its "phrase time" (Ermarth 1995), conversely the Frankfurt School's insistence on the existence of a coherent schema in the products and processes of popular and critical race theory urges a recognition of the centrality of Blackness to the culture industry's colonial capitalism. To the latter can be added a focus on an identity politics that traces anticolonial resistance as mapping across the (re)drawing of the African diaspora across international commodity circuits and this is particularly so with regard to music as per Ellis Cashmore's (1997) account of the *Black Culture Industry* and Les Back's (1996) *New Ethnicities and*

Urban Culture. Time and its temporality of consciousness is entwined with the structural relations of class, gender and race through which the capitalist circuits of colonial appropriation reverberate historically and into its contemporary iterations. Returning to the afore interview transcription, the central character of the interviewee evolves and matures throughout the to and fro of the narrative's circuitous weaving through iconic tropes and embodied native traditions of storytelling. In many respects the differences in the narrative style are illustrative of distinctions in the concept of technique when comparing the culture industry and artistic expression. The interviewee in their act of describing the anticolonial feminist icon deploys an artistic technique that is involved with the internal organisation of the depiction itself, with its internal symbolic logic. Conversely, the depiction and promotion of the anticolonial feminist icon in the culture industry is resonant with the mechanical reproduction processes of commodity capitalism in its appeal to facile, stylised tropes that are an objectification of the female subject. As Adorno (2001: 101) observes, the culture industry, "lives parasitically from the extra-artistic technique of the material production of goods, without regards for the obligation to the internal artistic whole implied by its functionality, but also without concern for the laws of form demanded by aesthetic autonomy". Whereby, the televisual mediated precision, of the simulacra of multilayered dimensions of anticolonial black feminism are merely further evidence of what Adorno (ibid.166), citing "Leo Lowenthal when he coined the term 'psychoanalysis in reverse'...that somehow the psychoanalytic concept of multilayered personality has been taken up by the cultural industry ... in order to ensnare the consumer ... in order to engage him psycho-dynamically" in an incessant existential pursuit of a confected sublimation of cultural identity. Contemporary advances in Artificial Intelligence (AI) accentuate and exceed the televisual mediations observed by the Frankfurt School in the 1960s. Indeed, in its integration of the body as subject and object of advertising inscriptive technologies 'Adsensory' (Odih 2016) Generative AI operates beyond Baudrillard's (1994) *Simulacra and Simulation*, observation of capitalist production of first-order simulacra of the real; second-order simulacra that is indistinguishable from the real and third-order simulacra that feigns its existence in material reality (i.e., simulation). For, Adsensory Generative AI manifests a fourth-order of simulacra that feigns its purpose to the potential of the body which is its subject and object. Diaspora is an attractive site for signs that are directed at bodily potential; this is because the migrant tales and narrative experiences

3 ANTICOLONIAL FEMINIST HUMAN RIGHTS   101

embedded in the habitus of immigrant communities cultivate imaginative listening and an embodied visuality of the hopes, dreams and aspirations of migration. Imagination as a realm of capitalist primitive accumulation is inherently unpredictable because it is imaginative; and thus, provide spaces for radical transgressive resistance, as I observed in my interviews with Nigerian creatives, Afrobeat artists. It was observed, that giving space for the creative ingenuity of the subaltern provides for enlightening appreciation of the contradictions and conflicts of the lived experience of the stereotypes and simulacra produced by the culture industry. Consider in this respect the following extract from my interview with the Nigerian-based Afrobeat music creative.

> *Interviewer:* **Pamela Odih**: *Can you tell me about your work around Afrobeat? How are you involved? I have looked at your art.*
>
> *Interviewee:* **Afrobeat Music Creative**: *So, I think when I started doing 3D, I was, in the University of Benin. That was around 2014, so I was fortunate to do my internship at one of the best animation studios in Nigeria that is Orange VFX studios. So, after that after I was doing 3D from one studio to the other. But later when I started doing it on my own, I was like what's, what can I do that is going to be different? Then I thought of doing different things like doing my own short movie; doing this doing thing that. But later I noticed that most of the client I was getting are coming from music. So, it's either foreign music or local music. There was a time I had the opportunity to work with Alicia Keys. So, and I also worked with one of our A list local artists Niyola [Eniola Akinbo]. So, when noticing these things, I decided to lean more towards creating music-influenced 3D. So, because now Afrobeat is a global product, so it's not a local music anymore.*
>
> *So I decided to now use my medium of 3D to showcase my talent alongside the already blown artists like our A list like Whiskey, Burna Boy because these guys are global already international. So, I just make my arts more around them. So, I think it resonates more with my kind of art. So instead of me, trying to reinvent the wheel. I decided to show my talents using these artists that are already international.* (Afrobeat Music Creative: Semi-structured qualitative interview, 19th January 2024)

The interviewee's description of music-influenced 3D is very resonant with the tradition of sculpture in traditionally native Nigerian culture. Whereby, similarly to West African art more generally, music, song and the sculpting of images of deity and spirits perpetuates the cultural anthropology of the society and identity of its people. In monotheistic West African countries such as Nigeria the symbolic meaning of sculpture is embedded within a belief system situating at its centre a "universal God of Creation" which is believed to have imbued "the world with a sacred energy, or life-force, which animates all things" (Naylor 1973: 8). The supreme energy, is believed to have been accorded a universal God, that in turn bestowed its spirit to a pantheon of gods; including those of nature several of whom were female deities that are worshipped in female cults. After the pantheon of gods, spiritual power is bestowed to the "primeval ancestors of the tribe" (ibid.). In its appropriate state the energy binds together the universe into a decorous ordered harmonious whole. In its disordered state discordant forces meddle with the order of things, intruding and disrupting its harmony. So as to reset the state of being and bring about the return of stability to the world, it is deemed necessary to placate the supernatural universe: "To correct the disorder, new life-force must be generated by the tribe to increase the power of the spirits" (ibid.). In their performance of ceremonies, festivals, sacrifices, ritual and prayers the tribe endeavours to assist the gods in their bringing back harmony to the metaphysical universe and stability to the material world. Sculpture plays an integral role in the attempt to subdue evil spirits and bringing the metaphysical forces of the world within the control of human interventions. In spiritual ceremonies sculptured images of figures are presented so as to invoke the approbation and presence of the tribal ancestors and gods. In so doing, "the spirits are summoned to dwell within the images, and to participate in the rites" (ibid.). Given the reverential accolade of the supernatural ascribed to the cosmological worldview there is little separation of spiritual beliefs from their daily existence, thus in Nigerian culture and society it is plausible that "they call upon the spirits residing in the sculptures during every phase of their lives" (ibid.). Consequently, it has been observed that sculptures and images of ancestors protectively survey tribal communities; that masks and figures watch over agricultural harvest celebrations; and "Other images ward off witches, invoke the spirits of war, and guard the graves of people who have recently died" (ibid.: 9). Furthermore, the sculptural figures are not merely "just temporary abodes for the spirits. The sculptures are links between man and the realm of the supernatural, possessing awesome powers of their own" (ibid.). While African sculptures represent the collective spiritual beliefs of the tribe they are created by an individual sculptor. Nevertheless, they tend not to claim individual authorship for their production in contrast with Western first world creatives; and yet despite not signing their work Western African sculptors are known within their communities. This aspect of sculpture as

3 ANTICOLONIAL FEMINIST HUMAN RIGHTS   103

communicative action is poignant to my discussion of Funmilayo Ransome-Kuti because of the significance of artistic praxis to her anticolonial feminism. It is my contention that it is possible to discern sculpture as a medium for an articulation of Nigerian ethnicity and a cultural political identity. The following discussion develops the concept of sculpture as both metaphor and materiality, of a contemporary anticolonial praxis that is situated in resistance to the commodification of anticolonial feminism by the capitalistic culture industry. In this respect consider the following extract from my interview with the Afrobeat music creative.

*Interviewer: **Pamela Odih**: And how do you make it distinctly Nigerian? You are using a very Western medium 3D [digital media]. How are you making it Nigerian?*

*Interviewee: **Afrobeat Music Creative**: Yeah, yeah, yeah. I think that's a very, very interesting topic and it's something I can discuss from now to tomorrow; but I would like to like, break it down. So, it's doesn't have scattered around the place. One of the most important mediums of art in Africa, precolonial era, I think it's mainly sculpture.*

So mostly in Africa, we do sculpture, some for religious purpose, some for aesthetic purposes. So we don't do much of painting before the Western people came, so we do more of if you go on the Internet, you see a lot of Benin and if you Ife art all around the place. So we are, we are this kind of people that believe in seeing the arts from the 3D perspective. You don't like those flats, so we love seeing the base, seeing the back, seeing the front and at times we we mostly lean towards the stylized and abstract kind of arts, you understand. So that's really influenced my artwork in as much as I really want to create characters that people can easily know or resonates with that art this is so and so artist, this is Burna Boy, I still want some influence [from] our stylized and abstract style in that art; so most times when you look at the eyes of the characters you can see that at times it is over exaggerated. It is big. It is bulgy and at times the mouth the eyes the proportion is not exactly realistic, but does that's art for me. Because you can't keep copying the genre exactly and now saying you have been creative about it, that's not creativity. You have to be a bit lean away from realism and create something that is out of the ordinary. You understand? So, my artwork is it's more stylized than umm Abstract than it is realism. So, and that comes from our own sculptural works, like the one you can find in Ife. You can find some in Iboko in the eastern side of Nigeria and uh Benin all around Nigeria. So, we are this kind of people that love 3-dimensional works so that I can see that's my basic motive of why I decide to make my characters not being realistic in the approach, yeah. (Afrobeat Music Creative: Semi-structured qualitative interview, 19th January 2024)

Specialist expertise publications on Nigerian sculpture emerged as a field of Western intellectual research activity in the 1960s; especially with regard to a series of exhibitions that coincided with Nigeria's celebration in 1960, of its independence from British colonial rule. October 1960 witnessed the Arts Council of Great Britain's staging in London, in collaboration with Nigeria, the foremost comprehensive loan exhibition of Nigerian art and sculpture (Fagg 1963). Prior to this exhibition, displays of Nigerian art were most probably looted treasures derived from the punitive expedition by the British of Benin City in 1897. An outcome of the raid was the looting of thousands of Benin bronze antiquities, which arrived in Europe having been unjustifiably pillaged by the brutal British as trophies of their wanton destruction of a civilised and cultured monachal dynasty. Surviving artefacts of Nigerian antiquity are believed to exist more commonly as a consequence of imperialist plundering; and also as having been protected during the later stages of British colonial rule, in which was practised indirect rule via traditional native leaders; as a consequence, the crafting of tribal and pagan art was little interfered with by the British rulers. An outcome of this, it has been observed, was "that the religious art, far from being snuffed out, often continued to flourish, only gradually impaired by the erosion of its spiritual basis" (ibid.: 20). The abundance of surviving Nigerian sculpture antiquity is also due to their material substance, which having to endure and withstand the geological climatic processes of sub-tropical erosion, were by necessity made of metal, stone and terra-cotta clay. Indeed, excavations of the alluvial beds of the Niger Delta reveal old land masses that had been broken down, carried by the river waters; and sedimented down in the alluvial beds, which traditionally adept potters using the principle of levigation would separate the finer clay particles from the coarser substances, with the latter heavier mineral participles swept along more quickly than the finer ones (ibid.: 22). Given that the Niger River from its source at the Sierra Leone, Guinea border through its crescent flows through Mali, Niger, Benin, Nigeria before disgorging in the Niger Delta, the terra-cotta material basis of ancient Nigerian sculpture is both symbol and a consequence of a communication between flows of people.

Nigerian sculpture is recognised for its distinctly locational expressive verve. Configurations of aesthetic techniques marking out the native sculptural form of the southern-western Nigeria region of Funmilayo Ransome-Kuti's Yoruba tribe reflect the rich cornucopia of tropical foliage. Sculptural carvings in modern times, as I have observed in my visits to Nigeria, embody the medium of the sub-Saharan verdure as they are borne abundantly from the tropicality of the circumferent rural area and echoing its *timbre*. Sculptural carvings of the Yoruba antiquity are the message of a spiritual, meta-physical and embodied relation to the external world, as evoked in the stone, metal and clay art that mediate the sculptural forms from east to west Nigeria. Nigerian sculpture can be classified according to numerous criteria; a prominent schema elucidates a useful distinction between ethnicity (tribe) and "style". Ethnic-tribe style refers, according to Jones (1973), to two different assemblages: "cultural – people speaking a common language, and social – people forming a traditionally independent political unit" (ibid.: 59). In terms of communities of Yoruba-speaking people, one can discern the second characteristic of Western African sculpture classification, that is a recognisable "style" that extends across the native land of the Western State (region) of Nigeria. Experts specialising in Nigerian sculpture distinguish the Yoruba style from that of the Benin palace style, whereby the latter refers to productions of Benin City craftsmen, which were confined by craft rituals to brass casting and wooden carvings meticulously controlled and distributed by the King of Benin (ibid.). These same experts also disagree on whether the technique of bronze-casting was introduced by the sixteenth-century Portuguese explorers, the first Europeans to transact and capture territories in Nigeria. Whereby, the prominent specialist in Nigerian antiquity sculpture, William Fagg (1950: 69) says of the theory of European origin, that there is little doubt that Portuguese soldiers did little to dissuade European scholars of this presumption and there is some evidence of traces of influence e.g., "same ideas of menstruation which produced the Parthenon metopes", but there is substantial evidence to the contrary in the theory of "the foreign origin of the best in Benin culture", whereby archaeological evidence more plausibly suggests, "that Benin owed something to Ife, 150 miles away, whose Oni had exerted spiritual overlordship over Benin since the early years of the founding of the Yoruba kingdoms; and the subsequent inquiries by Talbot and others leave no doubt that the Bini believe they learnt bronze-casting from Ife" (ibid.).

Applying the concept of "style" to Yoruba sculpture is in actuality even more complex than is initially perceived. It is dissimilar to the Classical sculpture style of the Greek, Roman and the Gothic style of Mediterranean ancient European worlds in terms of a uniformity of technique and visual culture across the representation of human, animal forms. Conversely, in Yoruba sculpture, "different materials and techniques have different styles" (Jones 1973: 60). The medium, in concurrence with the materiality of the cultural identity of the local community principally determines the style of the sculpture. Indeed, it has been affirmed that the earliest extant artefacts in sculpture created in African antiquity are in terra-cotta, and Nigeria holds the supreme primacy in its multitudes (Fagg 1963). Furthermore, remaining with a focus on material.

Thus, it has been observed that the sculpture art of south east and western Nigeria "tends to have different styles for different media" (Jones 1973: 63); where difference in styles is evident in the same media this exists in communication with tribal exigencies. In specific regard to the regions mostly populated by Yoruba people, the tendency of this tribe to build large urban communities partly explains the centrality of communication to the style making of the art and eclectic tribalism. Thus, in contrast to the Ibo tribe's aversion to expanding the population of the community beyond village proportions, the antiquity of Yoruba urbanism was seen to be based on a morphology of "fusion" (Fagg 1963). More specifically, it has been observed that in its native form there existed as a "pyramidal organization of the innumerable Yoruba kingdoms or city-states; if we consider the religious rather than the political aspect of divine kingship, then all these kingdoms are seen to form a greater pyramid, embracing all Yorubaland, and with Ife at its apex" (ibid.: 26). The style of Yoruba sculpture, although clearly defined by its medium and highly diverse; nevertheless, a highly influential narrative description derives from the often-cited book *Nigerian Images,* in which it is stated that the significance of the natural world to the sculpture production of the Yoruba tribe was productive of a style defined as "idealized naturalism".

Nevertheless, considerable variations of style distinguish and conjoin the sculpture of southern Nigeria and this complexity has been explained as thus, "the communities of south-eastern Nigeria are not isolated from each other but closely interconnected by a well-developed system of communication based on an elaborate network of trade routes and markets" (Jones 1973: 63). The issue of communication, as an integral feature of east to western Nigerian sculpture is discussed in William Fagg's (1967) *The Art of Central Africa; Tribal Masks and Sculptures,* where it is recognised that a "general absence of tribal sculpture among the eastern and southern peoples of Africa is not due to any inferiority in artistic capacity … A people may indeed lose their arts under the stress of cultural change (such as Africa is undergoing) but it is improbable that they can lose the capacity for art" (ibid.: 24). The inference here is that African nations that have preserved native arts have done so due to effectively communicating these traditions across generations. Integral to this, it is my contention, has been the role of poetry, oral literature and song to the success of the Yoruba tribe in preserving its sculpture tradition. Such observation is supported elsewhere as thus, by William Fagg (1963: 39).

> **Nigeria's reputation in the world of art rests at present very largely on the Ife-Benin tradition, on the fact that ancient Nigerians were able to make a reasonable approximation to the high arts of Egypt, Greece, Rome, India, Renaissance Italy and the western world in general; and educated Nigerians are not unjustly proud of this passport to the international club of the naturalistic arts.**

Indeed, during my interview discussion with the afore introduced Nigerian-based music creative we explored the applicability of methodological concepts of Western critical theory. The interview had previously explored traditional native Nigerian sculpture crafts so as to develop methodological practices which authentically reflected a consciousness of the world and an embodied relation to it. There is evidence of innovative ingenuity in the application of digital technology to create a music-sculpture that works with computer generated programmes similar to traditional Nigerian crafters in their dependency on the surrounding ecology as a medium for their message. In William Fagg's (1966) *African Tribal Sculptures; The Niger Basin Tribes,* there is detailed description of the extent to which the art of African tribes pertains to an aura as existing in their own individual universe such that the whole exceeds a sum of its parts. Closer elucidation of the Yoruba cosmological conception of world reveals geometric calculus and schema attune with the technical capital ascribed to cultural distinction of aspects of digital music technologies. Specifically, it is observed that, in south-western Nigerian artistic traditions there exists a

> Yoruba cosmological concept of an essentially square world founded on the number four and more especially its multiple, sixteen – a system which can be endlessly illustrated from Yoruba art and myth, from the birds on the beaded crowns of the Yoruba Obas, and above all from the odu of *Ifa* divination in which the order of the universe is both defined and applied to daily life. (Fagg 1963: 25–26)

Digital music-sculptures are highly evocative of the matrix form of Nigerian craft tradition that exists as a congregation of universes of art, rather than the Western classical notion of a singular universal tradition. According to Fagg (1966: 5) a craft tradition can only be described as "a multitude of universes of art" where its creatives are involved in "mutually exclusive with artistic horizons limited to the frontiers of each universe". Nigerian native tribal art was historically redolent with these characteristic features, whereby "the tribe is an exclusive 'in-group', which uses art among many other means to express its internal solidarity and self-sufficiency, and conversely its difference from all others" (ibid.). Speaking with the Nigerian Afrobeat music creatives in respect to their use of digital technology to express anticolonial sentiment, while formulating bridges between the old and new relevant intergenerationally to a Nigerian diaspora became evident that digital media's communality was a distinctly attractive feature. In their digital application to sculpture, just as with the Nigerian ancestry of their heritage, it was also perceived that, in tribal art communication is not a limit to the art in the same way that cultural capital delimits the reception of European art. For, it is believed that tribal art as created by the people of the tribe has as its purpose that of a clarity in its reception; indeed, the tribal artist, "is using a 'language' of form which all can 'understand', even though it is never out into words, their comprehension and his composition are intuitive to an extent rarely known in Europe for several centuries past" (ibid.: 6). In an exhibition catalogue book titled, *The Living Arts of Nigeria*, William Fagg (1972: 86) provides a brief mention of the influence of Nigerian wood-carving traditions on European art and conceptualises this in terms of a "recreative function" in terms of boundary cross between African and European commercialised imitation. Thus, for example it is stated by Fagg (ibid.) that inspirations for Cubism exist in African art.

It is a truism to say that there are many examples of Cubism – or something very like it – in African art, but masks are often a striking illustration of the breaking-up of surfaces into triangular and lozenge-shaped facets in order to catch the light as they move in the dance. (In fact, Cubism seems much more functional in this mobile sculpture than in modern painting). The Ibo headdress of the Maiden Spirit is of this kind, though its cubism is somewhat muted to show beauty (whereas it is exaggerated in the counterpart mask of the Elephant Spirit). The Gelede mask from the Yoruba which carries on its head an admirably (and rather early) motor car with passengers is an example of the readiness of this cult to adapt to the modern world, which has given it the durability to survive in Lagos itself until now. The long anthropozoomorphic mask from Epe is startlingly 'pop' in appearance; but a

3 ANTICOLONIAL FEMINIST HUMAN RIGHTS 109

little research would probably establish that similar masks were known before Dada and Duchamp, let alone the recycled Duchamp of the sixties. It would be going too far to say that the origins of each of the schools of modern art are to be sought in Africa, but at least the Africans had a remarkable knack of anticipating them (sometimes by as much as 2500 years). William Fagg (1972: 85)

In this respect consider the following interview transcription extract, derived from an interview I conducted with a Nigerian Afrobeat musician, who although a resident in Nigeria occasionally tours in England. The Anglo-Nigerian hybridity of their creative production is very much a product of the discerning and critically selective use of new music technology to sculpt their music profile and craft an audience community.

*Interviewer: **Pamela Odih**: And so, what was special about Fela Kuti's music; you said that there was a spirit?*

*Interviewee: **Afrobeat Musician**: I think I love him because also, so, I believe that he's more like a spiritual man when it comes to music, you know; because I believe that music is also spiritual. So that's also one of the things I love about Fela Kuti. We'll see sincerely, yeah.*

...

*Interviewer: **Pamela Odih**: ... How does the market reach out to the artist?*

*Interviewee: **Afrobeat Musician**: It's either that they are reaching through record labels or personally you as an independent artist you could just make sure you are dropping your content; your content online. Just reach, you know, record labels out there, who could sponsor you in one of the themes. Just put you out there as long as. You are available constantly on social media. That's or so another way that the Afrobeats are getting known through the younger ones and also the upcoming ones.*

*Interviewer: **Pamela Odih**: You said you are using social media to drop your work; how do you do that?*

*Interviewee: **Afrobeat Musician**: I do that through Facebook, Instagram ... You know, social media now is much more powerful; you can't compare it now than you know a few years ago. I think that I dropped something a few weeks ago and it got a lot of views. So I actually say that social media is one of the key points for younger ones that are going into entertainment in general. It helps a lot ... [Interviewer: What's the process?] Actually, now I have a company distributor called TuneCore based in the US. So I upload my songs there. It's actually where I make my realities also [real-time creative production]. So I upload my songs there; all you just need is to put a date of your release [music song release to the audience]. Then after that you have to [publish] the song; after* *that you have to make a campaign of the song. So as of now, since the song was dropping on the 14th as of now I am actually in the campaign season. Yeah, so that's what I'm actually doing right now.*

The interviewee's references made to TuneCore publishing provide illustration of how contemporary Afrobeat(s) artists are operating similarly to the native sculptors of traditional Nigeria tribal art; for as with their ancestors the Afrobeat(s) musicians in their use of digital music technology are sculpting materials foraged from the surrounding environment so as to craft channels of communication. In this respect the rhizomatic morphology of TuneCore is comparable to the clay sedimentation into the Niger Delta of broken away landmasses. Whereby TuneCore operates as a music publishing platform, that "has direct memberships with pay sources for musicians worldwide", it collects, from paying territories, the mechanical and performance royalties music artists earn from the streaming of their original songs on Spotify, TikTok, and video views on YouTube etc. (TuneCore 2024). The act of crafting a community of listeners for the artist's original Afrobeat(s) is facilitated by the TuneCore's dashboard, whereby the interoperability between TuneCore and the streaming company e.g., enables a seamless flow of digital data that the artist can use to craft a community of listeners. For example, the artists having connected to Spotify for Artists, so as to register the songs they have distributed, can view how well their songs are performing through TuneCore's advanced analytics and therefore sculpture their music in response to audience response; and in respect to the algorithmic profile, personalisation of their music as delivered to selected audiences via the streaming server.

The interview transcription extract provides further insights into the tribal diversity of the traditional African art on to which the Afrobeat artist is overlaying digital music technology. Expertise within the field of African sculpture has consistently highlighted the Western European ways of seeing art as an obstacle to recognising the resonances that interoperate in the creative arts of distinct localities and tribes. As Fagg (1970: 12) expresses it, the difficulties Europeans encounter in appreciating the diversity of African art and the differences between its tribal arts, is "because for two millennia past the national arts of the countries of Europe have been provinces within a single universe of art, whereas the African tribes have separate universes more different from each other than European art from Chinese". It is evident that much of the diversity stems from the fact that many of the tribes have evolved through their distinct historical trajectories and through this evolutionary process have refined a language in culture to communicate a shared ethnicity and belonging in the ecology of the surrounding environment. Returning my interview with the Afrobeat creative. The above interview transcription extract provides indication of the echoing of traditional West African artistry across the diaspora. Multiple dimensions of the interviewee's use of digital technology are resonant with the Yoruba art tradition which is the most prolific of Nigerian tribal art. Of particular resonance is the connection of digital music technology and urbanism. For, it has been long since recognised that Yoruba art has "strong tendencies to urbanism, organizing themselves in large and small city-states under divine kings of carefully limited power" (Fagg 1966: 21). In addition to a "variety of local cults, Yoruba religion and art are characterized by a number of universal cults of major deities, who clearly began as nature gods" (ibid.). Thus, the communicative action of Yoruba tribal art is based on a revered functionality as it is directed towards respect for the local cult of the deity. While very useful to my analysis of Yoruba native tribal art and its translation into the digital music sculpture of Afrobeat creatives, there is a limitation to William Fagg's theoretical framework, and this pertains to his consistent marginalisation of the influence of African women to the making of tribal art. In this area of specialism there are a limited number of academic writers reinterpreting the pieces exhibiting in Fagg's many catalogue writings, photographs and curated showcases on West African art. Preeminent, for my purposes, is Rowland Abiodun's (1989) *Woman in Yoruba Religious Images*. According to this writer, "From available archaeological finds mainly at Ile-Ife, the sacred city of the Yoruba, the presence and power of women would appear to be of great antiquity" (ibid.: 2). The author describes a brass figure pair that was discovered at Ita Yemoo in Ile-Ife in 1957 as providing some indication of the status of esteemed female subjects. "The female brass figure dresses as an important chieftain with all the regalia of office which is not in any way inferior to that of her male counterpart" (ibid.). With regard to the actual practice of sculpture, it is Abiodun's observation that while the craft guilds prohibitively denied access to females, it is possible to see in hair plaiting an area in which traditional sculpture was the preserve of female expertise. In focussing on festivals, it is possible to trace a heritage of female sculptures using this art to preserve cultural heritage and communicate authority in public civic spaces. Abiodun provides a detailed description of hair plaiting traditions in celebration of the Yoruba mythology of the river goddess Oshun; and in honouring the tradition cult members of Yeye Olorisha in Owe spend tremendous amounts of time plaiting their hair intricately so as to produce ornately styled hair for the annual Igogo festival in reverence to the Oronsen female deity (ibid.: 3). Adorned with elaborately plaited hair and traditional garments that cult members' parade at the Igogo festival conjures an "aesthetic atmosphere" infused with the meta-physical powers so ascribed. Consider in this respect the following quotation extracts; the first continues from Rowland Abiodun's (1989) *Woman in Yoruba Religious Images* and the second is derived from my interview with the 3D music-sculpture artist who provides digital art for Afrobeat musicians.

> **Besides adding to the power and beauty of the human face and head which is the focus of much aesthetic interest in Yoruba art, hairplaiting has an important religious significance in the Yoruba tradition. The hairplaiter/dresser is seen as one who honours and beautifies Ori-inu, lit. 'inner head', the 'divinity' of the Head, also taken to be the visible representation of one's destiny and the essence of one's personality... Seen in the above light, Oshun, the 'Hairplaiting Expert with the Beaded Comb' is believed to have the power to influence the destinies of men and gods, orisha, for better or for worse. Oshun's presence is crucial to the sustenance of life and order on earth. She is the source of potency for most if not all male-dominated cults like the Egungun 'ancestral masquerades', 'the collective male dead, whose voice is the bull-roarer', Gelede 'to honour our mothers' and Ifa 'the Yoruba divination deity'. Rowland Abiodun (1989: 3)**

> *Interviewer:* **Pamela Odih**: *Could you tell me about [the Afrobeat musician] Eniola [Akinbo] [Niyola]?*
>
> *Interviewee:* **Afrobeat Music Creative**: *So, concerning how I approached Eniola work. Eniola is an artist in which whenever you are working with her as an artist, you don't really need to overthink it. She has a very unique personality. She's very feminine and she, she does a lot of dances. Like she loves elaborate outfits like nails, beautiful hair and she, she has a very unique style of dance. So, I tried to depict one of those dancing. The last video I did and she really loved it. So, concerning Eniola's animation. I think it's something that is very straightforward because she sings different on different topic.*
>
> *She doesn't amount just one. You can listen to her song and it's about love and the other one is about victory and another one is about thanking God and different kind of song and even talking about what is happening currently. So, but for the songs I decided to go with the flow with exactly what she's saying and simultaneously trying to like.*

3 ANTICOLONIAL FEMINIST HUMAN RIGHTS 113

Still show our personality because he has this calm personality, but whenever she comes to the state and she really wants to perform; she's all over the place. She has this mad energy, so I tried to like do that in one of the video, I did where she was just looking and she was looking calm; and the other one, I did one in which she was just doing a household dance. That very unique dance with her lap. So, I don't. I don't over think it whenever I am working with artists that has their personality and identity already. So, I don't try to reinvent anything. I just try to study what are they going to do in this situation? OK, let me add fun to it. So that's what I do. (Afrobeat Music Creative: Semi-structured qualitative interview, 19th January 2024)

My reasoning in aligning the two quotations is to highlight similarities in their reverence for using sculpture to venerate female cults that seek to empower and celebrate the human right of women to extol communicative action. The link to anticolonial feminism here relates proximately to the British colonial era and its suppression of indigenous cultural identity, which was further curtailing in respect to the over layering onto gender differentiation within tribes, with an imposition of British patriarchal gender inequalities. Furthermore, both extracts refer to the aesthetics in the presentation of the female deity and the stylising of their racialised gender identity. The extent to which celebrating, valorising and sanctioning the parade in public spaces of race-based physical characteristics is related to human rights might be clearer if one considers the United Nations Declaration of Human Rights of 1948, "Everyone has the right freely to participate in the cultural life of the community, to enjoy the arts and to share in scientific advancement and its benefits". In more recent times campaigns feminists have sought to challenge colonialist abuses to human rights in terms of seeking to render illegal discrimination based on the racialised characteristics of hair. Indeed, with regard to hair and human rights, in October 2022 the United Kingdom's Equality and Human Rights Commission published non-statutory guidance to prohibit unlawful indirect discrimination related to hair (Odih 2025). The non-statutory guidance seeks to protect against institutional policies that are putting at a disadvantage, individuals who have similarly racialised characteristics based on their hair. These indirectly discriminatory practices restricted certain hair sculpting such as cornrows and dreadlocks, clearly harkened back to a colonial era of imposition and control of Black aesthetics and certainly related to the dark satanic enslavement of Black people who were deprived their humanity. It is in this sense that the Yoruba female sculpture art of hair plaiting relates to anticolonial feminist human rights.

Although technically complex and erudite in its expression, the description of the musician's use of contemporary digital technology is more familiar to the traditional Yoruba hair sculpture carried out by women, than it is strange. Experts on Yoruba art have long since observed, in respect to tribal dimensions, "It is the unity of art and belief which makes understanding and acceptance of the forms of art easy for members of the tribe, but correspondingly difficult for non-members, since they do not share the belief" (Fagg 1966: 6). The use of digital technology as a form of sculpture is communicatively functional within the digital community tribe; because they are acting within the medium, but correspondingly difficult for outsiders because they are not as emersed in the digital world. As described about traditional tribal art, it is "functional within the tribe but not outside it" (ibid.). In many respects, the creative quoted previously is emblematic of a dissimilarity between the functionality of African tribal art and the European cultural prestige of an indulgence of art in which it exists in human perception as for its own sake. Conversely, the creative describes an inherent functionality attributed to the art, rather than art for art sake; there is evidence of a committed endeavour to communicate with a tribe, albeit a digitally created and geographically dispersed group. Such activities are germane to African tribal art, in their focus on the universe of meaning communicated to their tribe and unlike European art's eclectic interloping between genre the African tribal artist "is likely to be biased by his own matrix of belief against responding to these universalities" (ibid.).

The interviewees spoke eloquently about the Nigerian arts and crafts of sculpture; and their respective attempts to translate this into digital music technology. In respect their thoughts and accomplishment in using sculpture as a metaphor and practice for their creative pursuits in mixed-media provided an original insight into the possibilities of decolonial feminist critical theory. Indeed, the political praxis of Funmilayo Ransome-Kuti was often ridiculed by the British colonial governors for its bricolage presentation of traditional Yoruba music cultivated into protest songs, coupled with the occupation of public space in the hosting of picnics and her fastidious letter writing—as per the many handwritten and typed letters held at the National Archives. In retrospect the materiality of arts, crafts, inscriptions and presentations of self in hair, garments etc., all pertained to sculpture. Collectively these artefacts are illustrative of the possibilities of an anticolonial feminist praxis that is imbued with the culture and society of its Nigerian heritage.

Timely Reminders; Anticolonial Feminist Human Rights Technocultural Boundary Crossing

The issue of giving entitlement to the articulation of the colonised experience is a deliberation, "accessible only from positions of relative privilege; voice becomes a tool that is available to work with because of ongoing colonial power relationships" (Coddington 2017: 317). Cognisant of these issues accounts of the feminist influences that shaped the Afrobeat protestations of the artist Fela Anikulapo-Kuti have provided close readings song text crafted by the Yoruba feminist collective led by his mother. Prominent within this genre is Stephanie Shonekan's (2009) examination of *The Revolutionary Songs of Funmilayo Ransome-Kuti [FRK]and the Abeokuta Market Women's [AWU] Movement in 1940s Western Nigeria,* in which the author describes becoming mindful of these protest songs having read Wole Soyinka's 1981 autobiography *Ake: Years of Childhood.* Thereafter, the influential biography of Johnson-Odim and Mba (1997) provided insight into the existence of the "FRK" archive of protest songs, composed by the AWU, hosted at the University of Ibadan Archives, Nigeria as part of the "FRK" collection. Shonekan description of examining and translating the lyrics speaks of a conscious awakening and embodied association with the texts. As is evident in the phrasing and articulation of approbation when providing inferences of their technique of close reading; narrated as thus: "While first examining the song texts in translation, I was struck by how closely connected these songs are to Fela's lyrical devices and political philosophy" (ibid.: 129). Pertinent aspects of the Yoruba native tradition in respect to mother-son maternal bonding are emphasised as indicative of just how this influence is transferred, "The Yoruba term for mother, *Iya* or *Iye,* has particular significance to this theory. *Iye* signifies a powerful bond between mother and child ... by all accounts, Fela was uniquely connected to his mother" (ibid.: 128–129). Conversely, my diasporic racial identity, while Nigerian, is British; I am London born from parents that immigrated to Britain in the 1960s from the south-eastern Igbo (Ibo) land of Biafra during the Nigerian civil war. My ethnic and racial heritage, ascendency from an oppositional tribe is as irrelevant as the colour of my skin, however it does inform my insistence on achieving critical distance in the analyses; a position less apparent in the afore described studies. Of particular distinction is my focus on political economy of human rights and the elicitation of the material components of anticolonial Nigerian feminism; as opposed to an emphasis on culture

116   P. ODIH

and society. Integral to this elicitation has been an investigation into the cultural industry's interpretation of Funmilayo Ransome-Kuti, to which I envisaged a Frankfurt School critical theory response to *Fela!* the musical. In riposte to critical theory's denunciation of agency in respect to the possibilities of political engagement using the medium of jazz, I discussed interviews conducted in recent times with Afrobeat creatives. In my interviews with the afore artists the metaphor of sculpture emerged as a means of articulating the functional communicative action of African tribal art. Rather than the European sentimentality of art for art's sake, the former endeavours towards communication as its principal purpose and this builds into their use of digital music technology as an uncompromising determination to be comprehended whereby, functional communicative action is practised by the Nigerian digital-music sculptor as a natural disposition to an anticolonial feminist antecedent embedded in the medium of Afrobeat. It is ultimately the intention of this chapter to identify the anticolonial feminist antecedents of Afrobeat and to theorise the extent to which resistance to the culture industry's commodification processes, has materialised a contemporary form of anticolonial feminist praxis which uses the medium of digital music technology as a means of West African Nigerian diaspora human rights sculpture.

References

Abiodun, R. (1989). Woman in Yoruba Religious Images. *African Languages and Cultures, 2*(1), 1–18. http://www.jstor.org/stable/1771702

Adejumobi, S. A. (2003); Affirmative Action and the Politics of Social Reform in a Global Context. *The Black Scholar, 33*(3/4), 32–36. http://www.jstor.org/stable/41069042

Adorno, T., (2001); *The Culture Industry*, London and New York: Routledge.

Álvarez, M., (2022); Monumentality and Anticolonial Resistance: Feminist Graffiti in Mexico, Public Art Dialogue, 12:2, 178–194, DOI: 10.1080/21502552.2022.2112349

Back, L., (1996); New Ethnicities and Urban Culture; Social Identity and Racism in the Lives of Young People, London: Routledge.

Baker, C., (2020) What female pop-folk celebrity in south-east Europe tells postsocialist feminist media studies about global formations of race, Feminist Media Studies, 20:3, 341–360, https://doi.org/10.1080/14680777.2019.1599035

Baudrillard, J., (1994); *Simulacra and Simulation*, Ann Arbor, Michigan: University of Michigan Press.

Bijl, P., (2017) Human Rights and Anticolonial Nationalism in Sjahrir's *Indonesian Contemplations*, Law & Literature, 29:2, 247–268, https://doi.org/10.1080/1535685X.2016.1268769

Byfield, J., (2003); Taxation, Women and the Colonial State, Egba Women's Tax Revolt, Meridians: Feminism, Race, Transnationalism, 2003, vol.,3, no., 2, pp. 250–77.

Byfield, J., (2012); Gender, Justice, and the Environment: Connecting the Dots, *African Studies Review*, April 2012, vol., 55, No., 1 (April 2012), pp., 1–12.

Cachalia, F., (2018); Democratic constitutionalism in the time of the postcolony: beyond triumph and betrayal, South African Journal on Human Rights, 34:3, 375–397, https://doi.org/10.1080/02587203.2018.1543838

Cashmore, E., (1997); *The Black Culture Industry*, London: Routledge.

Castledine, J. (2008); "In a Solid Bond of Unity": Anticolonial Feminism in the Cold War Era. *Journal of Women's History* 20(4), 57–81. https://doi.org/10.1353/jowh.0.0053

Coddington, K., (2017) Voice Under Scrutiny: Feminist Methods, Anticolonial Responses, and New Methodological Tools, The Professional Geographer, 69:2, 314–320, https://doi.org/10.1080/00330124.2016.1208512

Colonial Office (1947–1948); Note on Taxation of Women in Eastern Provinces, Colonial Office: Nigeria Original Correspondence. National Council of Nigeria and the Cameroons: Activities of Mrs Ransome-Kuti. The National Archives, Kew – Colonial office, Commonwealth and Foreign and Commonwealth Offices, 1947–1948, Reference: CO 583/293/1, National Archives, Kew, Richmond, TW9 4DU. Date of Visit: Tuesday 23rd April 2024; Booking Reference: RR147-950-06156K

Du Bois, W. E. B., (1903/1994); *The Souls of Black Folk*, [unabridged text as first published by A.C. McClurg and Co., Chicago in 1903], USA:Dover Publications.

Emard, K., & Nelson, L. (2021). Geographies of global lifestyle migration: Towards an anticolonial approach. *Progress in Human Geography*, 45(5), 1040–1060. https://doi.org/10.1177/0309132520957723

Engelmann, S. (2022); Pollution is Colonialism; Feminist Queer Anticolonial Propositions for Hacking the Anthropocene: Archive and Feminist Queer. *The AAG Review of Books*, 10(4), 33–35. https://doi.org/10.1080/2325548X.2022.2114761

Ermarth, E. D. (1995). Ph(r)ase Time: Chaos Theory and Postmodern Reports on Knowledge. *Time & Society*, 4(1), 91–110. https://doi.org/10.1177/0961463X95004001005

Fagg, W., (1950). A Bronze Figure in Ife Style at Benin. *Man, 50*, 69–70. https://doi.org/10.2307/2794524

Fagg, W., (1963); *Nigerian Images; The Splendour of African Sculpture*, London and New York: Frederick A. Praeger.

Fagg, W., (1966); *African Tribal Sculptures*, London: Methuen.

Fagg, W., (1967) The Art of Central Africa; Tribal Masks and Sculptures, London: Collins in Association with UNESCO.

Fagg, W., (1970); *African Sculpture*, Washington, D.C.: H. K. Press.

Fagg, W., (1972); *The Living Arts of Nigeria*, London: Macmillan.

Fela! (2010); Fela! the Musical, National Theatre Archive, National Theatre, London.

Felakuti.com (2023); *Story*. Available at: https://felakuti.com/gb/story/1938

Hornabrook, J., (2019); Gender, new creativity and Carnatic music in London, South Asian Diaspora, 11:2, 193–208, DOI: 10.1080/19438192.2019.1568663

Ibhawoh, B., (2014); Testing the Atlantic Charter: linking anticolonialism, self-determination and universal human rights, The International Journal of Human Rights, 18:7–8, 842–860, DOI: 10.1080/13642987.2014.951340

Johnson-Odim, C., (2009); 'For their Freedoms': The Anti-imperialist and International Feminist Activity of Funmilayo Ransome-Kuti of Nigeria, *Women's Studies International Forum*, 32, pp., 51–59.

Johnson-Odim, C., and Mba, N., (1997); *For Women and the Nation, Funmilayo Ransome-Kuti of Nigeria*, Urbana and Chicago: University of Illinois Press.

Jones, G., I., (1973); Sculpture of the Umushia Area of Nigeria, *African Arts*, Summer, 1973, Vo., 6. No. 4, pp., 58–63.

Kuti, F., (1984); Fela Kuti, Arena: Teacher Don't Teach Me Nonsense (Television Documentary, 30 November 1984), British Broadcasting Corporation (BBC). Available at: https://www.bbc.co.uk/programmes/p00jf0jg

Kuti, Fela., (1978/2011); *Fela Kuti, Konkombe Interview*. Available at: https://youtu.be/4waYY1HZ318?si=tGh7GXL6Jg1Nt7Q6

Labov, W. and Waletzky, J. (1967) Narrative Analysis: Oral Versions of Personal Experience. In (ed.) Helm, J., *Essays on the Verbal and the Visual Arts*, Proceedings of the 1966 Annual Spring Meeting of the American Ethnological Society, Seattle and London: University of Washington Press.

Moore, S. S. (2020). Between the state and the yard: gender and political space in Haiti. *Gender, Place & Culture, 28*(9), 1306–1326. https://doi.org/10.108 0/0966369X.2020.1846500

National Theatre Archive (2010); Digital Research Pack for Fela!, National Theatre Archive, London: National Theatre.

Naylor, P., (1973); *Black Images; The Art of West Africa*, Garden City, N.Y.: Doubleday.

Obiagu, A., (2023); Toward a Decolonized Moral Education for Social Justice in Africa, *Journal of Black Studies*, Vol., 54(3), pp., 236–263.

Odih, P., (2016); *Adsensory Financialisation*, Newcastle Upon Tyne: Cambridge Scholars Publishing.

Odih, P., (2025); *Challenging Hair Discrimination Through Racial Narratives, Industry Knowledge on the Economics of Hair and Counter Literacy Equality, Diversity Strategies.* Reference: SRG24\241531. British Academy and Leverhulme Trust. Small Research Grant, Researching Findings. London: BA/ Leverhulme Trust.

Ramírez, M., & Adzich, T., (2023); When monuments fall: anticolonial disruptions and decolonial urban practices (2022) Plenary Commentary, Urban Geography, 44:6, 1084–1092, https://doi.org/10.1080/02723638.2023. 2217619

Ransome-Kuti, F., (1947); "for Women: She Speaks for Nigeria / We Had Equality Till Britain Came", Daily Worker (London, August 18, 1947). Reprinted "We Had Equality till Britain Came", in (ed.) Wayne, T., *Feminist Writings from Ancient Times to the Modern World: A Global Sourcebook and History*, London: Bloomsbury.

Ransome-Kuti, F., (1947–48); *The Plight of Nigerian Women, Funmilayo Ransome Kuti, (President Abeokuta Women's Union and Member of the Pan-Nigerian Delegation)*, National Council of Nigeria and the Cameroons Activities of Mrs Ransome-Kuti, Nigeria, Colonial Office: Nigeria Original Correspondence. National Council of Nigeria and the Cameroons: Activities of Mrs Ransome-Kuti. The National Archives, Kew – Colonial office, Commonwealth and Foreign and Commonwealth Offices, 1947–1948, Reference: CO 583/293/1, National Archives, Kew, Richmond, TW9 4DU. Date of Visit: Tuesday 23rd April 2024; Booking Reference: RR147-950-06156K

Ransome-Kuti, F., (1949/2021); A Talk About Women, in (ed.) Russell, A., *Great Women's Speeches: Empowering voices that Engage and Inspire*, London: White Lion Publishing/The Quarto Group.

Salawu, O., (2019) Abàmì Èdá: Personhood and Socio-political Commitment in Fela's Music, Muziki, 16:2, 4–21, https://doi.org/10.1080/18125980. 2020.1781547

Shonekan, S., (2009); Fela's Foundation: Examining the Revolutionary Songs of Funmilayo Ransome-Kuti and the Abeokuta Market Women's Movement in 1940s Western Nigeria, *Black Music Research Journal*, Spring, Vol.29., No.1., pp., 127–144.

Soyinka, W., (1983); *Aké The Years of Childhood*, New York: Aventura/ Random House.

TuneCore (2024); *What is Music Publishing?* Available at: https://www.tunecore. co.uk/music-publishing-administration

United Nations (1948); Universal Declaration of Human Rights, United Nations. Available at: https://www.ohchr.org/en/human-rights/universal-declaration/ translations/english

Vasudevan, P., Ramírez, M. M., Mendoza, Y. G., & Daigle, M. (2023). Storytelling Earth and Body. *Annals of the American Association of Geographers, 113*(7), 1728–1744. https://doi.org/10.1080/24694452.2022.2139658

Walcott, R., (2015); Genres of Human: Multiculturalism, Cosmo- politics, and the Caribbean Basin, in (ed.) McKittrick, K., *Sylvia Wynter On Being Human As Praxis*, London: Duke University Press.

Zambakari, C. D. (2020). Interrogating Liberal Theories of Rights: An Analysis of Rights in the African Context. *Interventions, 22*(7), 860–878. https://doi.org/10.1080/1369801X.2020.1753550

CHAPTER 4

Communicative Human Rights and Colonial Digital Capitalism

O2 Academy Brixton, Street Level, 211 Stockwell Road, London SW9 9SL, December 2023, Photographer © Pamela Odih

© The Author(s), under exclusive license to Springer Nature Switzerland AG 2024
P. Odih, *Black British Postcolonial Feminist Ways of Seeing Human Rights*, https://doi.org/10.1007/978-3-031-71877-9_4

122   P. ODIH

Communicative capitalism is the notion that market capitalist values have colonised "the site of democratic aspirations, indeed, the mechanism by which the will of the demos manifests itself" (Dean 2005: 54). It designates an era of late neoliberal capitalism, "in which values heralded as central to democracy take material form in networked communications technologies" (ibid.: 55). Social media is emblematic of a situation in which social democratic and civil rights ideals of participation, access and inclusion have been reconceived in terms of the interoperability of networked apps and their global telecommunications. Consequently, capitalist notions are frequently inherent within the social media enterprise of interconnections and its production of disruptive fluctuates of affinity. Capitalism transforms dialogue into an entrepreneurial artefact of commercial choice and marketability. Political campaigns, anti-capitalist protest, revolutionary resistance are indiscriminately conduits for the mode of capitalist accumulation in which communicative practice is the focus of exploitative, extractive communication technologies.

Instead of producing greater accessibility and engagement, the proliferation of political dialogue, and "the deluge of screens and spectacles", enervates "political opportunity and efficacy for most of the world's peoples" (ibid.: 55). Amplified in speed, velocity and connectivity messaging in the dot.com internet era attracts optimism about the possibilities of democratising political engagement. Whereby, an abundance of messaging platforms and the colossal streams of communicative content circulating online in time/space compressed nano-seconds offers a signal of democratic potential. Maintaining an optimistic stance, it is presumed that the possibilities for affecting positive political change are multiplied exponentially in a situation of plentiful communication. Conversely, one can conceive the torrential outpouring of disentangling loquacity circulating as online speech as deficient in depth and political efficacy. Nevertheless, both propositions rely upon a "fantasy of abundance"; this is because "both optimists and pessimists are committed to the view that networked communications are characterized by exponential expansions in opportunities to transmit and receive messages" (ibid.: 58). The central issue of concern relates to the process of commodity fetishism in which the use value of the message is displaced by the exchange value.

It is notable that the communicative action feminism of Jodi Dean, in their pioneering formulation of "communicative capitalism", deprioritises and renders as largely irrespective the medium of the message. Such that the circulation of communication digitally and the circulation of messages through analogue channels are considered and treated as interchangeable

4 COMMUNICATIVE HUMAN RIGHTS AND COLONIAL DIGITAL CAPITALISM 123

features of communicative capitalism. Dean recognises that messages, in communicative capitalism, "are contributions to circulating content – not actions to elicit responses" (ibid.: 58). Nevertheless, discounting the medium of the message within dot.com media communication is a consistent feature of Jodi Dean's *Communicative Capitalism: Circulation and the Foreclosure of Politics*. The unmitigated parturition of the message from its medium is disputed and in so doing bringing into question the assertion that "uncoupled from contexts of action and application – as on the Web or in print and broadcast media – the message is simply part of a circulating data stream" (ibid.). Here and elsewhere Dean's work has some pertinent anticolonial significance in terms of a challenge to the colonising features of digital communication. As is evident in the following expression which can be formulated as of anticolonial concern, "the value of any particular contribution is likewise inversely proportionate to the openness, inclusivity or extent of a circulating data stream – the more options or comments that are out there, the less of an impact any one given one might make" (ibid.). Embedded within these statements referring to how "communicativity hinders communication" is a tautology. Whereby, in the absence of a specification of the medium, it is equally plausible to agree or disagree with the proposition. Alternatively, the approach to communicative capitalism adopted in this case study recognises unequivocally that the medium of the message signifies. Consequently, in the following analysis of social media and advertising inscriptive technologies, Dean's concept is reformulated into a focus on communicative digital capitalism.

Empirically focusing on Black music, and the promotion of the fateful 15th December 2022 music event at the O2 Academy Brixton, the case study engages with Jodi Dean's three fantasies of communicative capitalism and highlights each as specifically configuring the medium of the message. Firstly, it is argued that there exists in communicative capitalism the propensity towards a "fantasy of abundance" in which the deluge of communications online is reformatted as contributions into endless streams of dot.com data. This propensity is reproached for distracting attention away from the fact that the stream of abundance of online dispatches has precipitated "a shift in the basic unit of communication from the message to the contribution" (ibid.: 51). Secondly, the "fantasy of activity" involves a reformatting in which the political activity online is reformulated as engagement with the fetishist properties of this technology. More specifically, it is argued that "the fantasy of activity or participation is materialized through technology fetishism" (ibid.). Thirdly, the "fantasy of wholeness" relies upon the notion of a global totality "both imaginary and Real" (ibid.). Exchanges online are increasingly, according to Dean, less motivated by dialogue-based exchange. Rather, the abundance of content circulating in the dot.com spaces of social media appears intent on contributing to an incessant deluge of data flow. One easily agrees with the overall proposition that there have been expansive technological convergences. Conversely, the assertion that online messages have morphed into mere contribution, in my opinion, negates the specificity of the medium and the capacity of social media to amplify communication into digital advertising promotional culture. Consider this in respect to the following discussion of digital advertising disruptions on the social media platform, Twitter. In so doing, one gains a more complex understanding of the circuits of counterpublics and racialised cyberspaces that the pre-15th December 2022 concert tickets for the Nigerian Afrobeat artist Asake circulated through. It is my contention that the transformation of these social media messages into hyper-connected advertising, in which the communicative action of a mostly female populated Black Twitter cyber-sphere (that is hyper-subject to mass extractive primitive accumulation surveillance), contributed significantly to the exploitative condition of the concert's ticket selling.

Digital Advertising Disrupters: "Fantasy of Abundance"

In communicative capitalism, aspirations heralded as integral to democracy are now deemed to be realisable through the abundance of messages streaming through globally networked communication. Commentaries on its impact identify how both optimistic portrayals of accumulative engagements and pessimistic concerns about undifferentiated, indecipherable communications rely ultimately on a presupposition "that networked communications are characterized by exponential expansions in opportunities to transmit and receive messages" (Dean 2005: 58). The resulting "fantasy of abundance" tends not to recognise, according to Jodi Dean, the extent to which online messages circulate in streams of content that are detached from the specificity of the technological application, coalescing into an incessant "data flow". As such, individual messages are reducible to one another, functioning merely as a contribution to the unremitting circulation of online content. The "morphing of message into contribution" is detrimental to politics because the message is no longer a reciprocity of perspective and incentive towards engagement.

The exchange value of the message having displaced the use value has, according to Dean, become annulled the meaning of the message,

4 COMMUNICATIVE HUMAN RIGHTS AND COLONIAL DIGITAL CAPITALISM 125

constituting it as merely a contribution to the incessant data-streams of content. Communication in the online context, therefore, "functions symptomatically to produce its own negation". I appreciate that there are significant nuances in the argument presented; obviously, there is not the absolute insistent that all online messages are devoid of meaning. Clearly, capitalism does often times facilitate the continuation of communications into sustainable coherent engagement. Such observation illuminates the significance of exchange value and use value in discerning the value of online contributions. Obviously, commodities are not entirely without use. Some messages clearly have a subjective meaning and sustained impact on political consciousness. Nevertheless, it is an assertion that the overall global convergence framework, while some messages might make a difference, the overall impact of the time and space compressed (Harvey 1989) "infostream" is "the shift from message to contribution" (Dean 2005: 59). Continuous with this approach is the ascription to the messenger, a self-assured futility. Celebrated as expansive and accessible, the participatory asseveration of networked communication is widely appreciated. As has been observed, "People are fully aware of the media, the networks, even the surfeit of information". But the theory of communicative capitalism is despondent about the depth of engagement that flows from the appreciation of scale. For it is assumed that a dissimulation of knowledge is enacted by online users; "they act as if they don't have this knowledge, believing in the importance of their contributions, presuming that there are readers for their blogs" (ibid.). According to Dean, part of the explanation for user's acting against their realisation of the limitations of their contribution is that "the way networked communications induce a kind of registration effect that supports a fantasy of participation" (ibid.). Conversely, it is my contention that the conception of these fantastical aspirations of engagement theoretically involves a level of standardisation across dot.com technology that is far removed from the actuality of user experience. For example, digital advertising on the social media platform X (formerly known as Twitter) is designed to aggregate an abundance of user engagement, and it does so not in uniformed "infostreams" but rather through tracking disruptions, discontinuities and infinitely subtle differences between increasingly narrowly profiled users. Indeed, one might challenge the existence of "infostreams" in digital advertising and replace this instead with a model of communicative digital capital based on the capitalisation of "disrupters". In this regard, consider the following discussion of the business model of X (formerly known as Twitter).

According to Twitter, video is the fastest-growing advertising medium on its platform. Its vast volume of video circulation daily on Twitter is in excess of 2 billion video views. It is claimed that tweets with video content attract "10x more engagement" than all other formats of communication on the platform. Video ads with website buttons have "2x higher click-through rate" driving content to the client's website. Amplify Pre-roll is a short video advertisement that appears prior the main video and in so doing provides the client with the opportunity enhance audio viewing by aligning their brand with brand-safe video content. Mobile-responsive short-formatted videos, including subtitles or closed captioning, to attract sound-off viewing, drives online traffic, "93% of views" on Twitter (X Business 2023). Digital advertising agencies use the audience attraction of video and visual imaging to drive their marketing strategy on social media platform. Twitter offers specialised "inter-based tools" so as to target groups through digitally listening to their online streams and fragments of conversation. Content personalisation is refined through the use of Twitter engager targeting of users that have previously engaged with a client's content and also through custom audience lists. Monitor analytics can enhance audience engagement, by identifying the posts that have attracted higher levels of user engagement and informing advertising spend to boost their promotional reach. Thus, while video, Gifs and hashtags provide monitored analytics, the digital drive in social media advertising resides prominently within data-driven approach to determining content strategy (ibid.). Indeed, the use of multiple video advertising formats more effectively facilitates brand awareness and purchasing intent, whereby digital data-driven content pushed through Timeline Takeover, Amplify Pre-roll and Promoted Ads are all ad formats that are proven to play "a key role in the purchase funnel" (ibid.).

Twitter's digital data-driven audience targeting includes the following types of advertisements: Promoted Ads, Follower Ads and Trend Takeover. Artificial Intelligence (AI) is a major disrupter in each of these categories of advertising. Machine learning programmes in AI use algorithmic formula representing the relationship between variables to make predictions on digital advertising content strategy and marketing. Weblinks from Twitter to AI chatbot programmes are disintermediating customer support; indeed, the possibilities of applications for chatbots are growing exponentially. Of particular significance are advances in image recognition. According to Twitter, AI-powered computer visioning "searches for patterns within images" that a rapidity and detailing that exceeds human capability. AI application in natural language processing (NLP) evidences the immense ability of machine learning when applied to determining text

4 COMMUNICATIVE HUMAN RIGHTS AND COLONIAL DIGITAL CAPITALISM

or human voice patterns. The cultural nuances of whit, sarcasm and subtlety have in recent times entered into the terrain of digital colonisation with AI technology being able to "pull out context and more hidden meanings" (Kniahynycky 2023). Key Performance Indicators (KPI) chased by advertising and marketers are in this regard reflecting the game-shifting enhancements of AI digitality in respect to the enhancement in the measurements: engagement (retweets, etc.), performance (impressions), growth (consumers), return on investment (ROI) (conversion) (X Business 2023). In an article published on X Business and X Performance Advertising Performance Advertising and Campaign Measurement Resources, the following ideas are put forward to boost advertising performance: optimise conversion of tweets to specific audiences; "drive high value website traffic"; mobile marketplace app installation directly from X; app engagement campaigns; track results through X Pixel and Conversion API (X Business [Twitter] 2023).

In the autumn of 2023, the social media platform X (formerly known as Twitter) mooted the possibility of charging all users. Most analysts of capitalist communication technology were unsurprised by the mooted change in the business model of X. For it is a commonly held fact that the free non-subscription democratically accessible model, while successful for music streaming services, is failing in respect to Twitter. Part of the problem is the form of abundance that the platform generates. For it is apparent from the previous description of digital advertising that rather than, as Dean surmises, communicative capitalism produces an abundance that is merely contributions in an "inforstream", it is apparent from my discussion of digital advertising that the "fantasy of abundance" refers more accurately to an overaccumulation of advertising content generated by practitioners and also self-advertisers in equal measure. Consider this in respect to the following discussion of the promotional tweets produced from the Afrobeat Nigerian musician Asake from their Twitter account @ asakemusik—posted in the immediate aftermath and in the lead-up to the 15th December 2022 concert at the O2 Academy Brixton.

> I am devastated by the news that Rebecca Ikumelo who was in a critical condition since Thursday has sadly passed away. My sincerest condolences to her loved ones at this time. Let us please keep her family in our prayers. I have spoken to them and will continue to do so. I am overwhelmed with grief and could never have imagined anything like this happening. My team and I are still awaiting the full debrief back

from the Venue management and the Police to determine what exactly led to all the disruption caused and ultimately to Rebecca's passing. If you have any relevant information relating to this please do reach out to the Metropolitan police. Thank you. (@asakemusik 2022b)

Asake is a Nigerian Afrobeat music artist with an international profile, and with hundreds of thousands of followers on the social media platform Twitter, @asakemusik. The above-quoted Tweet posted on Twitter 17th December 2022 achieved 35.8K likes, 5691 retweets, 500 comments and 2.6m views (as counted: 1st October 2023). As part of the lead-up to the concert, on 11th December 2022 at 1:52pm, the artist launched a series of tweets promoting their December 2022 London concert tour. The initial tweet clearly and responsibly discouraged those without tickets, as thus: "AsakeLondon. Sunday 11th December. Update. Please do not come to Brixton Academy tonight if you do not have a valid ticket. Doors are 7pm sharp and usual security measures are in place. The show is completely sold out and there are no tickets for sale at the venue" (@asakemusik 2022a). While unalarming and ordinary text is evident, the semiotics of the Tweet inferred a more spirited interpolation of the more culturally attuned fan, for its denotative façade deploys a first-order semiological system (Barthes 1972) of an American Western bounty poster, with its sepia background, head and shoulder booking photograph, black cascading bold typeset and red insignia "update". The concert's promotional advertising text is inscribed into the first-order semiological system so as to produce a second-order semiological system, appropriating a cultural stereotype of the Black male's disproportionate representation within the criminal justice system. Digital advertising is meritoriously utilised in the artist's December 2022 timeline. The hyper-interconnectedness and interoperability of digital social media amplifies and multiplies the potentialities of fans promoting the event beyond an information transfer electronic word of mouth (Chi 2011: 44). Examining the @asakemusik tweet of 11th December 2022 at 1:52pm, its metrics suggest that information exchange is a minor aspect of the digital advertising enabled Tweet. For it achieved 236 comments, 1627 retweets, 127 quotes, 20.2k likes and 38 bookmarks. Social networking the tweet into individual networks appears as a primary pursuit of the social media users' interactivity with the @ asakemusik tweet. Indeed, communicative digital capitalism erases the political possibilities of online abundance, because the content it produces is an overaccumulation of user-generated advertising.

BLACK TWITTER, DIGITAL ADVERTISING DISRUPTERS: "THE FANTASY OF PARTICIPATION"

The cultural political impact of networked communications technologies is the primary focus of the communicative capitalist analysis of the foreclosure of politics in late capitalism. Dissimulated in the convergence between politics and promotional culture is the neoliberal marketplace conception of democratic entreaty. Indeed, communicative capitalism regards social dialogue as an abundant natural resource to be colonised through expropriation. Primitive accumulation of communication relies on extracting value from the raw uncapitalised fields of social dialogue that exist on the margins of commodity capitalism. Human rights and social justice dialogue are the latter-day equivalent of atavistic labour transposed into online communication. Consequent perhaps because of its ubiquitous familiarity, people have secured the right to be heard online, thus producing a situation in which the primary accumulative process involves exploited subjects continuously returning to the online to digitally labour at being heard.

In recent years writers have defined Black Twitter as a manifestation of communicative capitalism, in respect to the Black Lives Matter movement that blasted visually into civil rights political consciousness in the UK during the COVID-19 pandemic. Black Twitter refers colloquially to a micro-blogging collective of African-American and people from the African, Caribbean diaspora that have effectively used the social media platform to effect cultural political change and bring acutely into public consciousness issues of race, racism and racial discrimination. Academic writings advance a more sophisticated version of the phenomenon, having had pioneered a mode of analysis of social media, that focusses on the participatory infrastructure of the platform Twitter in terms of its "embedded, distributed modes of collectivity" (Prasad 2016: 50). Of particular relevance are the possibilities of trans-locational "posthuman coalitions" of affinity bonds created because of the platform's hegemonic capitalist-modelled dehumanising commodification of the Black body. Empirical studies of Black Twitter illuminate the technically astute, impressively literate and instinctive contrivances by which a disidentification with the "hypercapitalist composing practices of digital spaces" is proficient in the cultivation of counterpublics (ibid.). Such that, Black Twitter activism is defined "as a space of critical disidentification that mobilizes the hypercapitalist networking and composing logics of Twitter to create new forms of embodiment, humanity, and coalition" (ibid.: 68). Continuous with an affirmation of Black political engagement is the provocative belief that disidentification practices on Twitter have brought into being a Black Twitter, that is "far more than just a critique of racism and power to ensure survival. It also radically exposes, articulates and enacts new possibilities of freedom" (ibid.: 68). Indeed, through the devices of hashtags, memes, hyper-networked connections of transgressive semiotics, Black Twitter provides a site for the voicing and negotiation of Blackness apprehending the wider cultural anxieties of silencing of racial identity in the discourse of post-racial society (Stevens and Maurantonio 2018). Continuous with this genre is the notion that the technological mediation of anti-racist protests, in their insistence that the Black body matters, encourages a disidentification with the "hypercapitalist composing practices of digital space" and the "dehumanization of Black bodies" into posthuman avatars of affirmative action (Prasad 2016). Feminist writers on communicative action have nevertheless questioned the extent to which these online counterpublics sufficiently transgress the structuration of inequality offline. For example, Onanuga (2023) in their interrogation of patriarchy and homophobia in the Nigerian online magazine Zikoko argues that "speaking about their personal experiences on a public space becomes a way to build social capital and a step towards voicing their experiences and renegotiating their realities" (ibid.: 14). However, existing structural inequalities within the literary industry continue to limit the acclaim of this genre of writing, i.e. "the digital cultural production of non-fictional writing in Zikoko, a Nigerian blog" (ibid.: 15). Consequently, it argued that even where authors have worked beyond the dehumanisation of Black bodies in commercial digital spaces, their engagement with this space is undermined and devalued by the literary industry, often being "tagged [as] supplementary or secondary in the examination of societal realities" (ibid.).

BLACK TWITTER "SIGNIFYIN": "THE FANTASY OF PARTICIPATION"

"Signifyin" is defined as the performance of racial identity through exhibition of cultural competence with the denotative and connotative dimensions of racial identity. In online communications where the corporeal signifiers of the racialised body are imprecise and obscured, competence in signifyin decrypting becomes an authoritative aspect of Black cultural identity. Through the deployment of figurative language, circuitousness and inversive wordplay, signifyin allows for multiple meanings to be conveyed simultaneously (Florini 2014). It has been observed that historically signifyin has been a space for social critique, highlighting racial injustice and witnessing institutional racism. On the social media platform Twitter, signifyin evidences expressions of Black racial identity. Metadata devices such as Twitter hashtags provide opportunities for competing experiential knowledges of Black identity to be showcased, contested, negotiated and reformulated. The collaborative aspects of signifyin are easily transposed onto the Twitter architecture, as with the characteristic inclination to "dis[respect]" allied participations as part of verbal Black culturally gamified antagonisms (ibid.: 229). Signifyin, in its efforts towards a text-based oral performance of racial identity, traverses the patterns of popular usage of the platform. Video and image-based tweets, according to Twitter, attract the highest proportion of interactions and engagements. Crucially, "signifyin as oral performance via text-based social media" replicates the importance of language to Black cultural identity while also capturing the oral performance dimensions of mimicry in pronunciation, delivery and nonverbal cues. It achieves this through drawing upon the repertoire syntaxes of text-based speech, e.g. use of capitals, etc. Additionally, the dynamic gaming interplay of Black oral performance is captured in text-based signifyin through the velocity and speed of delivery. Indeed, with its capacity for simultaneous rapid exchange between multitudes of users, the quick-fire pace of Black oral performance via text-based communication is hyper-realised on the social media platform. Speed of delivery is enhanced by the tendency in this genre to disregard Black Vernacular English in preference for linguistic repertoires characterised by "phonetic spellings that convey specific pronunciations" (ibid.: 233). While nonstandard spellings of words are used as a standard practice by users as a workaround Twitter's 280 character limit, the Black Twitter cultural tradition employs phonetic spellings and abbreviations in a competitive gaming of competency in Black cultural literacy. Nevertheless, there is evidence of a convergence of standardisation of Black Vernacular English necessary for the creation of a community networked through experienced-based meaning. Linguistic systems, while competitively gamed, are bounded and stabilised by their reliance "on context embeddedness to convey meaning and nonverbal aspects of signifyin' performances" so as to constitute crucial components that enable decoding and comprehension (ibid.: 234). Signifyin' is attuned to Twitter as a condition its tendency to disembody, deracialise the subject into a data-stream of communication. For in this situation "the social and cultural markers of race take on great importance" (ibid.). Signifyin necessitates of the user a level of competitively acquired cultural knowledge of contemporary Black media, politics and popular culture. In post-racial discursive contexts, "Signifyin' on Twitter allows Black users not only to reject colour blindness by actively performing their racial identities but also to connect with other black users to create and reify a social space for their Blackness" (ibid.).

Frequently espoused in the writing on signifyin in Black Twitter is the communicative practices of Black culturally referenced humour. In the writing into history of race and racism, an often-cited aspect is the practice of humour through which racial trauma is excised. Humour as a response to condition of epidemic feature frequently, as evidence of the ability of Twitter to connect geographically dispersed or locationally isolated Black human bodies, is a proclaimed example of agency. Indeed, research has found communicative practices of humour in unbearable situation of health epidemic and racial trauma. For example, Cottingham and Rose (2023) in their study of African-American Vernacular English communicative practices in the expression of emotion and elevated epidemic risk in online spaces identify the "agency and creativity of this influential digital community while showing the variability of communication practices among a group facing disproportionate vulnerability to outbreaks and public health threats" (ibid.: 1954). Reassurance cultivated through the technologically mediated, performative acts of the cultural reappropriation of language through meme and hashtags is a trait defined, in Black Twitter literatures, as "signifyin" practice (Florini 2014). Writers identify the "rhetorical discourse" of Black humour as acerbic interventions into the modern-day misrepresentation of Black bodies evident in healthcare situations that have necessitated the separation of peoples from public life (Outley et al. 2021). Similarly, it has been a focus of writers within this genre to identify the hypermediated networking architecture of the Twitter platform to operate occasionally effectively in the circulation of health information. An often-cited example is the high-profile campaign, precipitated by death in August 2020 of the Black actor Chadwick Boseman, to raise awareness of the racial disparities in rates of colorectal cancer (Myrick et al. 2022). The para-social propensities of Twitter make it much more legitimate for communities of grievers, ordinarily unknown to each other, to come together in a space of public mutual recognition. Although albeit amplified by the conditions of intensification of mediated

4 COMMUNICATIVE HUMAN RIGHTS AND COLONIAL DIGITAL CAPITALISM   133

communications, during the COVID-19 pandemic it became evident that social media provided a space for the expression of "parasocial grief" for the loss of Chadwick Boseman. Research has professed associations between an uptick in members of the Black community seeking screening for colon cancer. Whereby, it has been reliably conjectured that "Twitter remains a viable space for collecting data that reflects user sentiment about para-social relationships with celebrities, including connections forged as a result of the celebrity's illness and death" (ibid.: 16).

An issue of great concern to social theorist analyses of Black Twitter is the extent to which the loosely moderated hypermediated architecture of social media enables too easily the networked "workshopping" and "viral weaponizing" of the racialised Black body (Hagen and de Zeeuw 2023). While it is not extraordinary to identify the weaponing of language in the pursuit of media propaganda, it is apparent that digital social media operates in conversely to the smooth communicative processes of analogue. For it is evident that the situational indexing of memes, slang terms and operational syntaxes undermines standardising processes and the pursuit of uniformity in the "effect of the word-as-poison on the mind-as-body" (ibid.: 13). In its labyrinthian algorithmically curated enclaves, communicative language may "function as subcultural synecdoches, gateways to a subterranean network of fringe communities" (ibid.). Consequently, in their efforts to retain political connotations across communities, the language communicating Black experiences of embodiment may unintentionally "forge an insidious ideological milieu whose effects remain hard to gauge" (ibid.).

Capricious, inconsistent and irregularly schematic provides an image of mutability in communicative practices defined as pervading Black Twitter. Whereby, it is depicted as a site of a contestation in the meaning of Black cultural and racialised sexual identities. The affordances of social media provide space for self-expression and the policing of the dynamic interplay of identity formation. Reneses and Bosch (2023), in their study of *Networked Masculinities in South Africa*, applied critical thematic analysis to discourses of masculine identity under the hashtag of a fictional male conference. Significantly, it was observed that contested notions of masculinity were embedded in socio-economic and cultural contexts, thus challenging an online/offline distinction, instead reaffirming the tendency for Twitter to reiterate existing socially structured conditions that limit the contestation of hegemonic masculinity. Elsewhere, the intersectionality of race, gender and sexuality is explored by writers in terms of the politics of "cancel culture". Whereby, the hypermediated architecture of Black Twitter and the rapidity of the circulation of its content are seen to amplify the consequences, for the "cancelled" and those that "cancel", in the praxis of "cancel culture" (Clark 2020). Whereby, it has been observed that an "evolution of digital accountability praxis" is being enacted in Black Twitter's culturally networked communities (ibid.: 88). In accordance with much of the writing in this genre, the direction of evolution in respect to the calling out of infringements of human rights and social justice is seen as positive. Conversely, platform's accessible enables spaces in which extant social problems, and their corresponding perpetrators, are being critically engaged with to become open territory for social elites to misappropriate the anger of minoritised people and its expression through the praxis of cancelling. As Clark (ibid.) expresses it, "The dominant culture's ability to narrativize the process of being 'cancelled' as a moral panic with the potential to upset the concept of a limited public sphere". A troubling consequence of which, as experienced by the elite, is that the ability of Black Twitter to harness the platform's architecture, rapidly identify harmful maleficent actors, deploy the "cancel" praxis precisely and afflict silence on the threat by starving it of an audience, amounts to an effective strategy. The "coalitions of the Othered are now equipped to execute a responsive strategy" and in so doing "elite public figures fall victim to their own worst fears: a realization that the social capital they've worked so hard for is hyperinflated current in the attention economy" (ibid.: 91).

Media witnessing, as a form of "mobile-mediated sousveillance" and citizen journalism, has also featured in the literature on Twitter and the cultivation of the Black public sphere (Richardson 2017). In the meagre cultural information spaces for Black commentary to enter the mainstream press, digital citizenship commentary provides opportunities for reportage on human rights violations. The rise of Black Twitter as a platform in which ethnic groups are more likely to share news content is plausible when one considers its ease of accessibility through mobile devices and the straightforwardness of its "hashtag folksonomy", which enables like-minded Black patrons of the platform to associate with each other (ibid.: 693). There is also the determination for Black journalists within the mainstream to similarly use the platform to Black witness and in so doing "question anew how our current political climate empowers or silences vulnerable voices" (ibid.). Citizen activism potentialities ascribe to Black Twitter the optimistic presumption of an authentic, vernacular, radical interventionist challenge to the hierarchical structures of media production. Similarly, it is argued that new media suffuses into contemporary politics enabling extraordinarily proximal relations between political leaders and their citizens. The outgrowth of "media-assisted citizen activism" in the hyper-connectivity of the platform enables ordinary people to engage and confront the politically powerful precipitating a plurality of democratic dialogue (Mpofu 2019: 88).

Memes, hashtags and other mimetic features of Twitter act as counter-hegemonic texts challenging the excesses of ruling-class power (ibid.). Black Twitter is optimistically conceived in this accord as a counterpublic sphere, a digital subaltern sufficiently distant from mainstream media to capture marginalised voices. Indeed, such thinking informs issues of Twitter and the bearing witness to police brutality, whereby the platforms' accessibility and the immediacy of circulating information convincingly perform a notion of authenticity while also raising concerns about morality, ethics and the dilemmas of circulating graphic images of racist brutality (Hawkins 2023). In response, academics have expressed the need for careful professional practice when studying the digital traces of the marginalised communities that constitute Black Twitter. This requires appreciating Black communities as enduring complex relations to institutional processes of gathering and archiving their data as citizen and settled peoples. In an attempt to formulate an ethics for public data, researchers have emphasised the imperative for a critically engaged recognition of the positionality of the researcher, implicit biases, the privileging of prevailing structured inequalities of power, and in so doing attempting to avoid reifying of race-based advantage (Klassen and Fiesler 2022). Marginalised communities exist in tentative relation to policing and governmental authorities. Thus, the collation of information, and especially in digitally amenable sources of data, provides further possibilities for the enhancement of already excessive surveillance trained on these marginalised Black communities. Ultimately, research into Black Twitter requires an increased level of professional care with regard to the heightened potentialities that the research will impact negatively on the community. Due diligence is a commonly articulated precursor to this area of research, for "when discussing risks and harms to research participants, regardless if it is through human subjects or public data research, what we are really contending with is justice" (ibid.: 10).

Instead of assuming a deontological intolerance to public data harms approach, much of the research in this genre is guided by a consequential

136   P. ODIH

fervour in which the social justice and human rights appeal of Black Twitter ameliorate the potential harms of exposing marginalised communities to greater levels of surveillance. The fecundity and hyper-connectivity of Twitter in these literatures are examined positively as multiplicative in the production of accessible, networked counterpublics in which marginalised communities appear to flourish. Indeed, a frequent feature of the Black Twitter genre is that marginalised Black communities cultivate counterpublics on the platform Twitter so as to challenge racism and connect in solidarity with others in their experiences of racial oppression (Ramirez and Williams 2022). The social cultural status of Black Twitter as a counterpublic is consistently ascribed in the literature, because it is so evidently founded on commentary of prominently racial issues and consequently "more likely to support communicative action" (Graham and Smith 2016: 445). Indeed, it has been advanced that the technological mediation of Black Twitter constitutes a veritable "digital counterpublic" that is facilitative of a critical pedagogy and political mobilising with respects to "symbolic and material forms of resistance to anti-Black state violence" (Hill 2018: 286). Black Twitter's networked counterpublic terrain enables configurations of anti-racist activism that inform and are informed by the platform's digital technoculture and in so doing provide "forms of pedagogy that reorganize relations of surveillance, reject rigid respectability politics, and contest the erasure of marginalized groups within the Black community" (ibid.).

Conceptions of Black social networks operating digitally online appreciate the cultural heterogeneity of the Black space and the coded interactions that demarcate the performativity of Black cultural identity in the Twitterverse (Williams and Gonlin 2017). The informatic-coded digital syntax of the hashtag, for example, provides a site for the pronunciation, contestation and arbitration of Blackness, seizing upon grander cultural anxieties encapsulating racial identity in the era of post-racial society (Stevens and Maurantonio 2018). Ethno-racial representation and signification are of peripheral concern as compared with the "digital-race assemblage" styled as "Blacktags" (Sharma 2013: 46). Specifically, the platform's network connectivity, conjoining with its trending algorithms and machine replicating composition, plays an integral role in the viral circulation of racial disruptions to the White hegemony of the Twitter network. Integral to this assumption is the notion of the digital architecture of Twitter as a purveyor of heterogeneous technological features that are brought together through dynamically shifting connections, which are emblematic of a radical thinking of race in terms of assemblages (ibid.: 54). Blacktags delineate a materiality emerging through how the racialised corporeal bodies of Black users mechanically connect with digital assemblages of informational logics that infrastructure the platform. In recent times I have developed the concept of adsensory to denote a neglected feature of these technocultural assemblages, i.e., the perspicacity of the body as subject and object of advertising inscriptive technologies. Earlier accounts of Black Twitter advance race as an assemblage so as to outline its constitution and emergence through networked relations online. Infused into these technologies are the power/knowledge contestations of informational logic and the technosocial processes that distinguish new media online. Viewed from a digital-race assemblage approach, Black Twitter is a condition and consequence of its community's exploration of "race as an emergent online relation, articulated by systemic software processes and informatic connections" (ibid.: 64).

Everyday lived experience as a feature of Black cultural identity has been a focus of writing in respect to exploring Black Twitter as extending the explanatory power of place in its making of connections locally with globally dispersed diaspora. Black feminist inroads here include studies considering the US South and the Global South as connected allies in the decolonising of digital social phenomena (Barlow and Smith 2019). Elsewhere, writers have explored the transnational scope of Twitter in respect to its ability to harness ethnic-cultural values and communicate these to a scattered diaspora. Molefe and Ngcongo (2021) formulate a critical perspective known as ubuntu, which is defined as being integral to the African ethnic-cultural value of critical humanism. In researching an online viral episode featuring a South African celebrity, the authors question the extent to which the notoriously confrontationally structured contribution architecture of Twitter is able to facilitate the harnessing to Black Twitter exchange of the cultural value of critical humanism. They conclude in the affirmative, arguing that a "robust view of ubuntu, whose application is demonstrated from the context of Black Twitter, ultimately seeks to make another person a better human even if it means public criticism" (ibid.: 26). Black Twitter is constituted here as a space for pan-ethnic, dynamic racial belonging. As an affirmative networked counterpublic, it foregrounds anti-racist critique eschewing the individualising silencing of institutionally racist mainstream communication structures. Black Twitter as a notion of networked critical engagement is constructed in these writing as a diametric opposite to the

138　P. ODIH

spectator-focused pseudo-Gemeinschaft (Goldman 1983) of the leisure spaces that pervade offline recreation. Continuous with this insight is the concept of Black Twitter as containing "competing ethnoracialized counterpublics" (Gutiérrez 2022: 100). Thus, writers have explored the impact on social activism of race and ethnicity operating relationally in a dynamic interplay in Black Twitter counterpublics. The Black Twitter universe is presented as enabling of critical engagement both against the system and within its diverse online communities.

The ease by which people express themselves online is regarded disapprovingly by Dean (2005). The increasingly apparent expressions of emotion and scripting of subjective thoughts that is proliferating online, induce a perception of "registering". Whereby, these thoughts in the action of writing are being articulated into language and received onto a platform. The notion here is the possibilities of achieving catharsis through expressing one's thoughts and acknowledgement for having thought. In this form of active contribution to the converging data-stream, there is a "registering effect", in which "one believes that it matters, that it contributes, that it means something" (ibid.: 60). Consequent of this impression people presume that enacting an activity that has significance despite the minimality of merely exchanging words on a blog, signing a petition or adding to a discussion group. Conversely, in reality, there is a fetishisation of these activities so as to disguise a more discordant displacement of resistance away from mainstream politics. The frenetic activity bustle of the fetish works to avert actual political engagement. Ultimately, this is because an inversion of activity is in actuality taking place, whereby the commodity fetishism of online communication technology involves ascribing to them a notion of political dimensionality, and in so doing obscuring their inextricable capitalistic mode of production. Consequently, it is observed that when we as users are actively doing politics on these platforms, we are in actuality engaging with the fetishist properties of the technology, which in return stand-in for politics. In other words, any engagement with a fetishism, no matter how eagerly enacted, is inevitably inactivity. Hectic online agitation at the boundaries of political discourse translates into inactivity. The sentiment here returns to the conception of online communication as ceaseless circular transmission of contributions, in which scarcely any sustained engagement is accomplished; instead, they "fail as messages in need of response, we might think of this odd interpassivity as content that is linked to other content, but never fully connected" (ibid.: 61). Paradoxically, then, the ceaseless circulation of contribution

4 COMMUNICATIVE HUMAN RIGHTS AND COLONIAL DIGITAL CAPITALISM 139

is depoliticising, not because of an unavailability of content; rather, it is because of the deficiency of capitalistic abundance. The technological fetish of politics happening through capitalist technologies sustains a privation on the part of the subject, namely that of shielding the fantasy that is the politically active citizen online, and doing so "by acting in the subject's stead" (ibid.: 63). Three features of the phenomenon, that is the operation of the technological fetish, are identified and detailed as generalisable to entirety of dot.com communication. The first *condensation* refers to the propensity for the complex conditions and capital resources integral to effective liberal democratic governance to be reformulated simplistically in a manner that can be resolved by more technology.

In respect to Black Twitter, one might relate the technologically fetish of condensation as operating in terms of presenting the platform's non-subscription as a facilitator of its wide usage among the Black community. The second technological fetish that operates in respect to the fantasy of participation is *displacement*. In engaging with the online as a site of politics, Dean observes a shift in its depth away from critically reflective discourse towards a myopic focus on the immediacy of the everyday. In so doing, displacing politics away from its material sites of political effectivity on the ground, in the ballot-box, into the cyberspaces and oversight of surveillance capitalism. Dean applies this second technological fetish operation to the ease by which cyber surveillance capitalist technologies track the #Blacktags of Black Twitter. The third technological fetish in operation is *foreclosure*. Whereby, the presentation of online technology as political requires the obscuring of the exploitative relations of capital and labour, natural mineral and their primitive extraction indeed all the processes of conflict and antagonism through which technology is manufactured. As Dean argues,

> Bluntly put, a condition of possibility for asserting the immediately political character of something, web radio or open-source code, say, is not simply the disavowal of other political struggles; rather, it relies on the prior exclusion of the antagonistic conditions of emergence of web radio and open source, or their embeddedness within the brutalities of global capital, of their dependence for existence on racialized violence and division. (ibid.: 66)

As one might discern, here as elsewhere, Dean conceptualises the fetishisation of politics into technology as interchangeable objects. In so doing, they overgeneralise and insufficiently appreciate the nuanced and complex ways capitalism operates to transform the medium its message and the subject into advertising.

It is my contention that the informatic coded syntax and memetic properties of the Twitter platform are critical in the construction of racial identity because they amplify its performative features. Social media appeals to the redistributive expression of racial identity. It accomplishes cooperative sociality despite the para-sociality of the medium's digital assemblage. The medium and the message of Twitter is advertising. Nevertheless, despite the discernible plausibility of my contention, it is not generally accepted among writings in the area of Black Twitter. For example, Harlow and Benbrook (2019) in their exploration of #BlackLivesMatter and the role of hip hop celebrities in cultivating Black identity through their use of the hastag make a clear distinction between constructing racial identity using the Blacktags and the practices of advertising. Thus, in the analysis of 2.67 million tweets in and around the 2014 Ferguson protests in the USA, it is their assertion that the "study found more celebrity tweets were framed as related to Black identity compared with marketing/self-promotion" (ibid.). Contrast this with my assertion that the technological architecture of Twitter is fundamentally geared towards the hyper-generation of advertising.

Returning now to the case-studied promotional tweets posted by the musician Asake prior to the 15th December 2022 critical incident at the O2 Academy Brixton, on 11th December the artist posted from their Twitter account a poster featuring the following statement: "Asake London … Please do not come to Brixton Academy tonight if you do not have a valid ticket". The tweet achieved 20k likes, 1714 retweets and 236 comments (count taken on 1 October 2023). Given the para-sociality of Twitter, it is plausible that the Tweet's immense volume of "like" activity is instrumentally deploying the original tweet as a means to expand the social networking of the individual users regardless of its informational content. Unpaid, affective digital labour is evident in the abundance contributions as users innovatively deployed their social capital in the crafting of memes and clickbait responses in competitive displays of technical dexterity and self-aggrandising social capital. It is in this sense particularly that the tweets are a form of digital advertising that is individualising and fragmentary, for the platform is particularly mercurial in its competitive tendency to convene and transform digital labour for purposes that work against the cultivation of mutuality.

Digital Disrupters: *"The Fantasy of Wholeness"*

According to Dean (2005), the communicative capitalist fetishising of dot.com technology operates by reformatting online communications into data-streams of contributions. The fantasy of belief in the participation of meaningful political engagement is accompanied by a "fantasy of wholeness" (ibid.: 66). In contrast to the generic ontologising that is evident in Dean's formulation of the fantasy of abundance and participation, their critique of the existence of a unity and wholeness in the global online is more appreciative of the nuances of technological architecture. As evident in their statement that "the internet provides an imaginary site of action and belonging. Celebrated for its freedoms and lack of boundaries, this imagined totality serves as a kind of presencing of the global" (ibid.: 67). Indeed, and furthermore, the online feigns to be global because its promise of universal coverage is a third-order simulacra, a simulation given its integral function as a vehicle for advertising. Thus, it is my contention that one needs to examine forensically digital advertising to comprehend the accelerated circulation of online social media contributions. For example, Twitter purports to primarily enable real-time, global open platform for news exchange, information dispersion and computer-mediated discussions. Consequently, one might suppose that the spectacular escalation of social media tweets merely maps onto the global reach of the platform's service provision. Conversely, recent investigations into the monopolist practices of the social media reveals practices intended to control the networking opportunities of its users, by limiting its inoperability to the making connections with its preferred partners. For example, as CMA (2020: 141) reveals, following Twitter's acquisition, in 2013, of the video sharing platform Vine, Facebook removed API access from its platform to Vine. Twitter in response discontinued Vine in 2016.

The inference in application to the case studied Twitter postings of Asake prior to the critical incident at the O2 Academy Brixton on 15th December 2022. The technological fetish operates to have formatted the Asake @asakemusik tweets as globally networked. In actuality, the interoperability between social media providers is subject to the fierce vagaries of international market capitalist competition. The centrifugal dissemination of the hypermediated @asakemusik tweets were also a consequence of Twitter's algorithms optimising the public profile and prominence of the tweet based on its processing of its digital stores of the digital footprint of its users. Part of the obstruction is inertia for users tend not to make the adjustments to their settings, preventing Twitter from combining the user's platform activity with the personal data information that it obtains from its partner organisations. Indeed, Twitter's aptitude in direct customer engagement is a competitive advantage that also provided conditions that were conducive to the spectacularly rapid circulation of the @asakemusik preconcert tweets. For it is my supposition that tweets published by the Black culture industry's international music artists are inherently spectacular; in so doing, they are capable of replicating the official promotional attributes of Twitter's advertising digital technology, but they accomplish this in less advertising metric and programmatic ways. Prominent features of Twitter Ads particularly enabling Black culture industry artists to replicate advertising channels to propel their tweets through the platform, are detailed in the following discussion. Whereby, the supposition being formulated here is that these features facilitated the amplification of the preconcert tweets of @asakemusik and in accordance with the programmatic automation of Twitter's architecture, but these advertising amplifying outcomes were underestimated by the Eurocentric cultural optics of the Metropolitan Police.

Firstly, in respect to Promoted Ads, ordinary, regular text/image/video tweets labelled as "Promoted" that the advertiser pays to appear in the search results/trending/official Twitter clients/timeline of a wider group or to engage their existing followers. In many ways promoted tweets are native to the Twitter user interface in as much as they can be retweeted, replied to, liked and refabricated into memes. Their tendency to seem native is enhanced by the fact that they may not appear on the advertiser's product page and its timeline, for they can be targeted at a discrete cohort of users and/or followers. The user sees the promoted tweet, initially at the top and later as they scroll through their timeline. They are able to reject the promoted tweet by clicking onto a relevant instruction, e.g. "I don't like this ad" (Twitter 2023). On 13th December 2022 at 2.24am, @asakemusik posted an image and text ♥ tweet, which read: London [red heart symbol]. The metrics of the tweet were quite impressive, in that it secured: 2979 retweets, 64 quotes, 43K likes and 21 bookmarks. In the absence of Twitter's "promoted" tweet label, it can be presumed that it was audited as authentically within the regular tweet category. Prior to this, on the 12th December 2022, @asakemusik posted a tweet with the artist wearing a mostly white puffer jacket in front of a tree festooned with freshly fallen snow, and the Twitter metrics for this tweet were even more impressive: 6275 retweets, 347 quotes, 98.5K likes and

36 bookmarks. Given that the latter preceded the former, the tweet established a sign-sequence that quite obviously signified the artist's arrival in London, preconcert promotion. In so doing, the @asakemusik tweet operated as a simulacrum of the purchasable features of Twitter's official digital advertising programme, i.e. Personalised Ads, Promoted Accounts, Twitter Trends and Trending, Promoted events. Integral to these features is Twitter's Ads auction API, where advertisers bid against each other to secure space/time to target its promotional display on the platform. Twitter claims that it examines the advertiser's auction bid in conjunction with its evaluation of the quality of the advertisement. Thus, it is conceivable that if the @asakemusik preconcert promotional tweets had been evaluated through Twitter Ads auction, it would have been subject to the refracted prism of commercially contradictory programmatic metrics that define Twitter's free speech policy. In its auction operating model, an advertisement automatically enters the auction once the campaign starts, and Twitter decides on which auction it enters premised on the "targeting criteria" that the advertiser submitted. Twitter's auction algorithm will compare the advertisement bid with others targeting the same interest, and the advertisement deemed to have excelled in this monetised competition is shown to the target audience. If the target audience carries out the billable action (e.g. clicks onto the advertisement), Twitter will charge the advertiser for that action, based on their "second price auction model" (Twitter 2023a).

Twitter has three types of advertising bidding: automatic bid (the bid is programmatically set by Twitter in real-time "to ensure competitive serve within the auction"). It is intended to "auto-optimize" the advertiser's bid so as "to maximize results at the lowest price (within the advertiser's budget)"; Maximum bid (based on predetermined agreement of the maximum the advertiser is "willing to pay for a billable action"; their "results will not be charged over this price"); and Target bid (an option in Twitter's "follower, website traffic, reach, app installs and app re-engagements campaign objectives" whereby the advertiser can decide how much they agree to pay per billable action). Twitter will then auto-optimise the advertiser's bid so as to "achieve a daily average cost that meets or beats [the] target". The advertiser pays the specific "average cost for all link clicks in a day" (ibid.). AI-assisted decision-making operates in this respect whereby advertising brokers reading the runes of a tweet's real-time metrics "can figure out the best creative combination that would facilitate acquiring the best results through real-time A/B testing" (Lee and Cho 2020: 336). So much of the tweet's amplification is therefore its data-driven advertising context and the automation of the programmatic buying of advertising space, "though data-based real-time bidding (RTB)" (ibid.). In their pursuit of "buying media" (time slot in an online advertising banner), the advertiser engages in "the purchase of a specific inventory of the media" (ibid.: 337).

Further to the issue of automation and the transformation of digital communication into advertising is the advancing field of Artificial Intelligence (AI) and the automation of oral and written discourse. With respect to the latter, writers on communicative capitalism and AI have raised concerns about the rise of the "algorithmic discourse generator", which is capable of automatically, rapidly generated journalist news text (Reeves 2016: 157). If as I am proposing, it is to be accepted that the phenomenon of Black Twitter is both condition and consequence of the social media platform's transformation of content into digital advertising, then the existence of automated communicative labour evidences the heightened existence of these processes. The advanced capabilities of generative-automated communicative labour to produce complex sophisticated algorithmic identities capable of mimicking the rhetorically attractive humanity of the literary productions emanating from Black Twitter present a challenge with regard to the political efficacy of this community. Equally as disconcerting are the advancements in the automation of spoken discourse. Of specific concerns is less the communicative labour challenges presented by interactive voice response systems, but rather the advances in natural language-processing chatbots. Writers have raised concerns about the cost-cutting pervasion of "therapeutic communication machines", ruing their displacement of person-centred encounters with virtual impersonal. Capitalist profitability is consistently sighted as the motivation momentum as it is evident that "like other forms of automated communicative labor, automated psychotherapy provides an impersonal whiff of human communicativity while allowing capital to eliminate the unpredictability, contingency, and expense of the speaking human subject" (ibid.: 160). Accepting this it is plausible that the current convergence of generative-automated communicative labour and digital advertising technology is rapidly colonising and dehumanising the sociality of Black Twitter with disconcerting outcomes in terms of social alienation and the displacement of labour into advertising artefacts of commodity capitalism.

4 COMMUNICATIVE HUMAN RIGHTS AND COLONIAL DIGITAL CAPITALISM 145

These economies of time in digital advertising space enable real-time buying to launch campaigns at optimal relevance to their target audience. Some indication of how this works is provided as thus: "Programmatic buying makes a request to the advertising network in real time for billions of advertising inventory provided by the media companies, and it takes less than 0.2 seconds to publish the advertisement maximising the advertiser's performance" (ibid.). It is my contention that a highly followed Black Twitter account, such as that of @asakemusik (485.4k followers in May 2023), can replicate the formal features of the Twitter programmatic digital advertising suite and in so doing amplify the flows and rhythms of the communication networks of the audience towards its live music events.

Timely Reflections

In 2021, the Competition and Markets Authority (CMA) published its research algorithms reduced competition and harm to consumers. Personalised pricing harms consequent of digital markets applying analytics to data aggregates as a basis of personalised advertising pricing is cited as a frequent cause for consumers to withdraw trust in online digital markets. Complex and opaque pricing techniques reveal further disquieting algorithmic systemic practices in which firms apply analytics to data aggregates so as to corroborate profiling inferences and inform personalised pricing architectures. In the 2021 report, the CMA stated, for instance, that the Financial Conduct Authority (FCA) had identified "that some home and motor insurance firms use complex and opaque pricing techniques to identify consumers who are more likely to renew with them". Having identified these consumers, the firms were found to "then increase prices to these customers at renewal each year, resulting in some consumers paying very high prices, many of whom are unaware of this". According to CMA, these complex and opaque algorithmically based pricing techniques "disproportionately affect older consumers and cumulatively over time can lead to large increases in prices, or the order of 100 percent or more" (ibid.: 14–15). Elsewhere, concerns have been expressed about disruptors in financial services, exploiting analytic algorithms applied to centralised datasets, so as to commercially target people/households unable to access standard financial products such as current and savings account. It is a point of concern that these technologically platformed branchless "neobanks", that "are largely targeting unbanked and disengaged segments of the market", are falling below the radar, for "the regulatory environment around startup banks and payment platforms remains unsettled" (PGIM 2021). Where this unbanked market segment is a condition of legalities, the centralising of their policing information provides for a potentially lucrative data-stream upon which to navigate the innovative fintech and rapacious pricing tariffs of digital banking disruptors. Consequently, it is plausible to argue that consumer segments, reliant on high-pricing tariff digital banking disruptors, pay more for their banking provision. One might extrapolate this argument further in respect to the digital platforms that facilitate the online purchase of concert tickets. In August 2021, the CMA published recommendation to the government as a result of its investigation into consumer protection with the online secondary tickets market. It is evident from the CMA recommendations that these online secondary ticketing services are not necessarily at market value, and thus, consumers acquiring ticket through this route pay more money. Furthermore, it can be ascertained from the CMA's recommendations that the online secondary ticket seller market's suspected breaches of consumer protection law have resulted in situations of hazard in respect to exceeding, in their ticket sales, the venue's crowd capacity. Hence, the CMA recommended "a ban on platforms allowing resellers to sell more tickets for an event than they can legally buy from the primary market" and also "ensuring platforms are fully responsible for incorrect information about tickets that are listed for sale on their websites".

In November 2022, the House of Commons Library published its report on the uncapped secondary ticketing market titled, *Ticket Resales.* In a chapter focusing on the use of computer bots to harvest tickets, the report details how in regard to the secondary ticketing market, the Digital Economy Act (DEA) 2017 criminalised the use of software application programme designed to automate the buying of ticket on mass while imitating this as human behaviour (i.e. bots). The next year, in July 2018, the Breaching of Limits on Ticket Sales Regulations 2018 was brought into force under the auspices of the DEA 2017 made it illegal to use automated computer programmes to buy tickets in excess of limits detailed in the terms and conditions of sale and where the buyer is seeking financial gain (ibid.). According to the more recent November 2022 House of Commons Library publication, it is the police that enforce the Breaching of Limits on Ticket Sales Regulations 2018. Thus, in regard to this case study, it needs to be appreciated that it was the Metropolitan Police's jurisdiction to have investigated suspected breaches of the Regulations, whereby the sanction for a breach is "unlimited fine" (ibid.). The Metropolitan Police also have available the use of the Criminal Justice and Public Order Act 1994 in regard to the unlawful ticket for entertainment events. Additionally, legal agencies have available the Consumer Rights Act 2015, which defines an "online secondary platform" as "a website or app where tickets are offered for resale, rather than where the first sale of the ticket is made by or on behalf of the event organiser" (ibid.). However, the Metropolitan Police, in respect to the Consumer Rights Act 2015, are reliant upon the secondary ticket market to report itself in regard to illegal practices, for "secondary ticketing platforms have a legal obligation to report to the police and event organisers any criminal activity they become aware of in relation to tickets" (ibid.: 9). It is in this area that digital policing's disconnection from local communities impacts on their ability to be intuitively aware of automated secondary market ticket selling presenting a crisis of accumulation.

For, it is my contention that the Metropolitan Police were insufficiently knowledgeable about the amplifying effect of digital media when directed at advertising internationally profiled Black music artists. Even the most cursory perusal through the online social media promotion of the 15th December 2022 concert at O2 Academy should have alerted concern about the prospect of a crisis of overcapacity. This section has involved a forensic sociological analysis of key elements of digital advertising that were deployed on Twitter as part of the promotion of the Asake concert. My overall conclusion is that communicative digital capitalism's exploitation of Black music promotional culture is disconcerting.

Given that the advertising visual culture of Black music cultures is already hyper-sensationalised, heightened by visual techniques associated with Black Twitter, and this, in combination with the automated computer programme harvested secondary market ticketing, in my opinion, produced a situation of heightened consumer demand for the O2 Academy Brixton, 15th December 2022 Asake concert. These circumstances magnified the simulacra of market-based ticket sale and in so doing amplified the *face-value* of the concert tickets. *Face-value* is networks of stock exchanged at a variable contextually determined par value, rather than a standardised market value. Indeed, the face-value trading networks that emerge have some resonance with a similarly motivated scenario that Debord (1990: 69) observes as a feature of the spectacle, and described as thus:

The ubiquitous growth of secret societies and networks of influence answers the imperative demand of the new conditions for profitable management of economic affairs, at a time when the state holds a hegemonic role in the direction of production and when demand for all commodities depends strictly on the centralisation achieved by spectacular information/promotion, to which forms of distribution must also adapt.

It is a central contention of this case study that the conditions that befell the victims of the O2 Academy Brixton, 15th December 2022 crowd crush, can partly be explained in respect to the spectacular digital capitalist exploitation of Black Twitter's informational promotion of the concert tickets. Thus, from a Black feminist anticolonial framework, the capitalistic exploitation of communicative action channelled through social media's promotion of the fateful concert is very plausibly a prime culprit.

References

@Asakemusik (2022a); AsakeLondon; Sunday 11th December. Available at: https://twitter.com/asakemusik

@asakemusik (2022b); @asakemusik. Dec 17, 2022. Available at: https://twitter.com/asakemusik

Apryl Williams & Vanessa Gonlin (2017) I got all my sisters with me (on Black Twitter): second screening of *How to Get Away with Murder* as a discourse on Black Womanhood, Information, Communication & Society, 20:7, 984–1004, DOI: https://doi.org/10.1080/1369118X.2017.1303077

Barlow, J., and Smith, G., (2019) What The Health (WTH)?: Theorising Southern Black Feminisms in the US South. Agenda. 2019;33(3): 19–33. https://doi.org/10.1080/10130950.2019.1668725. Epub 2019 Oct 20. PMID: 33013143; PMCID: PMC7531585

Barthes, R., (1972/2000); *Mythologies,* London: Vintage Books.

Chi, H., (2011) Interactive Digital Advertising vs. Virtual Brand Community, Journal of Interactive Advertising, 12:1, 44–61, https://doi.org/10.1080/15252019.2011.10722190

Clark, M., (2020); DRAG THEM: A Brief Etymology of So-Called "Cancel culture", *Communication and the Public,* Vol.5(3–4), pp., 88–92.

Competition and Markets Authority (CMA) (2020); *Online Platforms and Digital Advertising, Market Study Final Report,* 1 July 2020. Available at: https://assets.publishing.service.gov.uk/media/5fa557668fa8f5788db46efc/Final_report_Digital_ALT_TEXT.pdf

4 COMMUNICATIVE HUMAN RIGHTS AND COLONIAL DIGITAL CAPITALISM 149

Competition and Markets Authority (CMA) (2021); *Algorithms: How They Can Reduce Competition and Harm Consumers*, Competition and Markets Authority, Published 19 January, Gov.UK. Available at: https://www.gov.uk/government/publications/algorithms-how-they-can-reduce-competition-and-harm-consumers/algorithms-how-they-can-reduce-competition-and-harm-consumers

Cottingham, M., & Rose, A., (2023) Tweeting Jokes, Tweeting Hope: Humor Practices during the 2014 Ebola Outbreak, Health Communication, 38:9, 1954–1963, https://doi.org/10.1080/10410236.2022.2045059

Dean, J., (2005); Communicative Capitalism: Circulation and the Foreclosure of Politics, *Cultural Politics*, Volume 1, Issue, 1, pp. 51–74.

Debord, G., (1988/1990); *Comments on the Society of the Spectacle*, Trans. Imrie, M., London:Verso.

Florini, S., (2014); Tweets, Tweeps and Signifyin': Communication and Cultural Performance on "Black Twitter", *Television and New Media*, Vol. 15(3), pp., 223–237.

Goldman, R. (1983). "We Make Weekends": Leisure and the Commodity Form. *Social Text, 8*, 84–103. https://doi.org/10.2307/466324

Graham, R., and Smith, S. (2016). The Content of Our #Characters: Black Twitter as Counterpublic. *Sociology of Race and Ethnicity, 2*(4), 433–449. https://doi.org/10.1177/2332649216639067

Gutiérrez, A., (2022); Situating Representation as a Form of Erasure #OscarsSoWhite, Black Twitter, and Latinx Twitter, Television and New Media, Vol., 23 91) pp., 100–118.

Hagen, S., and de Zeeuw, D., (2023); Based and Confused: Tracing the Political Connotations of a Memetic Phrase Across the Web, *Big Data and Society*, January-June, pp., 1–16.

Harlow, S., and Benbrook, A., (2019) How #Blacklivesmatter: exploring the role of hip-hop celebrities in constructing racial identity on Black Twitter, Information, Communication & Society, 22:3, 352–368, https://doi.org/10.1080/1369118X.2017.1386705

Harvey, D., (1989); *The Condition of Postmodernity; An Enquiry Into the Origins of Cultural Change*, Oxford: Basil Blackwell.

Hawkins, D., (2023); "When you search a #Hashtag, it Feels Like You're Searching for Death:" Black Twitter and communication About Police Brutality within the Black Community, *Social Media and Society*, April–June pp., 1–12.

Hill, M., (2018); "Thank You, Black Twitter": State violence, Digital Counterpublics, and Pedagogies of Resistance, *Urban Education*, Vol.53(2) pp., 286–302.

House of Commons Library (2022); *Ticket Sales*, (ed. Conway, l., House of Commons Library. Available at: https://researchbriefings.files.parliament.uk/documents/SN04715/SN04715.pdf

Klassen, S., and Fiesler, C., (2022); "This Isn't Your Data, Friend": Black Twitter as a Case Study on Research Ethics for Public Data, *Social Media and Society*, October-December, 2022, pp., 1–11.

Kniahynycky, R., (2023); Artificial Intelligence: Terms Marketers Need to Know, X Business. Available at: https://business.twitter.com/en/blog/artificial-intelligence-terms-marketers-need-to-know.html

Lee, H., and Cho, C., (2020) Digital advertising: present and future prospects, *International Journal of Advertising*, 39:3, 332–341, https://doi.org/10.1080/02650487.2019.1642015

Molefe, M., and Ngcongo, M., (2021) "You Don't Mess With Black Twitter!": An Ubuntu Approach to Understanding "Militant" Twitter Discourse, Communicatio, 47:3, 26–49, https://doi.org/10.1080/02500167.2021.2001553

Mpofu, S., (2019) Jesus Comes to South Africa: Black Twitter as Citizen Journalism in South African Politics, African Journalism Studies, 40:1, 67–90, https://doi.org/10.1080/23743670.2019.1610782

Myrick, J., Willoughby, J., and Clark, M., (2022); Racial Differences in Response to Chadwick Boseman's Colorectal Cancer Death: Media Use as a Coping Tool for Parasocial Grief, OMEGA – Journal of Death and Dying, pp., 1–20.

Onanuga, A. O. (2023). Interrogating patriarchy and homophobia in Nigeria's Zikoko online magazine. *African Identities*, 1–17. https://doi.org/10.1080/14725843.2023.2227354

Outley, C., Bowen, S., & Pinckney, H., (2021) Laughing While Black: Resistance, Coping and the Use of Humor as a Pandemic Pastime among Blacks, Leisure Sciences, 43:1-2, 305–314, https://doi.org/10.1080/01490400.2020.1774449

PGIM (2021); Disruption in Service Sector Favours Leaders in Health, Finance and Logistics, PGIM Reports. Available at: https://www.pgim.com/press-release/disruption-service-sector-favors-leaders-health-finance-and-logistics-pgim-reports

Prasad, P., (2016); Beyond Rights as Recognition: black Twitter and Posthuman Coalitional Possibilities, *Prose Studies*, Vol., 38, No. 1, pp., 50–73.

Ramirez, M., & Williams, B., (2022); #Migente: Latinx Twitter's Reaction to the Super Bowl LIV Halftime Performance, Howard Journal of Communications, 33:1, 58–77, https://doi.org/10.1080/10646175.2021.1929581

Reeves, J., (2016) Automatic for the people: the automation of communicative labor, Communication and Critical/Cultural Studies, 13:2, 150–165, https://doi.org/10.1080/14791420.2015.1108450

Reneses, P., and Bosch, T., (2023) Networked masculinities in South Africa: the #MensConference as a case study, NORMA, 18:2, 106–121, https://doi.org/10.1080/18902138.2022.2051396

4 COMMUNICATIVE HUMAN RIGHTS AND COLONIAL DIGITAL CAPITALISM 151

Richardson, A., (2017) Bearing Witness While Black, Digital Journalism, 5:6, 673–698, https://doi.org/10.1080/21670811.2016.1193818

Sharma (2013) Black Twitter? Racial Hastags, Networks and Contagion, *New Formations*, Volume 78, Issue 78., pp., 46–64.

Stevens, L., & Maurantonio, N., (2018); Black Twitter Asks Rachel: Racial Identity Theft in "Post-Racial" America, Howard Journal of Communications, 29:2, 179–195, https://doi.org/10.1080/10646175.2017.1354789

Twitter (2023); *The Twitter Ads Auction*, Ads Help Center, Twitter. Available at: https://business.twitter.com/en/help/troubleshooting/bidding-and-auctions-faqs.html

Twitter (2023a); *How Twitter Ads Work, Twitter Ads Help Center*, Twitter. Available at: https://business.twitter.com/en/help/troubleshooting/how-twitter-ads-work.html

X Business [Twitter] (2023); *Twitter Ads Pricing, Twitter Ads Help Center*. Available at: https://business.twitter.com/en/help/overview/ads-pricing.html

X Business Outlook (2023); Digital Advertising – Search Results. X Business Outlook. Available at: https://business.twitter.com/en/search.html?limit=10&offset=0&q=Digital%20advertising%20&searchPath=%2Fcontent%2Fbusiness-twitter%2Fen&sort=relevance

CHAPTER 5

Decolonial Feminism, Civil Rights Refutation of "Colonial Mentality"

Pamela Odih Interviews Sandra Izsadore—December 2023. © Pamela Odih

In 1961 the illustrious portrait artist Brian Duffy photographed Fela Ransome-Kuti with his Afro-jazz ensemble for a Vogue magazine piece provisionally planned for its feature article spread on the early transformative years of the jazz boom, titled "Evening Looks and All That Jazz". The jazz fashion portfolio assortment parades in the forefront the 1960s professional model Judy Dent, attired in the pared-back eveningwear of the preeminent English fashion designer to Queen Elizabeth II, the Royal Warrant holder, Hardy Amies. Vogue's glimpse of the 1960s jazz scene's leading lights is a quintessentially Eurocentric aesthetic schema for the Swinging London of the 1960s, in its depiction of a Caucasian English professional model as the personification of Londonesque jazz cool. Fela Ransome-Kuti is positioned playing his trumpet adjacent to the model, he is attired in sharp designer wares. Koola Lobitos, were assembled in the late 1950s, while their multi-instrumentalist lead vocalist was at Trinity College of Music in London. They are pictured in the relief, as performing statues projecting from the photograph's flat background; caricaturised as a syncopating ensemble in similar pared-back Swinging jazz attire.

Having immersed himself in London's vibrant 1960s artistic scene and cultivated music affiliations with jazz aficionados, Fela Ransome-Kuti commenced his epochal quest to craft a "distinctive global sound" (Ajiola 2019). He recorded a jazz album in London and in 1963 on returning to Lagos, motivated by Radio Nigeria's weekly jazz programme, the artist assembled a jazz Quintet, which became a second version of Koola Lobitos, and later the Afrika 70 in 1970 (ibid.: 173). It is popularly believed that through creative experimentation with jazz-funk, indigenous Yoruba Nigerian, allied with Ghanian highlife and West African Creole, that the artist coined the name Afrobeat, in the late 1960s. In 1969 he journeyed to the USA where he encountered Sandra Izsadore and the civil rights activists Black Panthers, which had a profound impact on his political sensibility; for, it inspired him into pursuing new ideologically inventive directions for his art. Also omitted from the Eurocentric portrayal of African jazz in the Brian Duffy photography is any sense of the older Black female, neither seen or heard; but "Back in Nigeria, Fela's mother finances the RK label, which releases three singles recorded by Koola Lobitos in London" (FelaKuti.com 2024).

In 2018, Vogue publishes a retrospective that features the photograph. In this retrospective of the photographer Brian Duffy's Vogue October 1961 exhibition, there is evidence of a reflexive deliberation and a conscious attempt to establish racial identity. In a feature piece *The Beat Goes On*, Brian Duffy's photograph of the Koola Lobitos band is redescribed as "the snappiest of Vogue's round-up" (Vogue 2018). Emphasis is ascribed to racial heritage ethnic cultural identity, whereby the music genre is described as an "African highlife band" led by "Nigerian-born Fela Ransome-Kuti" who is described as forming the band, "while studying the trumpet in London". The chronology of the development of the music genre traces a colonial lineage in which, "Two years after his Vogue appearance", Fela Kuti is reforming "Koola Lobitos in Lagos" prior to "relocating to Ghana" where he is ascribed to have unilaterally "created Afrobeat, his popular fusion of jazz, funk and West African music" (ibid.). The political influence on Afrobeat is chronicled vaguely, merely referring to 1979 when, "he sought nomination for the presidency of Nigeria, but was barred from standing, and instead became a figurehead in the opposition to Nigeria's military regime" (ibid.). In an attempt to write into the fashioning of the legacy of Afrobeat, in June 2021 Vogue published its feature on the *5 Ingenious Forgotten Female Pioneers of Afrobeat You Should Know* by Adimora (2021). Afrobeat is described here as having been evolved, "When Fela Kuti introduced his ingenious Afrobeat sound – the disruptive genre founded on the harmonic backdrops of jazz, funk, highlife and soul, rooted in traditional West African rhythms and melodies – to the world" (ibid.). It is recognised that Afrobeat has transformed the African music landscape and Fela Anikulapo-Kuti is ascribed the appellation, "Afrobeat patriarch" (ibid.). The piece interpolates with an established aspect of African feminist reflection on the music genre i.e., to give voice to the female influences on the development of Afrobeat. Among the female influences referred to foremost of which, in accordance, with a cavalcade of articles, documentaries and features is the musician, Sandra Izsadore. The Vogue piece describes the latter's influence in familiar stylised and caricaturing prose whereby she is said to have been "A Black musician manager an activist – who was heavily affiliated with the Black Panther civil rights movement in the United States – encountering Izsadore was a turning point for Kuti's sense of political identity" (ibid.). The Vogue article describes her impression as mesmeric, "So profound was her impact that upon their meeting, Kuti fell hard for her principles of Black nationalism and colonial history, changing his name from Ransome to Aníkúlápó and altering his music to sonic attacks on Western dominance" (ibid.). Nevertheless, possibly as consequence of its brevity, the Vogue piece is highly reminiscent of the sensationalist depiction of the exotic female muse, casting her mesmerising persuasion on the vivacious artist Fela Anikulapo-Kuti. Cognisant of avoiding this popular media and intellectually facile stylisation, I endeavoured to provide an original new direction, based on a primary sourced qualitative interview conducted in December 2023 with Sandra Izsadore.

Decolonial Feminist Civil Rights as Human Rights, African-American Perspective

Arena – Teacher Don't Teach Me Nonsense is the programme title for a BBC documentary filmed in 1984, containing extracts from the Glastonbury music festival performance of Fela Anikulapo-Kuti and backstage interviews. In several of these extracts the artist pays homage to their earlier influences commencing with the Black African leaders that provided the philosophical basis for Pan-Africanist movement for independence from colonial rule. Ghana's first prime minister Kwame Nkrumah (1909–1972) is attributed rightful prominence in the artist's pantheon of pioneering pan-Africanists. In 1969 the artist arrived in the USA with his band, fuelled by great ambitions to cultivate a successful freelance career of his existing profile in West Africa. In the Arena documentary the artist recounts his first encounter with, a person the BBC documentary narrator describes as "one of the new generations of radical Black Americans, a woman called Sandra Izsadore". The narrator then states that, "he says that after his 'failure' to become an American she taught him how to be an African". The audio then interjects to the artist's own words and first-person statement of recognition to Sandra Izsadore, "She was telling me about Africa. She said don't I know that Africans taught the Europeans everything that they know today? I said, no; I said you're talking … She say 'there are books; there are books that are saying', I said: 'show me a book'. And she gave me Malcolm X to read" (BBC 1984). Sandra Izsadore is graciously known as the Afro-American empress of Afrobeat. Her book, *Fela and Me*, provides for a candid autobiography of her professional and romantic relationship with the artist. Consequently, my aim in interviewing her was less directed by the pursuit of sensational revelations. Rather, I was motivated to gain an appreciation of her as a humanitarian activist and feminist; so as to explore the impact of her feminist ideals on the formative political ideology of the artist. In this respect I undertook a close reading of *Fela and Me* only after our online interview so as to listen closely to her narrative self in real time—albeit with a transatlantic time lapse—of the meeting. Language and communicative action are heightened features of the online interview; there is a negotiated reality that emerges as strangers cohere a reciprocity of perspective in the time/space compressed conditions of the online Microsoft Teams environment. We spent several minutes at the start, sound and backdrop checking the virtual mediation. In retrospect we momentarily were sensing an impression of the event; actions that Goffman (1989: 125) discerns "'tunes your body up' and with your 'tuned-up' body and with the ecological right to be close to them" I was suitably in a position to listen attentively. Thereafter, we settled into a wide ranging, and consistently informed interview.

> *My music. I think it's important for our children throughout the diaspora to have music that address their consciousness; their needs and to bring some form of awareness. Not just for our diasporas; but to let it be known that we are all connected and the origin of that connection begins in Africa. So, it is important for me and for any other artist entertainers, be it male or female. What's important to convey is to 'use the music as a weapon' as Fela said. But to use it as a weapon to educate. And if you have noticed. America heard Fela when he said 'use music as weapon'.* (Interviewee: Sandra Izsadore, December 2023)

The notion of a decolonial feminism featured tentatively at first in the interview, initially pertaining to Afrobeat music as a decolonial political means of expressing the everyday experiencing of racism encountered by British born Black youths. Progressing thereafter, we explored decolonial feminism in its general formulation i.e., as a politically informed critical engagement of the intersectionality of gender, class and race in the regional context of internationally exploitative colonial capitalist forces. The regional context pertains to the environmental devastation of the primitive accumulation through extractive drilling of oil and mining of mineral resources from Nigeria's national resources entering into privatised circuits of capitalist accumulation. Decolonial feminists identify traditional patriarchy and capitalist expropriation as rendering women to be frontline casualties of the commodification of indigenous environmental knowledge; the dismantling of indigenous farming cooperatives and the privation of rural conservation rights avaricious to the application of copyright and privatisation through the land enclosure. *Decolonial Ecology* critically examines the "calamitous intersection of racial capitalism and systematic assaults on the environment, including human expressions" (Davis 2022: xv). Writing in the foreword to Malcom Ferdinand's *Decolonial Ecology*, Angela Davis reenvisages earlier episodes in the aftermath of her release from incarceration, establishing the National Alliance Against Racist and Political Repression and being informed by esteemed colleagues to incorporate into the popular education more focus on the connection between state violence, racism and the environment. While her politics had long since recognised "colonialism and slavery as the foundational historical oppressions" and thus of direct value to the decolonial feminist movement of the 1970s, it is more in recent times that she has explored "environmental racism" as "a crucial concept, one which advances our understandings of the strategic location of dumps and toxic waste sites and other practices that devalue the lives of Black, indigenous and Latinx people" (ibid.: xvii). In *Fela and Me* Sandra Izsadore in a chapter in tribute to Fela Anikulapo-Kuti's 1976 album *Upside Down* in which she features as a lead vocalist, describes her appreciation of the environmentalist concerns about oil extraction in Nigeria.

> But when people are being displaced in the Niger Delta due to oil spills that are not being cleaned up, one sees that the people's fight is unending. There are still gas flares that have been burning for decades, costing two billion US dollars and counting, causing acid rain, unemployment, and a myriad of health hazards in the Niger Delta. People must know that the struggle is never going to end.
> …
> There are things they don't dare do in their own countries – America, United Kingdom, or Italy. But they have the arrogant audacity to take away livelihoods, destroy communities, and cause ill health, leaving adult farmers and fishermen in the Niger Delta without means of existence. These are things they would never attempt in 'God's own country' without great consequences. Fela will be relentless, with his music against their atrocities. Izsadore (2019: 190)

The vividly described environmental desolation consequent of hazardously extractive oil and mineral mining prompted a renascence in the impetus of my critical reflections and writings on water ecology. Long before my interview with Sandra Izsadore I was aware of the environmental crisis consequent of the oil industry in Nigeria. Habitus inculcates one's predisposition towards the capital of a cultural form. Thus, explains the inculcation of my childhood listening to my mother's stories of rivers in Nigeria that had catastrophically been contaminated by toxic agrochemical pollutants and oil extraction chemicals. Such distressing environmental disasters became transposed into my Marxist ecofeminism and translated into my empirically based writing on financialised privatisation of water companies, breaches in European Union regulation, and the disturbance to water ecology from excess untreated raw sewage being pumped into the River Thames, with the latter improperly blamed on the demand of increased immigration into a densely populated urban city (Odih 2014). Additionally, my childhood wonderment of how it was that my maternal grandmother's red clay built home in an Ibo community situated in Nigeria's Delta State made solely from earth was visibly more resilient, environmentally sustainable and ergonomic than the shiny new buildings in the city of Lagos. As these thoughts sedimented into my habitus through childhood stories of collapsing city dwelling and the chorus of protestors that braved to challenge the architects of such disasters, it was evident that I had subconsciously transposed this witnessing into my studies of London's urban ecology (2019a, 2019b).

Indeed, in my study of aesthetic gentrification and the 14th June 2017 Grenfell Tower London fire tragedy my embodied capital of a cultural form transposed through my habitus as a Black British born first-generation daughter of the Nigerian Biafra diaspora informed my unique conception of adsensory urban ecology. For in the still smouldering ruins and acrid smoke infused air of the Grenfell Tower carcass that I visited soon after the 14th June 2017 blaze, I could see the ruinous consequences of the exasperated intersecting disordering of the urban ecology, ethnic diaspora displacements and capitalistic investment propertied urban planning. Through these primary observations, intellectual pursuits and conversations with Nigerian feminist allies such as Sandra Izsadore I define decolonial feminism as a praxis borne from resistance to the continued pervasion of gender racialised colonial discrimination in a regional context that has long since dismantled the perpetrating architecture of its colonialism. Françoise Vergès (2021: 10) expresses poignantly what it means to be a decolonial feminist stating that it is an embodied experiential praxis, dissuaded by nihilistic "empty ideologies" because it is to affirm the fidelity of the material and cultural conditions of struggle of the women in the Global South who have proceeded us in their fortitude and resistance. In this respect decolonial feminism, "means recognizing that the offensive against women that is now openly justified and acknowledged by state leaders is not simply an expression of a brazen, masculine dominance, but a manifestation of the destructive violence generated by capitalism" (ibid.). Consequently, decolonial feminism calls for the building of alliances across colonial difference; and in Black music cultures such vivacity nourished and inspirited the feminine soul of Afrobeat enabling its revolutionary mobilisation, by Fela Anikulapo-Kuti. Four main areas of mobilisation are specific to this analysis of decolonial feminist influence on Afrobeat.

Communicative Action. Occasionally, students of African descent engage me in conversation about the music and culture of the West African diaspora. Despite being knowledgeable in response, as one might expect the daughter of Nigerian parents that lived through British colonial rule, the gaining of independence and their immigration to Britain from Biafra at the beginning of the Nigerian civil war. These events have become impressed in my mind through migration tales and narrative expression, that melodically rhyme through our habitus. Consequently, I swiftly became fluent in the interview's African-American lyrical narrative framing, whereby, the interview was one and the same time about and of the feminine soul of Afrobeat, some indication of which is evident in her account of music as communicative action.

How it all began, was here in America, I never had any positive images of Africans and growing up in an all white neighbourhood seeing images of black people and none of these images ever showed black people in an elevated position. So as a young child I am thinking, well you know: When am I gonna turn white? I literally because my parents they never taught me. You know hatred has to be taught. And even though we were in that all white neighbourhood, I was never taught hatred. (Interviewee: Sandra Izsadore, December 2023)

Attention to language in discursive lyrical appellation and subjective meaning is a consistent theme of *Fela and Me*, commencing with the popularly held belief that the artist substituted the patronymic Ransome-Kuti with Fela Anikulapo-Kuti as a consequence of an African consciousness initiated by her tutelage. Izsadore (2019: 14) explains in her book that, "He [Fela] said 'Ransome' an English word was a slave word and a slave name. 'Kuti' in the Yoruba language of the Southwestern part of Nigeria means 'cannot die'. 'Anikulapo' means 'someone who has death in his pocket'. When one puts together both names, his full name comes to mean Fela, 'someone with death in his pocket and so cannot die'". Language mobilised as communicative action relates more to a transformation of the lyrics from songs of personal experience to critical political commentary on Nigeria. The artist named his residence Kalakuta Republic as derived from the epithet "Calcutta" "cell for rascals" ascribed by cellmates to the prison. The artist declared Kalakuta Republic an independent republic situated within the Federal Government of Nigeria; which provoked infuriation from the military government. While having been educated in Anglo-Nigerian institutions, in his native country, and several years of music study in Trinity College London, the artist preferred to write and compose lyrics in Pidgin English and perform using this vernacular associated with poor illiterate communities. Pidgin is known to be the lingua franca connecting opposing tribal resistance against a common ruling enemy. Adopting Pidgin English was therefore a provocative communicative action, fearless at inciting the wrath of the military, fearful of the political disenfranchisement of illiteracy. Tremendously noble pursuit but the wrath of the former would have deterred all but the bravest of musicians. It has been observed that the enhanced prominence of Pidgin English as the lyrical language of the artist's Afrobeat had displaced the "nonlexical syllables" of Yoruba chanting recitation composed in narrative format, a genre "that engaged the audience in a conversation about politics, colonialism, and oppression" (Cobo-Piñero 2020: 447). Nevertheless, it was the artist's transgressive use of Pidgin English that was to the annoyance and ire of the establishment. It has been observed that Pidgin served the artist's purpose particularly well because of its ability to transcend tribal linguistic repertoires, while also maintaining a sense of being regionally with the imprint of a local agency (Ogunfeyimi 2021).

"Why is it that African leaders usually don't mind when you speak and write in Queen's English, but the moment you speak the language of the common man, you become a target?", rhetorical decolonial quip in *Fela and Me*. Indeed, this acutely ascertained critique of neocolonial Nigeria interpolates well with some of the foremost civil rights advocates prominent in the USA, during her time with Fela Anikulapo-Kuti. Of particular significance to this era includes Angela Davis. Writing on Education and Liberation, from a Black women's perspective, as a chapter in *Women Race Class*, Davis (1983) draws attention to the immediate aftermath of the abolition of slavery as distinguished by the urgent need expressed by Black people for land, enfranchisement and the satiation of a deep-rooted desire, to redress hundreds of years of educational deprivation. Parallels exist between Angela Davis's notion of the emancipated slaves having a breakneck impatience for the acquisition of education and Fela Anikulapo-Kuti's acuity in mobilising Pidgin English to expedite the spread of listeners to his political message. For it is accepted, as depicted in the Broadway Musical, that Sandra Izsadore re-educated the artist, then her contribution parallels that of the many Black women and who rapidly responded to the ferocious pursuit of knowledge expressed by Black people having been emancipated from the brutally enforced prohibition on the literacy and education of enslaved people in the Northern and Southern states of America. Decolonial feminists highlight the struggle for the recognition of knowledge that fervently challenges the "Western-patriarchal economic ideology" of Euro-centric epistemology (Vergès 2021: 13). Suffice to say, in the transference of knowledge thought the communicative action of decolonial feminism, "The work of discovering and valuing knowledge, philosophies, literature, and imagination does not begin with

162   P. ODIH

us, but one of our missions is to make the effort to know and disseminate them" (ibid.: 14).

Matriarchal Ethics of Care. Reiterating an earlier expression of concern is necessary so as to prepare my discussion of care ethics. *Fela and Me* contains an account of the death of Funmilayo Ransome-Kuti, describing this tragedy as a consequence of her injuries sustained when military police raided Kalakuta Republic and hurled her out of a window "claiming that they did it so that she would not roast alive in the furnace they'd inflicted on Kalakuta" (Izsadore 2019: 15). The author's description of a grieving son suffering excoriating mental trauma hauling his mother's coffin in procession in a long march from Kalakuta Republic to Dodan Barracks in Obalende Lagos is heartfelt and powerfully symbolic. "Kalakuta Show" expresses some of the grief of the physical abuse perpetrated against his mother, and "Coffin for Head of State" is a defiant primal rage against the military regime describing the act of carrying his mother's coffin to the steps of Dodan Barracks is filled with emotional pain. Despite his lyrical witticism the verse about reaching the barracks gate asking whether "Obasanjo dey there" and placing the coffin down having declared the episode to be a "Movement of the People" for "Young African Pioneers" is an arousing and affecting testament. Significantly, in *Fela and Me* there is speculation about the content of the coffin, for, we are informed that "Fela, an African Nigerian, and Yoruba culturist to the core, was not likely to defy Yoruba culture and ancestral beliefs" (ibid.). But while suspicious of the content there is unanimity with regard to its symbolic meaning as an outpouring of grief, sadness and anger of the military police's politically motivated horrendous physical assault of his mother's body. It was also a protestation against the violation of the female body, which had become a terroristic assault weapon levied by the military police against political challengers to the 1976–1979 era of General Olusegun Obasanjo's regime. The political party "Movement of the People" had been white-listed and was disallowed to participate in the civilian election that secured, in 1979, the presidency of Alhaji Shehu Shagari. Accepting the long march to Dodan Barracks as in part motivated to protest against politically moti-vated violence against women, one might argue that it was an allied femi-nist act. It was in protestation of the physical violence perpetrated against his mother and also the violence meted out against his wives and female acquaintances resident in the Kalakuta Republic. For, in this instance and countless others "a direct attack on the black female as potential insur-gent" is a sexual repression that "finds its parallels in virtually every historical situation where the woman actively challenges oppression" (Davis 1971: 12). Furthermore, the use of sexual violence against the artist's wives was not solely an attack on their person, but also an attempt to immaculate and undermine the patriarchal power of Fela Anikulapo-Kuti in terms of his ability to protect his family. In her book *Fela and Me*, the author is uncharacteristically constrained in their description of the sexual violence perpetrated against the female witnesses of the military police's raid in 1977 of Kalakuta Republic.

In my interview discussion with Sandra Izsadore, it became apparent to me that the physical violence perpetrated against the female witnesses of the 1977 of military police's raid of Kalakuta Republic had a brutality reminiscent of the violent denigration of the Black female during slavery and colonial times. In *Toward a Decolonial Feminism*, María Lugones (2010) provides an account of "the coloniality of gender" that traces a legacy of dehumanising treatment of the Black female, starting with the dichotomous hierarchical distinctions between human and non-human integral to colonial modernity. Colonisation of Americas, Caribbean and Africa ideologically framed its illegitimacy by imposing the human, non-human dichotomy on the colonised so as to elevate the White Western man (ibid.: 743). It operated in conjunction with another dichotomy that distinguishing male from female. This latter distinction became the primary differentiator of civilisation and its separation from the animal world. "Only the civilized are men or women" (ibid.). In order to legitimate the enslavement of indigenous people and the forced transportation through the transatlantic slave trade, their human species was denied, classified not as human beings they were deemed equitable to organic cargo and animals. Descriptions of African slaves of this era were rife with animalistic denotations, connoting uncontrolled sexually wild non-human species. Conversely, the European White male epitomised the Western ideal of conquering civilisation and mastery over carnal bodily sensation. The European White female, although not his equal, was considered to be his human Other, "as someone who reproduced race and capital through, her sexual purity, passivity, and being homebound in the service of the White, European, bourgeoisie man" (ibid.). These dichotomous hierarchies endured into the first modernity and thus were part of the atrocious imposition of the colonial, gender system. While it was the case that the White female was subjugated, delimited of rights and defined in terms of her fecundity, she was nevertheless the "Other" to the gendered human male in the colonial dichotomy. Conversely, the colonised as positioned outside

164   P. ODIH

of the gender colonial dichotomy were non-gendered and treated as inherently uncivilised, thus it has been observed that the "behaviour of the colonized and their personalities/souls were judged as bestial and thus non-gendered, promiscuous, grotesquely sexual and sinful" (ibid.). This denigration of the colonised, provided an arbitrary justification for the coloniser to unleash, without restraint, its "civilising mission" to discipline, but not so as to create civilised White people, but rather to train the animistic propensies of the colonised against the ideal subject the White male. The inherent illogicality of this intent precipitated unrestrained violence. Consequently, the colonised were subject to unimaginable sexual violence and physical brutality so as to produce a gender coloniality in which "males became not-human-as-not-men, and colonized females became not-human-as-not-women" (ibid.: 744). One can begin to appreciate the legacy of the first modernity iteration of the colonial system as impacting, thereafter, on the colonial mentality of disciplinary actors and official systems of policing. Nevertheless, the ferocity of physical violence reigned upon the females present in Kalakuta Republic during its 1977 raid by the military police, was in excesses of that which might be inflicted on an animal. Listening to documentaries and reading through *Fela and Me* one gains a sense that the brutality of the police violence was in actuality directed at a dissidence evoked by the females, that were part of the entourage of 27 wives, and unnamed backing singers.

The gender coloniality of the first modernity in its denial of the colonised as belonging to the human species by necessity, so as to govern less overtly in respect to its monopoly of coercive power, allied with patriarchal structures in its acceptance of the colonised female as human. But it did so while retaining the heteronormative hierarchical gender coloniality that situates the White male at its apex and the White female as its civilised subjugated "Other". As defined by gender coloniality the Black female is doubly subjugated; for she is a human species that is both Other to the White male and its female Other. When in the immediate aftermath of Nigeria's independence nonelected officials were siphoning off Nigeria's resources, it was the symbolisms of gender coloniality that were repurposed so as to veil corruption in a guise of civility. The 1973 album, titled *Gentleman*, written and produced by Fela Anikulapo-Kuti, with musical accompaniment by Afrika 70, satirises the gender coloniality of neocolonialism. It distains a colonial mentality in which previously colonised people adorn the gender etiquette and attire of the colonised so as to perpetuate colonial inequalities to which they are extracting symbolic and material

5 DECOLONIAL FEMINISM, CIVIL RIGHTS REFUTATION... 165

gain. Through satire and acerbic lyricism such as "I no be gentleman at all o!; I be Africa man original" *Gentleman* seeks to provoke a decolonial consciousness. Accepting this it is my contention that the ferocious physical violence perpetrated against the female witnesses of the 1977 Nigerian armed forces raid of Kalakuta Republic was a horrific illegitimate punishment. The undue violence was to punish the women for their affront to the gender colonial hierarchy; because these women in their spectacular African-centric polygamous cultural display were rejecting the White female archetype and its subjugation to the White male patriarch of gender coloniality. For this contravention they were punished severely.

Indeed; apropos to the civil rights tutelage of Sandra Izsadore and her association with the Black Panthers, Angela Davis's writing on violence perpetrated against the Black female body, as a weapon of domination, provides further decolonial feminist explanation as why in the context of the 1977 police raid of Kalakuta Republic the matriarchal mother-subject was horrifically and brutally attacked. Of specific pertinence to this era includes Davis's (1971) writing, *The Black Woman's Role in the Community of Slaves*. In this article published in 1970s, by the journal The Black Scholars Davis challenges the notion of the Black matriarch; defining its repeated invocation "as one of the fatal by-products of slavery" (ibid.: 2). Particularly, frustrating and duly castigated by Davis is that "lingering beneath the notion of the black matriarch is an unspoken indictment of our female forbearers as having actively assented to slavery" (ibid.). The myth of Black female emasculation of the Black male is imbricated in an indictment of collaboration. For it is wrongly assumed that the enslaved female as matriarch and unifying force within the slave family enabled the slaveholder to sustain its wretched control over the enslaved community. Parallels exist here in respect to colonialism and its reliance on matriarchate at times when its male members of the community had been forcibly conscripted. It is proposed that both of these instances of matriarchy would more probably be spaces for resistance, rather than spaces of collaboration with the illegitimate dominating force of the occupier. Inherent in the essential concept of matriarchy is the female's embodiment of a socially recognised power. In both slavery and colonialism it would have been, as Davis recognises about slavery, "risky for the slaveholding class to openly acknowledge symbols of authority – female symbols no less than male. Such legitimized concentration of authority might eventually unleash their 'power' against the slave system itself" (ibid.). Furthermore, the notion of a matriarch household was more akin to plantation confected mythology for it presumes stable kinship structures; but mothers were often forcibly separated from their children and "Where families were allowed to thrive, they were, for the most part, external fabrications serving the designs of an avaricious, profit-seeking slaveholder" (ibid.). Consequently, Davis argues that the myth of the collaborating matriarchy needs to be shown to be contradictory, so as to reveal the complexity of Black female resistance to enslavement and to the shackles of colonial patriarchy.

It is Davis's contention that the Black female matriarch was neither a collaborator nor a passive recipient of her family's enslavement. But rather, "by virtue of the brutal force of circumstances, the black woman was assigned the mission of promoting the consciousness and practice of resistance" (ibid.: 3). Analyses of the intersecting power trajectories which enslaved women were subject to reveal spaces for resistance through the reproductive labour ascribed to the female in the homestead. Turning to the plight of the African female slave, domestic division of labour role was dictated by the White slave-owning elite as part of their monopoly of power; it was also woven into the native patriarchal traditions of the African communities from which the slaves had been forcibly extracted. But while "traditionally the labour of females, domestic work is supposed to complement and confirm their inferiority" for the Black slave female, Davis describes "a strange twist of affairs", whereby "in the infinite anguish of ministering to the needs of the men and children around her (who were not necessarily members of her immediate family), she was performing the *only* labor of the slave community which could not be directly and immediately claimed by the oppressor" (ibid.: 5). If one recalls here the placing by her son of Funmilayo Ransome-Kuti's coffin the act appears resonant of an appreciation of the reproductive labour of the matriarch as a form of powerful resistance to the dehumanising and excessive exploitation of the monopoly of power held by the British colonialist. This is because, as with the plight of the enslaved African female forcibly working in the plantations of the American states, domestic labour under colonial domination is the only meaningful labour for the sole purposes of the well-being of her family and community. As Davis expresses it, "Precisely through performing the drudgery which has long been a central expression of the socially conditioned inferiority of women, the black woman in '*chains*' could help lay the foundation for some degree of autonomy" (ibid.: 5; emphasis added). Similarly, the matriarch's ethics of care in colonial times was integral to the survival of her community. Not all people survived colonial domination; and what's more "Not all people have survived enslavement; hence her survival-oriented activities were themselves a form of resistance" (ibid.).

Returning to the spectacular demonstration of grief in which the artist Fela Anikulapo-Kuti marched in convoy to Dodan Barracks, Obalende carrying the coffin of his mother who had tragically died from injuries sustained by the military police was laying the coffin down and calling for the military leader Olusegun Obasanjo (1976–1979) to acknowledge the scene, all of which might be defined as bearing witness to the unifying power of the matriarch to incite resistance. It also needs to be recognised that residents in Kalakuta Republic at the time of the 1977 raid by the military police were many of the 27 wives of the artist. I mention this because they were also mothers to his children and many had experienced the brutality meted out during the raid. Writings by Angela Davis on policing and the incarceration of women of colour advance beyond the excessive focus on gratuitous violence as is evident in the mainstream "crime and punishment" framework. In accordance with the "new politics of imprisonment" the agency of the prisoner's experience is considered a valid source of knowledge. Consequently, listening to documentaries that have included extracts of testament drawn from interviews with members of the 27 wives, it is possible to assume these as valid insights into the appalling event. In an article titled *Deepening the Debate Over Mass Incarceration*, Davis (2014) developed further the notion that criminalisation is a means of population control to obfuscate crises in the socioeconomic conditions of capitalism. An area of Davis's thesis of relevance to the experiences of the 27 wives in terms of police brutality relates to the suggestion that neoliberal privation of social welfare systems as a consequence of debt restructuring and similar fiscal policies directly exacerbates existing situations of patriarchal control and financial dependencies of women. Nigeria in the 1970s was similarly subject to controls on state welfare provision. In these situations, as Davis later describes, women "who can no longer depend on welfare, are compelled to participate in underground economies and are thus subject to instant criminalization when they are penalized for their poverty" (Davis 2014: 17). Fela Anikulapo-Kuti's 27 wives in the absence of welfare provision were dependent on his patriarchal behest and were therefore unfairly condemned to be guilty by association when the military police raided his music emporium Kalakuta Republic.

Ethics of Justice. Sandra Izsadore's *Fela and Me* was co-authored with the University of California, Los Angeles (UCLA) graduate Segun Oyekunle. Perhaps this explains the nuanced detailing of Sandra's appreciation of Angela Davis's Black feminist activism. Segun's basis on their experience at UCLA enlightens an intriguing aspect of the decolonial feminist perspective, with regard to its alliance with African-American feminism in pursuit of a global decolonial feminist movement. According to Segun's account of the heightened activism at UCLA during the 1970s and 1980s, relation between "Blacks and African students in America" was a complex contentious issue. UCLA's Black student politics was nationally and internationally orientated, campaigning with equal vigour against anti-apartheid in South Africa and the discriminatory racist policing practices directed at Black communities. With regard to the latter the authors emphasise that "one must also remember that the FBI targeted Angela Davis and forced her out of UCLA" (2019: 78). The FBI's harassment of UCLA student protests was notoriously imperialist in its political persuasion and was evident in the ferocity meted out against students participating in anti-apartheid demonstrations. The Tent City occupations appear to have particularly attracted the wrath of the FBI as the authors describe, "The FBI was also very active during the Free Mandela protest and wanted to dislodge the Mandela 'Tent City' that was erected at 'The Pit' there in the center of UCLA Campus in protest" (ibid.). The Tent City was both a symbolic demonstration occupied by student and non-students demanding disinvestment in the South African apartheid regime, it was also an instance in the alliance of Black civil rights activism with Pan-Africanism. African students studying at UCLA had formed their own distinct affiliations, the Association of Africans in America (AAA) was one among others that were disproportionately monitored by the FBI and CIA. It was reputed that the FBI and CIA infiltrated the AAA, which was believed by the authors to have been an unnecessary pursuit, "because most were graduating and returning to their various homes in Africa and the United States, or they were securing appointments spread all over the country" (ibid.: 81). Conversely, it is posited that American officials seized the financing of AAA, described as thus, "The AAA, and its goals, was destined to fizzle out. It finally fizzled out. The money in their account was trapped in the account as the signatories dispersed everywhere. Probably trapped till today" (ibid.). Rather than interpret these as separate occurrences, when seen through the prism of Angela Davis's critique of the capitalistic criminal justice system in the USA, they are more plausibly part of the international spread of the coercive capitalistic processes that are systematically using intelligent surveillance and institutional discrimination against people of colour.

Angela Davis's (1971/2016b) account of *Political Prisoners, Prisons and Black Liberation* interrogates "a glaring incongruity between democracy and the capitalist economy" and in so doing reveals the ingenious means Black people have developed in their pursuit of resistance to the extended reach of the capitalist monopoly of extrajudicial power (ibid.: 27). Listening and reading expressions of agitation concerning the brutality of Fela Anikulapo-Kuti's encounters with the Nigerian military regime and subsequent civilian government of 1970s and 1980s, give credence to the immediacy and international reach of Angela Davis's writings on political prisoners. Indeed, three areas of specific influence warrant a brief descriptive detailing. Firstly, capitalism's monopoly of coercive control has meant that "the people are not the ultimate matrix of the laws and the system which govern them – certainly not Black people and other nationally oppressed people, but not even the mass of whites. The people do not exercise decisive control over the determining factors of their lives" (ibid.). Davis identifies how capitalist commercial interests permeate the legal rationalities and institutions that in the aftermath of the American Civil War assured in place, "the Black Codes, successors to the old slave codes, legalized convict labor, prohibited social intercourse between Blacks and whites, gave white employers an excessive degree of control over the private lives of Black workers, and generally codified racism and terror" (ibid.: 29). Secondly, a reconsideration of the political prisoner as the very embodiment of an ongoing revolutionary disruptive force intent on frustrating the ideological claim to legitimacy by the capitalistic criminal justice system. This is because for the political prisoner where their category of existence is unrecognised, their incarceration is based on a criminal offence unrelated to the actual political act of transgression; and or "often the so-called crime does not even have a nominal existence" (ibid.: 30). Ultimately, the political prisoner is incarcerated for having "violated the unwritten law which prohibits disturbances and upheavals in the status quo of exploitation and racism" (ibid.). Contravention of this unwritten law is what the political prisoner is punished for, when they are incarcerated for having evidentially committed a criminal offence and/or found guilty for participating in the schooling of others to become critically conscious of the unwritten law. Davis is particularly convincing in her contention that a deep-rooted ambivalence typifies the criminal justice

170   P. ODIH

system's detainment of the political prisoner: "Charged and tried for a criminal act, his guilt is always political in nature" (ibid.). While the political prisoner might have dissented racist unjust laws, they do so with the outlook of intending to transform their exploitative social conditions of materialisation.

A third feature of Angela Davis's conception of the political prisoner, which emerges in my interview with Sandra Izsadore in respect to her apprehension of Fela Anikulapo-Kuti's encounters with the Nigerian criminal justice system. In Davis's discourse on the political prisoner, critical emphasis is placed on the cynical dexterities by which the ideological apparatuses of the state are mobilised in order to "explain away the existence of the political prisoner" (ibid.: 33). In media and culture, the politically transgressive act is diminished to a criminal act "in order to affirm the absolute invulnerability of the existing order" (ibid.). Writing while incarcerated awaiting trial for harrowing capital felony crimes Davis was insistent that contributory correlations exist between the increased prominence of the Black Liberation Movement, other civil rights progressives and the expansion of "the judicial system and its extension, the penal system". These apparatuses of the criminal justice system become increasingly mobilised as "key weapons in the state's fight to preserve the existing conditions of class domination, therefore racism, poverty and war" (ibid.). The issues of racism are relatable to the African context in respect to the ideological power structures of European colonialism and British colonial Africa. Davis's concern about the imbrication of culture in underpinning fascism has an acute applicability to the repressive legislation augmenting the policing powers of the Nigerian military regime that Fela Anikulapo-Kuti encountered in its most audacious unconcealed brutality. Encountering these excesses of coercive control during the civilian government's rule was an inevitable feature of what Davis et al. (1971/2016a: 13) describe as "the necessity to resort to such repression" as "reflective of [a] profound social crisis, of systematic disintegration". During colonial governance and its prior and neocolonial imbrication, "Repression is the response of an increasingly desperate imperialist ruling clique to contain an otherwise uncontrollable and growing popular disaffection", which Davis et al (ibid.) believed would ultimately provoke collectively coordinated resistance and "the revolutionary transformation of society". The inevitability of the demise of the prison system is believed to be as a consequence of its existence "as an appendage of the capitalist state, as an instrument for class, racial and national oppression" thus, as of when capitalism becomes overwhelmed by its irresolvable contradictions its criminal justice system will also disintegrate.

Decolonising "Colonial Mentality". Interviewing Sandra Izsadore and subsequently reading her book enabled me to focus precisely on the decolonial feminist praxis of "de-thinking" "colonial mentality" and its distinction from the anticolonial feminism of Olufunmilayo Ransome-Kuti. In contrast to the absolute binary opposition of collaboration versus separation, decolonial feminists explore and optimise the strategic gains, in respect to the project of decolonialism, of aligning with mainstream feminism. These shifting proximal alignments in strategy might ultimately refer to differing aims and thus should not be perceived as seamless collaborations, as Davis (1971/2016a: 104) indicates in the following extract from *Freedom Is a Constant Struggle*, "Feminism insists on methods of thought and action that urge us to think about things together that appear to be separate, and to disaggregate things that appear to naturally belong together". Such processes of aligning together perceptibly distinct aspects of the struggle against racism were described during my interview with Sandra Izsadore. Indeed, in *Fela and Me*, there are numerous passages of reflexive introspection in regard to teaching Black Africans about American centric "Black consciousness". The author at times reads as though they are conflicted in their quest as an outsider, and that they perceived the African-American history of slavery as self-vindicating her right to tell the "truth" to the African people. As she expresses it, "I wanted Nigerian people to know the truth! That Black African-Americans were treated differently because of the color of their skin, and the same would happen to them too. This is the truth that was never taught in school or publicized on mainstream television" (Izsadore 2019: 100). But in many respects, this was already our embodied "truth", the lived epistemology antecedent in the resounding rhythms and defiant lyrics of Afrobeat. Indeed, I think Sandra Izsadore was sufficiently reflexively aware of the Black culture industry to appreciate its machinations in operation in the formulation of the story of her as beautiful exotica, enlightened visionary and muse. For, it is evident in my conversation with her that she was articulating a more supplicated and delicately nuanced narrative of her influence, as is implied in the following extract derived from *Fela and Me*.

> Every time I spoke to the press, and it was published, it was about a hot, paper-selling item. People were interested in what I had to say; and I was determined to speak my truth. It was so special to me to be

172   P. ODIH

in a country where Black people were everywhere and were in control. I felt free for the very first time in my life. At every interview, I was talking about the Black injustice in America, and the people were listening. Izsadore (2019: 190)

One might discern from the portrayal of her encounters with the music press media that these became platforms for Sandra Izsadore to convey a praxis of "de-thinking" of "colonial mentality", indication of the methodological basis of which is evident in the lyrical composition and production of Fela Anikulapo-Kuti's album titled *Sorrow, Tears and Blood*. Released in 1977 featuring the musicality of Africa 70, the album includes, alongside the title track, the song titled "Colo-mentality [Colonial Mentality]". In the following verses significant insights are evident as to the "de-thinking" that is made necessary by colonial mentality.

Colo-mentality

If you say you be colonial man
You don be slave man before
Them don release you now
But you never release yourself

I say you fit never release yourself
Colo-mentality
E be say you be colonial man
You don be slave man before
Them don release you now
But you never release yourself. Fela Anikulapo-Kuti (1977)

The tenacity and rapacious appetite for cultural appropriation evident in the capitalist culture industry and its tumultuous avaricious attraction to diversity is not to be underestimated. As Françoise Vergès (2021: 14) expresses it, "We should not underestimate the speed with which capital is able to absorb ideas and turn them into empty slogans. Why wouldn't capital be able to incorporate the idea of decolonization or decoloniality?". In Fela Anikulapo-Kuti's conception of "de-thinking" "colonial mentality" there is evident an acute precision in conceptual boundary differentiation so as to convey plausibly the enduring legacy of oppression that requires "de-thinking". Consequently, it is necessary not to entangle one's definition of colonisation with colonialism. The former, i.e., colonisation is a period of time in which the economic and political existence of a nation is dominated by the interests of another to which it has become a colony.

Conversely, in my reading of Marxist decolonial feminist accounts of colonisation it is clearly apparent that colonialism is discerned as a "process" of domination involving the appropriation of land and the subjugation of its human population. Etymologically the root word "colony" derives from Latin *colonia*, which refers to an established and settled land, and also emerges from Latin *colonus*, *colere* which respectively refer to the husbanding of settled land and its guarding (EtymologyOnline.com 2024). It is possible to trace antecedents of this etymological root in Marxist decolonial feminist conceptions of colonialism. This is because the colonialism which is the focus of Marxist decolonial feminism is the form of domination of land and subjugation of its people that emerges in the eighteenth century with the rise of industrial capitalism. Whereby in order to meet the resource requirements of its industrial capitalist metropolis, capitalism fuelled by imperialist ideologies sought out non-capitalised enclaves for primitive accumulation. Consequently, it is from this dialectical materialist conception of the trajectory of capitalism that Marxist decolonial feminists such as Françoise Vergès (2021: 15) define colonialism as "a process or a movement, a total social movement whose perpetuation is explained by the persistence of social formations resulting from this order". Colonialism in terms of the domination of land, the subjugation of its people and the primitive accumulative extraction of its resources is therefore a process that is directed associated with trajectories of capitalist exploitation.

Decolonial feminism is concerned with critically examining the intersections of race/gender/class intrinsic to colonialism's colonial matrix of power which pervades "all relations of domination, even when the regimes associated with these phenomena have disappeared" (ibid.). Accepting this, it becomes self-evidently inadequate to depict through a linear chronology an era of colonialism as having been purged by decolonial praxis. This is because "colonial situations" of exploitation, expropriation and domination can persist and be present even where the institutional structures and processes of administration of colonisation have long since been dismantled (Grosfoguel 2004: 320). Whereby, "colonial situations" refer to "the cultural, political and economic oppression of subordinate racialized ethnic groups by dominant racial/ethnic groups, with or without the existence of colonial administrations" (ibid.). These colonial situations can also refer to "coloniality" which in its recent form emerges from the extended history of capitalist European colonialism (Vergès 2021: 16). Decolonial feminism interrogates the European and other trajectories of coloniality, so as to challenge the gender, class and racialised

174   P. ODIH

discrimination consequent across the global onslaught of Western capitalism. As Vergès (2021: 16) expresses it, ignorance of the multiply radial centrifugal forces "of the circulation of people, ideas and emancipatory practices within the Global South preserves the hegemony of the North-South axis; and yet, South-South exchanges have been crucial for the spread of dreams of liberation" (ibid.).

Decolonising Human Rights, Timely Reflections

Human rights in the last one-and-a-half centuries were in an odd and artificial way always linked to the project of colonisation itself, before they more genuinely, became a part of the reverse effort of resistance against colonialism. Salil Shetty (2018)

On 22 May 2018, the Secretary General of Amnesty International (Salil Shetty) delivered a lecture at the London School of Economics (LSE) titled, Decolonising Human Rights. The December, of 2018, commemorated 70 years since the espousal of the Universal Declaration of Human Rights. Traversing the seven decades of its existence has been witness to radical progress forward in the securing of women's rights alongside crucial new frameworks for securing protections for civilians in areas of conflict, children and their families in war zone and in times of peace. Human rights in these situations relates to rights to which we are entitled by virtue of our being part of the human species; they also re attendant to the silences in mainstream human rights discourse pertaining to its implied subject being i.e., the White unencumbered male citizen. Consequently, feminist writers have sought to challenge the default subject of Western human rights discourse and in so doing opened into these discussions the significance of the domestic sphere of embodied relational existence. The Secretary General provides indication of which in their definition of the topic as thus, "I see human rights as the struggles of ordinary people to hold those in power to account – particularly power that is abused by those in government or corporations" (ibid.). In appreciation of the fact that in more recent times recognition has been ascribed to private and public face of human rights violation they state that, "It does not matter whether we are talking about this at the level of a violent husband, or an abusive landlord, or a government criminalising people because of who they are, or states playing games with people's lives at the UN Security Council. All of these are about the abuse of power against the powerless" (ibid.). It is this recognition of the public face of private violation that distinguishes the feminist human rights perspectives. Whereby, feminist human rights discourse has emerged as an interrogation of the public/private dichotomy evident in mainstream accounts of human rights. An axiomatic feature of this dichotomy is to absence the private sphere from protection inscribed in law, state policy and surveillance. Given that women and care dependants are more frequently associated with the private sphere, they are disproportionately vulnerable to human rights violations unforeseen by international state agencies, and local states either neglect these violations through blind-spotting the private sphere or tragically dismiss their occurrence as part of the "privacy" of the family and in so doing inhibit the interventions of legal structures and law enforcement agencies to police such rights violations (Gurr and Naples 2013: 20). Mainstream approaches retort with the insistence that women benefit from the broader achievement of the securing of human rights for populations. Such gains do little to ameliorate the adverse neglect that emerges from the decades of modelling human rights on the presumed needs of a male political actor. For, "the human rights of women are subsumed or delegitimized under the rubric of masculinized citizenship" (ibid.). In more recent times, feminists of colour have drawn attention to issues arising from a mainstreaming of feminists irrespective of their cultural location and racial identity, in the (mis)endeavour so as to produce a universalising "women's-rights-as-human-rights" framework which replicates the concerns of Western feminism. Feminists of colour concur that it is necessary to reveal the way in which human rights definitions and institutional structures for their implementation are predicated on notions of White Western masculinity, which have adverse consequences in respect to neglecting the specificities of women's experience. In critique of mainstream human rights, feminists of colour argue for the imperative need to interrogate the intersections of gender, race and class in respect to comprehensively appreciating differences in the experiences of human rights and their violation. In so doing, this will encourage "human rights scholars and activists gender opportunity to avoid essentializing women and imposing inadequate Western concepts of 'rights'" (ibid.: 21).

Examining from a perspective of intersectionality, the speech of the Secretary General of Amnesty International, Salil Shetty (2018) provides a means of framing the politics and praxis of decolonial feminist human rights crusades. This is because feminist human rights and the decolonial project have a shared history in the struggle against Western capitalistic colonialism. Indeed, in this chapter, in its focus on decolonial feminist challenges to the denigration of the Black matriarch, intrepid robust advocacy for an ethics of justice, and the insistence on de-thinking colonial mentality one can discern inextricable alliances between human rights and feminist struggles against colonialism. As the Secretary General observes, "the essence of human rights and decolonisation are basically the same thing: the struggle for freedom against the abuse of power" (ibid.). Whereby, in this shared historical framing it is possible to discern that "the modern human rights framework as we know it was born in the crucible of decolonisation" (ibid.).

It has been the principal aim of this chapter to view the past and the present of the decolonial feminist influence on the human right to the cultural political communicative action of Afrobeat. The cultural appropriation of this Black music culture by market capitalist forces is further evidence of the extent to which, and disconcertingly so, "human rights themselves have always been subject to efforts at colonisation: misappropriation and being manipulated for political ends" (ibid.). Consequently, the past and present of decolonial feminism is always its future in respect to the instability of capitalistic colonialism. As the Secretary General observes, "We need to recognise this for what it is, and in this sense the fight to decolonise human rights is a permanent one" (ibid.). Indeed, such prophetic ideals have never been more pertinent as the technological infrastructural expansion of the Black music industry is increasingly interpolating with that of capitalistic surveillance directed at controlling and political potency of Black cultural productions, a situation previously alluded to in the earlier and more recent writings by Angela Davis on the prison industry.

Even if we were to bracket-off the disproportionately high numbers of ethnic minority males mislaid within the USA's criminal justice system, "we would still learn a great deal about the relationship between capitalist economic systems and punishment practices by looking specifically at the situation of women" (Davis 2014: 17). Neoliberal privatisation, coupled with a contraction of the welfare state directly correlates with upward trends, in the USA, involving the disciplining and carceral punishment of women who in the absence of welfare provision were driven into iniquitous, illegal circumstances. Disproportionately high diagnoses of mental ill-health and psychiatric disorders among women in the prison system indicate correlations between disinvestment in psychiatric care provision increasing reliance on the domestic sphere and its patriarchal gender division of reproductive labour. Notions of the Black matriarch provide unconvincing explanation for the plight of single-families in which absent fathers have left women struggling to manage household finances. Vulnerable equally to the exorbitant interest rates of barbarous loan sharks and the irreputable debt re-financing credit agencies these mothers are more likely to have their poverty criminalised. In tracing the interconnecting links between these gender racialised processes of criminalisation, Angela Davis pioneered critical insights into "the global impact of the prison industrial complex" (ibid.: 20). Evidence is deepening about the detriment to fiscal spending on social services consequent of the financialisation that the World Bank and IMF have compelled debt ladened countries to comply with in order to enable debt restructuring. Davis observes this situation to be encouraging, "the replacement of expensive and unprofitable social services with prisons, often for profit, in Africa for example" (ibid.). Apparently, to no real surprise the largest employer across the African continent is the private security and private prison company—G4S (ibid.). Indeed, the company at G4s.com in brash grandiloquence publicises that it has global business operations presence in more than 85 countries, employing 800,000 people it is "one of the world's largest private employers". Angela Davis surmises that given its profiteering in the criminal justice system, of the USA, such companies have little incentive to challenge the systems of repression that use the carceral system to disenfranchise and disabuse Black people of their human and civil rights. Consequently, it is precisely because these companies are entrenched in the capitalist mode of production that their merchandising of carceral alternatives interoperates seamlessly with the third-party paid-access to policing data-bases and the commodity-form of surveillance capitalism. As Davis observes, those proposing "carceral alternatives such as parole, probation, house arrest, GPS bracelets, and other modes of carcerality that are parasitically attached to the prison system" are not really concerned with revolutionising the rooting of the prison system in capitalism; indeed, "I don't think they are thinking about democracy either" (ibid.). It is from this basis of injustice that Davis (1971/2016b: 36) convincingly proposes the distinct situation of the political prisoner to be that of the victim, "of an oppressive politico-economic order, swiftly becoming conscious of the causes underlying their victimization". That Angela Davis was writing this observation of the political prisoner in May 1971 while resident in Marin County Jail, heightens one's attention to the pertinence of the prose and integrity of its validation. During my interview discussion with Sandra

Izsadore a consistent reference was made to the valour and political heroism of Fela Anikulapo-Kuti.

On 4th September 1984 Fela Anikulapo-Kuti was arrested at Murtala Muhammed International airport in Lagos, Nigeria. On 8th November of that year, the Port Harcourt Zone of the Exchange Control Tribunal convicted the artist of intentionally attempting to export unlawfully, his own British pound sterling currency. He was convicted of this charge and sentence to five years' imprisonment. Amnesty International publicly expressed concern, "that the government's motive in prosecuting Fela Anikulapo-Kuti may have been political" (Amnesty International 1985). Indeed, on 1st January 1985 Amnesty International published an open letter, in which they denounced the integrity of the trial, proclaimed it to be "unfair" and categorically demanded that the artist should be either "re-tried in proceedings which are in accordance with internationally recognized standards of fairness, or else released" (ibid.). Amnesty International were particularly concerned that the artist had been given no right to appeal, statements were prejudicial as they were proven to have been elicited from the military government official that the artist had openly criticised. According to the human rights agency, there was compelling evidence to suggest that the arrest and imprisonment was politically motivated. It was stated that, "Brigadier Tunde Idiagbon, Chief of Staff, announced that the government would ensure Fela would be imprisoned for a long time, concluding: 'and I hope he will rot in jail'" (Amnesty International 2010). Furthermore, "there were allegations that important defence witnesses, including customs officials, were prevented from testifying at Fela's trial" (ibid.). These observations led the human rights organisation to assert that "in these circumstances his guilt as charged has not been adequately proven, and Amnesty International is concerned that he may be a prisoner of conscience imprisoned for his non-violent political behaviour rather than for any criminal offence" (Amnesty International 1985). Writing in the 1970s, while herself incarcerated, Davis expressed the imperative need for consciousness raising to defend those political prisoners, who had been persecuted and jailed for, in actuality, challenging the legitimacy of institutionalised racism to arbitrarily persecute and imprison Black people. If one is to accept that Sandra Izsadore conveyed in her relations with Fela Anikulapo-Kuti the human rights advocacy of the leading 1970s and 1980s civil rights activists then it is plausible she represented part of the movement towards "unity". In so doing, was part of what Davis (1971/2016b) describes as the collective challenge against "the merciless proliferation of the power of monopoly capital" (ibid.: 41) as part of the imprisonment of those that dare to challenge its institutionalised racist injustices. Ultimately, "No potential victim of the fascist terror should be without the knowledge that the greatest menace to racism and fascism is unity!" (ibid.).

REFERENCES

Adimora, M., (2021); 5 Ingenious Forgotten Female Pioneers of Afrobeat. You Should Know, British Vogue. Available at: https://www.vogue.co.uk/arts-and-lifestyle/gallery/forgotten-women-afrobeat

Ajiola, F., O., (2019); Fela Anikulapo Kuti, Afrobeat Genre and Socio-political Activism in Nigeria, *ASUU Journal of Social Sciences, a Journal of Research and development*, Vol., 6, Nos. 1 & 2, January & December, 2019; pp., 165–183.

Amnesty International (1985); *Nigeria: The Case of Fela Anikulapo Kuti*, Amnesty International, January 1, 1985, Index Number: AFR 44/002/1985. Available at: https://www.amnesty.org/en/documents/afr44/002/1985/en/

Amnesty International (2010); *Fela Kuti, PoC, Nigeria*, Amnesty International. Available at: http://static.amnesty.org/ai50/fela_kuti_en.pdf

BBC (1984); Interviewer, Fela Kuti, Arena: Teacher Don't Teach Me Nonsense (Television Documentary, 30 November 1984), *British Broadcasting Corporation (BBC)*. Available at: https://www.bbc.co.uk/programmes/p00jf0jg

Cobo-Piñero, R., (2020) Afrobeat Journeys: Tracing the Musical Archive in Sefi Atta's *A Bit of Difference*, Journal of Intercultural Studies, 41:4, 442–456, DOI: https://doi.org/10.1080/07256868.2020.1779200

Davis, A., (2014) Deepening the Debate over Mass Incarceration, Socialism and Democracy, 28:3, 15–23, DOI: https://doi.org/10.1080/08854300.2014.963945

Davis, A., (1971) Reflections on the Black Woman's Role in the Community of Slaves, The Black Scholar, 3:4, 2–15, DOI: https://doi.org/10.1080/00064246.1971.11431201

Davis, A., (1971/2016a); *If they Come in the Morning, Voices of Resistance*, London/New York: Verso.

Davis, A., (1971/2016b); Political Prisoners, Prisons and Black Liberation, in (eds.) *If They Come in the Morning, Voices of Resistance*, London: Verso.

Davis, A., (1983); *Women Race and Class*, New York: Vintage books; A Division of Random House.

Davis, A., (2022); Foreword, in Ferdinand, M., *Decolonial Ecology: Thinking from the Caribbean World*, Cambridge: Polity.

Davis, A., Magee, R., Soledad Brothers and Other Political Prisoners (1971/2016); *If They Come in the Morning; Voices of Resistance*, Forward by Bond, J., London/New York: Verso.

EtymologyOnline.com (2024); Colony. Available at: https://www.etymonline. com/search?q=colony

Felakuti.com (2024); Story:1986. Available at: https://felakuti.com/gb/ story/1986

G4S (2024); Who We Are. Available at: https://www.g4s.com/careers

Goffman, E. (1989). ON FIELDWORK. *Journal of Contemporary Ethnography, 18*(2), 123–132. https://doi.org/10.1177/08912418901800200

Grosfoguel, R., (2004); Race and Ethnicity or Racialized Ethnicities? Identities within Global Coloniality, Ethnicities, Vol. 4., Issue, 3., September, pp. 315–336.

Gurr, B., and Naples, N., (2013: 20); Sex and Gender, in (eds) Brunsma, D., Smith, K., and Gran, B., (2013:7); The Handbook of Sociology and Human Rights, London: Paradigm Publishers Boulder.

Izsadore, S., (2019); *Fela and Me*, with Oyekunle, S., Ibadan, Nigeria: Kraft Books Limited.

Kuti, F., (1977); Colo-mentality, in *Sorrow, Tears and Blood*. Kalakuta Label.

Kuti, F., (1984); Fela Kuti, Arena: Teacher Don't Teach Me Nonsense (Television Documentary, 30 November 1984), *British Broadcasting Corporation (BBC)*. Available at: https://www.bbc.co.uk/programmes/p00jf0jg

Lugones, M., (2010); Toward a Decolonial Feminism, *Hypatia* 25, no. 4 (2010): 742–59. http://www.jstor.org/stable/40928654

Odih, P., (2014); *Watersheds in Marxist Ecofeminism*. Newcastle upon Tyne: Cambridge Scholars Publishing. ISBN 978-1-4438-6602-6

Odih, P., (2019a); *Adsensory Urban Ecology (Volume One)*. Newcastle upon Tyne: Cambridge Scholars Publishing. ISBN 9781527523173

Odih, P., (2019b); *Adsensory Urban Ecology (Volume Two)*. Newcastle upon Tyne: Cambridge Scholars Publishing. ISBN 9781527524682

Ogunfeyimi, A., (2021) The grammar and rhetoric of African subjectivity: ethics, image, and language, Review of Communication, 21:4, 310–326, https://doi. org/10.1080/15358593.2021.2001842

Shetty, S., (2018); *Decolonising Human Rights*, Speech Delivered by Salil Shetty, Secretary General of Amnesty International, at the London School of Economics on 22 May 2018. Amnesty International.

Vergès, F., (2021); *A Decolonial Feminism*, Trans. Bohrer, A., London: Pluto Press.

Vogue, (2018); *The Beat Goes On*, Muir, R., September 2018 – Vogue Retro Article. Available at: https://www.duffyarchive.com/september-2018-vogue-retro-article/

CHAPTER 6

Decolonial Intermediation in Crisis Heterotopic Space

O2 Academy Brixton, Street Level, 211 Stockwell Road, London SW9 95L, March 2023, Photographer © Pamela Odih

© The Author(s), under exclusive license to Springer Nature Switzerland AG 2024
P. Odih, *Black British Postcolonial Feminist Ways of Seeing Human Rights*, https://doi.org/10.1007/978-3-031-71877-9_6

So as to operate within these conditions of extraordinary risk assessment, insurance premiums and hyper-vigilant digital policing surveillance, live music venues in urban inner-cities actively seek additional security routes proffered by Business Improvement District (BID) schemes. These are business-steered partnerships, which are created in order to deliver supplementary services to local businesses over a designated period (usually five years). In a report entitled Business Improvement Districts Guidance and Best Practice, the Department for Communities and Local Government describes the advantages of BIDs as thus: "They can be a powerful tool for directly involving local businesses in local activities and allow the business community and local authorities to work together to improve the local trading environment" (Gov.UK 2015: 4). O2 Academy Brixton as a subscribing member is actively involved in the Brixton BID's schema of integrating local music venues into communication and dialogue with the local authorities, policing regulators and governance. I intend to provide contextual information about the gendered and racialised heterotopic urban space in which the music venue O2 Academy Brixton was situated at the time of the 15th December 2022 fatal crowd crush. Ultimately, my objective is to apply decolonial feminist praxis so as to identify the operation of the matrix of colonial digital capitalism in rendering the private Black female subject as an object of public colonial digital capitalist surveillance. My principal contention is that despite an excitation into the hyper-digital surveillance of a disproportionately Black British female population in Brixton, London, the capitalistic technological surveillance matrix is insufficiently meeting the safety and security needs of this female community in public recreational spaces.

Davis (2003) as part of their exposé question "Are Prisons Obsolete?" provides insights relevant to the application of a decolonial feminist analysis of local community policing in respect to the human rights of Black women to have safety and security in public recreational leisure spaces. The plenteously detailed insights about the gendering of capitalistic policing services, renders further luminosity to the extent to which policing directed at protecting the security of women in public space is perforated by oppressive patriarchal ideologies and practices perpetuating the gendering of recreational space. Such contemplations are pertinent when international circuits of capital accumulation within the live music industry present as a local incident of tragedy as was evident on 15th December 2022 when O2 Brixton Academy hosted a live music concert for the Nigerian Afrobeat artist, Asake.

Decolonising Gender, Class, Racialised BIDs

BIDs can be established using several distinct routes, the most prominent of which involves either the local authority and/or local businesses rate payers coming together to form a cooperation. Having brought together a collective, the BID proposer is required to develop a proposal and submit this to the local authority for evaluation and if endorsed agreement to manage the ballot. Businesses that pay business rates, within the business district, and thus would be subject to the BID levy, are given a vote on the BID proposal—the ballot. Predicated on it achieving a simple majority in the balloted vote, the proposed BID is established. In its operation the BID will subject all businesses within its jurisdiction, to the levy—irrespective of whether they voted in support of the BID proposal (Gov.UK 2014). The balloting process through which the BID is created provides precedence for the decision-making and identification of the services, additional to the baseline provision of the local authority, that will be provided to local businesses. BIDs are potent instruments for precisely involving local businesses in local activities and facilitating local authorities to work collaboratively with the local authorities to advance and prosper the local trading environment. Established in 2014, Brixton BID accentuates as its mission statement the vantages of collaborative endeavour in respect to the cultivation of the Brixton district into "a sustainable and distinctive destination" (Brixton BID 2023a). Indeed, it was via Brixton BID's collaboration with the Night Time Industries Association (NTIA) that I came to appreciate that the former defines itself as an outcome of collaborative exchange with local businesses. As is evident in the following extract:

Interviewer *So, could you tell me about your campaign please?*

Interviewee *Well, our campaign was linked directly with the NTIA. Right. So, and in a sense, although we were linked with them, I suspect they had because they're a national organiser organisation. I suspect they have other organisations that that were connected to them that we weren't aware of. If you see what I am saying. Yeah, but our direct link was with the NTIA. Primarily because, primarily because the O2 Academy are night time venue, we are a member of the NTIA and we were concerned about the impact on the night time economy in Brixton; if that, if that venue remains closed for a long while. (Interviewee: Brixton BIDs Representative; Interviewed: August 2023)*

184   P. ODIH

Brixton BID is a not-for-profit cooperative of local business who have cohered around the aim to work together to progress their immediately local area. It is generally believed that the business-led partnership known as a BID emerged from a previous civic structure known as the Town Centre Managers.

Interviewer   *Can you tell me about Brixton BIDs? How were you developed? So, it's a Business Improvement District.*

Interviewee   *Business improvement district. Yeah, well. Most town centre area in Lambeth would have a Business Improvement District. Yeah. So, what happens is that you have, it's kind of a development on Town Centre Managers. If you see what I'm saying. So, it's a development in a very lateral way, but what happens is that. Businesses in the town centre area, they all pay a percentage of their business rates to an association called a BID. (Interviewee: Brixton BIDs Representative; Interviewed: August 2023)*

As per the finance structure of BIDs, it relates to a specific area in which a levy, proportional to the rateable value, is charged on all business rate payer in conjunction with the business rate bill. The levy extracted is used to fund projects and initiatives in the local area, and these are unlimited in their purposes, with the only restriction that they should not overlap an existing service provided by the local authority. In the Brixton BID, in excess of 500 businesses pay an annual levy that overlays the enterprises determined by the local business community. As is described in the following extract:

> *They then manage the organisation the BID. The businesses run the BID. And most people with more shop fronts; depending on your rateable value, you are fitted into that organisation [The amount that a business pays in their annual levy contribution is based on the rateable value, and it is proportional to the physical scope of the premises. Usually, businesses pay 1.5% of their rateable value]. Yeah. We are run by a Board of Governors who are made-up of local businesses. So, the O2 [Academy Brixton] would have been on our board. Oh the Lambeth because they pay; Lambeth Council because they pay a levy; they probably have been on a board. Organisation retail groups ... they would all be kind of represented in the bid, some would be on the board, some wouldn't be on the board. The board would then determine the priorities for the BID and what we get involved in and how we operate.*

Yeah, the idea of being that that money from the levy that we collect goes directly back into the local economy, either to promote the area as a destination. So, you increase the footfall that comes in. So, all the businesses would benefit or it would mean doing practical things like cleaning, litter picking, doing things that would make the destination welcoming for people; because the idea is that what you wanna do is drive more footfall into the area, so the business, be they retail or hospitality they would then directly benefit from that. Yeah. So, most BIDs as a basic thing they will do that; they will provide training they'll provide some level of security but that's how bids tend to work. And then we are accountable to the businesses who pay into the levy. They will be retail groups or they will be groups who won't be members of the BID.
Because their rateable value might be too low, so they're not in the BID, so to speak, but they will benefit from anything the bit does in the area. Yeah. (Interviewee: Brixton BID Representative; Interviewed: August 2023)

As is germane to BIDs elsewhere, Brixton BID operates on a five-year term, at the culmination of which there is a ballot among members, during which they are ascribed the opportunity to decide about the continuation of the BID. In respect to governance, the Brixton Business Improvement District (BID) manoeuvres via Brixton BID Development Company, which is a non-for-profit establishment established in January 2014 by local businesses. The BID is superintended by a board of local business leaders volunteering their time, and a modest Executive Team who conveys the BID business plan. Reportedly, "Since 2014 Brixton BID has invested over £1.75m exclusively in Brixton, with 10% of that money coming from external sources. The BID is 100% committed to improving Brixton for all" (Brixton BID 2023a). Throughout the year, the Board of Directors convene to progress strategic decisions concerned with improving the business district's commercial area. In summary, Brixton BID defines ethos and purpose as thus: "Better Business – We believe Brixton is stronger together. In partnership with you, the BID will promote Brixton's businesses, work with stakeholders to bring added value and make you save money through collective purchasing and funding innovative projects" (Brixton BID 2023a).

A consistent feature of interest as derived from the interview extract is the issue of space both within the premises that constitute the Brixton BID, but more intriguingly the internecine spaces that thread through the local civic governance and private businesses. Indeed, interviewee's description of the management of the internecine space of the District resonated with my existing knowledge of Michel Foucault's (1986) *Of*

Other Spaces. Foucault discerns that in this postindustrial era, "our experience of the world is less that of a long life developing through time than that of a network that connects points and intersects with its own skein" (ibid.: 22). In the above transcription extract, there is some reference also to the continued existence of a categorical, delineation of space into grids of functional distinction, e.g. the space in which littering has become a problem because it is unclear as to which authority should clear away the refuse discarded by humans that may or may not be residents of Brixton; as the respondent mentions the BID services these internecine spaces of clutter that exist outside the space of the local authority and private contractors, *it would mean doing practical things like cleaning, litter picking.* In Foucault's account *Of Other Spaces,* this internecine space can be defined as "a hierarchic ensemble of places". Collecting and disposing of litter orderly is resonant of "places where things had been put because they had been violently displaced", and then conversely to *doing things that would make the destination welcoming for people* is resonant with the "places where things found their natural ground and stability". Both of these places relate to "the space of emplacement" (ibid.). Such a space refers to the place of sustainable urban ecology, an embodied that is cultivated by its community as a subjectively infinite and inter-subjectively infinitely open space.

Conflations of Private Space with Public Security: Digital Surveillance Heterotopias BID

Existing in conjunction with "the space of emplacement", it can be discerned that the Brixton BID pays attention to quantitatively delineable civic spaces that exceed the existing baseline services provided by the Lambeth Council local authority. An example of which is the calculation of footfall and specifically, Brixton BID's collection of footfall data so as to provide digitally analysed intelligence-led data to the subscribed businesses in the District. Reading through the BID's Brixton Monthly Report—December 2022, it is evident that the anonymised, aggregated and General Data Protection Regulation (GDPR) compliant data has many of the characteristics Foucault ascribes to the grid-like matrix space of the "site". In this respect consider for following statistics derived from the *Brixton Monthly Report—December 2022:*

Where Do Visitors Come From?

Mobile network data allows us to understand the origin of those visitors who are detected by the sensor. This is summarised at the Local Authority level, Postcode Sector level, and alongside a distribution of distance travelled.

47% of visitors originated within Lambeth, up 2% from the previous month.

83% of the visitors sighted live within 0-10km to the site, similar to the previous month.

Long distance visitors represented 3% of total visitation, similar to the previous month. (Brixton BID 2023b)

Foucault (1986), in *Of Other Spaces*, describes a space of "extension" which preceded the space of "site" and replaced the space of emplacement. In the space of extension, there exist the possibilities of "an infinite and infinitely open space" which contrasts with the embodied contextually meaningful space of emplacement (ibid.: 23). In the above-cited spatial mapping derived from Brixton BID, the digital analytics relate not to a subjectively meaningful, contextually space of encampment but rather to the quantitatively grid like distribution of the space of "site". Whereby, "the site is defined by relations of proximity between points or elements; formally, we can describe these relations as series, trees or grids" (ibid.: 23). Clear parallels exist here between the epistemology of the space of site and that of the calculation of footfall provided by the Brixton BID anonymised, aggregated and GDPR compliant data analytics. Of particular significance is the procedure of measurement. According to Brixton BID, "Footfall is measured by the number of visits by the presence sensor located". In the digest, the metric of footfall is represented at the monthly and daily levels in conjunction with location metrics (Brixton BID 2023b).

The footfall analytics, provided to Brixton BID, by the telecommunication company O2, are also described as micro location insights, designed, in marketing logic, to drive an in-depth comprehension of crowd-level visitor volumes, consumer profiles and spending patterns. The O2's micro location sensor technology, that powers Brixton BID's footfall metric, can detect O2 registered customers within a small-scale geographic radius—anything as narrow as 2 metres to 50 metres (O2 2023). Installing the insights' sensor is relatively straightforward, and once in operation it is designed to detect O2 mobile phone users as soon as they enter the area of the coverage zone. In many respects, the O2 system represents a consolidation of existing sensor-based footfall technologies while also post-dated these in respect to its production of GDPR compliant anonymised data at high levels of accuracy. Less advanced in its proposition is video footfall counting systems that use an overhead Internet Protocol (IP) or Closed Circuit Television (CCTV) to visually record the numbers of people that traverse through the designated counting zone, feeding back this data to an exchange database unit. Closer approximation to the O2 mobile data sensor system is smartphone counting using mobile signals in respect to collecting Wi-Fi probe requests from individual smartphones, for these probe request signals as with O2's footfall counting; provides people count, records of dwelling time, data on customers returning to locations; and can generate "heat maps" of coverage areas most likely to be visited. Although the latter system's reliance on Wi-Fi provides a level of digital automation, its currency in tracking returning customers, rather than anonymously aggregating mobile phone users, presents ethical issues with regard to GDPR and this, coupled with its reliance on smart phone users to have their Wi-Fi being switched-on, further undermines effectivity (Windmill Software 2023).

By way of some alternative, there are opt-in mobile phone apps that are more GDPR complicit because the user has agreed to install the app, but this feature is also a hindrance to the extent of footfall coverage as it's reliant on scaling-up the installation of the app to a critical mass. An alternative method that avoids generating personally identifiable information is thermal sensor, which identifies numbers of people by measuring body heat. But this requires IP or CCTV camera to verify the data (Windmill Software 2023), and this digitalised data in which the body is subject and object of observation (adsensory) is too easily aligned with bio-political governmental rationalities. Considering and discounting these afore options one can better appreciation to concession to utilise the O2's Motion Micro Location Insights, which, as the company describes, provides "accurate location data insights drives in-depth understanding of crowd-level visitor, profiles and patterns" (O2 2023). Its micro location insight sensors in the small-scale area focus can provide extensive customer profiling, behaviour and dwelling times about its mobile phone users detected in the coverage area. Its ability to produce anonymised, GDPR complicit, aggregated data that is extrapolated so as to represent specific populations, sets it over and beyond its rivals in terms of the making of the District into a site that is effectively colonised by digital capitalist surveillance technologies. For the data gaps in wireless radar sensor people counting or people-sensing units connected to on-street IP or CCTV cameras, programmed to use non-tracking real-time counting logs so as to algorithmically learn, detect and differentiate people along consumer profiling dimensions, all present disruptions to the conjoining of the colonising and financialising intentions of Smart City surveillance technologies.

Gendered Space and Security: Digital Surveillance Heterotopias BID

Indeed, the data analytics calculating the demographic profile of consumer footfall also connect with their classification into spending power categories, and these overlay the following additional categories of data, resulting in a financial composite of the digitally colonised consumer detected to have entered the District and in so doing contributed to anonymised aggregates detailing "footfall"; "Visitors to the City Centre" (age, spend power, visit frequency, gender, time of arrival); "where do visitors come from"; "Spend data"; "social media". Thus, for example, in December 2022 bulletin, it was stated that "overall footfall in November 2022 saw a 10% decrease with respect to the previous month" (Brixton BID 2023b). It is also possible to discern that the gender profile by month suggests a slightly higher prominence of females. Given that the most prominent age cohort visiting the District is 25–34, one can plausibly discern that the District's documented increase in the volume of "very high" spend power in November 2022 was mostly driven by 25–34 females. It is evident that retail analytic data provides for a breakdown into demographic categories, card payment method, arrival and departure time durations, and patterns of spending, and this analytic exists at the level of monthly retail activity. For example, in December 2022, "visit frequency" analytic showed a decrease to 10%, whereby "visit frequency is defined as the number of unique days a person visits the vicinity of the presence sensor" (ibid.). In the digest, females constituted the largest gender profile by month. The digest's analytics about arrival identify that approximately 8% of the arrivals to the city centre were at 12pm (measured as the hour of first time sighting). The digitalised retail analytics provided in the December 2022 digest provide data mapped from the home Internet Service Provider of the human individuals picked up by the "presence sensor"; the stated source of this data is the telecommunications company O2. Analytics on spending power, provided in the digest, derive from the financial services provider VISA, and these profile spending with merchants using VISA are seen in Brixton's postcode district SW9. These grids of coordinated digital analytics are very reminiscent of the space of a thoroughly digitally colonised and financialised "site", described by Foucault (1986) as "defined by relations of proximity between points or elements; formally we can describe these relations as series, trees, or grids" (ibid.: 23). The issue of concern here is that the digitally colonised grid lends itself to a financialisation of monetarily lucrative cohorts and the definancialisation of others. Recognising that the UK's Equal Act 2010 and European Court of Justice 2011 ruling forbid sex-based discrimination in the provision of financial services (Odih 2016), it remains an imperative to observe critically convergences between demography and financial services in Smart City metrics. For these analyses can all too easily provide justification for the withdrawal of financial services provision and the dispossession of less financially lucrative consumer cohorts—as has been evident in the use of Smart City metrics to close banking branches and remove ATMs from neighbourhoods. Smart City metrics converge with the technical rationalities of adsensory financialisation, in which human bodies are subject and object of advertising inscriptive technologies which, in turn train the biopolitics of algorithmically calculated health interventions. Smart City metrics when aligned with Smart City biometrics during the coronavirus 2 (SARS-CoV-2) COVID-19 pandemic provided vital information for the creative arts, heritage sector and live performance industry to receive direct emergency funding and a financialised structure of aide (e.g., "repayable finance", "Live Events Reinsurance Scheme") in respect to the Department for Culture, Media and Sport administered £1.57 billion Culture Recovery Fund (DCMS 2023). Black and South Asian ethnic minority communities in the United Kingdom's capital city, were disproportionately afflicted by the COVID-19 pandemic and it is evident that the higher rates of cultural sector organisations supported in London (funding estimate of £494m) reflected the pandemic's excessively incommensurate demographic coverage. In these higher rates of financialised recovery funding, is evident illustration of a biopolitical confluence of Smart City biometrics and financial services directed at the live music entertainment industry.

Private People in Public Space: Digital Social Media Surveillance Heterotopias BID

As with the calculative mechanisms applied to the space of site more generally, the collection of data that quantitatively pinpoints human action and its occupation in space, is not without its technical problems. First and foremost is the issue of anonymity, issues of which have been anticipated by the Brixton BID in its emphasis in ensuring that the data is anonymised, aggregated and General Data Protection Regulation (GDPR) compliant. But the problems of the data of the space of site are even more extensive, for as Foucault (1986: 23) anticipated,

> [A] problem in contemporary technical work is well known: the storage of data or of the intermediate results of a calculation in the memory of a machine; the circulation of discrete elements with a random output (automobile traffic is a simple case, or indeed the sounds on a telephone line); the identification of marked or coded elements inside a set that may be randomly distributed, or may be arranged according to single or to multiple classifications.

These problems of technical work in the mapping of the space of site are magnified in respect to the application of digital technologies. Indeed, Brixton BID demonstrates some awareness of these in a published statement entitled *Background—About the Data and Limitations*. Firstly, it details the technical method of mapping the space of site, that is the Brixton District, and its footfall as thus:

> The mobile phone device of O2 users establishes connection with the presence sensor when passing near it. In the process, the presence sensor identified the device and O2 provides Movement Strategies (A GHD company) with anonymised, aggregated and GDPR compliant data of the visitors. Advanced modelling is applied to extrapolate volumes to all presence in the city, not just those on the O2 network. This is a novel dataset, currently in use by a limited number of BIDs in UK. It supplements traditional footfall information by understanding 'who is the visitor'. Brixton BID (2023b)

According to Foucault the challenge of the space of site (and also emplacement) arises for humankind in expressions of demography and social scientific calculation. For the problem of the human site is less than that of numbers in respect to capacity; for it is "that of knowing what relations of propinquity, what type of storage, circulation, marking, and classification of human elements should be adopted in a given situation in order to achieve a given end" (Foucault 1986: 23). The social scientific mapping of the space of site conjures into being conundrums of proximity that multiply in their complexity as part of the mapping process. As

Foucault expresses it, "Our epoch is one in which space takes for us the form of relations among sites" (ibid.). Part of the intricate difficulties of proximity is because, as Foucault observes, "despite the whole network of knowledge that enables us to delimit or to formalize it, contemporary space is perhaps still not entirely desanctified" (ibid.). Applying the latter term to the retail analytic digest, discussed previously, as compiled by Brixton BID, there is some consistent evidence of limitations and self-imposed restrictions in the types of data made available to analyse. For example, although having access to gender and age profile, the Brixton BID digest does not present analytics on race, ethnicity and British citizenship.

While it is evident that in the analysis of spending an area of personal has clearly become desanctified, the Brixton BID analytics have observed, and/or imposed, limitations to the racial colonialisation of its District by digitalised capitalistic analytics. In this sense, as Foucault observes about the space of site more generally, "perhaps our life is still governed by a certain number of oppositions that remain inviolable, that our institutions and practices have not yet dared to break down" (ibid.). Foucault refers here to the Western modernist delineating of spaces into public and private, with the latter associated with familial relations and the former is conceived of as social, cultural productive space of work as distinct from leisure. These oppositional spaces are informed in their obstruction by "the hidden presence of the sacred" (ibid.). In speaking with a representative of Brixton BID and reading through a sample of their monthly retail digests, it is my opinion that there exist in these analytics a sense of self-imposed limits as to the extension of its spatial mapping into those areas phenomenologically assigned as sacred. Indeed, for example, the Brixton BID digest of December 2022 does extend its reach into the gathering of data on consumer spending (calculated "through a combination of several measures (e.g., mobile device cost, frequency of upgrade, home postcode and a number of other behavioural inputs)") but insists that it is protecting the sanctity of personal privacy; for instance, it states: "Due to privacy constraints, postcode sectors from which the visitation at the site is lower than 10 people are shown as O" (Brixton BID 2023b).

Brixton BID's commitment to privacy in its collation and presentation of its District's retail analytics is also evident in its approach to the mapping of immaterial cyberspace. The cyber immaterial form of space exists in conjunction with the homogeneous material space of the retail analytic grid; it is "the space in which we live, which draws us out of ourselves, in which the erosion of our lives, our time and our history occurs, the space that claws and knaws at us, is also, in itself, a heterogeneous space" (Foucault 1986: 23). Aspects of the immateriality of this latter space are defined by Foucault, as relating to "utopia", and these "are sites with no real place" (ibid.: 24). It is my observation that the part of the Brixton BID retail analytics for December 2022, that refers to digitalised data about social media, presents cyber features pertaining to virtual communities and spaces online that are in actuality what Foucault describe as "sites that have a general relation of direct or inverted analogy with the real space of Society" (ibid.), i.e. spaces of site that are utopias. According to Foucault, utopias "present society itself in a perfected form, or else society turned upside down, but in any case, these utopias are fundamentally unreal spaces" (ibid.). Reading through the retail data analytics present in the December 2022 Brixton BID digest, the category of data catalogued as social media is exceedingly reminiscent of space of sites that are in actuality utopias. Firstly, the digest provides a Word Cloud of words which most frequently featured on social media posts in December 2022. The concept of Word Cloud is self-evident, an inverted analogy of the meteorological formation of that is an aerosol accumulation of water particulars suspended in the sky. Conversely, the cyberspace cloud is a simulacrum of collections posted in cyberspace and thus a digital phenomenon that exists in unreal digital space.

Adjacent to the presentation of the Word Cloud, in the Brixton BID monthly digest, there is positioned a bar chart graph depicting the volume of tweets related to the city centre at specific data points from 3rd July 2022 to 25th December 2022. Unlike the unreal space of the Word Cloud, the aggregation vertical bars on the chart are actual totalities of volumes of the unit of analysis. Remaining with this bar chart, intersecting its vertical axis is a horizontal line that indicates the metric described as "average polarity", which the graphic's notes labels as the "average positive/negative rating", i.e. a sentiment metric derived from the volume of tweets. The latter is an increasing commonly used social media metric derived from the marketing strategy of monitoring mentions and discussions of the company/organisation/brand on social media (Hootsuite 2021). Integral to this marketing practice is the technology of social listening, which is the technique of real-time observing across social media channels for mentions of a particular company's brand and related keywords. In the Brixton BID monthly digest for December 2022, the social listening technique is, in addition to monitoring, being applied to extract negative/positive sentiment analysis, and it does so through overviewing an entirety of online conversations related to its brand, organisation and related products. In digital marketing practice, social listening is proactive in its tracking and surveillance of brand-related conservation, and this is contrasted with the reactive practice of social monitoring. This is because the former involves real-time overview of online chatter in conversational format, which provides channels for the brand to intervene into a stream of online talk in response and/or facilitate the direction of a chat about the brand. According to the digital marketing appreciation of this process, social listening can track changes in mood sentiment in real-time, tap into sharp spikes in brand mentions to alert the company of a problem affecting its service users, enable a surfing of the zeitgeist of fleeting and erratically popular trends, and cultivate online virtual communities about the brand, organically (ibid.).

Given that social listening and social media monitoring analytic tools are increasingly a basic feature of social media analytics, one may question the extent to which these capitalistic programmes are providing any other than at most pseudo-Gemeinschaft fleeting associations between users. Furthermore, even a cursory pursual of the social listening product suite of the leading market providers provides some indication of the extent to which these programmes are merely sweeping through the social media scape and indiscriminately churning massive volumes of digital data aggregates into multitudes of the same differences. For example, in contrast to the organic nuanced ethnographies of consumer cultural profiles, social media analytics can provide simulacra of cultural diversity in their use of social media listening tools that segment users according to location, demographics and language. An example of which is the Hootsuite Insights analytic, which is described as taking, "listening a step further by giving you data from 16 billion new social posts every month. Boolean search logic can help you find meaningful trends and patterns you might miss by monitoring keywords and hashtags alone. You can then filter your searches by date, demographics and location to find the conversation most relevant to you" (ibid.). Despite the incredible price tag associated with these off-the-peg social media analytics, they are plausibly less expensive than the social media analytics of a BID District such as Brixton's. This is because Brixton BID's localised and engaged situation within the District means that their social analytics are pre-staged by nuanced, embodied, experience-based ethnographic knowledge of their District, and in so doing the cultivation of an insider perspective of the online and offline space of the District as a complex heterotopia. Such diligence is plausibly to be considered as more expensive than the quick and easy indiscriminate cyber-scrapes provided by the off-the-shelf social media analytic industry. As can be discerned in the following account of the Brixton BID's discerned, consideration of the space of the District as a heterotopic space.

With regard to the analytics that collate social media postings on Twitter and analyse, these are positive or negative rating in their reference to the Brixton BID District. The analytic is clearly based on actual data in terms of volume of tweets (approximately 3–3.5K); the measures of the "average polarity" analysis in terms of negative and positive tweets are more resonant of virtual ethnographic space. Similarly, the Brixton BID December 2022 retail digest provides a computer-generated Word Cloud map of terms (drawn directly from posts on Twitter and thus powered by Twitter) most frequently posted in the month of December 2022. In this utopian space of the Word Cloud can be seen, even at the higher and bolder levels of font size, a mixture of objective nouns such as "academy", "concert", "Asake", and subjective adjectives "crush", "protection", etc. Further reflection on the December 2022 digest and its presentation of social media retail analytics in terms of network science modelling of the social media postings and Word Cloud analytics, there appears to be a mixture of refrain for the sacred in its intersecting trajectories into the civic and commercial spaces of retail analytics. One might theorise this configuration of commercial extensions and retreating boundary management as evocative of the type of space that Foucault defines as a "heterotopia". The description of this space, as provided by Foucault, is eloquent and prosaic warranting an extended quotation.

> There are also, probably in every culture, in every civilization, real places – places that do exist and that are formed in the very founding of society – which are something like counter-sites, a kind of effectively enacted utopia in which the real sites, all the other real sites that can be found within the culture, are simultaneously represented, contested, and inverted. Places of this kind are outside of all places, even though it may be possible to indicate their location in reality. Because these places are absolutely different from all the sites that they reflect and speak about, I shall call them, by way of contrast to utopias, heterotopias. (Foucault 1986: 24)

Social media, computer-mediated communication and its congruous online time compressed inverted reality are all indicative of heterotopic space. For when considered as heterotopic social media spaces they all involve "a sort of simultaneously mythic and real contestation of the space in which we live" (ibid.). Foucault ascribes to the study of this form of space, the name heterotopology, and although reluctant to bequeath, a social scientific schema sets out sufficient principles to enable its application to a review of social media retail analytics in respect to Brixton BID. For it is my contention that a self-imposed retreat from intrusive investigations of online digital cultures differentiates Brixton BID from the colonial digital capitalism of social media analytics. This is particularly evident in five aspects of the heterotopic online social media space: (1) community curation of crisis heterotopias versus algorithmic analytics; (2) "the other city" versus pseudo-Gemeinschaft; (3) insolvable diversity versus micro-market segmentation; (4) absolute chroniques versus accumulation of time and (5) space of illusion versus meticulous colonies. The afore discussion is a brief description of the Brixton BID's analyses of heterotopic social media space, and the evaluation is aimed to illustrate its differentiation from colonial digital capitalistic social media analytics. However, as the analysis progressed, it became increasingly evident that the BID technological data gathering of the social media use of its population is resonant with colonial digital capitalist technologies of digital policing and thus, compounding the irregularities of these various systems. It is evident in the following discussion of the gender racialised irregularities of live facial recognition (LFR).

Racialised Digital Gaze, Private People in Public Space: LFR Surveillance Heterotopias BID

Unsurprisingly, the arrest rate is low. Already this year, the Met has scanned 125,000 innocent Londoners with facial recognition – only 0.1 per cent of scans led to an arrest. Some scans lead to misidentifications and innocent people being wrongly investigated. It's a terrible use of taxpayers' money. But the worst cost is our liberty. High crime rates make us less free but so too does Orwellian policing. Live facial recognition has no place in London. Big Brother Watch (2024)

In July 2020, Dame Cressida Dick provided witness evidence to the Home Affairs Committee, on the Work of the Commissioner of the

Metropolitan Police Service (MPS). Among questions posed about the Black music industry and the policing of live music events, the issue of live facial recognition (LFR) was raised in respect to public concerns pertaining to whether the technology's algorithms were biased and discriminatory. It was highlighted that a study, reporting in 2019 and conducted by the University of Essex, found that only "20% of facial recognition matches being correct, and being disproportionately inaccurate on black, Asian and female faces" (Home Affairs 2020). The then Commissioner fervently challenged the accuracy of the reported deficiencies in the accuracy of LFR technology, largely depreciating the role of LFR in frontline policing decision-making. Whereby, it was stated: "We are very comfortable with it in terms of potential, as people might say, bias. However, the most important thing is that we use it very openly. We do have lots of checks and balances and the most important one of those is that it is not the tool that makes the decision, it is the two officers in the chain after the machine has said, 'That could be Cressida'". Researching in 2023, the subject of LFR and racial equity reveals a shifting strategic practice in which automation features more prominently.

In an article entitled "Facial Recognition Technology", the MPS provides insights on the expanding field of public space captured by LFR. Some indication of which is described as thus: "LFR cameras are focused on a specific area; when people pass through that area their images are streamed directly to the Live Facial Recognition system" (Metropolitan Police 2023a). We are reliably informed that the LFR system is stocked by a "watchlist", which is "a list of offenders wanted by the police and/or courts or those who pose a risk of harm to themselves or others" (ibid.). Concerns about the potential of vast scope of people that might be included in the afore categories (and other stated in the Standard Operating Procedures for LFR) are insufficiently ameliorated by the assurance that "LFR is not a ubiquitous tool that uses lots of CCTV cameras from across London to track every person's movements. It is a carefully developed overt policing tactic to help locate a limited number of people the police need to find in order to keep London safe" (ibid.). In 2021 the National Physical Laboratory was awarded a research contract to conduct a test evaluation of facial recognition for the MPS and South Wales Police (SWP). Data collection and the empirical research took place in July and August 2022, during which time the National Physical Laboratory analysed the facial recognition technology version titled "NEC Neoface V4 using HDS Face Detector", which are currently utilised by the MPS and SWP for the biometric facial scanning, that is Live Facial Recognition, Retrospective Facial Recognition (RFR) and Operator Installed Facial Recognition (National Physical Laboratory 2023: 2). The results of the study are highly revealing and immensely disconcerting from a feminist human rights perspective. We are further informed that, according, test evaluation conducted by National Physical Laboratory (2023), the True-Positive Identification Rate (TPIR), "is identical for all demographic sub-groups, and with no demographic performance variation in TPIR", performance is considered to be "equitable" for Retrospective Facial Recognition (RFR), and a similar result was identified for Operator Initiated Facial Recognition (OIFR) (ibid.: 3). With Life Facial Recognition the situation is more complex. Firstly, its biometric scanning operates differently as thus:

> **Live Facial Recognition (LFR) compares a live camera video feed of faces against a predetermined watchlist to find a possible match that generates an alert. The recognition accuracy of Live Facial Recognition is measured in terms of: True-Positive Identification Rate (TPIR) – the rate of successful recognition when subjects on the watchlist pass through the zone of recognition. False-Positive Identification Rate (FPIR) – the rate of incorrect recognition (i.e., false positives or false alerts) when subjects not on the watchlist pass through the zone of recognition. National Physical Laboratory (2023: 3)**

It is a feature of the National Physical Laboratory's technique that they used "a range of watchlist sizes and face-match thresholds" and that "for summarising operational performance" they used "a face-match threshold of 0.6 which is the default setting of the Neoface facial recognition software" (ibid.). Key findings on LFR were published in March 2023, in the National Physical Laboratory report titled, "Facial Recognition Technology in Law Enforcement Equitability Study". It is noted that "the range of variation in True Positive Identification Rate due to demographic effects was the same as that due to environmental effects" (ibid.). Drilling down into the data it is revealed that: (1) "At face-match threshold 0.6, the ethnicity-gender group with the best TPIR was the Asian-Female group, and the poorest TPIR was for the Black-Female group"; (2) "At face-match threshold 0.6, the observed variation in TPIR for the different age groups was statistically significant, TPIR improving with subject age";

(3) "False positive identifications increase at lower face-match thresholds of 0.58 and 0.56 and start to show a statistically significant imbalance between demographics with more Black subjects having a false positive than Asian or White subjects" (ibid.: 4–5). Thus, a key equitability finding relates to the use of face-match thresholds lower than 0.6, whereby "at face-match thresholds lower than 0.6 FPIR equitability will depend on settings of the operational deployment, including size and composition of the watchlist, and the number of crowd subjects passing through the zone of recognition during the deployment" (ibid.: 5). Recognising this the authors recommend the following operational deployment of LFR: "Given our observations on the demographic variation in FPIR, we would recommend, where operationally possible, the use of a face-match of 0.6 or above to minimise the likelihood of any false positive and adverse impact on equitability" (ibid.). Furthermore,

> **FPIR [False-Positive Identification Rate] EQUITABILITY**
> Equitability is dependent on the face-match threshold settings and on the size and demographic composition of the LFR watchlist or RFR reference database.
> The demographic variation in the non-mated score distribution does not affect equitability if settings are such that the chance of a false alert is very low. However, if settings allow for a higher number of false alerts, these are likely to occur disproportionately within Black and Asian ethnicities. National Physical Laboratory (2023: 22)

In summary, it can be discerned that LFR is unable to achieve an equitable score for Black female ethnic minorities because this group has a low representation in the watchlists that contain the image of criminals and those suspected of committing a crime. Thus, it is because Black women are less represented in the criminal justice system, the policing technologies that excessively policing surveillance the public spaces that Black women populate are more likely to misrecognise them and produce false alerts.

With regard to the case study of O2 Academy Brixton incident, a Freedom of Information request was issued in April 2023, requesting information about the face-match threshold that was used in any Live or Retrospective Facial Recognition analysis applied to the crowd. On 5th April 2023 (09:50 BST), the Metropolitan Police issued *Statement on Release of Research into Facial Recognition Technology*. It is notable that the issue of face-match threshold and false match rates was highly simplified as thus:

The findings conclude:

- There are settings our algorithm can be operated at where there is no statistical significance between demographic performance.
- ACCURACY: When used at a threshold setting of 0.6 or above, correct matches (True Positive Identification Rate) were 89%. The incorrect match rate (False Positive Identification Rate) was 0.017%. The chance of a false match therefore, is just 1 in 6000 people walking past the camera.
- DEMOGRAPHIC DIFFERENCE: When used at a threshold setting of 0.6 or above, any differences in matches across groups were not statistically significant. This means performance was the same across race and gender.
- Retrospective Facial Recognition: The true positive identification rate for high quality images was 100%. This is the best performance possible. (Metropolitan Police 2023b)

While it was clearly the Metropolitan Police's intention to address public anxiousness around LFR, the simplification of the National Physical Laboratory research findings into a false binary in which matching the face-match threshold of 0.6 is deemed ethically good and lower is depicted as ethically bad, has the effect of raising suspicion about the entire spectrum of the metric. Consequently, it was really unsurprising that the Metropolitan Police's announcement of an intention to use LFR to support its policing of the coronation of King Charles III was received with an upsurge of renewed scepticism. Specifically, the Metropolitan Police in a press release posted prior to the coronation declared its intention to use LFR in the following public notices: "We intend to use facial recognition technology in central London. The watch list will be focused on those whose attendance on Coronation Day would raise public protection concerns" (Metropolitan Police 2023c) and "Live Facial Recognition is one of a number of tactics for the #Coronation security operation. Our tech used cameras made by Swedish company Axis. We do not use Hikvision cameras. Our use of LFR has been independently scrutinised – read more [NPL 2023]" (@MetPoliceEvents 2023). The human rights group Liberty, which is a member of INCLO (the International Network of Civil Liberties Organizations), has for some time campaigned against police in the UK using facial recognition. Indeed, in the critical pronouncements of a 2022 publication, it described facial recognition as thus, "This is gross violation of your human rights" (Liberty 2022). The Metropolitan Police is described as one of two forces that are spearheading this surveillance technology, and accused of using facial recognition to scan "hundreds of thousands of faces" at among events, the Notting Hill Carnival. Liberty describes facial recognition as thus, "Police facial recognition works by measuring and 'mapping' a person's unique facial features. These 'maps' are then converted into a numerical code to be matched against the codes of faces on secretive watch lists" (ibid.). Their definition of LFR corresponds with that of the Metropolitan Police, but it is notable that their labelling of "retroactive" technology is different from the former's RFR. Liberty persuasively argues that both LFR and retroactive technologies identify biometric data based on unique human facial dimensions and do so when capturing images from surveillance cameras scanning "everyone insight" in a crowded area.

> @metpoliceuk on 25th August 2024 posted to X (formerly known as Twitter) an announcement about its policing of the Notting Hill Carnival, it was stated that "in light" of violent disorders "a Section 60 has been authorised for the Carnival area from 6.05pm to 2am" (@metpoliceuk 2024). Later that day the posting announced an upgrade of the Section 60 as thus: "A Section 60AA order has been authorised in the Carnival area for the same period. 'It gives officers the power to order the removal of face coverings being used to conceal a person's identity. Anyone refusing such an order can be arrested'" (ibid.). On 26th August 2024 an extension to the time period of the enforcement of the issued Section 60 and Section 60AA "in force in the Carnival area until 2am" was announced (ibid.). Given that live facial recognition camera feed is subject to algorithmic system biases between different demographic groups and the Metropolitan Police Service recognises the validity of the Court of Appeal ruling in the Bridges Vs South Wales Police (2020) which determined "race and gender as being particularly relevant considerations for FRT" the issue of Section 60 and 60AA public order notices appears to be a troubling potential condition for the expansion of technology that continues to have flawed levels of biometric system performance across the key demographic of race and gender. (Metropolitan Police Service 2024f)

While legimately concerned about the facial recognition technology of LFR, Liberty (2022) is raising acute concerns about "retroactive" version of this technology. Whereby, it describes as thus the potentially limitless stock of image capture, "Retroactive facial recognition also turns every photo or video available to the police – including any you upload to social media – into a possible surveillance tool" (ibid.). Furthermore, Liberty (2022) provides, albeit descriptively, suggestion that the facial recognition technology misrecognises the biometrics of Black minority ethnics and particularly females. Significantly, they present an argument about efficacy to which I largely concur. That is the notion that increased efficacy in the accuracy of the technology "would lessen the problems with facial recognition is false" (ibid.). Stating further that "history shows that surveillance technology will always be used to monitor and harass people of colour. More accurate tech would only make thus easier and discriminatory policing worse" (ibid.). A similarly articulate and plausible riposte was directed at the @MetPoliceEvents post of 4th May 2023, whereby Liberty stated, "Police #FacialRecognition has indeed been independently scrutinised by the courts which said police use broke human rights, equalities and data protection laws #BanFacialRec" (@Libertyhq 2023). Although not the focus of Liberty's complaint, an additional area of concern about LFR and RFR is the financial service's incorporation of this technology in its service provision, fraud protection and risk assessment. It is necessary to briefly describe this area as it has relevance to the case study question: Why do Black people pay more for their music? For it is my contention that the incorporation of LFR and RFR into insurance actuarial calculations is one of the reasons why *Black people pay more for their music*. So as to substantiate this supposition I have identified advances in the use of facial recognition in the live music entertainment industry and also advances in the use of facial recognition within the insurance industry, with a view to identifying interrelations between these innovations. In summary, a convergence of AI with digital biodemography and GPS directed at public spaces presents a menace to the protection of the privacy and liberties of law-abiding citizens. Where these technologies are aligning as is evident in the digital underwriting of the live music entertainment industry, it is my contention that at the intersection of these digitally colonising AI data-streams is emerging an amplification of racial profiling, monitoring, surveillance and hyper-risk assessment of Black people and Black music cultures. While I can categorically state that I do not have a criminal or police records, such declaration should not be the threshold by which we condone the pervasiveness of surveillance technology and LFR.

"Seize the Opportunities of Data and Digital Tech to Become a World Leader in Policing" is a key chapter in the Metropolitan Police Business

Plan 2021–2024, and a consistent business theme since the initial iteration of the 2016–2020 digital strategy. It is significant that the pursuit of opportunities in digital policing has advanced from an operational strategy for the re-engineering of office technology and its cloud productivity, to becoming an integral analytical tool of the policing frontline. Digital policing is a prominent feature of the Policing Vision 2025, and Metropolitan Police's prioritising of this articulates with the National Digital Data and Technology Strategy 2020–2030. Digital policing was decidedly present in the police statements delivered in the immediate aftermath of the 15th December 2022, O2 Academy Brixton critical incident during the Afrobeat concert of the Nigerian artist Asake. Indeed, the prominence of digital policing language, rhetoric and practice expressed the Metropolitan Police's commitment to the role it ascribed to digital policing in the provisioning of enhanced "and more granular data analytics to identify trends, causal factors and situational awareness" (ibid.: 37). It is envisaged that this analytical tool will enable an efficient informational policing, thus providing more available time for frontline police officers to concentrate "on preventative action locally" and provide a more contextually knowledgeable response. As the business plan expresses it: "By building out technical links through our API strategy with broader partner agencies, we facilitate the ethical exchange of richer information in a more responsive manner to enable better delivery of the right support to those that need it most" (ibid.). With specific regard to this section's document-based case study examination into the visualisation of images of minority ethnics in respect to the O2 Academy Brixton critical incident, a consistent finding is evidence of a commodification in the centralisation of digital data. The Metropolitan Police's enrichment of its Single Online Home has been prominent in what the MPS describes as improving "the digital channels available to citizens and businesses for the reporting of crime and accessing of essential prevention and protection information" (ibid.). For its enabling technological infrastructure, facilitated through digital policing, is intended to achieve an acceleration in "the analysis of information in support of intelligence and investigatory activities". Axiomatic with the digital technology facilitation of Single Online Home has been an enhancement in the capacity to share digital material across forces in articulation with national and international agencies. As the business strategy expresses it, "Through the use of collaboration tooling we are improving the sharing of digital material with our partners across the criminal justice service and making proceedings for victims, witnesses and officers more flexible and convenient so that they are less intrusive and improve the overall experience" (ibid.).

Acknowledging concerns raised about the prominence of data analytics to the MPS's future ambitions, it has invested further in improving its service to the public in respect to privacy rights. But, its fervour for notoriously privacy-depleting and human rights dispossessing market-based data-rich information, technology and digital analytic capabilities presents new and evolving challenges that destabilise MPS's assurance of securing privacy rights. It is a contention of this case study that the centrality of data-driven analytics to MPS's operations does indeed produce calculable improvements in policing outcomes; however, it is my contention that this achievement is at a costlier disbursement to the market-based capitalisation of privacy rights. Indeed, a primary contention of this case study is that the centralisation of data sharing, facilitated through digital business operations, is integrating the MPS further into capitalist policing technology markets and the consequential discriminatory commodification of racialised, gendered data subjects. The determination of MPS to advance its LFR technological surveillance is precipitating expressions of immense concern by human rights activist organisations, prominent among which is Big Brother Watch. In response to the British Chancellor Jeremy Hunt's announcement in spring 2024 that UK police forces will receive, it is estimated, "£55.5 million" to support the adoption of facial recognition technology, Big Brother Watch published the following statement: "The U.K. is increasingly an outlier in the democratic world in taking this approach, with European countries, the EU, U.S. states and cities banning or severely restricting law enforcement use of LFR" (Big Brother Watch 2024). Given that LFR is more likely to misrecognise and produce false alerts for Black women, it is a human rights concern that the UK police force nationally intends to expand its use of LFR that biometrically (mis)scans Black human faces and (mis)recognises these against a criminal watchlist that has insufficient numbers of Black females to circumvent systematically producing false identifications. Expanding this strategy will merely further erode the sense of belonging of Black British female subjects, for the UK police force in "relentlessly deploying Orwellian live facial recognition in crowded public places [is] turning innocent people into walking ID cards" (ibid.). In specific regards to the case study of Brixton and the use of technological surveillance to increase the security of women more generally

Countering Rationalities: Safe Spaces for Females in Crisis Heterotopia

Violence Against Women and Girls (VAWG) designates a form of violence and abuse perpetrated by men against women. Across the year prior to O2 Brixton Academy's 15th December 2022 tragedy statistics for VAWG, crimes were dispiritingly elevated. Some indication of which is discernible from the Metropolitan Police Service data for Brixton North, from May 2021 to March 2024, record of the violence and sexual offences percentage of crimes at 22.7% with a total of 1540 VAWG incidents; Brixton Windrush records for this period is 19.5% with a total of 1828 VAWG incidents; similarly, Myatt's Fields recorded 26% with a total of 858 VAWG; and Brixton Acre Lane for this period 24.1% with a total of 1620 VAWG (Met Police 2024). With regards to homicide victims in London in 2020 the Metropolitan Police Service recorded male victim 104; female victim 29; with 56 where the ethnic appearance recorded as "black" and 48 where the ethnic appearance recorded as "white" (Met Police 2024). In 2022 homicide victims in London was recorded as 80 male and 28 female; with in the category defined as "officer observed ethnicity" 39 white and again a disproportionately high number at 48 for "ethnic appearance of black" (ibid.). These crime statistics are a disconcerting insight into the urban context in which the O2 Academy Brixton music venue is located and the very distinct experience of racialised female subjects with regard to their vulnerability of VAWG being perpetrated against them. In an attempt to address the situation of a gendering in the experience of public recreational space, Brixton BID has introduced several initiatives, which appear resonant of a decolonial attempt to restitute the human right for women to feel safe and secure in recreational space. Significant aspects regarding some of the initiatives are that they depend less on hyper-digitalised surveillance of Black females, in order to increase street security, but rather the focus is on reclaiming their sense of belonging to a diaspora of Black Britains.

On 30th December 2021, Brixton BID posted to its website an announcement of its *Walk and Talk Initiative*, subtitled Safe Day and Night. The initiative is described as thus,

> **The Walk and Talk initiative is part of Central South's proactive response to address local concerns about violence against women and girls (VAWG). These have become ever more prevalent following the**

shocking abduction and murder of Sarah Everard from our BCU, and wider concern about violence towards women, harassment and misogyny. The idea is simple: Local women, going for a walk with female officers in their neighbourhood. The opportunity is to talk to female members of the community about their experiences, concerns and suggestions on how they can make them feel safer. Brixton BID (2021)

Walk and Talk is first and foremost the community's curation of crisis heterotopias versus algorithmic analytics. In 2021, Brixton BID published a series of reports detailing the outcomes of its twinning with Harlem 125th Street Business Improvement District. Such a pairing was an innovative expansion of the spatial boundary management of the BID organisational structure. It was recognised that resonances exist in the racial and ethnic diaspora of Brixton (London, UK) and Harlem (New York City, USA). Furthermore, "both BIDs are located in communities with a long and rich history of being the epicentres for a convergence of diversity, informed by a high percentage of its population being of African descent, representing various parts of the diaspora, living and working within the BID's borders" (Brixton BID 2021). The collaborative association between the two BIDs was established out of shared principles and values regarding equality, community and social justice. Reflective of these values, Brixton BID emulated Harlem BID's 2020 Canvas for Change initiative, in which local business and local neighbourhoods had collaborated in the creation of street mural depicting floods of emotions, collective grief and hope in the midst of the pandemic and the community's demand for social justice.

In its emulation of Harlem BID's artistic cultural political initiative, Brixton BID invited artistic representations in support of the 40th anniversary of the Brixton Uprising of 1981, the heritage of the Windrush Generation and recognition of the global Black Lives Matter movement. According to the Brixton BID's press release about the initiative, activities and participation pertaining to the introduction of the Canvas project would be venerated through video, photography and the audio testimonials of drawn from local community. These memorialised material artefacts would exist alongside social media hashtags with the expectation of building a multi-media digital archive of the project that would be hosted at the Black cultural Archive on Windrush Square. Furthermore, it was a stated aim that "this activation will take place in preparation for the large-scale mural of 1970s leading social justice activist Olive Morris that will

6 DECOLONIAL INTERMEDIATION IN CRISIS HETEROTOPIC SPACE 207

transform Dorrell Place in 2022 to mark Olive's 70th Birthday". Resonances can be observed between this memorialised exhibition of British and American Black artistic vernacular and the type of space that Foucault (1986: 24) describes as "crisis heterotopias", whereby these spaces are defined as "privileged or sacred or forbidden places, reserved for individuals who are, in relation to society and to the human environment in which they live, in a state of crisis". Parallels in this respect are self-evidently portrayed in the Brixton BID description of itself and the Harlem BID as experiencing a shared defining moment during the COVID-19 pandemic and also in relation to racialised social injustice. We are informed that the Harlem Community's 125th Street district is one of the most significant and expressive landmark streets in New York City; its allegoric symbolism is particularly evident in its bearing as a double name that of Martin Luther King Jr. Boulevard. The internationally renowned Hotel Theresa, location in Harlem, has hosted acclaimed human rights advocates including Fidel Castro and Malcolm X. Correspondence exists here with its sister community of Brixton, which is similarly a multi-ethnic district that has undergone significant cultural political change. Directly associated with the arrival of Empire Windrush in 1948, the growth and settlement of the African Caribbean community in Britain is irrevocably tied to Brixton. It has been a juncture in the anti-racist struggle, witnessing in 1981 the community's struggle with racism erupt into the Brixton Uprising. Brixton's rich cultural, political history is increasingly chronicled in the "only" national heritage centre dedicated to memorialising and preserving the histories of African and Caribbean people in Britain, the Black cultural Archives situated on Windrush Square, Brixton London.

The crisis heterotopia status of the Brixton (London, UK) and Harlem (NYC, USA) twinned Districts was heralded as the scaffolding of a "bridge connecting both communities", with a view to exchanging ideas on how to "protect the historic values of both Harlem and Brixton and preserve the African American/African-Caribbean legacy" (Brixton BIDs 2021). Additionally, it was envisioned that the twinning will precipitate an increase in tourism and also "an exchange of e-commerce products and services" (ibid.). Whereby, e-commerce is emphasised as "vital in the creation of jobs, development of infrastructure and can contribute to the overall economic health and wealth of both communities and the cities they are located in" (ibid.). Integral to the communication of the e-commerce strategy, it is evident, is social media. Indeed, the press release about the twinning, as with most of the recent publications from the BID, involves an encouragement to circulate and to distribute the content into the immaterial space of social media. In so doing, and in transitioning the crisis heterotopia into cyberspace, social media becomes an online extension of the crisis heterotopia. Thus, it is of little surprise that the social media analytics published in the Brixton Monthly Report—December 2022 contained in its sentiment analyses multitudes of words that spoke and exclaimed an existence of crisis around the Asake concert crowd crush tragedy of 15th December 2022. It is also probable that these online channels intersected and supportively engaged with the Metropolitan Police's social media and online investigative enquiry call for images and video-footage taken during the tragedy to be submitted into the police's online portals. But here also there appeared to be a gender racialised disproportionate representation of Black females.

This is partly due to the fact that Brixton BID had gained a profile as a prominent member of the alliance seeking to Save Brixton Academy. Indeed, in a press release, published on the 11th of the May 2023, the Managing Director of Brixton BID described the motivation for supporting the campaign to save Brixton Academy quite definitely in terms of the purpose of the BID. As they express it, "Whilst artists dream about performing in Brixton, our business community is proud to be home of such a venue. Not only is it one of our key cultural destinations, the Brixton Academy contributes positively to the local economy as well as opportunities for our community. We stand by the Brixton Academy" (Brixton BIDs 2023c).

Within the press release the BID speaks defiantly about its support for O2 Academy Brixton and details its active engagement in the campaign. It provides readers with a clear blueprint of how to participate favourably in the campaign, as thus: "We need the industry to stand up, work alongside us, the Night Time Industry Association and Save Our Scene to champion a campaign to show the importance of this business and protect this space by submitting representations of support to Lambeth Council" (ibid.). At the time of the press release just under 115,000 people had signed the petition by S.B. to save Brixton Academy, and readers were urged that "in order to stop this happening we need to get as many representations to Lambeth Council by Midnight on Monday 15th May 2023" (ibid.). The press release footer contains the social media share icons and email share icon. It is noticeable here and elsewhere (in my interviews with key members of the campaign) that the BID retained a specific line of support which emphasised the value of the venue for the local economy.

Furthermore, by assuming this strategic response, the BID provided further indication that it is working within the law-and-order maintenance remit assumed by BIDs in recent times. Indeed, an increasingly cited value-for-money indicator of the operation of Districts in which a BID levy is extracted from business rate payers is the business cost decrease derived from a reduction in crime. The Black British post-colonial feminist, West African diaspora perspective articulated, thus far is in advocacy of decolonial strategy in respect to an inherent scepticism of liberal ideology pertaining to protect women's safety within the night time economy; in respect to its promulgation of a 'colour-blindness'.

Kimberlé Crenshaw (1988: 1282) identifies how colourblind' antiracist agenda "tend to focus only on single issues" and in so doing mitigates against an appreciation of the extent to which intersecting structural inequalities compound the vulnerability of Black women to an amplitude of racism. I therefore concur with the assertion that, "Recognizing that identity politics takes place at the site where categories intersect thus seems more fruitful than challenging the possibility of talking about categories at all" (ibid.1299).

Such observations of the intersections between the immaterial spaces of social media and the legal channels of law, order and policing governance provide further insights into the crisis heterotopic space into which hundreds (if not thousands) of messages were posted into during the 15th December 2022 crowd crush and in its immediate aftermath. Social media postings of images, audio-visuals capturing the horror of the critical incident, were postings into the forbidden online liminal places reserved for individuals, social groupings and forms of social interaction that are in relation to the human environment in a situation of crisis. It is my contention that the Brixton BID in its previous initiatives mapping transatlantic Africa and Caribbean diaspora with the USA and its other racial heritage identity initiatives successfully cultivated its associated social media spaces as safe spaces for crisis heterotopia. Consequently, it is unsurprising that witnesses and concerned members of the community sort out these spaces into which to vocalise and visualise their shock, horror and grief during and in the immediate aftermath of the critical incident of 15th December 2022. But it is my observation that these safe spaces within the crisis heterotopias were marginalised at crucial times early into the police investigation, in which they appeared to be technical rational opposition.

Timely Reflections

Police were called at 21:35hrs on Thursday, 15 December to the O2 Academy on Stockwell Road, SW9 following reports that a large number of people were attempting to force entry to the venue. Officers, London Ambulance Service (LAS) and London Fire Brigade attended and found a number of people with injuries believed to have been caused by crushing. Eight people were taken by ambulance to hospital, four of whom remain in a critical condition. LAS treated two other less seriously injured people at the scene. An urgent investigation is under way led by detectives from Specialist Crime. Cordons remain in place at the location as officers continue work at the scene. Nobody has been arrested.

Commander Ade Adelekan, Met Police Gold Commander, said: This is an extremely upsetting incident which has left four people critically ill in hospital. My thoughts and prayers are with them and their families. A police investigation has been launched, and it will be as thorough and as forensic as necessary to establish exactly what happened last night. The scene will be examined by specialist officers, CCTV will be viewed, every witness that we can make contact with will be spoken to and all other lines of enquiry will be followed. Officers are remaining in the area to provide reassurance to the local community in and around Brixton. If you have any information or concerns, please speak with them. I am aware of video being shared on social media. I would ask people to be sensible about what they share, and not to post material that will be upsetting to those affected by this incident. Where force has been used by police officers, those officers know they have to be accountable for their actions. The Met's Directorate of Professional Standards will view all material, including Body Worn Video footage from the officers at the scene. In relation to a clip being widely shared, I can confirm that no police dogs were deployed to the location. Any witnesses who are yet to speak with police are asked to call 101 ref 6725/15Dec. If you have mobile phone footage that may assist police, please make contact via @MetCC on Twitter. We will provide further details about ways to share footage in due course. (Metropolitan Police 2022—16 December [04:57 GMT])

When one considers the Metropolitan Police press statement as an instance in the making visual of the critical incident enquiry, it becomes apparent that a "synoptic" mode of visualisation is in operation. I have elsewhere (Odih 2016, 2019a, 2019b) conceptualised contemporary digital surveillance technologies as constitutive of a new mode of reciprocity of perspective defined as "ethico-synoptics". The concept of synoptics emerges from Mathiesen's (1997) critique of Foucault's (1991) panopticon in respect to the latter in sufficiently releasing a situation, as stated by the former, in which the many are watching the many. By examining the limits of Foucault's (ibid.) panopticon in terms of its limited emphasis on technologies of the sign (Odih 2010) and examining the limits of Mathiesen's (1997) synoptics in terms of moral judgement, I formulated my concept of "ethico-synoptics", which refers to a social phenomenon facilitated by the materiality of digitally visual communication technologies in which the many are making ethical judgements in their irregular watching of the many. It is my contention that ethico-synoptics are prevalent in the digital policing technologies of the Metropolitan Police, and this has discriminatory outcomes for Black ethnic minorities. Having explored this further in respect to the Metropolitan Police digital policing strategy documents, it is a contention of this case study that ethico-synoptics are embedded in the operational blueprint of the digital policing strategy 2021–2025. In so doing, it reproduces the business model of digital policing along with the financialising propensities of its client-model, both of which have relevance to the means by which policing surveillance information enters into circuits of capitalist market commodification and discriminatorily punitive actuarial calculations of risk populations. All which failed to anticipate and protect against the 15th December 2022 crowd crush fatalities.

References

@ Libertyhq (2023); *Police #FacialRecognition has Indeed been Independently Scrutinised by the Courts which Said Police use Broke Human Rights, Equalities and Data protection Laws.* Liberty. Available at: https://twitter.com/libertyhq

@Metropolitan Police Events (2023); *Live Facial Recognition is One of a number of Tactics for the #Coronation Security Operation.* Available at: https://twitter.com/MetPoliceEvents

@Metpoliceuk (2024); Section 60 has been Authorised for the Carnival Area. Available at: https://x.com/metpoliceuk/status/1827637405064507547

Big Brother Watch (2024); City A.M. – The Notebook: Facial Recognition CCTV is Orwellian. But it Also Doesn't Work, Big Brother Watch. Available at: https://bigbrotherwatch.org.uk/press-coverage/city-a-m-the-notebook-facial-recognition-cctv-is-orwellian-but-it-also-doesnt-work/

Brixton BID (2021); *A Bond Across the Pond. A First of its Kind Twinning Joins Two Important Business Improvement Districts (BID) and Forges a Bond Across the Pond in Two Radical Communities of Colour*. Brixton BID. Available at: https://brixtonbid.co.uk/content/uploads/2021/06/BID-Twinning-Brixton-Harlem.pdf

Brixton BID (2023a); *About Brixton BIDs*. Available at: https://brixtonbid.co.uk/about/

Brixton BID (2023b); *Brixton Monthly Report – December 2022, Brixton Business Improvement District*. Available at: https://brixtonbid.co.uk/content/uploads/2023/02/LPR_Brixton-BID_-Levy-Payer-Report-Dec-2022_2022_11_v1.pdf

Brixton BID (2023c); *Save the O2 Academy Brixton*. Available at: https://brixtonbid.co.uk/save-the-o2-academy-brixton/

Foucault, M., (1986); *Of Other Spaces*, Foucault, M., and Miskowiec, J., *Diacritics*, Vol.16, No. 1 (Spring, 1986), pp. 22–27.

Foucault, M., (1991); *Discipline and Punish; The Birth of the Prison*. trans., Sheridan, A., London: Penguin Books.

Davis, A., (2003); *Are Prisons Obsolete?* New York: Seven Stories Press.

Department for Culture, Media and Sport [DCMS] (2023); *Cultural Recovery Fund Data Report*. Available at: https://www.gov.uk/government/publications/evaluation-and-data-report-for-the-culture-recovery-fund/cultural-recovery-fund-data-report

Gov.UK (2014); *Business Improvement Districts; Information and Guidance on Business Improvement Districts*. Department for Levelling Up, Housing and Communities and Ministry of Housing, Community and Local Government. Available at: https://www.gov.uk/guidance/business-improvement-districts

Gov.UK (2015); *Business Improvement Districts: Guidance and Best Practice*, Ministry of Housing, Communities and Local Government. Available at: https://www.gov.uk/government/publications/business-improvement-districts-guidance-and-best-practice

Home Affairs Committee (2020); *The Work of the Commissioner of the Metropolitan Police Service*, Home Affairs Committee, House of Commons. Available at: https://www.met.police.uk/SysSiteAssets/media/downloads/force-content/met/about-us/stride/macpherson-hasc-transcript%2D%2D-met-commissioner-july-2020.pdf

Hootsuite (2021); *What is social Media Analytics? Everything You Need to Know*. Available at: https://blog.hootsuite.com/what-is-social-media-analytics/

Liberty (2022); *Facial Recognition / What is Police Facial Recognition and How Do We Stop It?* Liberty. Available at: https://www.libertyhumanrights.org.uk/issue/what-is-police-facial-recognition-and-how-do-we-stop-it/

Mathiesen, T., (1997); The Viewer Society, Michel Foucault's 'Panopticon' Revisited, *Theoretical Criminology*, Vol. 1(2), pp., 215–234.

6 DECOLONIAL INTERMEDIATION IN CRISIS HETEROTOPIC SPACE 213

Met Police (2024); *Top Reported Crimes, Brixton Windrush; Brixton Acre Lane; Myatt's Field, Metropolitan Police.* Available at: https://www.police.uk/pu/your-area/metropolitan-police-service/brixton-acre-lane/?yourlocalpolicingteam=about-us

Metropolitan Police (2022); *Four People Critical Following Incident in Brixton,* Metropolitan Police, News – 16 December 2022 [04:57 GMT]. Available at: Four_people_critical_following_incident_in_Brixton.pdf

Metropolitan Police (2023a); *Facial Recognition Technology,* Metropolitan Police. Available at: https://www.met.police.uk/advice/advice-and-information/fr/facial-recognition-technology/

Metropolitan Police (2023b); Statement on Release of Research into Facial Recognition Technology, New Scotland Yard. Available at: https://news.met.police.uk/news/statement-on-release-of-research-into-facial-recognition-technology-464791

Metropolitan Police (2023c); *The Coronation of His Majesty the King and Her Majesty the Queen Consort,* Deputy Assistant Commissioner Ade Adelekan, Metropolitan Police. Available at: https://news.met.police.uk/news/the-coronation-of-his-majesty-the-king-and-her-majesty-the-queen-consort-466199

Metropolitan Police Service (2021a); *Metropolitan Police Service, Business Plan 2021–24.* Metropolitan Police. Available at: https://www.met.police.uk/SysSiteAssets/media/downloads/force-content/met/about-us/met-business-plan-2021-24.pdf

Metropolitan Police Service (2022a); UPDATE: Statement from Chief Superintendent Colin Wingrove on O2 Brixton Academy Incident, Metropolitan Police, News - 16 December 2022 [16:46hrs GMT]). Available at: UPDATE_Statement_from_Chief_Superintendent_Colin_Wingrove_on_O2_Brixton_Academy_incident.pdf

Metropolitan Police Service (2024f); The Metropolitan Police Service Facial Recognition Technology: Understanding Accuracy and Demographic Differences, Metropolitan Police. Available at: https://www.met.police.uk/SysSiteAssets/media/downloads/force-content/met/advice/lfr/new/understanding-accuracy-and-demographic-differences-v3.pdf

National Physical Laboratory (2023); *Facial Recognition Technology in Law Enforcement Equitability Study,* Final Report, Mansfield, T., Middlesex: National Physical Laboratory. Available at: https://science.police.uk/site/assets/files/3396/frt-equitability-study_mar2023.pdf

O2 (2023); *Micro Location Insights – Detailed Movement Data From O2.* Available at: https://www.o2.co.uk/documents/456036/1067287/O2_Business_Micro_Location_Insights_0121.055_FINAL.pdf/fe06a775-7d4e-ae23-68ed-050b28d1e419?version=1.0&t=1615800453580

Odih, P., (2016); *Adsensory Financialisation*, Newcastle Upon Tyne: Cambridge Scholars Publishing.

Odih, P., (2010); Advertising and Cultural Politics in Global Times. Farnham: Ashgate. ISBN 978-0-7546-7711-6

Odih, P., (2019a); Adsensory Urban Ecology (Volume One). Newcastle upon Tyne: Cambridge Scholars Publishing. ISBN 9781527523173

Odih, P., (2019b); Adsensory Urban Ecology (Volume Two). Newcastle upon Tyne: Cambridge Scholars Publishing. ISBN 9781527524682

Windmill Software (2023); *People Counting: Eight Technologies to Measure Footfall*. Windmill Software. Available at: https://www.windmill.co.uk/footfall-technology.html

CHAPTER 7

Post-colonial Feminist, Interpolation

Pamela Odih interviews Jane Bryce, March 2024. © Pamela Odih

The politically confrontational album *Beasts of No Nation* (credited with Afrika Egypt 80) had not endeared Fela Anikulapo-Kuti to the Nigerian authorities, with its insurgent lyrics castigating their debased colonial mentality. In chorus with growing disquiet, the artist disparaged the neo-colonial ties beneath the (post)colonial façade adjourned by monetarily opportunistic public officials. But the utmost derision is reserved for (post) coloniality and its manifold trajectories of enduring control. As expressed in the following extract from the original to the 1989 album sleeve of Bêtes Sauvages Sans Nationalite (*Beasts of No Nation*),

> C'est le premier ministre Botha, *(d'Afrique du Sud)* Il dit,
> 'Ces soulèvement vont faire ressortir la Bête en nous' !!!
> Et Botha, c'est le pote à Thatcher et Reagan
> Et à d'autres dirigeants aussi
> Et c'est tous ceux-là
> Qui tiennent a nous faire cadeau des droits de l'Homme !
> En somme, des animaux quiveulent gratifier des humains de leurs droits!
> Mais cela ne se peut.
> Ces Bêtes sans Nation sont une société pourrie.
> Ces Bêtes sans Nation sont la [Oturugbeke] confusion totale.

Beasts of No Nation was composed, arranged and produced by Fela Anikulapo-Kuti. It was originally recorded at Recordisc, Lagos, with recording engineer Ignatius Ibebuike, and mixed in Paris, at Studio Plus 30, Rue De Annelets, France. Mixing engineers: Lyric Co-ordination, Uwa Erhabor; Cover painting design, Ghariokwu Lemi Arts Company, Lagos State, Nigeria. The Egypt 80 musicians are accredited as "personnel". The copyright notice for the vinyl that I possess reads as thus: "© 1989, 2014 FAK [Fela Anikulapo-Kuti] under exclusive license to Knitting Factory Records INC. All rights reserved. Unauthorised duplication is a violation of applicable laws. FELAKUTI.COM". It is significant to detail these production and licensing issues; this is because, as pronounced in Chris May's 2015 inner sleeve jacket note, *Beasts of No Nation* is a thoroughly "post-colonial" album. It states specifically "Beasts of No Nation, originally released in 1989, was an indictment of the corruption and repression in post-colonial Africa" (May 2015). It is my contention that in the aftermath of his release from imprisonment in 1986, the political praxis of Fela Anikulapo-Kuti transformed from its rooting in anticolonial, decolonialism, towards an engendered post-colonial intervention into the neocolonial public/private context of human rights in Nigeria. This chapter case studies an interview with the artist, published in *Index on Censorship* in 1989, and it does so through the use of feminist post-colonial analysis so as to account for the political effectivity of the agency, deployed by Fela Anikulapo-Kuti, in his engagement with the Western capitalistic culture industry.

Transformational Post-colonial Praxis

When listening to the album it is immediately noticeable that it is constituted by a single track that envelopes both sides of the vinyl LP. The jacket sleeve designed by Ghariokwu Limi contains a montage of images depicting Britain's political leader Margaret Thatcher, USA's Ronald Reagan and South Africa's P.W. Botha as therianthropic beast/humans, alongside which is situated a Nigerian political leader in civilian attire cravat and leopard skin hat with protruding horns derived from a species of ruminant artiodactyls. The inspiration for the album was borne from a moment in which Fela Anikulapo-Kuti was attending an Amnesty International rally in New Jersey, having been released from prison in 1986. The artist was incised by an occurrence while viewing P.W. Botha, on US television, bemoaning the uprising against apartheid. The album cover to the original 1989 edition of *Beasts of No Nation* makes reference to the episode. P.W. Botha is believed, in the television programme, to have said: "This uprising will bring out the beast in us", and this is referenced as "Pietta Botha, U.S. TV June '86". Infuriated and infused by the symbolic violence and brutal rhetoric of the invocation, Fela Anikulapo-Kuti was compelled to write and release in 1989 the album, *Beasts of No Nation*.

Further visual indications of the album's traversing of human and civil rights activism relate to the album title *Beasts of No Nation*. Its title constitutes the acronym BONN, which, it has been suggested, provides a resistant denotation to the Third Reich of Nazis Germany (May 2015). The notion that the album represents a "post-colonial" era that has superseded a pervious colonial era, is depicted at the level of the aesthetics and visual materiality of the album in respect to the album's sleeve's inclusion of characteristic tropes of decolonial praxis. For example, the images of protest placard-bearing activists wearing Black Panther berets depicted as resisting the neoliberal co-option of non-governmental organisations (NGOs) into the capitalist commodity-form. The placard provocatively reads: "Human Rights is Our Property". Collectively, the denotations of the album sleeve coalesce in the connotation of intersecting "post-colonial" forces. Reading and re-reading the album sleeve I became intrigued about: What was the "colonial" to which the cultural politics of the album is now "post"? Indeed, the sign-systems convey a multiplicity of traversing powerful connotations, impressing on the need for theoretically sophisticated definition of "post-colonial".

Bill Ashcroft's (2001) *Post-colonial Transformation* provides a critically informed exploration of the indigenous people encountering European colonial expansion during its crest in the nineteenth century. Issues pertaining to the study of anticolonial resistance and the legacy of colonialism as conditions of existence in the aftermath of the colonial occupation collectively form the focus of a post-colonial study. In this aspect of post-colonial examination, significant emphasis is placed on the conflicts and contradictions evident in "the centuries-long advance of European modernity [which] had been radically accelerated during the eruption of capital-driven, late-nineteenth-century imperialism" (ibid.: 1). Ashcroft focusses on "the huge contradiction of empire ... between the geographical expansion, designed to increase the prestige and economic or political power of the imperial nation, and its professed moral justification, its 'civilizing mission' to bring order and civilization to the barbarous hordes" (ibid.). He challenges the acclaimed restitution that the colonial occupation by European nations advanced the medical expertise and infrastructural capacities of the colonised nations. While it can be evidenced that substantial advances were achieved during the Western colonial occupation, there is little evidence to suggest that the indigenous population would not have achieved these advances through their own purposes in due course. This is to recognise the existing capabilities of the indigenous nations and in so doing appreciate that "the striking thing about colonial experience is that after colonization post-colonial societies did very often develop in ways which sometimes revealed a remarkable capacity for change and adaption" (ibid.: 2). One may discern from this that Ashcroft's definition refers in actuality to post-colonial transformations in which the exploration instigates a positive appreciation of "the resilience and adaptability of colonial societies" (ibid.). Rather than ascribe the colonised nations to have been subdued by an inherent inept passivity, a post-colonial analysis observes the manifold ways, "colonized cultures have often been so resilient and transformative that they have changed the character of imperial culture itself" (ibid.). Thus, in respect to a study of Fela Anikulapo-Kuti's promotional activities in 1989. The newly released album *Beasts of No Nation* while the "transcultural effect" of this and other aspects of his repertoire are varied and not seamless, they provoke an insistence on recognising the dynamic creative agency of populations responding to the colonial legacy within the post-colonial era. In this sense the album is part of a repertoire of praxis directed at a cultural and political engagement with the *sui generis* of power relationships operating transacting within European colonialism.

Postcolonial studies developed in the 1980s as a means to bestowal an accreditation to the wealth of the cultural productions emerging from those societies that had been previously colonised and subject to colonialism. Ashcroft plausibly argues that the genre was not initially designated as a "grand theory", but rather that it was considered to be "a methodology: first, for analysing the many strategies by which colonized societies have engaged imperial discourse; and second, for studying the ways in which many of those strategies are shared by colonized societies, re-emerging in very different political and cultural circumstances" (ibid.: 7). In order to signify its critical methodological application, Ashcroft directs us in the use of a syntax, "A simple hyphen" so as to connote value in the emphasising "strategies and practices in postcolonial reading and writing" (ibid.: 10). In this book postcolonialism (without the hyphen) refers to the tradition of postcolonial studies, and post-colonial (with the hyphen) refers to a praxis directed at disrupting colonial modernity in respect to its legacy, revisionist positivity and neocolonial reinvigoration. As Ashcroft (ibid.) expresses it,

> The spelling of the term 'post-colonial' has become more of an issue for those who use the hyphenated form, because the hyphen is a statement about the particularity, the historically and culturally grounded nature of the experience it represents. Grounded in the practice of critics concerned with the writings of colonized peoples themselves, it came to stand for a theory which was oriented towards the historical and cultural experience of colonized peoples, a concern with textual production, rather than towards the fetishization of theory itself. The hyphen in 'post-colonial' is a particular form of 'space-clearing' gesture (Appiah 1992: 241), a political notation which has a very great deal to say about the materiality of political oppression. In this respect the hyphen distinguishes the term from the kind of unlocated, abstract and post-structuralist theorizing to which Shohat and Stam object.

Writers within this genre of praxis recognise that the "post" in the hyphenated post-colonial can be simplistic in its assertion of "the situation in a society 'after colonialism'" (ibid.). Furthermore, this genre finds it difficult to escape the linear chronology of the Western epistemology within which it writes. As Ashcroft (ibid.: 11) contends,

Undoubtedly the 'post' in 'post-colonialism' must always contend with the spectre of linearity and the kind of teleological development it sets out to dismantle. But rather than being disabling, this radical instability of meaning gives the term a vibrancy, energy and plasticity which have become part of its strength, as post-colonial analysis rises to engage issues and experiences which have been out of the purview of metropolitan theory and, indeed, comes to critique the assumptions of that theory.

It is my contention that in the aftermath of his release from imprisonment the political praxis of Fela Anikulapo-Kuti transformed from its rooting in anticolonial, decolonialism, towards a post-colonial intervention into the neocolonial public/private context of human rights in Nigeria. An indication of the intersectional complexity of the "post" to which *Beasts of No Nation* is positioned necessitates a feminist epistemological critical analysis. Consequently, my research methodology explored feminist critical readings, which led me to an iconic interview with Fela Anikulapo-Kuti, conducted by the journalist and academic Jane Bryce as part of a commissioning by the left-wing journal *Index on Censorship*. Examining further the publishing outlet, it became evident that *Index on Censorship* complemented favourably with my research focus on human rights. Indeed, in 2024 *Index on Censorship* describes itself as thus:

Index on Censorship is a nonprofit that campaigns for and defends free expression worldwide. We publish work by censored writers and artists, promote debate, and monitor threats to free speech. We believe that everyone should be free to express themselves without fear or harm or persecution – no matter what their views. Index's aim is to raise awareness about threats to free expression and the value of free speech as the first step to tackling censorship. Index relies entirely on the support of donors and readers to do its work. *Index on Censorship* (2024)

First published by *Index on Censorship* in October 1989, "Animal Can't Dash Me Human Rights" is the article which principally contains transcription extracts from an interview panel, featuring Jane Bryce, that interviewed the artist Fela Anikulapo-Kuti. Having enjoyed reading the article, I decided to see whether I could interview the author so as to provide a "post-colonial" analysis of the interview itself and render it as a "post-colonial" intervention in its own right.

Thankfully, after a significant amount of communication networking, in March 2024, I received a reply from the Head of Department (HoD) of Language, Linguistic and Literature, Faculty of Humanities and Education, the University of the West Indies, Cave Hill Campus, Barbados: Dr. Korah Belgrave. I was informed that Prof. Emerita Jane Bryce would be in contact with me. Shortly after which Prof. Emerita Jane Bryce contacted me via my Goldsmiths University of London, and we agreed the terms of an interview. The hour-long interview took place on Wednesday, 13th March, 13:10hrs to 14:10hrs online using the software Microsoft Teams. Speaking with Prof. Emerita Jane Bryce was significant at several layers of relevance to my research; firstly, she had seen Fela Anikulapo-Kuti in concert at the Brixton Academy in the early 1980s, and secondly, as part of an interview panel of journalists, she questioned Fela Anikulapo-Kuti while in London several years after his release from prison. Thus, securing an interview with Prof. Emerita Jane Bryce was a tremendous scoop for my research. The following discussion explores the interview first published in print in October 1989, in the journal *Index on Censorship*. The interview along with Fela Anikulapo-Kuti's reasons for participating is considered as a "post-colonial event" directed at interrupting, via communicative action, the portrayal of the Nigerian regime as proportionate in its policing of anti-neocolonial demonstration. The account commences with a redefinition of the interview as a "post-colonial encounter". Whereby, Louis Althusser's (1971a) conception of Ideological State Apparatus (ISA) in conjunction with the concept of "interpellation" is counterposed with Bill Ashcroft's (2001) notion of "interpolation" so as to describe the making of a "post-colonial event" and explore its impact in disrupting neocolonial ideology. The discussion progresses onto a review of Jane Bryce's (2022) initial interview as a "post-colonial" challenge to the cultural-economy of neocolonial economics and then concludes with a reconceptualisation of the chronology of the "post-colonial" and an appraisal of its transformative impact. A continuous thread that weaves through these three sections of discussion is my March 2024 interview with Prof. Emerita Jane Bryce.

Post-colonial Feminist Refracted Beginnings

On Tuesday, 12th March 2024, 17:10hrs, I was delighted to have received a confirmation reply to my request to interview Prof. Emerita Jane Bryce. The response I received was itself a fascinating artefact in its reflexivity and meditation on our negotiated reciprocity of perspective in the joint-construction of the interview. The email I received immediately prior to the 13th March 2024 interview read as follows:

> *OK Pam, I'll be there. I like the direction of your research and will of course do anything I can to help. But I think I should disabuse you re 'influence on the artist's work in regards to human rights and social justice' - unless you meant to write influence of? Because the interview certainly would not have influenced Fela in any way! Apart from this, I'm sure we can have a productive chat. Till tomorrow, Jane [Bryce].* Prof. Emerita Jane Bryce (Email correspondence: March 2024)

The email is emblematic of the refracted beginnings that arise as a consequence of the "theoretical sensitivity" (Strauss and Corbin 1990) of a grounded theory methodological approach in its subtleties of empirical meaning making. Periodically stepping back, and pausing for the reconsideration of the interview's thematic properties is an integral component of the refracted beginnings of the interview. In the weeks and months prior to my correspondence with Prof. Emerita Jane Bryce inductively and deductively generate data had been painstakingly processed through the matrix of grounded theory coding to elicit general categories of data (open coding); consider the dimensions and characteristic of categories of open-coded data (axial coding); and examine the emerging thematic networks of data (selective coding) so as to develop tentative assumptions that are basis for the "theoretical sampling" of ongoing cases/individuals. I came across the 1989 interview featuring Jane Bryce while data analysing material derived from journalist interviews in the music press. Linking categories of data at the dimensional level (axial coding) was highlighting patterns of standardisation in the journalism of the music press that distinguished at a higher level of complexity, Jane Bryce's interview that was originally published in *Index on Censorship*. The more I studied the bibliographic archiving of the interview, the more intrigued and appreciative I became about the prestige ascribed to the article; for it was re-published in April 2022 as part of the "Special report 50 Years of Index on Censorship; 1982-1991". Moving between inductive and deductive thinking in the iterative process of inference and verifying patterns of relationships that exist within the data confirmed the distinct value of the interview. As I mentioned to Jane Bryce, when at the start of our interview, I asked for an account of the background that led to the original interview, to which she responded intriguingly.

Interviewee [Prof Emerita Jane Bryce]   *Well to be honest with you I don't remember exactly where it took place. I think the recording studio. And it was a group interview. So, the questions were coming from the group. And I don't remember who else was there. The reason why I was included, which presumably because I had recently returned from Nigeria where I had been living. This was 1990 I came back from Nigeria in 1988; and I was a freelance journalist. So, anything Nigerian I was writing about. That's the basic background. Why Fela, would have been given a group interview and why Index on Censorship would have been interested in featuring him, is because by that time he was a major star. Everybody knew about him he was notorious. He performed, the first time I ever saw him he was in Brixton so you know he had been coming to England and performing for several years by the time. And yeah, he was very popular. But of course, his notoriety arose largely from his political taunting of the regime and his outspokenness and the fact that he had been in jail.*

Interviewer [Pamela Odih]   *You just mentioned that you saw him in Brixton. Could you tell me a bit more about that; that's really fascinating*

Interviewee   *Well before I went to Nigeria. I went in very early 1983. I had been hearing about Fela; it must have been 1982? He came to England to do concerts and one of them was at Brixton? What was the venue had been called then? I don't remember that either, this was all so long ago. And anyhow, I went along to the concert. I can't say I enjoyed it a lot. I hadn't really been exposed to the music very much at that time. I didn't understand its local significance. And I found his macho posturing very off-putting. But it was when I then started to go to the Shrine in Lagos and seeing how he interacted with a local audience, that is when I really understood Fela's significance. And by that time I understood Pidgin so I could follow the to – and – fro of the dialogue and so on. I very much fell in love with the music. Yeah.*

Interviewer	*I think that the venue you might have gone to was the Brixton Academy? ['Yeah it must have been the Academy'].* *And what was the atmosphere like? What was it like in the Brixton Academy? I know the outside of the venue but I am not familiar with the interior. ['You've never been to a concert there?']. Not, no I just know the outside.*
Interviewee	*Right. Well, it was like a lot of places in those days. A bit grungy. Very crowded; everyone was standing. I don't remember there being any seating at all. A very excited electric atmosphere and a lot of noise; a lot of drinking. Yeah, it was that kind of venue.*
Interviewer	*And how was the crowd being managed?*
Interviewee	*I don't remember the crowd being managed at all. The crowd was managed from the stage by Fela himself. There just weren't the same safety procedures in place in those days as there are now. The whole thing was very unpoliced.*
Interviewer	*How did Fela manage the crowd then? It would have been a packed venue. How did he manage the crowd?*
Interviewee	*Not in any obvious way. He wasn't telling anybody what to do. Just by shear charisma. By the fact that everybody was watching him; everybody had gone there. For him. Everybody knew his music. So it was; I suppose a sort of collective agreement that we were all there for that purpose.*
Interviewer	*And what was definitive about his music around that time? I think we're are at 1983, 82? Was it a Nigerian crowd?*
Interviewee	*It was very much a mixture. I would say. Being Brixton there would be a lot of Nigerians, but Black British people there and erm. But a lot of white fans as well. Erm, I think a thing about the music was; well, you've been studying Fela so you know. But erm the way he was fusing funk and jazz and his use of instruments and dancing. And the whole sort of package: the Fela package. Which was very exciting, very electric. And very different from anything most of us had seen before. Certainly, it was different from anything I had seen before.* Prof. Emerita Jane Bryce (Semi-structured interview: March 2024)

Recognising post-colonial studies to involve examinations into the early history of colonisation, through to resistance by indigenous people to colonialism and then a critically informed exploration into the condition "post" the dismantling of colonial structures, the interview commissioned by *Index on Censorship* is emblematic of a post-colonial event. My reasoning is indebted to Bill Ashcroft's (2001) *Post-colonial Transformation* and the conception therein of "interpolation", which in itself is a direct challenge to Althusser's (1971a) conception of "interpellation". But ultimately, my thinking is indebted to Herbert Marcuse's conception of "introjection". Whereby, in *One Dimensional Man*, Marcuse (1964) identifies how in advanced capitalist societies the pervasive spread of a technological rationality that is adjusted to operate in accordance with the apparatus of capitalist accumulation is undermining the critical distance enabled by "introjection". The introjecting reflection of the inner-self in terms of its difference from the outer-world is a "two-dimensional" process because the inner is different from the external world. So, the inner-dimension transposes the external world and in so doing realises discontinuities which it seeks to resolve. The inner-self which is the human's unique dimension and trajectory in the world, Marcuse argues that it is becoming increasingly, and he uses the concept of "whittled down" (ibid.: 13), to say that it is less original in terms of providing a unique sense of experience. The inner-self in terms of reflecting the external world is transforming its ability to be a force that is separate from the external world. This is happening because that inner experience has become increasingly subject to the scrutiny, investigation and examination of sciences that have claimed to know the inner-self. Such that, this private space is becoming so invaded by scientific forces that claim to know the inner-self; the influence of these sciences is now so powerful, for example psychology; and scientific management is so influential that collectively these sciences are presenting such a formidable truth to which we have become vulnerable to its exploits. Consequently, and in so far as the culture industry is pervaded by attacks on the two-dimensionality of introjection, it is a site of the perpetuation of one-dimensional thought. The products and processes of the industry in so far as they are pervaded by technological rationality are programmatically disinclined towards alternative ways of structuring their manufacture, other than in terms of one-dimensional society.

226 P. ODIH

Post-colonial Feminist Critical Theory: Beyond "One Dimensional Man"

One might have discerned the supposition I am building concerning the orchestration of the interview panel in which Jane Bryce participated so as to publish in *Index on Censorship* extracts of questions posed to Fela Anikulapo-Kuti. In Marcuse's construct of "one-dimensional society" and "one-dimension thought", the case studied interview event can be interpreted as a product and process of a music culture industry, which has become pervaded by the technological rationality of scientific management and advertising psychological modelling of the music artist. Enfolded into the capitalist ideology of the one-dimensional culture industry, the interview event and its participants might be conceived as objectified within the limited parameters of one-dimensional thought. A situation in which the thought sciences have become so powerful to the culture industry's scientific management that it is presenting a bewildering truth about knowing the inner-self of the industry's culture and society. A truth that we as participants in the culture industry have become vulnerable to in terms of how we then read our inner-self and so that inner-self that should be unique, creatively autonomous and very different from the external world is starting to become more and more the same as this world. As a consequence of the way in which the mind sciences have actually sort to know the inner-self give it a name ("1989 Interview"), give it a label ("Interview by Jane Bryce for Index on Censorship"), give it a category ("Special Report 50 Years of Index on Censorship"). But of these naming and categorising processes are all part of the colonising of the inner-self by the outer-world of the capitalist consumer society. Whereby, "The manifold processes of introjection seem to be ossified in almost mechanical reactions. The result is, not adjustment but mimesis: an immediate identification of the individual with his society and, through it, with the society as a whole" (Marcuse 1964/2002: 12). Thus, and in summary, if one were to apply Marcuse's critical theory to the interview and conceive it as a one-dimensional event contrived to further inculcate a one-dimensional thought within the music industry, then to participate in the event is to acquiesce to its colonising capitalistic subjectivity. While this conclusion might be plausibly applied by an outsider to the event, having spoken with Prof. Emerita Jane Bryce, it is clear the application of *One Dimensional Man* to the interview published in *Index on Censorship* might be too limited and misconceived. The contention here is the limitation in Marcuse's

7 POST-COLONIAL FEMINIST, INTERPOLATION   227

prevision of a technological rationality provides limited scope to conceive of the independent agency of the autonomous subject. Other than the invitation to provide a journalistic interview piece for *Index on Censorship*, why was Jane Bryce motivated to participate in the interview panel for the *Index on Censorship* article? Was she *hailed*? In this respect consider the following extract from my interview with Prof. Emerita Jane Bryce conducted on 13th March 2024, in which she speaks about her experience of visiting Fela Anikulapo-Kuti's club in Lagos Nigeria called the Afrika Shrine.

Interviewer **[Pamela Odih]**	*You said you have been to the Shrine, that's amazing. You said you have been to the Shrine in Lagos is it; where was the Shrine?*
Interviewee **[Prof Emerita** **Jane Bryce]**	*The Shrine was Fela's club in Lagos. In Ikeja, Lagos. And erm, yes I used to go, I used to go a lot. I was based, in Ife, which is 100 miles from Lagos. But I would go to Lagos for fun, to have fun and the Shrine would be the place I would go and erm it is a memory that I treasure.*
Interviewer	*What was what was distinct about it? Yeah, yeah. Could you tell me about the shrine? That's actually quite interesting about the space, just how it was being.*
Interviewee	*Well yeah. You arrive on the street; but because the Shrine is on the street there are lots of people selling stuff all up and down. And outside the Shrine itself there's a table selling the most enormous [contraband] that you have ever seen … And erm you'd go inside the Shrine and it is basically just this shed like space. Absolutely without thrills of any kind. It had kind of battered metal chairs. But also, a big space for dancing up in front. And the toilets were at the back. And as the evening wore on, they became more and more disgusting. You know there would be stream of urine running across the floor that you would have to step over. So, the place smelt. It was not in any way refined. But you'd go there.* *You know you'd get there may be about 10:00, o'clock and gradually the band would start to play in a desultorily sort of way. And it would play for an hour or so. Completely by itself, without Fela, and then suddenly there'd be this change in the atmosphere and Fela would*

storm down the central aisle and he would just take the stage and he would start, you know, blowing his saxophone or playing the keyboard, or he would just start singing. Or he would start his Yabbis as he called them, which was the dialogue with the audience, and the place would just wake up. And it was like electricity had struck. And then he would play, and yeah, the Queen's would dance. I remember at one time he had them in a cage over the stage, but generally they would just be along the front of the stage. And it would go on until 2:00 in the morning, and then you would have to find your way back across Lagos hoping that the armed robbers didn't get you. It was an exciting time.

Interviewer And then so you mentioned the Queens, OK, could you tell me about how, what were your views about how they were being represented? What were your views? It's quite significant. Yeah. Yeah.

Interviewee I was a young woman. I was a young feminist. I was in Nigeria to research a PhD on Nigerian women's writing. So, I was very much attuned to or sort of sensitive to sexism of any kind, and obviously Fela was completely, unabashedly sexist. He was, you know, a macho patriarch. And I suppose to a young British woman, the way the Queens were represented. Well, they represented themselves. I found it very shocking at first. But I also, you know, I was in Nigeria long enough. I was there for five years. I was there long enough to understand that bringing those kind of attitudes was actually unhelpful. It was unproductive because a lot of those women were working class. Well, they were all pretty much working class apart from, you know, the. The one he 'married' that in the US. Was obviously not. She was. She was an activist. But the young Nigerian women who used to join his, his compound The Republic, as he called it: Were often running away from home. They were running away from all sorts of things like forced marriage or whatever it was, and they would find a place that Fela's Republic and they would become one of his dancers. And I do not believe that they felt exploited. I don't believe that they were put upon. I believe that it was a structure within which they had a *function and they were dancing for one of the most famous musicians, probably at that time the most famous musician in Nigeria and in Africa. And you know, a world figure. So, sexism was just part of his schtick. He was he was; he was the king. There was no doubt about that. So that's my answer.* Prof. Emerita Jane Bryce (Semi-structured interview: March 2024)

In the above transcription extract Prof. Emerita Jane Bryce speaks incisively about the accusations of sexism and sexual exploitation that were directed at Fela Anikulapo-Kuti. She provides insights into the ambiguities and contradictions incurred as a feminist drawn towards the artist's music venues and its resounding Afrobeat. Indications of self-questioning and internal dilemma in having to reconcile feminist ethics with Fela Anikulapo-Kuti's Western African patriarchy reverberate throughout my interview with her. Reading through the *Index on Censorship* interview article, I can perceive more prominently these tensions, contradictions and dilemma as having provided a steer to the questions posed to Fela Anikulapo-Kuti. Such complexity of predicament exceeds Marcuse's conceptual architecture of introjection. Whereby, the application of Marcuse's notion of mimesis as a result of the ossification of introjection into that of the culture industry in my opinion inadequately abridges the fluctuating complex reconciliation of feminist ideals that appears to have taken place in regard to the Jane Bryce interview that formed the basis of the *Index on Censorship* case studied article. As illustrated in the following extract of my interview in which is revealed insights into the intersectional negotiations of class and economy relevant to defining gender differences in the creative industries of 1980s Nigeria:

Interviewer [Pamela Odih]	*You mentioned in respect to your academic profile and career that there has been a focus on Nigerian women writers among your portfolio of work. It is often referred to in respect to his mother as being a significant political force in terms of his work. I wondered what are your views about the influence of Funmilayo [Ransome-Kuti]?*
Interviewee [Prof Emerita Jane Bryce]	*Well, I never met her I wish I had. You know she was one of the; I met women like her. Because one of the things I was doing in my research and also, I was a freelance journalist in Nigeria. So, I did a lot of interviewing of*

very outspoken very strong forging careers for themselves mostly in journalism. But in other areas too. She was extraordinary because she. Extraordinary is the wrong word. What I am trying to say is that she comes from a background where women stand up and speak for themselves. But of course, she was educated. And that was the great thing about her. That she could lead the women who were less educated and she did that in Abeokuta in starting to lead literacy groups and that kind of thing. And became this very dynamic political force. And Fela revered her.

Interviewer And one of things that I have notices is that she [Funmilayo Ransome-Kuti] has quite a significant profile now in the culture industry. I wonder what are your views about how she is being represented in the culture industry? In the Nigerian culture industry and the products and process of mass popular culture in Nigeria. There's quite an industry around here isn't there? … There were a series of high profile concerts, that seem to now tell a narrative her which I think is obviously very significant. But I am interested how, for example there was a sort of concert called Fela, which toured and etc., And I wondered the extent to which she has become almost like a folk idol. And the extent to which we are seeking a sort of not a mythology but a set of narratives are being woven around who she is and what she represented.

Interviewee You are talking about the musical, Fela the musical? [interviewer: Yeah! That's it, that's it. Fela the musical]. Yeah. She was given a very high profile. I think that maybe that's the politics of today finds that necessary because it's very much otherwise; Fela's story is very much that of, you know the male star. And perhaps we find it necessary to introduce another way; or to find another way of looking at him. But at the same time, she was very significant. And as I said her did revere her which was one of those contradictions. One of those interesting contradictions about Fela. That he could have all these women at his beck and call; and not think anything of it. And have them shaking their arses on the stage and all

                                            *the rest of it. But he also had this tremendous respect for
                                            his mother. That part is not mythological in any sense.
                                            But yet she probably has; is in the process of being mytholo-
                                            gised. Partly in her own right; but partly because she pro-
                                            duced such a remarkable son. And not just him but his
                                            elder brother was a doctor and ended up working for the
                                            UN [United Nations]. So, they were a remarkable fam-
                                            ily. They were one of those pre-independence families who
                                            really sort of shaped the future of Nigeria. So, it's a way
                                            of linking him back to an earlier time.*

Interviewer   *Linking him back to an earlier time? That earlier time
                    would be defined as?*

Interviewee   *To the colonial era and the beginnings of resistance to
                    colonialism. And the formation of the kind of politics
                    that would emerge after independence. So, he comes from
                    a tradition of resistance within his own family I would
                    say. And that is probably what; what appeals to people
                    now.* Prof. Emerita Jane Bryce (Semi-structured inter-
                    view: March 2024)

The conflicts Prof. Emerita Jane Bryce conveys about having to negotiate her feminist values so as to interview Fela Anikulapo-Kuti are reminiscent of the contradictions I encounter with feminist's that apply uncritically
the writings of Louis Althusser. With this caveat in mind, the following
discussion examines the relevance of the concept of the "interpellation" of
the individual into becoming a subject so as to formulate a theoretical
basis of Jane Bryce's interview with Fela Anikulapo-Kuti as an iconic post-
colonial encounter.

Post-colonial Feminist Subjectivity: Interpellation and Ideological State Apparatuses

Althusser's (1971b/2014) account of communication media and "The
Ideological State Apparatuses" has potential of framing the products and
processes of mass popular culture and its music industry as integral to the
reproduction of the relations of capitalist production. Althusser advances
a formulation of capitalism that is distinct in regard to its negation of the
Classical Marxist primacy of materiality as the prescience for the class

struggle between the alienated proletariat and owners of the means of production. This is because Althusser recentralises the role of State in positioning its purpose into the terrain of political practice. The resulting theory of the State distinguishes "between state power (and those who hold it) and state apparatus", and also an additional reality that exists alongside the Repressive State Apparatus (RSA) "but is not conflated with it" (ibid.: 75). Althusser coined the latter as Ideological State Apparatuses (ISAs) and argues convincingly for the incorporation into Marxist dialectical materialism the relevance of ideological struggles cascading from the specialised institutions of the State, that, in co-ordination by the State, operate as apparatuses of reproduction of the relations of capitalist production. In *Ideology and Ideological State Apparatuses*, Althusser states that Repressive State Apparatuses such as the police courts and prisons exist at the limits of "non-physical violence" and the use of "physical violence". They are brought to the forefront when the ISAs' operation of ideological conditioning and repressive is proving to be ineffectual. Within his provisional list of ISAs is included "the Publishing and Distribution Apparatus" (ibid.). As with all ISAs the latter has institutions and organisations that correspond with every level of its operation. In this regard, the *Index on Censorship* organisation dovetails with the agencies and agents involved in the production of communication.

Althusser (1971a) elsewhere also uses the term Communications ISA to refer to an ideologically manufactured cultured industry, whose various organisations constitute a system that mirrors the operational constitution of other ISAs. Whereby, for example, "the communications ISA (press, radio and television, etc.)" is distinction from the Repressive State Apparatus whereby the former is not as with the latter belonging "entirely to the public domain" (ibid.: 144). The Communications ISA is part of the "private domain" just as "Churches, Parties, Trade Unions, families, some schools, most newspapers, cultural ventures, etc., are private" (ibid.). Communications ISA is observationally operational in the public domain; thus, the distinction between the private and public sphere refers to the realm of ideality. But this is not to assume an absence of materiality; for example, the case studied interview published in *Index on Censorship* has objective materiality as a published artefact available in print and electronic form. Material relations enacted and embodied the interview event. Thus, the operation of the Ideological State Apparatuses has formidable material reality, as Althusser (1971b/2014) expresses it: "each ISA, although defined as ideological, is [sic] not reducible to the existence 'of ideas' without a concrete material support. I mean by this not only that the ideology of each ISA is realized in material institutions and material practices, that is clear. I mean something else: that these material practices are 'anchored' in non-ideological realities". Take, for example, the culture industry as part of the Communications ISAs, while embedded in material transactional relations it is also anchored by the creative productions of real human subjects. Althusser surmises these features as characteristic of all ISAs, described as thus:

> **An Ideological State Apparatus is a system of defined institutions, organizations, and the corresponding practices. Realized in the institutions, organizations, and practices of this system is all or part (generally speaking, a typical combination of certain elements) of the State Ideology. The ideology realized in an ISA ensures its systemic unity on the basis of an 'anchoring' in material functions specific to each ISA; these functions are not reducible to that ideology, but serve it as a 'support'. Althusser (1971b/2014: 77)**

In respect to the regulation of subjects in and through the Communications ISA, it is necessary to distinguish Repressive State Apparatus from ISAs. Whereby, the former functions partly through ideology but predominantly through the imposition of violence, and this is the converse of ISAs because they "function massively and predominantly by ideology, but they also function secondarily by repression, even if ultimately, but only ultimately, this is very attenuated and concealed, even symbolic. (There is no such thing as a purely ideological apparatus)" (Althusser 1971a: 145). When referring to the culture industry's Communications ISA function, the notion of violence can be the threat of discipline, exclusion for the breach of its codes of practice, punishment for licencing infringement, state censorship, etc. Furthermore, given that the role of the ISA is to reproduce the relations of capitalist production, its power composition mirrors the existing structured inequalities consequent of the power of the ruling class; "insofar as it is ultimately the ruling ideology which is realized in the Ideological State Apparatuses" (ibid.: 146). Accepting this it is also self-evident that ruling class can sustain its position of superiority without securing hegemony over the State Ideological Apparatuses. Returning, in my thoughts, to the case studied interview with Fela Anikulapo-Kuti, the Communications ISA in which the culture industry operates is a prime target for the ruling class' pursuit of hegemony. For it, as all ISAs, is directed by the State's role in the reproduction of ruling class ideology with the Communications ISA achieving this, "by cramming every 'citizen' with daily doses of nationalism, chauvinism, liberalism, moralism, etc, by means of the press, the radio and television" (ibid.: 154). But one and the same time, it is because this ISA communicates ideas, symbolism and discursive interaction, the securing of ruling class hegemony is not permanent stable and everywhere guaranteed. Its basis in communicative self-expression makes the Communications ISA a site for contestation and resistance, which places in constant jeopardy its pursuits of hegemony. As Althusser (1971a: 147) explains,

> **The class (or class alliance) in power cannot lay down the law in the ISAs as easily as it can in the (repressive) State apparatus, not only because the former ruling classes are able to retain strong positions there for a long time, but also because the resistance of the exploited classes is able to find means and occasions to express itself there, either by the utilization of their contradictions, or by conquering combat positions in them in struggle.**

In summary, just as Althusser's theory of Ideological State Apparatus leads him back to Classical Marxist conjecture on the superstructure and therein the State, so it is that my application of this to the culture industry leads me to consider the necessity "to distinguish between State power (and its possession by …) on the one hand, and State Apparatus on the other" (ibid.). Althusser contends that the State apparatus is constituted by two entities: "the body of institutions which represent the Repressive State Apparatus on the one hand, and the body of institutions which represent the body of ideological State Apparatuses on the other" (ibid.: 148). It is important to recognise that Althusser contends that the Ideological State Apparatuses are not mostly repressive in their function, but rather they are predominantly ideological, and this is both a site of contestation and reproduction of the relations of production. Consequently, if I am to apply Althusser's notion of Communications ISA to describe the function of the case studied culture industry interview of Fela Anikulapo-Kuti, it is necessary to theorise subjectivity and the subconscious human identity as a function of ideology.

In Althusser's (1971b/2014) formulation of the concept of "interpellation", one can advance forward a critical account of Marcuse's one-dimensional thought, and in so doing develop a theory of how the ruling class subdues the revolutionary potential of an oppositional thinking Communications ISA. This is partly because the concept of "interpellation" recognises that "there is no ideology except by the subject and for subjects" (ibid.: 188). Axiomatic to this conjecture is the supposition: "there is no ideology except for concrete subjects (such as you and me), and this destination for ideology is only made possible by the subject: in other words, by the category of the subject and its functioning" (ibid.). The assemblage of the subject is basic to all ideology; at the same time, we need to forthwith adjoin "that the category of the subject is constitutive of every ideology only insofar as every ideology has the function (which defines it) of 'constituting' concrete subjects (such as you and me)" (ibid.). Althusser quotes St Paul's *Logos* and the pertinent truism that we live our humanity and experiential being in ideology. Such platitudes provoke a hackneyed reaction of disclaim in their inconceivable remarkability. Althusser describes this antiphon as part of *recognition* the first of the two basic functions of ideology, the second being *misrecognition*. One may discern the proposition being tentatively proffered is the extent to which the interview with Fela Anikulapo-Kuti, which was published in *Index on Censorship*, was an instance of "ideological recognition". Althusser presents the concept of "ideological recognition" in respect to a broader premise: "all ideology hails or interpellates concrete individuals as concrete subjects, through the functioning of the category of the subject" (ibid.: 190). Such an assertion presents a bifurcation situating individuals as distinct from the category of the concrete subject. Althusser counteracts this direction of drift by stating that "there is no concrete subject that does not have a concrete individual as its support". Indeed, it is demonstrably the case that "ideology 'acts' or 'functions' in such a way as to 'recruit' subjects among individuals (it recruits them all) or 'transforms' individuals into subjects (it transforms them all) through the very precise operation that we call *interpellation or hailing*" (ibid.). Althusser states clearly that he premises interpellation on the empirical occurrence of the everyday situation of a hailing "by (or not by) the police: 'Hey, you there!'". Whereby, two strangers are at this time/space connected through one hailing "Hey, you there!" and the other responding. Althusser registers as a response, the other stranger turning around or gesturing an acknowledgement of receipt of the hail. The intriguing feature here is as to why in a crowd of individuals two strangers connect in terms of a recognition to the hail. As is described as thus,

236   P. ODIH

> If, to offer readers the most concrete sort of concreteness, we suppose that the theoretical scene we are imagining happens in the street, the hailed individual turns around. With this simple 180-degree physical conversion, he becomes a *subject*. Why? Because he has recognized that the hail 'really' was addressed to him and that 'it really was he who was hailed' (not someone else). Experience shows that the practical tele-communications of hailing are such that hailing hardly ever misses its mark: verbal call or whistle, the one hailed always recognizes that he really was the one hailed. Althusser (1971b/**2014: 191**)

The inclusion in Althusser's description of the instigator of the hail, "Hey, you there!", as a police constable, provides some circumstantial basis as to why the recipient of the hail responds in a street scene to the hail. This is because individuals become subjects when they actively involve their self and subjectivity in the ritualistic norms and practices of law enforcement. It is notable that Althusser discounts the response to the hail as having basis in the assumption of guilt. As he expresses it,

> This is a strange phenomenon, after all, one that cannot be explained by 'guilt feelings' alone, despite the large numbers of people with 'something on their consciences'. Or is it that everyone always has something on his conscience and that everyone confusedly feels, at least, that he always has accounts to render or obligations to respect – if only the obligation to respond to every hailing? Strange. Althusser (1971b/**2014: 191**)

Given the a-prior acculturation of those within the street scene to the expectations, normative codes, legal rights and moral obligations assumed of people present in the semi-public space, it is plausible that everyone within the scene harbours an anticipation of the possibility of themselves being the subject of a hail. Consequently, at the moment of responding to the hail, the individual is recognising their pre-existing acculturation and anticipation to be its subject. Some illustration of the complexity of the concept of the hail is evident in the following extract from my interview with Jane Bryce's about her interview with Fela Anikulapo-Kuti, published in 1989 in the journal *Index on Censorship*.

Interviewer	*If we think about his work as communicative action. If we*
[Pamela Odih]	*think about the style of his; the way he communicated within the interview. What are you views about the way that he used language? Because he is known for using Pidgin in his lyrics but in the interview, its, Standard English that he is using.*
Interviewee	*Absolutely. Yeah, I was thinking about that when I re-*
[Prof Emerita	*read it yesterday. Fela was a very clever person. You know*
Jane Bryce]	*as I say. He came from an educated family which means he is a member of the elite. There is nothing working class his background. He was highly educated. You know all this. You know that he was sent to London to study music, and all the rest of it. He was extremely articulate. And it comes through in that interview. He was talking to a bunch of British journalists and he spoke the Queen's English. And he could communicate very effectively. But at different levels.* Prof. Emerita Jane Bryce (Semi-structured interview: March 2024)

Jane Bryce in the above extract describes the artist Fela Anikulapo-Kuti as using a simplified form of English language known as Pidgin, which she infers was consciously used when addressing local audience. The suggestion is that Pidgin English has its roots in West African British colonialism and that it was prominent in the interpellation of individuals into subjects of British colonialism. It is also inferred in the interview extract that the artist purposefully utilised Pidgin as a mode of resistance to standard English lingua franca of post-independence Nigeria. Accepting this contention places one at odds with a model of the hail which positions its actors in a linear chronological response. In some anticipation of this critique, Althusser introduces a level of complexity to accommodate the notion of a multi-directionality of hail/response.

Complexity is added to the mix in respect to Althusser recognising that the hail and response can be concurrent, simultaneously, and/or in a reverse succession whereby the response (e.g. turning around) prompts a hail. So as to reconcile these situations as neither anomaly nor misrecognition, it is Althusser's (1971b/2014) reasoning that "the existence of ideology and the hailing or interpellation of individuals as subjects are one and the same thing" (ibid.: 191). Thus, it is surmised that "ideology hails or interpellates individuals as subjects" (ibid.). If it is accepted that ideology is all enveloping, it is plausible to contend that the formation of the individual outside of ideology is in actuality happening within ideology. As it is explained in the following statement: "What really happens in ideology thus seems to happen outside it. That is why those who are in ideology, you and I, believe that they are by definition outside ideology: one of the effects of ideology is the practical denegation of the ideological character of ideology" (ibid.). Ideology never decries its existence; it never proclaims, "I am ideological". In so far as the individual is always already a subject within ideology. Consequently, it is conceivable that "ideologies never stop interpellating subjects as subjects, never stop 'recruiting' individuals who are always-already subjects" (ibid.: 193).

Althusser provides a pertinent example of interpellation in respect to Christian religious ideology, and this has application to my research enquiry into the ideological circumstances which *hailed* Fela Anikulapo-Kuti and Jane Bryce into the interview event that was published by *Index on Censorship*. The connection I am attempting to formulate in applying Althusser's conception relates to the Afrika Shrine nightclub, in Lagos Nigeria. In Althusser's conception of Christian religious ideology, the interpellation of the individual as a subject is premised on the ultimate Subject that is its deity and God. My equivalence here is the religious iconography ascribed to the Shrine nightclub. In 1972, the Fela Anikulapo-Kuti transferred his ensemble to a more capacious venue, situated in the courtyard of the Empire Hotel in Surulere, Lagos (FelaKuti.com 2024). Previously, a popular nightspot, but with the decline in the attractiveness of highlife, the music venue had fallen into disrepair. The artist renames it the Afrika Shrine and inspirits its revival. It becomes a vibrant destination in its rebranded theming of feature dance club and progressive cultural political salon patronised by the "Lagos demi-monde" alongside prominent African and American cultural figures (ibid.). This is a vibrant era in the artist's profiling of the female contribution to his music ensemble. It is noted that the artist adds six additional female singers to his band Africa 70. The vocal contribution enhances the call and response echoes of traditional Yoruba native music, which consolidates as an Afrobeat signature. It is around this time that the artist releases three impressive proto-Afrobeat albums with his band Africa 70, using his name as Fela Ransome-Kuti. These albums feature highly sexually provocative images of female on the album jacket sleeve: *Open & Close* (1971); *Afrodisiac* (1972/1973); *Shakara* (1972). His critics seize on these sexualised images to disparage the reputation of the artist's Afrika Shrine. In riposte a counter-narrative depicts the Afrika Shrine as having been modelled originally on the Mbari Artists and Writers Club in the university city of Ibadan (ibid.). The Mbari Artists and Writers Club was established in 1961, a year after Nigeria had achieved its independence from British colonial rule.

The eminent novelist Wole Soyinka (cousin to Fela) had co-founded the Mbari and cultivated it as a space for young people to gather in discussion and optimistic reverie about Nigeria's post-colonial future. Fela Anikulapo-Kuti also envisioned his venue Afrika Shrine "as a performance space and progressively minded salon" (ibid.). To this philosophy was added a "community hub" focus, "dedicated to improving the lives of the 'sufferheads'", which was the name he ascribed to the struggling "downtrodden, urban poor" who were often the inspiration and political motivation for his music (ibid.). In these aspects, of the Afrika Shrine, can be elicited features that appear pertinent to Althusser's conception of the interpellation of religious ideology. Whereby, the Afrika Shrine can be observed as an iconographical destination of pilgrimage for the forlorn and destitute, which invited them as individuals and interpellated them as subjects into the community's spiritual orthodoxy. Such a proposition appears to be supported by accounts of Fela Anikulapo-Kuti's outreach to destitute individual in the local community, welcoming them as subjects into the Afrika Shrine. According to Fela.Kuti.Com (2024), "Every year, Fela took dozens of young Lagosians off the streets and gave them a new start in life with jobs and responsibilities at the Shrine". Parallels emerge when one aligns the outreach of the Afrika Shrine with Althusser's idea of the interpellation of religious ideology in its address to individuals, in order to transform the individual into a subject "free to obey or disobey the call, that is, God's commands" (Althusser 1971b/2014: 195). In Christian religious ideology, the multiplicity of individuals interpellated as religious subject is only conceivable, "on the absolute condition that there is a Unique, Absolute *Other Subject*, namely, God". So as to differentiate the Christian religious deity and divine being to which the individual is hailed into becoming its subject, Althusser introduces the syntax of the capital "S". It is my supposition that just as the interpellation into religious ideology presupposes an idol, so it is that the interpellation into the ideology of Afrika Shrine presupposes the existence of a unique absolute Subject, Fela Anikulapo-Kuti. Some indication of this supposition is inferred in the following description of the chains of benevolence that threaded through the interpellation of individuals to become subjects of the philosophy of the Afrika Shrine: "literally hundreds of families living nearby depended on the club for their livelihoods, directly or indirectly. The Shrine was also active in local health and education initiatives" (FelaKuti.com 2024).

The Shrine remained the retreat for Fela Anikulapo-Kuti until his death in 1997. Thereafter, the venue fell into disarray, with neither restoration nor rebuilding possible due to the lease on the land ending at the point of the artist's death. Parallels exist here with Althusser's (1971b/2014: 196) conception of "the admirable necessity for the duplication of the Subject into subjects and of the Subject itself into a Subject-subject". In 2000, the New Afrika Shrine was built by the artist's family, with the project managed by his eldest daughter Yeni and eldest son Femi. The financing for relocating the venue and the building of the new Afrika Shrine was derived from a substantial proportion of the income gained from the licensing of their father's back catalogue. Parallels can be discerned here with the notion articulated by Althusser (ibid.) of the "mirror-structure". Whereby the New Afrika Shrine can be considered as a mirror of the structure of the original Shrine's ideology, engaged in interpellating individuals as subjects in the name of the absolute deity Fela Anikulapo-Kuti. According to Althusser, this means that ideology is centrifugal in its placing at the centre the Absolute Subject which then "interpellates around it the infinity of individuals as subjects in a double speculary relation such that it subjects the subjects to the Subject" (ibid.). Significantly, the New Afrika Shrine is noted to follow a similar philanthropic ideology as the original venue. Whereby, it can be free to enter the venue, with public access being granted most hours of the day, interpellating "locals and overseas visitors, rich and poor, black and white" (FelaKuti.com 2024).

Returning to the interview of Fela Anikulapo-Kuti, which was published in *Index to Censorship*, bringing together the afore discussion, an Althusserian proposition might that the interview panel—among whom was the feminist Jane Bryce—were invited to the event as individuals and interpellated as subjects of the Absolute Subject Fela Anikulapo-Kuti. The case studied *Index to Censorship* piece might be alternatively construed as per Althusser's "duplicate mirror-structure". In so doing, the latter at one and the same time ensures that: "(1) the interpellation of individuals as subjects; (2) the mutual recognition between subjects and Subject and among the subjects themselves, as well as the recognition of the subject by himself; (3) the absolute guarantee that everything really is so" (Althusser 1971b/2014: 197). According to Althusser, the culmination of these three-triple system of subjectification is that "the subjects 'go': they recognise that 'it's really true', that 'this is the way it is', not some other way, that they have to obey God, the priest, De Gaulle, the boss, the engineer, and love their neighbour, and so on. The subjects go, since they have recognised that 'all is well' (the way it is), and they say, for good measure: *So be it*!" (ibid.).

Althusser's conception of interpellation provides some pertinent insights in respect to explaining why the interview panel with Fela Anikulapo-Kuti, in which Jane Bryce participated, was enabled to take place and achieved publication in *Index on Censorship*. Whereby, although abstract and somewhat complex in its formulation of subjective consciousness, interpellation provides for Althusser a means to trace the "functioning of the superstructure and its mode of intervention in the base" (ibid.: 270). Althusser also raises issues that indicate his reservation about "the problem of the total process of the realization of the reproduction of the relations of production" (ibid.). In respect to my study of an interview within the culture industry, Althusser's expressed concern to decipher the contribution of Ideological State Apparatus (ISA) in the process of the reproduction of capitalist relations of power has relevance. According to Althusser, "It is only within the processes of production and circulation that this reproduction is *realized*. It is realized by the mechanisms of those processes, in which the training of the workers is 'completed', their posts assigned them, etc. It is in the internal mechanisms of these processes that the effect of the different ideologies is felt (above all the effect of legal-ethical ideology)" (ibid.). Consequently, when viewed through this lens my case studied interview can be seen a reproducing relations of capitalist production in respect to its capitalist processes of production of the interview and its circulation as a commodified text. But, Althusser himself released that this model of the operation of ISAs was too simplistic. If it is to be accepted that "in a class society the relations of production are relations of exploitation and therefore relations between antagonistic classes", then my case studied interview is more than a sum of its parts, i.e. a mere reproduction and circulation of the diatribes of a commercialised excessively indulged music idol. This is because antagonistic relations between classes will disrupt the smooth operation of the reproduction of the relations of production. Furthermore, and particularly pertinent to the case studied interview, these class struggles are not an outgrowth of differing levels of technical contribution to the interview's capitalistic processes of production and circulation. For, as Althusser recognises, "In fact there is no 'technical division' of labour except in the ideology of the ruling class: every 'technical' division, every 'technical' organization of labour, is the form and mask of a social (= class) division and organization of labour" (ibid.). Consequently, my case studied interview needs to be recognised in terms of "the reproduction of the relations of production" as a class undertaking that is "realized through a class struggle which counterposes the ruling class and the exploited class" (ibid.). Althusser urges Marxist critical theory that ideology is integral to the reproduction of the relations of production, not merely accessorising the material conditions of capitalist exploitation, but rather, the ISAs are site of intensive struggle, conflict

242   P. ODIH

and the potentiality of revolutionary change. Thus, Althusser postulates that "to adopt the point of view of reproduction is therefore in the last instance to adopt the point of view of the class struggle" (ibid.).

In summary, Althusser argues that ideologies are perpetuated in both Repressive State Apparatuses (RSAs) and Ideology State Apparatuses (ISAs); only the latter functions predominantly in the reproduction of ideology. The relevance of Althusser's observation to my analysis of the case studied interview with Fela Anikulapo-Kuti relates to situation of the culture industry as a Communications ISA in which ruling class ideologies are realised through its products, processes, rituals and practices. The basis of Communications ISAs in expressive, creative dialogue renders this as a site for struggle and resistance as well as perpetuating inequities in the relations of capitalist production. Specifically,

> [T]he class struggle in the ISAs is only one aspect of a class struggle which goes beyond the ISAs. The ideology that a class in power makes the ruling ideology in its ISAs is indeed 'realized' in those ISAs, but it goes beyond them, for it comes from everywhere. Similarly, the ideology that a ruled class manages to defend in and against such ISAs goes beyond them, for it comes from elsewhere. Althusser (1971b/2014: 271)

It can be deduced that class struggles in ISAs emanate from within in terms of competing ruling class ideologies (e.g. generational differences) and also from elsewhere encompassed by the State's regulation. Returning now to my case studied culture industry interview with Fela Anikulapo-Kuti, it is conceivable that this event while intended as an instance of the reproduction of capitalist class relations was also the situation of conflicting class-based dialogue. Taking into account the feminist principles and perspective of at least one member of the interview panel (Jane Bryce), it is evident that the culture industry interview site was also an intersectional gender/race/class struggle against the former patriarchal ruling class and their response to the threat of the ascendency of feminism in the new ISA (inferred in the above interview transcriptions). As Althusser expresses it, the situation of "continuous class struggle [is] first against the former ruling classes and their positions in the old and new ISAs, then against the exploited class" (ibid.).

If it is to be accepted that the ISAs depict "the form in which the ideology of the ruled class must necessarily be measured and confronted", then the ideological stance of my case studied interview with Fela

Anikulapo-Kuti that was published in *Index on Censorship*, was not created in the ISA. For, as Althusser expresses it, "ideologies are not 'born' in the ISA, but from the social classes at grips in the class struggle: from their conditions of existence, their practices, their experience of the struggle, etc." (ibid.: 272). This latter observation is consistent with the concept of interpellation, whereby the individual is hailed as a subject to the ideology. Nevertheless, there are limitations in respect to the extent to which Althusser's conception of ISAs adequately contends with the agency of the individual and the potentiality of their resistance to ideology attempting to interpellate them into becoming its subject. Consequently, it is my observation that while interpellation might explain the centripetal gravitational pull experienced, in my case studied interview event, there are some limitations in the application of this framework, the most prominent of which is the extent to which the interview panel used the event to "interpolate" bourgeois interview context, so as to elevate Fela Anikulapo-Kuti's vision of an anti-neocolonial challenge to the cultural-economy of British colonial mentality.

Refracted (His)tories of the Political Subject: Interpolating Feminist Post-colonialism

In 1989, *Index on Censorship* published a transcription of a panel interview with Fela Anikulapo-Kuti, featuring the feminist cultural critic Jane Bryce. In April 2022 the article was re-published as part of the journal's "Five decades in review". In their preamble to the interview text, the editors describe the wider context as "the year that made the modern world". Indeed, 1989 was an astonishing year that "saw walls, real and metaphorical, come down across Eastern Europe, while China's crushing of students in Tiananmen saw a more assertive global power". The preamble text then proceeds to introduce the interview subjects as thus, "Fela Kuti, the godfather of Afrobeat, was a thorn in the side of Nigerian politicians in the 1970s and 1980s. He talked to JANE BRYCE for Index in 1989".

Several years prior, to the original *Index on Censorship* publication (in 1986), Fela Anikulapo-Kuti had been released from a long imprisonment widely viewed to have been punishment for the artist's outspoken criticism of the Nigerian government. Unequivocal in its denunciation of Nigeria's postcolonial relations with the British Prime Minister Margaret Thatcher, its international dealings with President Ronald Reagan and ferment

244   P. ODIH

incredulity at South Africa's apartheid President P.W. Botha, the *Beasts of No Nation* album was released in 1989 as part of the band's international tour of Europe and the USA. Observing these circumstances, the case studied interview embarked dauntlessly in its showcasing, to a wider European audience, of the artist's outspoken condemnation of government corruption, police repression and the postcolonial exploitation of his native country. Indeed, it is my contention that the case studied interview was distinctly impressive in its dexterity, effectively "interpolating" the neocolonial chronicle of Nigeria's post-independence fiscal policies and macro-economic development. To appreciate this accomplishment and influence in shaping the artist's treatment of the interview as a postcolonial intervention, it is necessary to detail the concept of "interpolation".

Bill Ashcroft's (2001) *Post-colonial Transformation* critically engages with Althusser's concept of interpellation in respect to limitations in the latter's formulation of agency. Principal to this critique is the notion that "the colonial subject may engage imperial culture by using it as a communicative medium or consuming it as cultural capital" (ibid.: 45). Irrespective of the process of utilisation, it is argued that engagement with imperial culture is intensely involved with consumption and production; the magnitude and force of this implication is such as to present the potentiality of transformation in the hegemony of the dominant culture itself. Analysing these happenings of autonomous agency has proved a complex endeavour. As Ashcroft expresses it, "The most contentious problems in post-colonial theory continue to be those hinging on the capacity of the colonized subject to intervene in colonial discourse to contest it, change it or generally make the voice of the colonized heard" (ibid.). A jeopardy inherent in colonial discourse theory is the formulation of "absolutes" and their depiction as an impervious hegemony accomplished in its totality effect of silencing resistance to colonialist delineation. Whereby, colonial theory in its perpetuation of absolutes presents the colonial discourse as capable of devouring, systematically unravelling and dismantling anticolonialist intransigence. Ironically, if such a totality were to exist, it would have subverted the flourishing of postcolonialism as an area of literary studies. Conversely, Ashcroft enlists the following post-colonial supposition: "Gayatri Spivak's now notorious question – Can the subaltern speak?" (ibid.). In his envisaging of a porous hegemony, through its continuous embattlement with itself and Others, there emerges aspects of an appreciation that "in practice, the cultures apparently 'silenced' by this process nevertheless continue to exist, and not only develop their own operations and revisions but develop coherent strategies of self-determination with the new discursive tools at their disposal" (ibid.). In this respect consider the following extract from my interview with Prof. Emerita Jane Bryce.

Interviewer [Pamela Odih]

I am interested in, just going back to his mother, so she is known the be anticolonial in her politics. And how might you describe his politics? In terms of the anti-colonial, decolonial, postcolonial where would you situate his politics and how would you situate his politics? From the interview?

Interviewee [Prof Emerita Jane Bryce]

From the interview it is fairly simple because there was a military regime in Nigeria at the time; it was extremely repressive. He had been jailed. He had emerged from jail but he was still being harassed and hounded. So he was anti the military very much so. But it would be very hard to say that Fela was pro-democracy. He was not really in any sense, conventional sense a political person. He was anti a lot of things. He stood for Black liberation I would say. His main political education, apart from getting in the home through his mother and so on. Was from being in the US in 60s and the Black power movement. That's what I think really what shaped him. As his life went on he became more and more eccentric. When he started talking about himself as the 'Black President'. How he could rule Nigeria. He had really lost touch with reality, I think. I don't know if you are aware of how far he went in this light. Towards the end of his life, he had a traditional healer in his entourage and he must of known that he was sick by this time. He absolutely refused to have any kind of conventional therapy and he was convinced that this healer would cure him of whatever it was. Of course, he didn't and it became full-blown AIDs which he died of. This is what I am saying. Fela was an educated person. Who in a sense, gave himself over to the semi-mystical form of traditional worship which is not something he had grown u with at all. He grew up in a Christian family. So politically I would say that he was a figurehead who

> *represented black liberation. But he was not a conventional political figure. He didn't have a manifesto. He didn't have a platform. He was an oppositional figure. That's what he was.* Prof. Emerita Jane Bryce (Semi-structured interview: March 2024)

My immediate reflection on the above interview extract is that it provides consistent indication that despite the behemothic scale and imposing presence of the colonial legacy in Nigeria and its powerful linguistic constraint on subjects, the artist Fela Anikulapo-Kuti appeared never to be immobilised by the hegemony of colonial power. Moreover, in his engagement with the capitalist Western culture industry, the artist demonstrated that resistance to coloniality "need not *necessarily* mean rejection of dominant culture, the utter refusal to countenance any engagement with its forms and discourses" (Ashcroft 2001: 47). In Fela Anikulapo-Kuti's participation within the case studied interview, there is evidence of how the agency of the subaltern reveals itself through the consumption and production spaces, which serve to reproduce colonial discourse and power. Despite these apparent contradictions to mainstream colonial theory's absolutes, it continues to perpetuate, "its theoretical crippling of the subject's agency (or at the very least the perception that this is the case), and on the other because political action usually implies a binary separation of the 'colonized' ad 'colonizing' which locks resistance into an imperialist paradigm" (Ashcroft 2001: 47). Indications of the subaltern giving voice to oppositional thinking and alternative strategies of self-determination are evident in the above interview extract, in which references are made to Black liberation and the Black power movement. Issues raised about the artist's presentation of "eccentric" behaviours in actuality provide a more sophisticated insight into the complex discursive tools utilised as part of a subaltern refusal. It is not my intention to rationalise the irrationality of responding to a deadly pandemic with the indeterminant efficacy of "conventional therapy".

Thoughts are drawn further into Ashcroft's (2001) exploration of the phrase: "the subaltern cannot speak". If one assumes its meaning is not a negation of voice, then it plausibly signifies that the subaltern is only able to articulate outside of the "discourse of power" from their integration within this discourse. But this is the experience of all language, as the speaker only has available the lexicon and repertoire of the language, that is utilised to articulate their opposition. Furthermore, the (his)tory of struggles against colonialism has involved resistance to subjectification by those subjected to objectifying and subjectivising modes of regulation. Nevertheless, and despite the constrictions of language forming subjectivity, transformational disruptions to colonialism have been achieved. Thus, it is necessary to conceive of an approach to post-colonial agency which accommodates "the central function of language in 'forming' subjectivity" and corroborates "the capacity of the colonized subject to intervene in the material conditions of suppression in order to 'transform' them" (ibid.: 47). Ashcroft's concept of "interpolation" provides a means to theorise post-colonial agency by colonised subjects. It does so by appreciating that "the most effective post-colonial resistance has always been the wrestling, from imperial hands, of some measure of political control over" cultural production and entering "into the 'scene' of colonization to reveal frictions of cultural difference, to actually make use of aspects of the colonizing culture so as to generate transformative cultural production" (ibid.). Integral to this post-colonial theory of agency is a critically informed focus on the "way the colonized subject 'interpolates' the dominant discourse", whereby the concept specifies far-reaching practices of resistance (ibid.).

Ashcroft positions interpolation as a counter to Althusser's conception of interpellation and does so in respect to a focus on "the process by which colonized subjects may resist the forces designed to shape them as 'other'" (ibid.). Interpolation provides insights into the strategies employed by subjects interpellated into colonial discourse, to refuse and counter its ideology through autonomous acts of counter-discursive agency. Interpolation involves intervening into hegemony of colonial discourse through the deliberate and strategically prudent insertion of interruptions into its signifying systems, rhetorical codes and discursive practices. It is my contention that rather than a smooth process of being interpellated into the Communications ISA of the culture industry, post-colonial agency involves subjects interpolating the *hail*, and in so doing introducing counter-discourses of resistance to its power. As Ashcroft (ibid.) proposes, the strategy of interpolation "involves the capacity to interpose, to intervene, to interject a wide range of counter-discourse tactics into the dominant discourse without asserting a unified anti-imperial intention, or a separate opposition purity". Similarities correlate this description of interpolation, with the circumstances of the participants of my case studied interview with Fela Anikulapo-Kuti, which was published in *Index on Censorship* in 1989. Whereby, the event provided opportunities for the political positionalities of the invited participants to be mobilised in a dialogic

248 P. ODIH

engagement with the culture industry interview as a mode of transmitting colonial capitalist ideology. Some indication of which is evident in the following interview transcription extract:

Interviewer [Pamela Odih] *Interviewee [Prof Emerita Jane Bryce]*	*So as an oppositional figure he is opposed to; what is the point of opposition? What was the focus of his opposition? Well, you know his music. So, you know the kinds of things he sings about. He sang against apartheid. But he also sang against oppression in his own country and lot about the military and what the military had done to him. The attack on his compound. The throwing of his mother out of the window, you know her resulting injuries. Meant that he really hated the military. So, he was against army control. He was against. He was a liberationist. He wanted freedom for the Black man. But I don't think he was very sophisticated about how he viewed that freedom.* Prof. Emerita Jane Bryce (Semi-structured interview: March 2024)

The interview extract provides a valuable insight into the particularity of post-colonial interpolation in respect to autobiography, situational circumstance and the complex mosaic through which counter-discourse agency can be mobilised. The interviewee, in their awareness of Fela Anikulapo-Kuti's tortured relation with policing law enforcement and internationally recognised experience of human rights violation, navigated the rationale of Communications ISA so as to convey oppositional version of the artist's political efficacy. When we consider the way that the capitalist culture industry operates to reproduce dominant hegemony, it is easy to appreciate the strategic importance and immense value of interventions from within the system that while not dismantling it refuses to leave the status quo intact. As Ashcroft expresses it, "Fundamentally the process of insertion, interruption, interjection which is suggested by the act of interpolation, is the initial (and essential) movement in the process of post-colonial transformation" (ibid.: 48). Following on from my interview with Prof. Emerita Jane Bryce in their description of Fela Anikulapo-Kuti's political activism, it is evident that the ascription of the individual with the title of "post-colonial subject" might not be readily assumed even though

7 POST-COLONIAL FEMINIST, INTERPOLATION   249

their transformational contribution is mutually accepted. Consider in this respect the following aspect of my interview:

Interviewer [Pamela Odih] *I have been reading work by an Arab feminist writer called [Prof] Ella Shohat. And what interested me a lot is the way she talks quote sceptically about post-colonial and she writes 'post' with a hyphen 'colonial'. She talks about how this hybridity and this focus on fragmented cultural identities; how it works against a sort of political effectivity; works against a sort of more grounded politics of anticolonialism for example. In you discussion there about how the way in which towards the end of his career he became almost quite caught up in the mythology of around him. I wonder might that be an illustration of how the notion of the post-colonial in terms of hybridity or the post-colonial in terms of cultural fragmentation might have undermined his work? If that was a direction that he was moving towards. Less towards the anticolonialism of his mother towards a post-colonial approach? Or do you think he was post-colonial in any way?*

Interviewee [Prof Emerita Jane Bryce] *Post-colonial is a word that Fela would have laughed at he wouldn't have taken it serious. He didn't use those kinds of terms. I would say anticolonialism was where he came from because that's what his mother stood for and black power was the other thing. Cos it is very specific to the United States; but has its application in other places where Black people have been oppressed. But it is hard to see Black people being oppressed in Nigeria in the same as you see them in the states because it is a Black ruled country. And I think that's what he brought to the table really. Was that he was prepared to criticise his own government. And the government of other Black ruled countries in Africa. So in that sense you could call him post-colonial if you wanted. Because he didn't buy into the kind of post-independence idealism that saw having a Black government as the solution and that everything having to flow from that. When of course we are looking back to the 80s and we are now twenty years on from Independence and* *so he had seen what had happened. They had had the Biafran War which had set Black on Black. They've had all sorts of political upheavals and coups in Nigeria. So what he saw really quite clearly was the hierarchies that arguably the British left behind. The ascendency of military … that what he is able to stand against. And somebody of his background; his elite background coming out to expose is what gave him an incredibly passionate following amongst ordinary Nigerian's because they were the victims obviously.* Prof. Emerita Jane Bryce (Semi-structured interview: March 2024)

At the start of the above extract, the interviewee seems to rebuff my tentative ascription of the terms post-colonial as a means of organising the political praxis of the artist's activities in the late 1980s through to his passing. She then proceeds to set out an alternative account of the artist's politics prior to returning to the notion of an ascription of post-colonial. In so doing, the interview extract illustrates the ways in which counter-discourse agency works within postcolonial studies so as to negate post-colonial critique being ascribed to them, and they do so as strategy for the transformation of post-colonial critique. As Ashcroft (2001: 48) similarly describes in respect to Orientalism: "By operating inside the discourse of Orientalism, for instance, these intellectuals negate the Orientalist construction that have been ascribed to them. It is through this process of negation that they are able to become selves as opposed to the identity of mere others that they inherit". It is my view that the 1980s and 1990s political praxis of Fela Anikulapo-Kuti can be described as post-colonial in respect to explaining the artist's use of the tactic of "insertion" into the 1980s emerging genre of post-colonial activism; also, in so far as the artist's use of post-colonial techniques such as reappropriation, interjection and discontinuities sought to interrupt the hegemony of British colonialist discourse.

POST-COLONIAL FEMINIST CRITIQUE: DECENTRING NEOCOLONIAL CULTURAL-ECONOMY

Interviewee [Prof Emerita Jane Bryce]

Kwame Nkrumah's preferred term Neocolonialism I think applies to Nigeria in the 1980s. That was a neocolonial situation where, those who had the means were fighting over the resources and were appropriating power. And

> *that's why the series of military coups. Because the soldiers saw the opportunity and being in power in Nigeria means you 'chop!'. You have access to the money. That's why this term post-colonialism; you know it's an academic term really isn't it? I'm not sure how useful it is to try and box Fela into that category because he saw the world much more in black and white terms. I mean that both literally and metaphorically. It seemed yes, he was anti-corruption, and he was anti-elitism, anti-the Big Man in Nigeria. I don't remember; it's one of his songs where he talks about Nkrumah. But Nkrumah obviously was the first African leader and he had this vision for the united states of Africa. And his career was essentially ended by CIA intervention; and all of that Fela would have been against. He would have been against American meddling in African affairs. And in that sense, I mean you use the word nationalism, before we started talking. And he was very much a nationalist in that sense. I would have been Africa for Africans and the white man had no role in it.* Prof. Emerita Jane Bryce (Semi-structured interview: March 2024)

Generational differences aside, the intersectionality of post-colonial feminism compares favourably with the anti-neocolonial political activism of Fela Anikulapo-Kuti at the zenith of the artist's 1980s international Afrobeat appeal. Celebrated for advancing post-independence, Black consciousness, in Nigeria and Africa as a whole, by the 1980s he was using his revolutionary imprint to articulate the incredibility of the fiscal policy and neocolonial acquiescence made by the political regimes in his native country. The anti-neocolonial philosophy of the Ghanian politician Kwame Nkrumah (1909–1972) is evident in the artist's music portfolio in the aftermath of their release in 1986 from imprisonment, having been found guilty for breaching legal regulations for exporting foreign currency. The 1989 album *Beasts of No Nation* epitomised the mélange of Nigerian vernacular lyricism and Pan-Africanist oracular prose that distinguished the mid-1980s political maturation of Fela Anikulapo-Kuti's Afrobeat genre. As Ashcroft (2001) observes of other post-colonial cultural production, language features in the artist's Afrobeat music as part of his "personal and cultural voyage" (ibid.: 48). In the artist's use of Pidgin English, there exist elements of the incorporation into the lexicon of his Afrobeat, elements of British colonial linguistic repertoire so as to decolonise its denigration and subjectification of the colonial subject. Indeed, the cultivation of Pidgin English as his lingua franca of resistance to British colonialism is consistent with a post-colonial strategy also identified by Ashcroft, whereby "despite their ideologically 'contaminating' influence, colonial languages can be, and have been, vigorously adapted, their imperial assumptions abrogated and the language appropriated for the specific needs of post-colonial self-determination" (ibid.). Such acts are indication of the potentiality of resistance by the subaltern subject. The efficacy of these acts is dependent upon the opportunity available to insert the language-turn into the streams of discursive power deployed by the colonial discourse and in so doing disrupt its hegemony. A strategy Ashcroft (2001: 48–49) describes as thus:

> However, this strategy of appropriation is itself part of a broader strategy of interpolation. The post-colonial writers may appropriate the language, but he or she must insert that text into the Western-dominated systems of publishing, distribution and readership for the strategy to have any effect. This entry into the system of commodity production is a material instance of the post-colonial subject's intervention into dominant discourses of various kinds, such as history, literature, philosophy – indeed, into any hegemonic form of cultural production. While it is most obvious in literary textual production, the process of interpolation covers the full breadth of the 'cultural text'.

In the mid-1960s, Kwame Nkrumah, while president of the newly independent West African country Ghana, published his groundbreakingly prophetic, *Neo-colonialism, The Last Stage of Imperialism*. Commencing with the foreboding observation that imperialism was plausibly entering its most utterly treacherous stage, the book critically explores the perfidious larceny strategies of "Old-fashioned colonialism" in retreat. "In place of colonialism as the main instrument of imperialism we have today neo-colonialism" (Nkrumah 1965: 4). Distinguishing the essence of neocolonialism, Nkrumah draws attention to the circumstances in which "the State which is subject to it is, in theory, independent and has all the outward trappings of international sovereignty". But, in actuality, "its economic system and thus its political policy is directed from outside" (ibid.). The techniques of coloniality are various, in respect to neocolonialism; nevertheless, they can be situated within a spectrum of direct to indirect control. In respect to the former, these include the imperial power conducting an offensive raid and garrisoning the sovereign territory of the neocolonial state and seizing operation of its government.

More frequently, neocolonialism involves the indirect control by an imperial state through the means of economic or monetary mechanisms. Nkrumah described situations in this regard, in which the government policy of a neocolonial state is reigned through transactional obligations to prioritise the importation of the manufactured products of the imperial state to the exclusion of competing products sourced from other market economies. Additionally, it was observed that a neocolonial state can indirectly be controlled through international monetary structures that unleash power by their "provision of civil servants in positions where they can dictate policy, and by monetary control over foreign exchange through imposition of a banking system controlled by the imperial power" (ibid.). Observing elements of these strategies of neocolonialism, in an atmosphere of political intimidation, injustice and oppression, Fela Anikulapo-Kuti's Afrobeat became a rallying vocal point for disaffected Nigerians, especially the youth who were particularly affected by the dire economic outcome of the Structural Adjustment Programme (SAP) imposed in 1986 by the government of General Ibrahim Babangida. Nigeria had been a bona fide member of the International Monetary Fund (IMF) a year after achieving independence from Britain in 1960. It was at this time the country was rapidly transitioning from an agro-petrol economy into an oil-based economy with crude oil extraction constituting 80% of the Federal Government income and approximately 95% of its foreign exchange earnings (Isiani et al. 2021: 6). The economic crisis, of the early 1980s, precipitated by a fall in the price of oil, had dramatically blighted the Nigerian economy. Accepting the IMF's SAP measures required the devaluation of the Naira, the liberalisation of imports, privatisation initiated by a large-scale retrenchment of the state from the public sector, the deregulation of public utilities, removal of agricultural subsidies, rationalisation of the civil service and extension of market-based capitalism to Nigeria's fiscal management. In return, Nigeria was qualified for the structurally adjusted loans that were required to service the outstanding loans which in their repayment were consuming a vast proportion of the country's foreign exchange earnings from the export of goods and services. Indeed, an immediately evident consequence of subsidy removal was the compounding of the existing incapacities of petroleum-led manufacturing and transportation. The government's inability to track wage rises against

254   P. ODIH

epidemic inflation rendered the civil service and public sector vulnerable to inexcusable corruption and bribery. As Nkrumah (1965: 4) predicted, so prophetically, "The result of neo-colonialism is that foreign capital is used for the exploitation rather than for the development of the less developed parts of the world. Investment under neo-colonialism increases rather than decreases the gap between the rich and the poor countries of the world".

Post-colonial Feminist Rhizome Mapping Economic and Freedom of Expression Human Rights

Concerns relevant to feminist economics of sub-Saharan Africa are often prominent in the field of feminist human rights, such that it is conceivable to identify distinct aspects of a post-colonial praxis that aligns these areas. Issues pertaining to the gendered processes of neocolonial progression were raised during my interview with Prof. Emerita Jane Bryce, whereby we spoke about the militarisation of the political enforcement of the International Monetary Fund (IMF) and World Bank's imposed debt restructuring programmes that restrained Nigeria's fiscal policy in the 1980s. We discussed this from a post-colonial feminist perspective in terms of the collusion with social structural and historical patriarchal processes that had played a distinct role in exacerbating the gender inequality of colonial power. The global economic restructuring of African nations undergone in the 1980s manifested very distinct gender dynamics in Nigeria. This is because global economic and political change overlay a legacy of patriarchal British colonialism which had denatured native structures of support evident in the daily lives of women and caring communities. The impact of these processes has been to render Nigeria's disproportionately numerous population of young people vulnerable to politically induced impoverishment and excessively militarised policing of civil rights protestation. Post-colonial studies into "sex and gender" and human rights point to the lives of poor women so as to illustrate how they "are disproportionately women of color and disproportionately shoulder the burden of the economic and social dislocation resulting from gendered, racialized, and internationalized processes" (Gurr and Naples 2013: 15). In the following discussion, I examine the Jane Bryce's interview with the artist Fela Anikulapo-Kuti in terms of his music's anti-neocolonial appeal to young population, and the gendered power implications of his attempt to cultivate a politically informed nationalist Nigerian nationalist consciousness.

Observing these crippling conditions of IMF imposed neoliberal marketisation, Fela Anikulapo-Kuti used music to articulate resistance to the neocolonial conditions that were causing impoverishment and precipitating civil unrest protests. Politically provocative albums such as the 1989 release of *Beasts of No Nation* (credited, Egypt 80 personnel) had not endeared him to the Nigerian political authorities, with its insurgent lyrics castigating the debased colonial mental health of Buhari. "Na craze world be dat oh; No be outside Buhari dey; Na craze man be dat oh". Incredulity was more severely unleased against the dispositions of Nigeria's previous enslavers, colonial rulers, enacting neocolonial human rights custodians. Disparagement of the British expressed mercilessly in the song's lyrics to Verse III of *Beasts of No Nation*,

Dem go hold meeting oh, Dem go start yab human
Animal talk don start again
Dash dem human Right
How animals go know say dem no born me as slave
How animals go know say slave trade don pass
Dash dem human Rights.
Animals wan dash us human rights
Animals can't dash me human rights.
Give dem human Rights.
Animals must talk to human beings.
I beg you make you hear me well well.
Human Rights na my property
You can't dash me my property
Some people say why I dey talk like dis
No be talk like dis dem take to carry me go prison oh.
No be me dey talk na Prime Minister Botha dey talk oh.
Him say - 'this uprising will bring out the beast in us' (quote).
(Chorus) This uprising will bring out the beast in us.
Botha Na friend to Thatcher and Reagan.
Botha na friend to some other leaders too.
And now dem wan dash us human Rights.
Animals wan dash us human rights.
(Chorus) Many leaders as you see dem. Etc.
Beasts of no Nation Egbe ke gbe na bad Society
(Chorus) Beasts of no Nation Oturugbeke.

Reparation for Britain's role in the transatlantic slave trade is implicitly themed in the song lyrics and explicitly guided the artist's indignation of the obsequiousness in the reluctance of leaders to raise the issue at every opportunity. Defiant, as always, the artist valiantly pursued Britain's colonial legacy through the cultural political lyrics of his music and cultural political protestations. It was evident in the promotional interview conducted in London, by the academic Jane Bryce, while raising the political profile of his newly released album *Beasts of the Nation* in 1989. In April of that year, a thousand fully armed Nigerian police descended on Asero Stadium in Abeokuta in "Operation silence Fela" on the occasion of the artist's first concert since being released from jail; thus, when asked whether he was apprehensive about returning to Nigeria, it is poignant that he responded intrepidly, stating, "They want to scare me off coming home, but nothing they can do will keep me out of my country. I must go home. I've been through prison before, practising for the future. I learnt how to get bored. That's all they can do to me. There's no way they can prevent me from going back" (Anikulapo-Kuti 1989). Notwithstanding the significant generational difference that distinguish Afrobeat(s) Nigerian musician artists in recent times, from the pioneering Afrobeat cultural political interventions of Fela Anikulapo-Kuti, it is my contention that in *Beasts of No Nation* and Jane Bryce's interview there is evidence of a contemporary critique, which in its time-shifting positionality to the neocoloniality of Nigeria's relation to Britain's 1980s Thatcherite neoliberalism allies with "post-colonial" feminism. It is my view that these issues concerning the cultural-economy of neocolonism were interpolated into Jane Bryce's interview with Fela Anikulapo-Kuti and in so doing provided for an additional level of praxis in respect to the post-coloniality of the interview.

Interviewer [Pamela Odih] *And referring back to the article. In the article I think these are your contributions here when you talk about Structural Adjustment. He talks about it as well. He talks about the IMF and issues there in terms of locking Nigeria into various forms of financial dependency with its previous imperial domineering control structures … I wonder what are your views there in terms of why he was looking at Nigeria's relation to is previous coloniser Britain? … It comes through in the article as well that there are very real tensions in respect to how he views, not only Nigeria's relation to its previous colonisers but also*

7 POST-COLONIAL FEMINIST, INTERPOLATION 257

how Britain was relating; and he speaks about, in the article he speaks about Thatcher, America as well. … There are a couple of sentences in the article in which he speaks about Thatcher commenting about Nigeria and he takes offence to it. I wonder what are your views there? In the interview what were you picking up about how he was trying to position his politics in terms of Britain's in the 80s influence? … How did. You appreciate what he was saying?

Interviewee [Prof Emerita Jane Bryce]

Obliviously I appreciated it a lot because I knew exactly what he was talking about and not an admirer of Margaret Thatcher myself. Basically, it was no surprise that, that was Fela's position: The ex-colonial power should get the hell out of Nigeria. What he was aware of that he understood was that there was this consensus going on at the highest level between the current rulers and the ex-colonial power as to how the resources would be used and distributed and who would be in power and so on. He would have been against all that he was very much against all that. But again you see, it wasn't all white people; he didn't hate all white people. But again you see he had white friends; white British friends ["Manager"]. I don't know if you have come across a book called Bricolage by John Howe? [I indicate through my facial expression]. Alright, John Howe was a writer, journalist and writer who spent time with Fela; lived with him in the Republic; stayed with him at the Kalakuta Republic and his written a – you should try and get hold of it; a book called Bricolage and his name is John Howe … He's got an essay on Fela. John knew him very, very well and when Fela would come to London he would stay with John. So you know there was; and don't forget there was; he knew London, he had studied there. So it wasn't a blanket hatred of white people. It was a quite; you know we were talking about his politics; he was able to make that political distinction between the people who were manipulating things behind the scenes and ordinary people. And erhm. When he says that the world needs information about Nigeria of course the information about Nigeria came at that time from white journalists working in Nigeria. So all of that Fela understood very well. And I am sure that is why he would have agreed to this interview because this would have been one of his ways of getting out information as he saw it. Prof. Emerita Jane Bryce (Semistructured interview: March 2024)

The transcription extract is pertinent also to Ashcroft's (2001: 49) observation that the (post)colonised in their manifold tactics of engagement with imperial discourse are more efficacious as catalysts for change when they interpolate the cultural hegemony of the mainstream. Consequently, and according to Ashcroft, effective post-colonial critique is inextricably embedded in the conditions of its critique. More specifically, "Even those discourses which represent themselves as 'revolutionary' have a heavy investment in the mainstream, are themselves heavily involved in the political culture they are opposing" (ibid.). Such insights reinforce my supposition about the post-coloniality of the interview, in which Fela Anikulapo-Kuti was the interviewee, and the outcome of which was published in *Index on Censorship* in 1989. In the following description of the interview content, it is my intention to provide some features to illustrate the deployment of interpolation, which evidence the working assumption that "rather than a necessarily conscious and theorized policy, interpolation describes the range of strategies by which colonized people have historically empowered themselves through a calculated appropriation of aspects of the dominant discourse" (ibid.). Complexity in applying the dimensions of interpolation is an issue further illustrated towards the end of my interview with Prof. Emerita Jane Bryce, as thus:

Interviewer [Pamela Odih]	*How would you describe therefore your interview with the group. So, there was a group of British journalists; and so, you are all interviewing Fela. So, now that we have spoken about those issues around post-coloniality etc., representation and the culture industry. How would you, now reflect upon the interview? I mean it's a brilliant interview and it's got such a high acclaim as well as accolade for being in the journal in its entirety. Now that we've spoken about the complexities in his positionality in terms of his politics: How would you describe now the staging of that interview? Or what it represented? What did the interview represent do you think?*

Interviewee [Prof Emerita Jane Bryce]	*Well, this was, [Ibrahim] Babangida was in power so by this time in the 80s we had the [Muhammadu] Buhari coup; Babangida took over, and then of course the next coup after that was [Sani] Abacha; but that happened a couple of years later. So, it was very – erm how can I put this? It was of concern, to a lot of people that Nigeria the so called 'giant of Africa' - you know with its incredible resources and its population; its numbers and so on - was going through these terrible political upheavals and repression and disorder basically. And so, you get an individual like Fela that the – let me just say though I don't know where else the interview would have appeared I have no idea. But anybody there to interview Fela would have been representing, I imagine a left-wing journal. I don't think the Times or the Telegraph would have wanted to carry an interview by Fela. He was a renegade. Look at it from whatever direction you want. He wasn't, he represented himself and what he said may have been the truth as he saw it; but he wasn't a respectable person. He was an artist, who saw the world in a certain way. A maverick and a renegade and an extremist. He was all those things. Which made him very interesting, very exciting; but didn't make him necessarily reliable as an informant. Yeah? So I think that's also interesting in terms of how he expresses himself. Because he has quite deliberately presented himself as someone who can speak English to the English. Because he knows that's what he represents: That he is all those things. Clever guy, very clever.* Prof. Emerita Jane Bryce (Semi-structured interview: March 2024)

In the above extract there is some indication of the strategies and tactics of counter-discourse that were perceived to have been deployed by Fela Anikulapo-Kuti as part of his wider praxis and also in interview published in *Index on Censorship* in 1989. Indeed, in the published interview the artist is clearly interpolating between the culture industry setting and his motivation to insert into the agenda of the event, critical discourse about the political regime in Nigeria. He asserts that "people are starving in Nigeria", proceeding then to identify and disparage the military President Babangida's neocolonial sycophancy. He insists, "My country has become a 'settlement', a refugee camp. Anybody in any kind of authority, such as the army or police, uses the word 'settle' for bribery. If you're in any kind of trouble, you 'settle' it, before they let you go. When Babangida came to England to see Margaret Thatcher, Nigerians said he came to 'settle'" (Anikulapo-Kuti 1989). In the interview, he highlights the corrosive impact of the culture of bribery in respect to security, whereby seemingly arbitrary curfew restrictions had seen people's human right to freedom of association violated. Describing the situation as thus, "We have a law called 'Wandering'. The police start arresting people from 5pm onwards, even if they have an address and a job. Police stations have become banks; the Commissioner is the bank managers. They lock you up for weeks or months or even years without charge. Many people die in jail" (ibid.). In the interview, Fela Kuti spoke disconcertedly about the inevitability of large-scale civil disturbance, stating that "It was like putting a match to gas. People wanted to resist the acute oppression that is happening in my country. The first little riot was in Lagos State University". Conditions for ordinary people were impoverished, but it was the civil protests of the intelligentsia and university students that provoked the coercive brutal wrath of the policing authorities. Fela's concerts became a lightning rod for excessive policing control, with "Operation Silence Fela" existing as a known repressive policing strategy to thwart and prevent the artist's live appearance; for these were opportunities to challenge the postcolonial policy adopted by the military regime. It is notable that Fela Anikulapo-Kuti did not see these incidents in isolation but rather as part of an orchestrated assault on a pan-African Black consciousness of defiance against the colonial imposition of the neoliberal market-based economics of SAP. Additionally, it is evident that Jane Bryce and the interview panel were keen to make links aligning neocolonialism; IMF imposed neoliberal debt adjustment strategies and the impoverishment of generations of young Nigerian people. As is evident in the following extract from the published *Index on Censorship* interview:

> Some time before this, in April, the government had received information about student meetings at which a protest was being planned, Fela's concert was scheduled for 8 April in Asero Stadium in Abeokuta. But before the concert over 1,000 fully armed police descended on the town in 'Operation Silence Fela' ... 'When we arrived in my bus at the outskirts of Abeokuta, we saw this barrage of police cars and armoured vehicles, 15-20 of them in a line, blowing sirens, coming slowly towards us. I said to my band, "We're not going to play tonight". Police sur-

rounded the stadium and threatened to shoot anyone who went near it. It was a very big operation. That's what the government does in order to scare people. That was to have been my first student gig since I left jail. Many students came from all over the country for the show. The authorities felt that if Fela got there and started to talk about the elections, the Debt-Equity Swap, the things I always talk about, to 20,000 students, it would definitely cause unrest. So, they stopped me from playing'. Anikulapo-Kuti (1989: 12)

In the interview extract, there is consistent evidence of critical aspects of post-colonial feminist human rights discourse. Of principle significance is the interview panel's emphasis on the intersectionality of race, class and gender in respect to the hostility meted out by the police force directed at the young student protesters. Post-colonial feminists interrogate interconnections of capitalist colonialism, in regard to the operations of patriarchy and the inequalities of gender, class, race that are consequent of the intersectionality (Romero 2013: 79). In my discussion with Prof. Emerita Jane Bryce, it became more apparent to me the necessity for post-colonial feminist economic analysis of SAP's impact on local communities, firstly, to displace a tradition of economic theory that assumes the male as the single-axis of enquiry, and secondly, to incorporate into analysis the significance of examining the outcome of SAPs for those involved in non-economically productive labour such as care work. It is in this respect that I was able to discern the human rights direction of the initial interview with the artist Fela Anikulapo-Kuti. For the interviews detailed emphasis on the students impacted by the police's closing down the artist's performance scheduled to take place in Asero Stadium, there is clear movement towards a patriarchal foreclosure of the students' right to communicative action. In their detailing of the incident, the interview panel, which included Jane Bryce, rendered visible a violation which would have been dismissed as excessive patriarchal control. Given that students inhabit a liminal space at the juncture of non-economic adulthood and parental dependency, the interview panel made their marginalisation visible. The case studied interview—in highlighting the consequences for the students of the police's crackdown on the artist's Afrobeat concert—bring to the fore interlocking axis of oppression in terms of intergenerational experiences of the racialised, gender, classed subject. Of particular significance, therefore, is Jane Bryce and the interview panel's role in interpolating into the interview with Fela Anikulapo-Kuti attention to the injustice as a

262   P. ODIH

breach of Article 27 of the United Nation's (1948) Universal Declaration of Human Rights, in which it is stated:

> **Everyone has the right freely to participate in the cultural life of the community, to enjoy the arts and to share in scientific advancement and its benefits.**

Post-colonial feminists of human rights emphasise "the significance of social, political and historical context", which "makes multiple marginalizations visible; and establishes programs and policies that treat social positions as fluid identities operating simultaneously" (Romero 2013: 85). Without a post-colonial dimension to the case studied interview, the militarisation of the closure of the Fela Anikulapo-Kuti concert and its intersectionality of impact on the student population would have been less likely to be recognised as a violation of the human right to communicative action. In respect to the mentality of this regime and its impact on the vulnerable minds of the youthful student generation, the artist described the situation of the police raid as thus, "I know the mentality of my people. We talk and laugh. But I knew that we were really suffering. The students may have motivated people, but everyone joined in. It was a popular uprising. The theme was, 'Babangida must go'. Half the country rose up, starting in Ibandan then Lagos, Aba, Enugu and Benin" (Anikulapo-Kuti 1989: 12).

Nevertheless, Fela's ire was always more incensed by the avoidance of the British to take responsibility for the ongoing injurious legacy of its colonial empire. In the 1989 interview this wrath is directed fervently at the UK's prime minister as thus, "Margaret Thatcher said that the Nigerian economy is buoyant ... You cannot come to Nigeria and tell Nigerians that our economy is buoyant. She has no political mandate. But then Babangida says she is the best leader in the world. Can you imagine how stupid he is?". In many respects the broadside, obliquely veiled criticism of the British and American political leaders, is allied with the transformative processes of interpolation. This is because, as Ashcroft (2001: 50) expresses it, "interpolating process begins in a different model of imperial hegemony from the conventional view of it as a vertical and hierarchical structure". Some indication of the complexity of colonial exchange and the ambivalences of colonial reality is depicted in the alternative modelling, that is the rhizome. Ashcroft argues plausibly that in the morphology of the rhizome can be conceived a more nuanced conceptualisation of the territorial expansion of imperial power. To which I concur, because in physical biology the radial branches of rhizomes extend laterally from multiple decentred axial nodes and thus are diametrically different from the vertically hierarchical growth structure of the single nuclear tap root. It is conceivable that imperial power is invested in the mythology of its expansion as being comparable to a hierarchical vertical tap root, but in actuality in its response to resistance and discontinuities imposed by conditions and context, imperial power is more plausibly depicted by the morphology of the rhizome. Whereby, it is a decentred system of axials and laterally trajectory networking branches.

In Fela Anikulapo-Kuti's critical account of the UK's then Prime Minister Margaret Thatcher, there is evident a sophisticated tracing of the British neocolonial influence along discontinuous legacy structures, discursive practices and cultural-economies that propagate laterally and vertically just like a rhizome. Here as elsewhere there is evidence of post-colonial tactical thinking in the artist's refusal to accept the unities, binaries and hierarchical thinking of colonial mentality. For it is evident that the hegemony of colonial power operates in and through multiple axials of intermittently radicle lateral and horizontal branches. The provenience of colonial imperialism has limited inherent coherence, as Ashcroft expresses it, "There is no 'master-plan' of imperialism: the greatest advancement of cultural hegemony occurs when it operates through an invisible network of filiative connections, psychological internalizations and unconsciously complicit associations" (ibid.). Consequently, the artist's aslant into a tirade against Margaret Thatcher, etc., as seen through a post-colonial lens, is part of a transformational process of interpolation in which the myth of centrality is displaced for a notion of a legacy of colonial power that operates rhizomatically through discontinuous laminations and branches latticed into complex enfolding. Nevertheless, the notion of vertically rooted power perpetuates in colonial discourse and in so doing distracts attention away from the complexity of colonialism, as Ashcroft (ibid.: 51) states:

> The intermittent and rhizomic nature is the most difficult thing to combat because it operates alongside a mythology which asserts the presence of the tap root, the canon, the standard, the patented. It is this myth of power which the categories of marginality are addressing, not the intermittent, overlapping and intertwining nature of its actual operation. In this way the categories which we see reproduced in criti-

264   P. ODIH

cal reading – such as women, native, migrant – evolve as reproductions rather than subversions of imperial discourse.

Fela Anikulapo-Kuti's forthright challenges to the political governance of Nigeria's postcolonial relations with Britain, coupled with the ferocity of his lyrics in respect to the Nigerian military government, led to numerous arrests, detentions and incarcerations. It is particularly evident here and elsewhere in terms of the interview staging and dialogue that the artist deployed transformational post-colonial acts to insert into the event, modes of depicting counter-discourse, directly challenging the neocolonialist precepts of the dominant discourse. Indeed, it is evident that in mobilising the technology of the culture industry music interview, Fela Anikulapo-Kuti was able to use this event as a vehicle for critical engagement with the Nigerian political regime and their violation of his human rights. In so doing, the artists provide illustration of the case studied interview as being in one and the same time, a space for the reproduction of colonial ideology, and a space for resistance to colonial ideology. This is because the rhizomatic structuring of colonial power proliferates the fractures and ruptures that are an inevitable consequence of the potentiality for the colonised subject extricated as an entity with its own agency. "No system of control, no discourse, can ever operate with absolute consistency" (ibid.: 52). This credence has particular verity when both the colonial discourse and its counter-resistance are structured rhizomatically as was evident in both the above discussed colonialist commentary by the then British Prime Minister Margaret Thatcher and the counter-discourse of Fela Anikulapo-Kuti. In such a situation, Ashcroft (ibid.) observes that "because both discourse and counter-discourse are rhizomatic, interpolation is already partly a function of our complex subject position within this diffuse structure of social and power relations". This interpolation of similarly structure discourse is clearly evident in the case studied interview, which was published in *Index on Censorship* in 1989. For, as a product of the capitalist culture industry, the music interview is entangled into the rhizomatic trajectories of neocolonial capitalism; the artist Fela Anikulapo-Kuti and his music ensemble were also inextricably entangled into this capitalist structure. Consequently, one can attribute the dexterity by which the artist was able to interpolate the interview by inserting into it his counter-discourse, is because both discourses share a rhizome morphology. Consequently, as Ashcroft (ibid.) expresses it, "Interpolation obtains its insurgent effectiveness from the capacity to intervene in the dominant

7 POST-COLONIAL FEMINIST, INTERPOLATION 265

discourse at any number of scattered points on the rhizome of social and political interaction". Such astute observation has implications also for conceptualising the post-colonial interpolation of Jane Bryce, who as a feminist constituted a further layer onto the complex rhizome of socio-economic and political interaction during the case studied interview. Some indication of which is evident in the following extract derived from my interview with her:

Interviewer [Pamela Odih]	*When I am writing this up, I'd like to be able to do justice to your feminism, Professor Jane Bryce. So how would I describe your feminism? So that I am able to be clear. And this is the reason tried. And it's been a fascinating discussion. And we are at the end now. And it was worth every email that I have sent trying to find you ... So how would I be able to now do justice to your feminism? How can I describe; please could you tell me your feminism.*
Interviewee [Prof Emerita Jane Bryce]	*Well, I don't have a particular kind of feminism. I just call myself a feminist. I have always, I mean I suppose I cut my teeth on the early. What took me to Nigeria was the early days of Black American women writers being published in London, Toni Morrison, Alice Walker. that generation of women writers who had been published in the States. But in those days, you couldn't necessarily get books across borders so easily. So, when they started to be published by British Presses, they were unknown in England, although it seems absolutely incredible now. I'm talking about the late 70s, the early 80s. And I was one of the few people who was writing about black culture. One of the few white people who was writing about black culture. And there weren't that many black journalists about in those days. And so, I had the opportunity to do a lot of reviewing. And that was what sparked my interest. I grew up in Africa myself, so I kind of I was working towards wanting to go back and do something and I decided that I would go to Nigeria and do something on Nigerian women's writing. But I was very idealistic, very sort of romantic actually, because I thought I would do a wonderful celebratory work on Nigerian women's writing along the lines of what people were starting to say about Black American women writers. And when I got to Nigeria, I realised it was a completely different story ...*

So, I turned it around at that point and decided that I had to approach it from a more cultural perspective and look at what was being published locally. Romance fiction, journalism; and how women related to writing at all these different levels. And so. this is a long answer and I can't really give you a short answer. How do I see my feminism? I think I learnt how to be a feminist in Nigeria. I wouldn't want to call myself. I mean, I can't call myself. I can't align myself as a Black feminist because that's obviously ridiculous because I'm white. But I would say that I learnt a lot from Nigerian women. About gender politics and that shaped my feminism and I so there isn't a label for that, I don't think. But that's the explanation.

Interviewer   *Yes, would you consider yourself to (post)colonial feminist in respect to having emerged from an artistic tradition that sought to actually unsettle various colonial dichotomies, and epistemologies ways of knowing, etcetera. So it's post-colonialism could be seen as an intervention into particular colonial representations and epistemologies. Might that be a bit closer to see you as?*

Interviewee   *Yeah, that'll do. That will do because I mean, throughout my career, I retired seven years ago. But so, for most of my career post-colonialism was the dominant methodology in literature. In the universities and since then, obviously other things have emerged. Very much to do with, you know, different kinds of gender representation and decolonialism. But post-colonialism, yes, I'm quite comfortable with that. Yeah.* Prof. Emerita Jane Bryce (Semi-structured interview: March 2024)

Accepting that the contradictions, conflicts and tensions in colonial discourse produce fractures and fissures across which a counter-discourse can inveigle its interpolation in acts of transformational agency, it is conceivable that counter-positionalities will inevitably intensify the rupture in colonial hegemony. Ashcroft (2001) makes a similar observation but reigns back from detailing the difference in the transformation process that is achieved by post-colonial feminist interpolations. For he merely states that "interpolation redefines the nature of 'resistance' by revealing the diversity of subjective agency within the dominant territory. The successful disruption of the territory of the dominant occurs, not by rejecting or vacating that territory but by inhabiting it differently" (ibid.: 52). Although, in his account of "Tactics and Strategies", Ashcroft provides insights into a diversity of techniques, he is less theoretically detailed in terms of feminist post-colonial theory. With this in mind the following section has as its primary objective that of detailing Jane Bryce's interview with Fela Anikulapo-Kuti, in terms of a post-colonial feminist interpolation that tactically utilises strategies.

TIMELY REFLECTIONS

Jane Bryce's contribution to the panel that interviewed Fela Anikulapo-Kuti was impactful because of her feminist ideals, and evidently as a consequence of the rhizome structure of neocolonial power that pervades the capitalist culture industry. It is discernible from the original interview's published transcription that the interpolation of counter-discourse, because of the rhizomic configuration of the interview setting's interpersonal power relations, required both "tactical" and "strategic" techniques, and this has gender implications. Firstly, it needs to be reiterated that

> Ideology services the interests of the ruling classes, it is not static or unchangeable, and its materiality means that it is also contradictory, fragmentary and inconsistent and does not necessarily or inevitably blindfold the 'interpellated' subject to a perception of its operations. Ideology itself is rhizomic. The rhizome explains the very complex system of opposition and complicity which characterizes the relationship between post-colonial subjects and imperial discourse. This field is already fractured, heterogeneous, ubiquitous. This is why a binary model of resistance can contend with no more than the myth of the tap root of cultural identity and the 'trunk' of cultural control. Ashcroft (2001: 53)

The interview with Fela Anikulapo-Kuti, published in *Index on Censorship* in 1989, is an example of the way neocolonised groups occupy the cultural-economic spaces of imperial power and in so doing interpolate its colonial hegemony. Post-colonial feminist insertion into these spaces introduces a further dimension of complexity into which the intersectionality of gender/class/race scatter onto the rhizomic structures of power of the colonial discourse and its counter-discourse, realisation of a cultural reproduction of gendered power knowledge relations which it also seeks to disrupt. Thus, the presence of feminist post-colonial discourse is strategic in its endeavour to seek out and dismantle gender inequalities inherent in colonial discourse, but it is also tactical in that it manoeuvres less about long-term planning and more about transforming chance situations into opportunities to insert post-colonial feminist challenge. The presence of feminist positionality negotiated an orbit tracing the institutional power structures of the music interview, weaving across its formal networks so as to interpolate its boundaries and fortified predilections towards the cultural reproduction of gendered inequalities. Ashcroft (ibid.: 54) attributes diversity in the creative impact of interpolation to be a product of one's habitus and its predisposition towards what Bourdieu (1990) theorises as capital of an immaterial/cultural form. Ashcroft (ibid.) states that because tactics involves "the appropriation of habitus which cultural capital involves", it is less likely to "itself disrupt the dominant discourse", but rather "it provides the means by which such disruption and transformation may take place". It is my contention that the presence and participation of Jane Bryce within the case studied interview setting provided a crucial setting for her feminist principles to intervene into the patriarchal intent of the capitalist culture industry and in so doing introduce transformative realisations. Transforming the verbal interview into a published academic text enabled Fela Anikulapo-Kuti's anti-neocolonialism to be presented to a new audience of feminist critical theory while also mapping onto the rhizome structures of colonial discourse and forcing post-colonial feminist ruptures in all of these discursive power relations. Consequently, it is my contention that Jane Bryce's presence and participation in the interview evidences not only that "the subject actively engages the dominant discourse within those fractures through which its tactics, operating at the level of everyday usage, may transform the discursive field" (ibid.: 55), but it is also illustration of the capacity of post-colonial feminist discourse to interpolate gender inequities integral to imperial power and force through the resulting fractures a transformative agency capable of disrupting the cultural hegemony of colonialism.

REFERENCES

Althusser, L., (1971a); *Lenin and Philosophy and Other Essays*, Trans., Brewster, B., New York and London: Monthly Review Press.

Althusser, L., (1971b/2014); *On the Reproduction of Capitalism; Ideology and Ideological State Apparatuses*, Trans., from French, Goshgarian, M.G., London, New York: Verso.

Anikulapo-Kuti, F. (1989). "Animal can't dash me human rights." Interview with Jane Bryce, *Index on Censorship*, *18*(9), 12–13. https://doi.org/10.1080/03064228908534717

Ashcroft, B., (2001); *Post-Colonial Transformation*, London: Routledge.

Bourdieu, P., (1990); The Logic of Practice, Trans., Nice, R., Stanford, California:Stanford University Press.

Bryce, J. (2022). 'Animal can't dash me human rights'. *Index on Censorship, 51*(1), 76–78. https://doi.org/10.1177/03064220221084534

Felakuti.com (2024); Story:1986. Available at: https://felakuti.com/gb/story/1986

Gurr, B., and Naples, N., (2013); Sex and Gender, in (eds) Brunsma, D., Smith, K., and Gran, B., The Handbook of Sociology and Human Rights, London: Paradigm Publishers Boulder.

Index on Censorship (2024); *Index on Censorship; A Voice For the Persecuted*. Available at: https://www.indexoncensorship.org/category/about-index-on-censorship/

Isiani, M. C., Anthonia Obi-Ani, N., Obi-Ani, P., Chidume, C. G., & Okoye-Ugwu, S. (2021). Interrogating the International Monetary Fund (IMF) Policies in Nigeria, 1986–2018. *Cogent Arts & Humanities, 8*(1). https://doi.org/10.1080/23311983.2021.1932283

Marcuse, H., (1964/2002); *One-Dimensional Man, Studies in the Ideology of Advanced industrial Society*, London and New York: Routledge.

May, C., (2015); *Beasts of No Nation, Jacket Inner Sleeve to Beasts of No Nation* by Fela Anikulapo-Kuti, Knitting Factory Records INC.

Nkrumah, K., (1965); *Neo-Colonialism the Last Stage of Imperialism*, London: Thomas Nelson and Sons, Ltd.

Romero, M., (2013); Race, Class, and Gender, in (eds.) Brunsma, D., Iyall Smith, K., and Gran, B., *The Handbook of Sociology and Human Rights*, London: Paradigm Publishers.

Strauss, A., and Corbin, J., (1990); *Basics of Qualitative Research; Grounded Theory Procedures and Techniques*, London: Sage.

United Nations (1948); Universal Declaration of Human Rights, United Nations. Available at: https://www.ohchr.org/en/human-rights/universal-declaration/translations/english

CHAPTER 8

Post-colonial Challenges to the Spectacle of Black Music Culture

O2 Academy Brixton, Street Level, 211 Stockwell Road, London SW9 95L, March 2023, Photographer © Pamela Odih

Debord's (1990) *Comments on the Society of the Spectacle* observes a particularly pertinent contradiction in the pursuit of absolute spectacular surveillance. The contradiction relates to the impracticalities of processing the avalanche of information gathered by proliferating surveillance technologies, and the exacerbation of this illogicality by a gaming competitive pursuit in which "control comes to over-value his agents, as well as his opponents" (ibid.: 81). The resulting situation is one whereby each of the state, para-state and private companies apportioning surveillance, "all subtly united around the executives of raison d'État aspires to its own private hegemony of meaning" (ibid.). Similarities exist in this respect to the liberal democratic resistance strategies employed in the online petitions opposing the licence suspension of the O2 Academy Brixton in the aftermath of the 15th December 2022 critical incident. Indication of the immense cultural significance of the online petition strategy was evident when in early May 2023 it was recorded that a petition entitled "Save Brixton Academy" had achieved in excess of 50,500 signatures. Commenced by S.B. on 26th April 2023 and petitioned to Lambeth Council, its text reads as a compelling clarion call for Lambeth local authority to appreciate the community's economic and affective capital investment in Brixton Academy. It is notable that the petition text does not make reference to the venue's corporate title, i.e. O2 Academy Brixton. But rather, it subverts the branded commercial capital of the venue, preferring the affective and local cultural-economy of the venue. Indeed, the impassioned expression of dedication to the local is realised through the vernacular of the text, and because it represents an important artefact of the mellifluous community's concern, it is transcribed in full as thus:

> **S.B. started this petition to Lambeth Council**
> Brixton Academy is an iconic London music venue and should this cease to be so, another part of the musical landscape and history is lost forever.
> What happened there was a tragedy, but caused by people. People without tickets, security taking back handers etc. Revoke the security firm's license and bring in someone adequate recommended by the police (security having been alleged to take back-handers to allow people into gigs, surely lies at the heart of those without tickets attending). Bring in new security procedures including crowd control to ensure a repeat doesn't happen, but let's not turn this venue into soulless flats as would more than likely happen in the event of permanent closure.
> I personally have been to hundreds of gigs in my lifetime, many of them here and I have never once felt like safety was an issue!

8 POST-COLONIAL CHALLENGES TO THE SPECTACLE OF BLACK MUSIC... 273

The loss of this venue would also have a devastating affect on the local economy!

So please, let's help keep music live and Save Brixton Academy! (Change.org 2023a)

Change.org brands itself as an online petition service that "is proudly people powered". Its business model presents the platform to be free of charge for ordinary people to create petitions, but it caveats this by stating that in order to remain free at the point of use it requires financial investment in the form of contributors, who support by helping petition starters be connected to supporters and by financing for the promotion of their petition. Click through the Change.org provides further insight into the commercial function of a promoted petition, for these are in actuality advertisements; indeed, the organisation describes them as such: "Promoted Petitions are advertisements, allowing you to have your favourite petitions discovered by thousands of potential supporters. Similar to boosted posts on Facebook or sponsored tweets on Twitter, promoted petitions let you pay to show any petition (including your own) to other potential supporters on change.org or our distribution channels" (Change. org 2023c). We are informed that by agreeing to finance a promoted petition, the supporters are facilitating its exposure to a wider audience or potential supporters and thus increasing its impact. The opportunity to finance the promotion of a petition is available for most host on the platform and the financier can be the petition creator and also its signatories. The exchange-rate of paid promotion to circulation is described as thus: "On average in the US or the UK, $100 invested by promotions, a petition will be featured to 2,000 people on the Change.org website or via email" (ibid.). A second source of revenue involves the supporter becoming a subscriber to the Change.org platform and in so doing contributes to the revenue income that supports the media technology and administration of the platform. One discerns from this business model mechanisms of market capitalism in operation.

It is a feature of the capitalisation of online petitions that the Change. org platform allows multiple petitions on the same subject matter. For instance, when searching the platform on 19th May 2023, it was immediately evident that several other petitions with the theme of saving Brixton Academy were being featured. Indeed, these similarly themed petitions were positioned in competition as indicated by the metrics of signatories and signature targets that if achieved enable the petition to increase its profile on the platform. Such is illustrative of the petition started by B.W. entitled "Save Brixton Academy from Permanent Closure". Although containing a similarly worded statement to that of S.B., when reviewed on 19th May 2023, it had achieved over a hundred signatures and significantly less than the 200 signature target that would boost the likelihood of the petition attracting more profile by featuring in the platform's Recommendations. More nuanced data concerning the motivations and meaning that informed the petitions is available under the platform's allocated space for signatories to enter their Reasons for Signing. So, for example, in B.W.'s petition, its only signatory posted the following entry: "It's an old venue that should stay for the real local Brixton community it's a long established building leave it alone always destroying history stop". Adjacent to the comment is the familiar heart icon, thus indicating that the comment itself is subject to the sign-values of competitive capitalising metrics on the Change.org platform. Although posted two weeks prior to 19th May 2023, the posting had achieved zero likes. Conversely, by this date, S.B's petition had achieved 110,708 signatures with a new target aim of 150,000 signatures; achieving this target would bestow it with the accolade of being among the "Top signed on Change.org". In the three weeks prior to the 19th May 2023 review, it had achieved a multitude of Reasons for Signing, with the following posting, similarly worded to the previously described, having secured 61 heart sign-valued agreements: "Ridiculous scapegoating response to a tragic incident. Absolutely no reason for the venue to be closed as thousands of successful and safe gigs over the years have shown" (Change.org 2023a).

Other similarly themed petitions include those that make positive reference to the cooperation, in the investigation and licence review, of Academy Music Group (AMG), the O2 Academy Brixton's licence holder. Consider in this regard the following extract from such a petition: "Please sign and share to play your part in protecting UK's music venues and support the AGM in this battle against closing yet another historical music venue in London and let's hope artists can take to the beautiful venues stage again as soon as possible" (Change.org 2023c). One gains a sense, from this brief review of Change.org petitions themed on saving O2 Academy Brixton, that if this was their sole intention, *why did the numerous campaigns not collaborate to formulate one petition?* For their strategy of individual petitions modelling on the same theme merely fractured the constituency of signatories, its sign-value and thus undermining the

8 POST-COLONIAL CHALLENGES TO THE SPECTACLE OF BLACK MUSIC... 275

effectivity of the petition as a liberal democratic resource available to consumer citizens to articulate disagreement.

On 15th May 2023, S.B. posted an "11th Hour" announcement, alerting signatories to their petition that the deadline was approaching for the Night Time Industries Association's (2023) Support the Campaign to Save Brixton Academy request for "patrons" (members of the concerned public) to complete an online statement of campaign to Lambeth Council licensing committee to further the impact of the closure of the venue. Specifically, the Night Time Industries Association's (NTIA) campaign letter required signatories to forward the letter to Lambeth Council. The NTIA letter template contained reference to the history of the Brixton Academy in respect to the pantheon of internationally renowned artists that had performed at its live events; mention of the venue's importance to the local community in respect to employment and local businesses, and it was suggested that the revocation of the venue's licence would displace audiences onto illegal and unlicenced live music events. The following extract provides some indication of the extent to which the NTIA petition consequentially positioned its defence of the O2 Academy Brixton licensee in its attempt to reverse the revocation of the venue's licence.

> **Reference Application: 23/00773/PRMREV: 'Review of premises licence' Brixton Academy, 211 Stockwell Rd, London SW9 9SL**
> ...
> I have not lost sight of the tragic incident that occurred in December, but would respectfully ask you to consider working with AMG and the venue to learn from what has happened and enhance the licence to ensure that this could never happens again.
>
> I would ask you to carefully consider the evidence I have laid out above, the subsequent resulting community impacts of closing this iconic venue on the four key licensing objectives, and the damage that will be caused to the local economy and culture.
>
> At this moment I would urge all involved to step forward and engage in productive and meaningful discussions, with an aim to resolve the current challenges and present a unified position on delivering the safe and effective management of this space in the future. (Night Time Industries Association [NTIA] 2023, https://www.ntia. co.uk/save-brixton-academy/)

Debord's (1990) comments on advertising surveillance technology make reference to a phenomenon in which the conspiracy to defend the spectacle is integral to its continuity, because the tactics employed in conspiring to perpetuate the spectacle's functioning are also constituted from that which is spectacular. Thus, the conspiratorial defence of spectacle, "in a relatively confidential manner", uses anonymity as a guise of authenticity, for if famous people were deployed, we would equate this as engineered by the spectacle fielding its stars in a defensive strategic strike. Anonymous people bring a sense of possibility that these are everyday people, expressing genuine concern, and this has more value and cache to the embattled spectacle. As Debord (ibid.: 75) describes, "lucid texts are beginning to appear, anonymously, or signed by unknown authors – a tactic helped by everyone's concentration on the clowns of the spectacle, which in turn makes unknowns justly seem the most admirable". Alongside mobilising, anonymous concerned folk, as a frontline of defence, the spectacle conspires with "pseudo-critiques" to manufacture its own adjudication. Some indication of which is provided by a Night Time Industries Association (NTIA), publication on 15th May 2023 entitled, *The Prodigy, Muse, Skunk Anansie, NME, Mixmag Join 20,000 Music Fans in Campaign to Save Brixton Academy*. The publication describes a campaign Save Brixton Academy, launched by NTIA, that had concluded in May 2023. As part of the campaign the following activities were reported to have taken place: "delivered over 20,000 Representations to Lambeth Council, gaining support from The Prodigy, Muse, Defected, Mixmag, NME, Music Week, Skunk Anansie and many more, on top of the 107,000 music fans which have signed the change.org petition to keep the Brixton Academy open". The letter campaign has some semblance of the simulacra of anonymous communal concern, but the evidence of pseudo-critique requires a further level of critical analytics. For the publication is mostly constituted by quotations from night-time economy industry representatives, and on closer inspection, the quoted sources appear to be colluding from opposing perspectives, as is evident in the following extracted quotes:

> Michael Kill CEO NTIA: 'We have been overwhelmed with the level of response to this campaign, with over 20,000 representations made by music fans to Lambeth Council with support from The Prodigy, Muse, Defected, NME, Mixmag, Music Week, Skunk Anansie and many more'.
> George Fleming CEO Save Our Scene: 'The response to this campaign has been immense and further highlights the public's desire for Brixton Academy to have a future as a live music venue ... Lambeth Council must do everything they can to preserve Brixton Academy.

8 POST-COLONIAL CHALLENGES TO THE SPECTACLE OF BLACK MUSIC... 277

Displacing a community would be a dangerous move which could result in a lot more work for themselves and the Met police.'

Gianluca Rizzo MD Brixton BID [Business Improvement District]: 'The huge support for the Brixton Academy with 20,000 letters submitted to Lambeth and thousands of messages across all social media show the importance of this venue. However, we cannot forget that a delayed decision has a negative impact on Brixton businesses, in fact since its closure, over half a million pound per week is being lost in visitors spending. Let's turn the lights back on for Brixton.' (NTIA 2023)

According to Debord (1990: 75), pseudo-critique is the performance of contrasting opinion engaged in debate directed ultimately at the defence of the spectacle. It is in this theoretical sense the one is conceiving here a level of performativity in the above expressions of concern about Lambeth Council's adjudication. For at least two of the representatives, i.e. NTIA and BID, are condition and consequence of Lambeth Council's local government authority. In this sense their submissions are similar to the phenomenon described by Debord as thus, "In some cases, with issues that threaten to become controversial, another pseudo-critique can be created; and between the two opinions which will thus be put forward – both outside the impoverished conventions of the spectacle – unsophisticated judgement can oscillate indefinitely, while discussion around them can be renewed whenever necessary" (ibid.). Indeed, it is uncanny identifying resemblances in the technique of spectacular journalism, and the NTIA's publication features such as "computers programmed in critical thought" might explain the content which is a series of industry representative quotations: "facsimiles of famous weapons, which only lack the firing-pin"; "a lateral critique, which perceives many things with considerable candour and accuracy, but places itself to one side ... Not because it affects some sort of impartiality" (ibid.: 76); all of these pseudo-critique technics have an eerie manifestation in the NTIA text.

The appeal to the spectacle in respect to Black music cultures and its implications for the construction of risk evaluation requires an additionally nuanced appreciation of agency, subjectivity and identity. *Why, given our popular knowledge of algorithmic capitalism and the commercialisation of petitions, would individuals invest their human capital in the production of capitalistic metrics for the survey industry?* Such insights are axiomatic to the methodological logic of the unstructured interview, and hence, I conducted qualitative interviews with several campaigners involved in the above-mentioned O2 Academy Brixton petitions. Central objective of the qualitative interviews was to focus on agency and so doing ascertain the subjective meaning making that motivated campaigning activities directed at reinstituting the O2 Academy Brixton as a music venue.

Petition Makers: Subjectivity, Identity and the Structuration of Resistance to Spectacle

On 26th July 2023, I spoke with a prominently active advocate of the campaign to reinstitute the O2 Academy Brixton. The interview commenced with a mutual acknowledgement of the high profile of their petition. The interviewee animatedly recalled having been in bands since they were 18, visiting the Brixton Academy innumerable times, seeing countless bands, stating, "I think lockdown was the last time I went there… can't tell you how many times I have been to the O2 Academy Brixton; well into the 50s 60s times". Intrigued about the venue's interior, I asked about the legendary stage area and Art Deco interior décor, to which they replied: "It's actually my favourite venue in London. It's got a slope, so wherever you are you can see the stage which is handy for people. And it's got two platforms either side for disability seating. I know my stepmother she's got accessibility issues and she's been on that side bit before and it's amazing and it's so well thought out". The architecture of the interior seems to be designed to stage the performer and provides the audience with a wide panoramic visual marvel.

> And also the way it looks inside, without being inside [I had mentioned to the interviewee that I have never been inside the venue] – you could probably google pictures of the interior – it looks like you're outside but inside. There's like these two towers either side that have got some amazing architecture and statues on the them; and there's like artificial trees looking like a skyline, so when you look up it looks like you're outside at night.

Although they had not been to the venue since before look down, it had been intended to see a punk -band called Rancid, but this was transferred to the Wembley Arena due to the closure of the O2 Academy Brixton. It was advanced that the punk band's upgrading of their show to Wembley Arena was a "big jump for them, to be fair, but they still managed to sell it out". Interested in this band's rerouting of their show as providing me with a trajectory to focus on the Asake show's capacity issues, I suggested that Rancid's initial booking might have underestimated the audience numbers. To which, the interviewee replied, "I think that they may have under estimated how big they are in the UK, yeah. But they may well have added an extra night or two which has been known to happen in the past – you know. When a band sells out a gig so quickly, they are like 'oooh we have space in our calendar let's add another date'".

My interview questions became drawn to parallels in the crowd capacity management of the Asake Afrobeat band that played on the 15th December 2022, because it is perplexing why the venue hosts were previously able to manage capacity effectively with mainstream popular music bands. To which the interviewee responded:

> I think there was like a perfect storm of things that went wrong and there needs to be a massive investigation as to what really went on. I have read a lot in the media about people turning up way in excess of capacity without tickets. I read somewhere that like, a thousand people turned up that didn't have tickets. There's all sorts of stuff that is not necessarily founded or proven. There is a lot of here say. But I think there's a lot of investigation that needs to happen.

The interviewee reiterated their belief that the venue can hope safely and that it's been proven as operating safely. Indeed, this concurs with Ticketmaster, which in its interconnection with AMG and O2, has made inroads with the 2019 launch of SafeTix described as "Ticketmaster's pioneering anti-counterfeit encrypted digital ticketing technology" (Ticketmaster 2024). But that this was predicated on people abiding by the rules. Curiously, it was said that people arriving without tickets was not usual to music venues, and that it not a "venue specific" occurrence. But what was unusual was the percentage of customers that arrived without tickets, as they expressed it, "If you have twenty percent turning up without tickets then anywhere is going to have a problem". I was intrigued by their suggestion that a "perfect storm" had precipitated the venue's 15th December incident.

> [Interviewer: people turning up without tickets, what other features of the perfect storm?] Well, like say, people felt embolden because there was rumours going around that the security staff were taking backhanders for ticketless people. Whether that's true or not I do not know. When something goes like that, gets spread around people feel emboldened; so they feel like 'I can turn up without a ticket, cos I can just pay this guy 20, 40, 50 quid or whatever and they will let me in. And then people decided just to rush the doors as well. There's all sorts of rumours about the police involvement or lack of, at certain points during the whole scenario.

Keen not to determine a single cause, it was repeatedly stated that "people were culpable across the board potentially". But that the most likely culpability was "a thousand people turning up without a ticket". I asked as whether they thought the venue hosts had culpability, to which it was replied,

> AMG, the Academy Media Group … as I say I don't know. There needs to be an investigation to find exactly what happened there's obviously a hearing about the licence coming up, in September. You would like to think that something has been investigated behind the scenes there are not just going into the licence hearing without that sort of information to hand to make this decision.

Mention of the licence hearing and the Summary Review of the licence provided a trajectory into the interviewee's direct participation in campaigning. Thus, I asked as to whether they have contributed to the making of representations on behalf of the venue. To which it was stated that

> I have worked in close association with NTIA, Night Time Industries Association. And based on the campaign that I had already started on the petition they invoked getting people to do their representation to the Council and they received probably close to 25,000 letters of representation. All addressing the key areas of the licence.

The connection between the interviewee and NTIA was also of interest:

> [Interviewer: How did you get involved with NTIA?] They reached out to me via Twitter, much like yourself. These guys know what they are doing, they are heavily involved in the night time industries, so it was quite a relief for me to have somebody of their calibre involved. Because I found myself thinking I am way out of my depth I didn't expect it to go so big [Interviewer: It went big]. At the moment it is like 115,000 signatures on that petition and I was hoping that it would hit a 100. 'Wow that's a 100 people' Wow that's amazing'.

I erroneously informed the interviewee that I thought it was 150,000 petitions that had been gained, but in actuality it was 115,000 as

> they keep moving the target [which had moved to 150,000]. I checked the other day after you had messaged me. Because I hadn't looked at it in a while because the timeline had elapsed from putting representations … I had a quick look and thought, 'it has slowed right off. It's been a 115,000 for a couple of months now. I am still blown away by how many people helped and supported that petition.

The interviewee's account of their interaction with the metrics of the online petition's platform, along with their elevation of NTIA within a subjectively perceived cultural field, all seemed relevant to my ongoing reading of the writing of Pierre Bourdieu. Most particularly, Bourdieu's account of the relation between habitus (one's predisposition towards forms of capital) and the field (structured forms of social relations) is detailed in an often-cited interview with Loïc J.D. Wacquant (1993).

Whereby the respondent's habitus relates to their sense of identity and agency, seen here as mediating their interpretation of the metrics of the petition, the metrics are meaningful as artefacts signifying recognition of the immense labour invested into the construction of the petition. At a more structural level, the field in which NTIA is perceived as proficient, resembles a "field of power". Whereby in the structured social relations that define NTIA, there exists a "structural homology" with the mechanisms that reproduce "a system of differences and distances, resolving thereby one of the fundamental problems which confronts all 'elites', namely the management of their internal divisions" (ibid.: 19). Bourdieu marks a discontinuity with Marxist economic determinism, for the focus on the field of power is less directed by the need to uncover the existence of a capitalist elite and instead focuses on "the space of positions that may be characterized trough their properties" (Wacquant 1993: 21). Thus, in the field of power exist positions that one can only occupy if one possesses the highest value of the capital of a cultural form and of a material form that it defines. Consequently, the field into which the NTIA is situated is "structurally homologous" to the field of power to the extent to which in its practice there is evidence of its possession of the material and immaterial capital approximating their highest form in the field of power.

Notice that Bourdieu eschews the focus on individuals, nor classes of individuals focussing instead on the actions and practice of power. It is in this sense that I similarly deviate from a focus on the power of individuals within the NTIA and try to make comparison with the individual agent, i.e. my respondent. Rather, it is my intention to focus on the relations between the NTIA with other organisations that constitute the associations that collaborate to make representations on behalf of the commercial business and personnel that operate in the night-time economy. Relations between these organisations and the field of power can be expressed and discerned in terms of material capital but also more effectively expressed as relations defined by capital of a cultural form. Thus, when the respondent referred to being "way out of my depth" when compared to the NTIA's expertise, this relates to capital of a cultural form and much less so to culture of a material, financial form. In many respects it is to the advantage of the NTIA to cultivate a sense to which others within the field ascribe it with capabilities that exceed those of the individual agent, for in so doing that ascribe it with value worthy of seeking its association. It is in this sense that one may argue that it represents "a system of differences which defines a historically given division of the work of domination" (ibid.: 22). Significantly, it needs to be particularly recognised here that the prominence of the field relative to the individual in Bourdieu's schema does not assume passivity and acquiescence in respect to the activity of the individual agent. Rather, the field is a site of struggle for the capital of a cultural and material form upon which it is defined. The individual agent is in competitive struggles with others to embody and acquire the capital of the field, which motivate their actions within the field. Accepting this, one gains a more nuanced appreciation of why individuals are so committed in their endeavour to pursue social justice through the survey industry's technology of the online petition. More specifically, one gains in Bourdieu's account a substantial insight that is lacking in Debord's conception of spectacle making, i.e. a notion of subjective consciousness and agency. Integral to Bourdieu's account of agency and its operation with structure is the notion of habitus, and the significance of capital that exists in a cultural form, as a basis of alienation and social distinction. It is my contention that cultural reproduction explains much of the labour invested in the making of an online petition, axiomatic to this is the distinction ascribed to social and technical types of capital of a cultural form. In this respect, consider the following annotated description of their setting up the online petition and the capital of a cultural form that was relevant to this impressive accomplishment.

When discussing with me the process of commencing the online petition, the interviewee said of the overall success, "I'm still blown away by how many people helped and supported that petition". Encouraging me to probe further as to the practice and technique employed to accomplish the immense support gained, and in so enquiring it was necessary for me to change the method from semi-structured to a narrative interview, which seemed to work, in the interviewee's construction of a linear narrative of practice. In the following transcription extract the respondent provides insights into the reasoning and motivation behind the petition's initial construction.

I woke up one morning and I got an article on my phone about the academy closure and I was like 'this can't happen'. What happened there was a massive

8 POST-COLONIAL CHALLENGES TO THE SPECTACLE OF BLACK MUSIC... 283

tragedy and no one should go to a gig and not come home, that's the truth. But the fault is not with the venue. There may be like some issues that need addressing of the venue. I read like the doors need strengthening, 'then do it'. Make sure it happens. Make sure that becomes a venue again because the local economy is suffering around there. They are losing half a million pounds a week that the venue's closed. That's a lot of money and there is probably businesses closing left right and centre because of it. So, I woke up one day and when I read that they are article about it being closed and that they had requested asked the permanent revocation of the license, I was like 'that venue needs to be a music venue still' they can't convert it to flats or whatever they would want to do with it afterwards. I know it's a listed building, but there are ways they can still make it into flats and keep the façade and what not. So, I was like, 'there must be a petition for this', I am gonna go and sign it. So, I went and had a look on change.org and there wasn't, so I was like, well there needs to be and I thought someone needs to do this and 'I'm someone, why don't I do it? (Interviewee, Brixton Academy Petition Creator, July 2023)

The interviewee's narration of a thought processes and introjection foremost to their decision-making also provides empirical illustration of the interrelated boundaries of cultural reproduction between the creative arts and music industry. While evidently co-associated through economic capital, the latter is also ascribed with symbolic assets. As Bourdieu explains,

On the one side [of the space of power] there is predominantly economic capital (property, assets, titles to property, high income), which is also endowed with symbolic properties – this economic capital can be invested, for example, in the realm of culture, where it is converted into symbolic capital by the purchase of art works, the creation of foundations, the financing of 'civic' activities, etc. (Wacquant 1993: 23)

Interrelated but differently conceived exists "capital of the cultural kind", which, Bourdieu theorises, "can be empirically measured by the possession of educational credentials, the ownership of 'high' cultural goods such as paintings, and by practices which are so many titles to cultural nobility" (ibid.). Although one form of capital can, in particular conditions, be converted into another, material capital and capital of a cultural form have their mode of "acquisition, transmission and accumulation" (ibid.). Illustration of the accumulation of a capital of a cultural form associated with technical aptitude and the use of technology to organise relations between human individuals is evident in the following extract, derived from the above-detailed interview:

Interviewer	*Did they not try to approach you to combine your petition with theirs? [referring to the existence of multiple petitions seeking similar aims in respect to the O2 Academy Brixton summary licence review]*
Interviewee	*No not at all. Like I say, the only people I heard from was NTIA. And they kind of; they kind of liaised with myself Brixton BID and Save Our Scene. It was like a combined effort between [us]. I was putting updates to the plans that NTIA were coming up with to do the representations. You do an update because you email 115,000 people to do the representations and if we get one in five we're going to get like 25,000 emails [using NTIA's letter template] sent to the Council, which happened.*
Interviewer	*So, you have 25,000 emails that go to the Council. You've got 115,000 signatories on your petition. What has been the outcome?*
Interviewee	*I think they all go forward towards the hearing now. So I guess we see what happens. This is a touch of wait and see.*
Interviewer	*How will they influence the outcome? The outcome is a licence review.*
Interviewee	*Well. Hopefully like the letters of representation, will have the impact of they do address the areas of concern for a licence, such as public safety, protecting children, all of that sort of stuff and the letter that was it was a template that was set up by NTIA and basically you put your name and address to it and then it got emailed off. Some people, added their own bit in their personal touch to it. So that was quite like nice to read about as long as it addressed those areas of concern. Hopefully they're there. They pay attention. (Interviewee, Brixton Academy Petition Creator, July 2023)*

Some indication of the conversion of economic capital into symbolic in the field of the online survey industry is evident in the overall business model of the online petition platform provider Change.org. For it insists that "Change.org is a Public Benefit Corporation overseen by a nonprofit governing board – The Change.org Foundation – which also oversees Change.org Programmes, the charitable activities of the Foundation". The corporation claims that its hybrid governance structure makes it possible for it "to combine the ambition and growth trajectory of tech company with the mission-focused stewardship of a nonprofit". The hybrid configuration of the corporation, it claims, makes it "the world's largest nonprofit-owned tech platform for social change" (Change.org 2023). With regard to the creation of an online petition, the originator's technical capital can be converted into economic capital when they enrol a third-party sponsor to assist in their attracting of supporters, "by paying to promote their petitions as advertisements to a wider audience on Change. org" (ibid.). And this process of conversion from technical to economic capital differs from the Change.org and other means of obtaining funds and that is the Subscriber model. Whereby, the latter involves the direct giving of economic capital to Change.org to "Power the platform".

Conversely, interviewee detailed previously appears unmotivated to supplement the corporation's Power the platform, Subscriber non-for-profit scheme and more directed, if at all, to the prospects of gaining third-party sponsorship of a campaign. Indeed, it may be discerned from the previous interview extract that the respondent's focus relates less towards economic capital, for their approach to the civic activity of online petition campaigning resonates with the transmission and accumulation of capital of a cultural kind. Bourdieu refers in this respect to immaterial capital cultivated as part of an individual's predisposition towards particular forms of cultural capital inculcated in and through their habitus. Whereby, habitus relates significantly to the embodied historically present cultivation of values, ideas, tastes, and cultural and technical affinities. As Bourdieu (1990: 56) expresses it, "The habitus – embodied history, internalized as a second nature and so forgotten as history – is the active presence of the whole past of which it is the product". Accepting this, practice is defined less as an outcome of structured social relations and more as a structuration between agency and external determinations. As Bourdieu (ibid.) expresses it, "This autonomy is that of the past, enacted and acting, which, functioning as accumulated capital, produces history on the basis of history and so ensures the permanence in change that makes the individual agent a world within the world". Bourdieu is keen to emphasise the immediacy of habitus, its flexibility and adaptation in coinciding with the current context. The organisational habitus of Change.org is therefore considered here as constituted through "the habitus [which] is a spontaneity without consciousness or will, opposed as much to the mechanical necessity of things without history in mechanistic theories as it is to the reflexive freedom of subject 'without inertia' in rationalist theories" (ibid.).

Consequently, it is not to assume that the opportunities of one's habitus are without limits, for it is an accumulation of the experiential and material basis of capital, and the structural limitations of class, race, gender, etc., which lead to an unequal distribution of these capitals, will permeate the conditions and consequences of one's habitus. Let us consider in this respect the interviewee's reaction, upon realising that there did not already exist a petition on Change.org to campaign against the closure of the O2 Academy Brixton venue. In their statement "I'm someone, why don't I do it?" it is evident an entrepreneurial enthusiasm that is apparently undaunted by the formidable task and effort necessary to challenge a process of the revocation of a music venue's licence. The long haul of the task is extenuated by the inequities of access to the capitals that define the field of arts, music and performance industry. Given that, as Bourdieu (ibid.: 64), "the entrepreneurial spirit or the propensity to invest, economic information is a function of one's power over the economy" unless the individual agent positioned powerfully within the field accomplishing an entrepreneurial quest is daunting to say the least. This is because accessing the economic capital to fulfil the inspirited task is made more difficult by the fact that its accumulation is not premised in totality on one's skill, talent and competency, but rather economic power relies also on the immaterial capitals of distinction. As Bourdieu expresses it, "Economic competence, like all competence (linguistic, political, etc.), far from being a simple technical capacity acquired in certain conditions, is a power tacitly conferred on those who have power over the economy or (as the very ambiguity of the word 'competence' indicates) an attribute of status" (ibid.).

Bourdieu's reference to the limits of technical capacity as a pivotal basis for the accumulation of economic power might initially appear contrary to the mode of capital accumulation within the computer-mediated knowledge economy. Within which the online survey industry is primarily situated, in its manifestation as an informationalised, technologically mediated, knowledge propelled field of digital data capital accumulation. However, a closer reading of Bourdieu's *Logic of Practice* accedes significant complexity ascribed to a sociology of technology that exceeds the focus on technique per se and instead focuses on the social and cultural conditions of technical capacity. Some indication of which, as evident in the following extract derived from the above interview:

> You know why don't I just start it and I sent it around to a few friends and saying 'guys I have just started this can you put you name to it, because it won't publish it until you get like five signatures so my band mates all signed it straight away, passed it on to people. I posted it on my face book and on my Twitter and then it started getting shared.

8 POST-COLONIAL CHALLENGES TO THE SPECTACLE OF BLACK MUSIC... 287

The enduring friendships called upon in the technical process of the interviewee's setting up the online petition are reminiscent of the long-lasting and resilient aspects of one's habitus that Bourdieu identifies as integral to the cultural reproduction of technical capital in an organisation's institutional practice. As Bourdieu expresses it, "This durably installed generative principle of regulated improvisations is a practical sense which reactivates the sense objectified in institutions" (ibid.: 57).

Referring more specifically to technology in respect to the interviewee's online petition, the regulated improvisations to which Bourdieu refers relate to the formal and informal technical practices involved in creating the petition. Established procedures regulate the technical process, but the accomplishment of the task also relies on impromptu actions and creative innovation. For instance, the interviewee described to me their surprise the morning after launching the petition to see the rapid success of the petition, which they describe as thus:

> It started getting shared; and then the following morning, I woke up and then I was over a thousand signatures because the lead singer from Garbage had like signed the petition and twitted it. And I was like 'Oh dear this is gonna, this is gonna go' [chuckle]. And then other famous bands joined in and started tweeting about it. I had a list somewhere of bands that I noticed had tweeted it. I was like this is incredible. You know the support that I got; like Graham Coxon from Blur tweeted about it. Skunk Anansie, I know Skin was very spoken – outspoken is probably the wrong word – was very vocal in her support of the venue. Chemical Brothers the Prodigy. The list was, I was just blown away. And these were bands I listened to and they are all supporting just little old me, who thought we needed to do a petition to start, to save Brixton Academy.

It is evident from this catalogue of networked social capital exchange that "regulated improvisions" is an apposite terminology for the actual practices required to accomplish a successful online petition, whereby technical skill refers only to a dimension of the technological process. For it is evident that the collaboration of social and cultural capital renders efficacious a technical capital that is "produced by the work of inculcation and appropriation that is needed in order for objective structures" which are themselves the product of a long cultural history, "to be reproduced in the form of the durable, adjusted dispositions that are the condition of their functioning" (Bourdieu 1990: 57).

A socially and culturally imbued technical skill was quite evidently integral to the accomplishment of the successful online petition. Axiomatic to this expertise is the existence of resonances between the technical capital of the organisational habitus of the survey platform and that of their users. As Bourdieu expresses it, "The habitus, which is constituted in the course of an individual history, imposing its particular logic on incorporation, and through which agents partake of the history objectified in institutions, is what makes it possible to inhabit institutions, to appropriate them practically" (ibid.). Because the elevated value of the capital in its technical form is arbitrary, sustaining its distinction through symbolic violence, the acceptance by the organisation's habitus of the user's technical capital requires a reciprocity of perspective, which exists at the level of skilled practice of the human body. Accepting this, one can argue that the online petition platform's organisational habitus is a foremost determinant in the regulation of participants, such that it defines as illegitimate the technical inputs of the non-human body, e.g. blocking computer-automated inputs. As Bourdieu explains, "The habitus is what enables the institution to attain full realization: it is through the capacity for incorporation, which exploits the body's readiness to take seriously the performative magic of the social, that the king, the banker or the priest are hereditary monarchy, financial capitalism or the Church made flesh" (ibid.). Consequently, the technical capital that enables the accomplishment of the establishment of a successful online petition is cultivated in an embodied form with regard to the application of skill. As Bourdieu expresses it, "Property appropriates its owner, embodying itself in the form of a structure generating practices perfectly conforming with its logic and its demands" (ibid.). In this regard, consider the following extract derived from the interview with the online petition creator, as detailed previously:

Interviewer *I noticed there were, one or two other petitions they haven't flown. They have got a couple of hundred signatories.*

Interviewee *They kind of piggybacked off me. But I saw a couple of them popping up and I thought they are probably doing it for. What do they call it? Like trying to get followers and likes I guess. I didn't do it for any of that reason at all. I just did it for the pure love of the venue and wanting to see it remain a live music venue. I think these people just saw the traction mine was getting and decided to pop them up as well. See if they could get like 'oh I get some likes and follows', blah blah blah and stroke their egos. I have no ego in this. I just love the venue. (Interviewee, Brixton Academy Petition Creator, July 2023)*

Bourdieu's framework of cultural reproduction, in so far as it comprehends embodiment in respect to habitus, provides a further nuanced intelligibility of how subjectivity becomes manifest in the application of technical skill. Such a realisation is useful with regard to appreciating the symbolic value ascribed to the embodied labour invested in creating the online petition. According to Bourdieu, a homogeneity connects the culturalised member with the habitus of the organisation. Such that their practices are naturalistically intelligible when read through the habitus of the organisation, and mostly taken for granted, a situation that Bourdieu describes as an "objective homogenizing of group or class habitus that results from homogeneity of conditions of existence", and it is this occurrence that "enables practices to be objectively harmonized without any calculation or conscious reference to a norm" (ibid.: 58). A homogenising of organisational habitus resembles the successful petition maker's encounter with the habitus of the platform and organisational culture of the online survey petition provider. This is because a resonance between habitus partly explains the exhibition of an objective meaning motivating the creation of the petition, whilst the subjective intention remains less necessarily apparent. As Bourdieu expresses it, "Perfectly and immediately successful adjustment to the objective conditions provides the most complete illusion of finality, or – which amounts to the same thing – of self-regulating mechanism" (ibid.: 62).

One can discern from these parallels with the application of technical skill to the making of the online petition as immediate impression is to present a finality of objective meaning, whilst shielding a need to clarify self, subject and subjectivity integral to such activity. Nevertheless, one should avoid focusing excessively on that which appears to be objectively valid and subjecting this to immanent economic law. This is because, as Bourdieu explains, "the 'rational' habitus which is the precondition for appropriate economic behaviour is the product of particular economic condition, the one defined by possession of the economic and cultural capital required in order to seize the 'potential opportunities' theoretically available to all" (ibid.: 64). Consequently, if one were to attribute economic rational habitus as the primary motivation behind the respondent's application of technical capital in pursuit of the making of a successful petition, this would require ignoring the fact that "the habitus is the principle of a selective perception of the indices tending to confirm and reinforce it rather than transform it, a matrix generating responses adapted in advance to all objective conditions identical to or homologous with the (past) conditions of its production" (ibid.).

Thus, while the respondent is utilising their technical capital to create the petition and mobilising social capital in promoting and circulating the petition, the economically rational habitus of commercial gain is less realistically evident. This is because the respondent is clearly reading the field in terms of a play of capitals of a cultural kind and appears mutualistically motivated to utilise these capitals to mobilise the conditions which might set forth a fairer evaluation of the future of the music venue. As Bourdieu describes in respect to the nature of habitus, "It adjusts itself to a probable future which it anticipates and helps to bring about because it reads it directly in the present of the presumed world, the only one it can ever know" (ibid.). It is quite evident that the respondent's ambition is constrained a realisation of what is possible and what is possibly limited by power. One might surmise that the disposition of the respondent is pragmatically realist in its navigation through the field and decision-making in respect to how and when to invest capital as to further advance their aims in respect to the field. As Bourdieu insightfully explains, "This disposition, always marked by its (social) conditions of acquisition and realization, tends to adjust to the objective chances of satisfying need or desire, inclining agents to 'cut their coats according to their cloth', and so to become the accomplices of the processes that tend to make the probable a reality" (ibid.: 65). It is in this respect that my understanding of the motivation to create the online petition campaign evolved into the intellectual development of the concept of "community intermediation".

Primarily formulated through coding the transcription of the interview with the petition creator, the concept of "community intermediation" refers to both human interaction and non-human artefacts that function within the live music industry to create channels of communication between governance authorities, policing and local communities in respect to the embedding of a live music venue into an inner-city urban residential district. "Community intermediaries" are members of the local inner-city residence in propinquity to the live music establishment that actively intermediates between the venue, local government and policing authorities. While primarily involved in knowledge exchange and acculturalisation, it can be discerned also that community intermediation invariably assumes a mediation role, referring specifically to the interviewee that led the creation of the high-profile online petition to reinstitute Brixton Academy as a music venue. Their embodied labour involving capital of a cultural form is less plausibly described as transactional rational economic habitus and more incisively discerned as community intermediation. Of specifically insightful instance of which is evidenced in terms of the interviewee's account of their encounters with the mainstream news media that approached the interviewee as a consequence of the substantial profile of the petition. For these encounters, according to the interviewee, involved having to navigate misrepresentation of the O2 Academy and prompt the interviewee into producing a newsworthy soundbite. Conversely, their "love" for the venue translated into activities intent on opposing the tabloid industry's counterfactual spectacular portrayal of the music venue and the ethnic minority clientele that it popularly attracts. Consider in this regard the interviewee's description of their engagement with the mainstream press on the subject of the O2 Academy Brixton critical incident on 15th December 2022.

Interviewee   *It's quite an emotional subject to be honest. You know, it's a really emotionally charged subject because people lost their lives. And I'm not media trained or anything like that. I'm just a guy who sat at home who loves to go to gigs. And I had like news, the journalists reaching out to me, had to do an interview with the ITV. BBC have interviewed me like that. Not all of it got used because someone got murdered outside the club, like outside the venue on the same day I did an interview. And they were like, well, the optics aren't good for that. So probably best not, say, save Brixton when someone's just been stabbed outside; you know.*

Interviewer   *So how did they use your material? Yeah. So how did they; so with the BBC TV, how did they use the material? That was a very subtle negotiation that they had to make.*

Interviewee   *They didn't use the petition at all that day. Obviously, the article was obviously all about like the murder that happened; and rightly so. You know that's way more important. You know someone lost their life in that incident as well. But again that was outside the venue this one venue was closed at the time absolutely nothing to do with the venue but it's just the optics from a news point of view don't look good if you're saying save Brixton on the one hand by the way someone.*

                …

Interviewee	*To be honest that's the longest interview I have had [referring to the interview I was currently conducting with the interviewee]. No really after sound bites [laughter]. Obliviously this is a different sort of project to what I have been doing. Obviously, I've been; not a project I've been talking to press previously, so they obviously just want their little headlines and sound bites: 'So oh could you say that again on the camera? Because we wanna catch that right; cause that's a nice little bit to put in there. And you're like, OK. (Interviewee: Brixton Academy Petition Creator; Interviewed: July 2023)*

A significant and particularly impactful aspect of the respondent's community intermediation relates to the role of the petition in challenging the rumour machine that was perpetuating sensationalist and spectacular claims about the ticketing anomalies of the 15th December 2022 O2 Academy Brixton event. But this challenge to rumour making was sometimes conflictual and contradictory shifting in its defensive and offensive strategies. Indeed, a feature of spectacular defence, evidenced in the save Brixton Academy campaigns, is the spectacle's capacity to generate and mobilise rumour, as Debord expresses it: "To this kind of counter-journalistic false critique can be added the organised practice of rumour which we know to be originally a sort of uncontrollable by-product of spectacular information, since everyone, however vaguely, perceives something misleading about the latter and trust it as little as it deserves" (ibid.: 76). The spectacular journalistic tactic of rumour is consistently evident in the radio documentary discussed previously, particularly in its use of vaguely sourced witnesses, making many unverifiable accusations of bribery and corruption. For in the absence of legal adjuration, criminal sanction and/or conviction, the BBC's accusations were merely rumour spreading, which in my opinion veered dangerously close to liable and slander, and despite exonerating culpability, nevertheless, spectacular accusations of bribe taking by doorkeepers risked besmirching the reputation of the security guard fatally injured in the crowd surge. Given the BBC's charter of objectivity, the rumour mongering was all too easily adopted unquestionably as plausible. In this sense they became what the sociology of advertising describes "as 'pace-makers'", which can be defined as thus, "those whom others in their milieu come to follow and imitate – but this time moving from spontaneity to control" (ibid.: 77). For it is clearly the case that the BBC documentary facilitated the extension of surveillance technologies mapping the directions made plausible for investigation by the rumour making about bribery and corruption carried out by those responsible for keeping secure the entrance of O2 Academy Brixton.

Cognisant of the Brixton community's commitment to the long since established iconic entertainment status of the venue, it would appear that the BBC Radio 4—File on 4 documentary in its spectacular audience capture reporting of the 15th December 2022 tragedy also prepared conditions conducive to the local authority bypassing the previously effective mediation of the venue's key community intermediaries and embarking on a unilateral reinvestigation of the health and safety of the premises. On reflection, Debord (1967/2014: 104) also provides a particularly apposite analytical observation in *Society of the Spectacle*, which is expressed as thus: "The task of the various branches of knowledge that are in the process of developing spectacular thought is to justify an unjustifiable society and to establish a general science of false consciousness". It is in this sense that the BBC Radio 4—File on 4 documentary of the 15th December 2022 tragedy can be said to have contributed to the spectacle of rumours that circulated about the security staff, accusations of bribery and forgery in respect to the touting of tickets. That these rumours existed was confirmed in the interview conducted with the petition creator and was further reiterated in an interview with a senior member of the organisation Brixton BIDs. For example, with regard to the former interviewee, consider the following extract:

Interviewee	*I don't know. I don't like. I say that side of things [referring to the excess tickets were available] there needs to be an investigation as to what.*
Interviewer	*Yeah. Do you reckon the artist could have done more Asaki the Afrobeat artist?*
Interviewee	*Well, I don't have any off about what happened inside, but from what I can gather he did tell people to calm down and stop surging; because apparently there was a lot of surging inside. From what I've read.*
Interviewer	*Yeah, I looked at, yeah. [referring to the Asaki pre-concert tweets]*
Interviewee	*And he did apparently tweet out: "If you haven't got a ticket, don't come". I don't know. I haven't seen it because he's not an artist I follow, to be honest. I'm into a totally different style of music to like, you know.*

Interviewer	*They call him Nigerian, afrobeat. I hadn't heard of him either before either.*
Interviewee	*No, he's probably more famous than ever now, but for the wrong reason.*
	…
Interviewer	*Do you think he should have enabled his fans to be more cautious in terms of the fact that it was sold out? Because he did actually tweet a couple of days before that it was sold out. And and yet people continue to actually think that they could buy tickets.*
Interviewer	*Hmm, well if he's told his people that he is sold out and all the websites were saying sold out, you can't buy tickets, and then you're relying on 3rd party sales such as your Viagogos and whatever ones the big boys are using for 3rd party sales of their tickets. I can't remember what the resales of Ticketmaster and Live Nation are called, but if they're saying sold out, then there's tickets popping up on net, which is in theory someone has already bought the ticket and they're gonna sell it and not use it. I don't know what more the artist could have done to be honest. (Interviewee: Brixton Academy Petition Creator; Interviewed: July 2023)*

The Brixton Academy petition campaign's creator provides a nuanced illustration of their community intermediation between the spectacle of counter-journalistic false critique, irregularly systematic practice of rumours, their fact-based experience of the live music ticketing industry and their orchestration of the online petition to save the venue. There is also evidence of tensions in their attempt to reconcile these opposing stories, and this multifarious task is particularly challenging because of the spectacular complexion of this form of rumour. Originating as "a sort of uncontrollable by-product of spectacular information" (Debord 1990: 76), the proliferation of sources of the rumour's manufacture and distribution enable credible facts and sensational speculation to become inseparably intertwined. For example, limitation in the ticket selling systems of legitimate vendors became entangled with the spectacular information circulated in the BBC's File on 4 broadcast programme. The latter's investigative theatrical genre is very reminiscent of the rumour manufacturing role of the "media/police" (ibid.: 55), who appear somewhat oblivious to the adage that requires appreciation of the multiple of anecdote is not data. As Debord observes, the "media/ police rumours acquire instantly – or at worst after three or four repetitions – the indisputable status of age-old historical evidence" (ibid.). Furthermore, "By the legendary authority of the spectacle of the day, odd characters eliminated in silence can reappear as fictive survivors, whose return can always be conjured up or computed, and proved by the mere say-so of specialists" (ibid.). The overall impression effect of these spectacular articulations is, as Debord describes, an experience of "uncertainty organised everywhere". Amidst universally disorientating uncertainty, substantiation gives way to supposition, and as is "often, domination will protect itself by false attacks, whose media coverage covers up the true operation". Cognisant of this mesosphere of spectacular allegation, the community intermediary's petition to save O2 Academy Brixton has provided a seemingly popular, albeit defiantly capitalistic, counter-offence. When framed according to Debord's analysis of the spectacle, the online petition has resonance with "the organised practice of rumour" in which "rumour began as something superstitious, naïve, self-deluding" and through the advanced capitalist enterprise of computer-mediated online petitioning has more recently evolved into advertising informationalised surveillance (ibid.). The petition creatives at the helm of the online campaign for signatories wield tremendous largely unmoderated counter-journalistic power. Thus, as Debord (ibid.: 76–77) observes, "More recently, however, surveillance has begun introducing into the population people capable of starting rumours which suit it at the very first signal".

Accepting this, the online petition is at one and the same time a technology of spectacular surveillance and, as a practice of community intermediation, evidence of resistance to the spectacle. Nevertheless, for this to be effective, and according to Debord (1967/2014: 117), it must achieve "an emancipation from the material bases of inverted truth". Such an astounding achievement is with difficulty accomplished by the isolated individual online petition creative and nor by the "atomized and manipulation masses" (ibid.). Referring directly to the revolutionary action of the online petition to save O2 Academy Brixton, its pseudo-Gemeinschaft of a digitally programmed computer software generated community is, in actuality, a miniscule challenge to the spectacle's "material bases of inverted truth". This is because its technological rationality and speculative gaming is an integral feature of the DNA of the capitalist spectacle. Thus, and according to Debord (ibid.), "By rushing into ... reformist compromises or pseudo-revolutionary collective actions, those driven by an abstract desire for immediate effectiveness are in reality obeying the ruling laws of thought, adopting a perspective that can see nothing but the *latest news*". For in their uncritical reiteration of the "bribery" and other rumours, the

BBC Radio 4—File on 4 documentary, and many of the smaller petition said to be piggy backing on the highly subscribed Change.org *Save Brixton Academy*, hastily reproduced the pseudo-revolutionary consciousness of the spectacle. For the hastily speculative gaming of the pseudo-revolutionary self-aggrandising, isolated manoeuvers perpetuates a disorientating "delirium". Such that, and as Debord prophetically advises, "A critique seeking to go beyond the spectacle must *know how to wait*". It is my contention that longue durée of the reproduction of capital of a cultural form distinguished the field of online petitions directed at saving the O2 Academy Brixton as a live music venue. While they were all limited by the procedural operations of the online platform Change.org, the networked connections, technical and social capital of the most successful—in terms of signatures—meant that it could scale up and gain prominence in its field more quickly than its competitors. Indeed, in their willingness to collaborate with others, the latter petition, in my opinion, approximated more closely an alignment with the "historic mission of establishing truth in the world". According to Debord (ibid.), this is unable to be achieved by isolated agents, "but only and always by the class that is able to dissolve all classes by reducing all power to the de-alienating form of realized democracy – to councils in which practical theory verifies itself and surveys its own actions". Such attributes were, indeed, more evidently on display in those instances (as the interviewee describes) in which the petition creative (as discussed previously) collaborated with NTIA and Brixton BIDs in respect to their joint representations to Lambeth Council's summary licence review of the O2 Academy Brixton. In collaboration with these agencies, the isolated petition creative approximated more closely what Debord describes as a situation in which "individuals [are] 'directly linked to world history' – there where dialogue has armed itself to impose its own conditions" (ibid.).

References

Bourdieu, P., (1990); The Logic of Practice, Trans., Nice, R., Stanford, California:Stanford University Press.

Change.org (2023); What does it mean to promote a petition? Change.org. Available at: https://help.change.org/managing-petitions

Change.org (2023a); *Save Brixton Academy, S.B. Started this Petition to Lambeth Council.* Change.org. Available at: https://www.change.org/p/save-brixton-academy-savebrixtonacademy

Change.org (2023b); *Save Brixton Academy from Permanent Closure, Ben White Started this Petition*, Change.org. Available at: https://www.change.org/p/ save-brixton-academy-from-permanent-closure

Change.org (2023c); Why this Petition Matters, by D.P. - Change.org. Available at: https://www.change.org/p/save-brixton-acadamy-from-closure?source_ location=tag_

Debord, G., (1967/2014); *Society of the Spectacle*, Trans. Knabb, K., Berkeley: Bureau of Public Secrets.

Debord, G., (1988/1990); *Comments on the Society of the Spectacle*, Trans. Imrie, M., London: Verso.

Night Time Industries Association (2023); *The Prodigy, Muse, Skunk Anansie, NME, Mixmag join 20,000 Music Fans in Campaign to Save Brixton Academy*, Night Time Industries Association (NTIA), 15th May 2023. Available at: https://www.ntia.co.uk/over-10000-representations-sent-to-lambeth-council-to-save-brixton-academy-says-ntia-sos-brixton-bid/?_ga=2.8464674 8.457519409.1684503913-

Ticketmaster (2024); Our Story. Available at: https://business.ticketmaster.co.uk/ why-ticketmaster/our-story/

Wacquant, L. J. D. (1993). From Ruling Class to Field of Power: An Interview with Pierre Bourdieu on La Noblesse d'État. *Theory, Culture & Society, 10*(3), 19–44. https://doi.org/10.1177/026327693010003002

CHAPTER 9

Conclusion: Feminine Soul of Black Critical Theory

O2 Academy Brixton, Street Level, 211 Stockwell Road, London SW9 9SL, December 2023, Photographer © Pamela Odih

© The Author(s), under exclusive license to Springer Nature Switzerland AG 2024
P. Odih, *Black British Postcolonial Feminist Ways of Seeing Human Rights*, https://doi.org/10.1007/978-3-031-71877-9_9

In a piece originally published in the 1960s and entitled *Perennial Fashion*, Adorno directs specific disenchantment at jazz music. While most aspects of Adorno's critique regarding the structural form of jazz apply generally to the 1941 *On Popular Music*—regarding the standardisation and pseudo-individualisation—*Perennial Fashion* contains several insights original to the African and American history of jazz. Adorno (1997) applies a reactionary archaeology of jazz so as to arrive at his usual termination of derision and discord with this genre of music. It is therefore unsurprising that he insists that the "African elements in jazz" although seemingly primitive and naturalistic, "was from the very beginning integrated into a strict scheme" (ibid. 121). He contends that this integration is not entirely the outcome of scurrilous marketing practices. For, it is his belief that the propensity of rigidification and commercialisation transpire from the genre itself. "The abuse of jazz is not the external calamity in whose name the puristic defenders of 'real' unadulterated jazz furiously protest; such misuse originates in jazz itself" (ibid.). Using, terms that contemporarily are perceived as offensive, although germane to the 1960s context when writing, Adorno identifies the roots of jazz in the transatlantic slave trade of the eighteenth and nineteenth century; and its attenuation with the rise of industrial capitalism. He uses this era's formulation of the as a basis for the claim the commercial exploitation of jazz is rooted in jazz itself. Borne from the captivity of human enslaved people, jazz was a means of oral history to bear witness to the depravity and inhumanity of the capitalist-driven state sponsored capture and transportation of human beings. Adorno cynically deploys the role of music stating that, "The Negro spirituals, antecedents of the blues, were slave songs and as such combined the lament of unfreedom with its oppressed confirmation" (ibid.). The proposition being that jazz rather than a catalyst for agency merely is an expression in musical form of the experience of enslavement and unfreedom in a totalitarian system of inhumane exploitation. Furthermore, according to Adorno (ibid.) it is difficult to isolate the definitively "authentic Negro elements in jazz" this is because the White lumpenproletariat were also a ruthlessly exploited aspect of the capitalist driven slave trade as they were moved in and out of the lowest positions of the paid labour market in respect to its replacement by enslaved people and newly emancipated slaves. The total effective rendering of the Black experience as an authentic element of jazz according to Adorno is that of pseudo-individualisation. The latter relates to a situation in which jazz is marketed as "consumer art" created especially for the audience listening; it is "The particular

9 CONCLUSION: FEMININE SOUL OF BLACK CRITICAL THEORY 301

effects with which jazz fills out its schema, syncopation above all, strive to create the appearance of being the outburst or caricature of untrammelled subjectivity – in effect, that of the listener – or perhaps the most subtle nuance dedicated to the greater glory of the audience" (ibid. 125).

According to Adorno, this promise of a personalised ingenuity is inevitably unrealised, mainly because of the need to remain within the creative boundaries of the genre, so that it can be recognised as audibly jazz; even when the artist is expressing their creative music through improvisation—it has still to be audibly jazz. For, Adorno (ibid. 131) an overall consequence of these features is that jazz is a Delphic esurient passion:

> Art is permitted to survive only if it renounces the right to be different, and integrates itself into the omnipotent realm of the profane which finally took over the taboo. Nothing may exist which is not like the world as it is. Jazz is the false liquidation of art – instead of utopia becoming reality it disappears from the picture. (ibid.)

The Frankfurt School's collectives of mainly German intellectuals originally affiliated, in the 1930s, to the Institute for Social Research at the University of Frankfurt are contiguous with a trajectory in Karl Marx's (1857/1973) *Grundrisse* that views advancing communication technology as a capitalist accumulation, dialectical imperative. Adorno's (1941) *On Popular Music*, provides insightful misgivings and graphical trepidations that have relevance to the (pseudo)standardising technological processes within the contemporary music industry. As a member of the Frankfurt School's Jewish diaspora Adorno's refugee migration away from Germany, in 1933, with the rise of the Third Reich, clearly sedimented into his consciousness the extent to which propagandist authoritarian can inveigle and mobilise into standardised formulaic syncopations, manufacturing and distribution of popular music. Consequently, Adorno's critical theory was actuated by what he perceived to be mechanical reproductions automated into technical delivery and lyrical constructions of jazz. Notwithstanding, the existence of a degree of commercialised cliché jazz creative production speaks to the racialised historical context of Black experience. Counterposed to Adorno's intransigence to recognising the interpretative capacities of human subjectivity, writers professing the political effectivity of Black music cultures have frequently drawn upon the insights of W.E.B. Du Bois (1903) *The Souls of Black Folk*. Du Bois applies intellectual erudition and critical thinking in discerning that, "After the

Egyptian and Indian, the Greek and Roman, the Teuton and Mongolian, the Negro is a sort of seventh son, born with a veil, and gifted with second-sight in this American world, – a world which yields him no true self-consciousness, but only lets him see himself through the revelation of the other world" (ibid. 3). Du Bois, in this respect provides for an alternative reading of Black music emerging from the capitalist culture industry. Whereby, they can be discerned as expressions of the conflicts and contradictions of the lived experience of being Black in a society in which the definition of self-conscious belonging is embodied by Whiteness. Similarly, Afrobeat while needlessly afflicted by capitalistic commercialism is borne from the expression of a way of seeing beyond the colonial veil that obfuscates and refracts the integrity of Black consciousness. In seeking to give voice to local experiences of internationally colonial influences on Black vernacular culture, Afrobeat invited an awareness of the history of the Black West African diaspora in a situation in which generations in the aftermath of British colonialism have struggled to recognise subjectively a "true self-consciousness"; in so doing, challenges the colonial tropes of Black music as emotional catharsis and or melancholic entropy. For, its emergence in times of struggle with colonialism is evidence of the inspiriting, revivalist, cultural political effectivity of a music that pierces through the veil of obscurity and speaks truth to power. As a survivalist pedagogy, Afrobeat affirms that Black experience generations in the aftermath of colonialism is in actuality "gifted with second-sight" in a (post)colonial world. Afrobeat as a pedagogy of resistance informs conscious awareness of what Du Bois defined as "a peculiar sensation, this double-consciousness, this sense of always looking at one's self through the eyes of others, of measuring one's soul by the tape of a world that looks on in amused contempt and pity" (ibid.). Furthermore, Du Bois develops the notion of a separation from self and the ways of seeing the Black racialised subject, in terms of the concept of "two-ness" stating that, "One ever feels his two-ness – an American, a Negro; two souls, two thoughts, two unreconciled strivings; two warring ideals in one dark body, whose dogged strength alone keeps it from being torn asunder" (ibid.).

9 CONCLUSION: FEMININE SOUL OF BLACK CRITICAL THEORY

TIMELY REFLECTIONS: LIMITS OF SMART CITIES, DIGITALLY POLICING CRISIS HETEROTOPIAS

It has been the primary objective of this book to identify the anticolonial, decolonial and post-colonial antecedents of Afrobeat and critically examine the political efficacy of their mobilisation in the affirmation of communicative action as a human right.

On 15th December 2022 at the O2 Academy Brixton tragedy cruelly snatched away the lives of 33-year-old Rebecca Ikumelo and 23-year-old Gaby Hutchinson. The following statement headed a renewed appeal for witnesses: "Today (Thursday, 15 June [2023, 06:00]), detectives have renewed their appeal for witnesses to the incident at the O2 Academy Brixton, as the families of the victims pay tribute to their loved ones six months on" (Metropolitan Police 2023g). The news release contained appeals for further information made by members of the victims' family and the police. We are informed in the publication that significant volumes of information have been collected by the police as thus, "Over the last six months, officers have reviewed hundreds of hours of CCTV, social media footage and police body worn video, as well, as interviewing a significant number of witnesses and reviewing forensic evidence" (ibid.). But despite this abundance of information gathered the Detective Chief Inspector assigned as the senior investigating officer suggested that it was not sufficient, as can be discerned from the following statement: "It is of the utmost importance that we work out why the surge happened, for the families of those who never returned home, and those who were injured and traumatised" (ibid.). Additionally, significant is that the Detective Chief Inspector placed emphasis on the possibility of the existence of some as yet unknown footage that might be the epiphany, as they expressed it:

> We know there were thousands of people there and that many will have seen what happened. Footage shared on social media immediately after the incident showed dozens of people filming on their phones … We are grateful to everyone who has come forward so far, but we still need more information from those who were there that evening. Please do not assume we have the information or images you are in possession of. We are especially interested in video footage from that evening. (ibid.)

The focus on a possible disclosure, elucidated from crowd sourced footage conspicuously contradicts the news media reports of the Detective

Chief Inspector's 15th June statement. For example, the BBC (2023) in an article entitled, *Brixton Academy Crush Victim's Families Still Seek Justice*, report the Chief Inspector as saying of the criminal investigation that the potential offences included: "corporate manslaughter, criminal negligence manslaughter, unlawful act manslaughter and health and safety at work offences, along with violent disorder and offences against the person or assaults". Indeed, a focus on corporate manslaughter indicates a very different direction of investigation when compared to the Metropolitan Police (2023g) news release's emphasis on the immediate percipients of the crowd crush. Further indication of a shift or consolidation of the investigation towards the organisation and thus a structural focus is evident in the Police Witness statement delivered on 3rd May 2023. Whereby, the Metropolitan Police (2023h) accused Academy Music Group (AMG) of failing to agree that concerns had been reported in February 2020 pertaining to "the weakness of the [external entrance] doors". And that since the Summary Review of Licence hearing, 16th January 2023, AMG had focussed too narrowly "on preventing the 'crowding around the front doors of the premises'" (ibid.). Consequently, it was the Metropolitan Police's stated view, "AGM appear to regard 'the incident' simply as the gathering of the crowd outside the entrance to the Academy [O2 Academy Brixton] and the 'uncontrolled manner' of their entry. What happened inside, however, is as much a part of the incident as what happened outside, if not more so: the fatalities occurred in the foyer" (ibid.). As a consequence, the Metropolitan Police conclude the witness statement with the declaration: "The MPS has lost confidence in the Premises licence Holder. Regrettably, the agreed "variation solution" suggested to the sub-committee at the review hearing on 16 January has not been successful in identifying the remedial measures which need to be in place before the Academy can safely re-open" (ibid.). It has been the overall and consistent observation of this book, that the 15th December O2 Academy tragedy has significance to the corporation and its organisational management. However, it is my contention that the organisation's conduct needs to be placed within a wider context pertaining to the policing of Black music cultures and culture industry's colonial digital capitalist marketising of Black music culture.

Digital Policing of the Crisis: "Seize the Opportunities of Data and Digital Tech to Become a World Leader in Policing", is a key chapter in the Metropolitan Police Business Plan 2021–2024; and a consistent business theme since the initial iteration of the 2016–2020 digital strategy. It is significant that the pursuit of opportunities in digital policing has advanced from an operational strategy for the re-engineering of office technology and its cloud productivity to becoming an integral analytical tool of the policing frontline. Digital policing is a prominent feature of the Policing Vision 2025 and Metropolitan Police's prioritising of this articulates with the National Digital Data and Technology strategy 2020–2030. Digital policing was decidedly present in the police statements delivered in the immediate aftermath of the 15th December 2022 O2 Academy Brixton critical incident during the Afrobeat concert of the Nigerian artist Asake. Indeed, the prominence of digital policing language, rhetoric and practice expressed the Metropolitan Police's commitment to the role it ascribed to digital policing in the provisioning of enhanced "and more granular data analytics to identify trends, causative factors and situational awareness" (Metropolitan Police Service 2021a: 12). It is envisaged that this analytical tool will enable an efficient informational policing thus providing more available time for frontline police officers to concentrate "on preventative action locally" and provide a more contextually knowledgeable response. As the business plan expresses it: "By building out technical links through our API strategy with broader partner agencies, we facilitate the ethical exchange of richer information in a more responsive manner to enable better delivery of the right support to those that need it most" (ibid.). With specific regard to this chapter's document-based case study examination into the visualisation of images of minority ethnics in respect to the O2 Academy Brixton critical incident, a consistent finding is evidence of a commodification in the centralisation of digital data. The Metropolitan Police's enrichment of its Single Online Home has been prominent in what the MPS describes as improving "the digital channels available to citizens and businesses for the reporting of crime and accessing of essential prevention and protection information" (ibid.). For its enabling technological infrastructure, facilitated through digital policing, is intended to achieve an acceleration in "the analysis of information in support of intelligence and investigatory activities" (ibid.). Axiomatic with the digitally technology facilitation of Single Online Home has been an enhancement in the capacity to share digital material across forces in articulation with national and international agencies. As the business strategy expresses it, "Through the use of collaboration tooling we are improving the sharing of digital material with our partners across the criminal justice service and making proceedings for victims, witnesses and officers more flexible and convenient so that they are less intrusive and improve the overall experience" (ibid.).

The Spectre of Automated Ticket Selling and Hyper-Advertised Black Music Cultures: A consistently stated intention of the MPS is for it to become "a data-rich organisation". Indeed, the pursuit of data enrichment pervades the language and rhetorical construction of its business strategy, decision-making and procurement of frontline policing technology. As is evident in the following statement on knowledge and data management: "We have established a Data Board which oversees the delivery of the Data Strategy and our progress towards the Met Direction ambition to become a data driven organisation" (ibid. 38). Advances in policing technologies is profligate and market-driven, similarly determined it the MPS's ambitions to keep pace of developments in Artificial Intelligence (AI); and this is resolutely steadfast. As it expresses, "Our plan is to harness the use of machine learning and other forms of Artificial Intelligence. This is essential to help us keep pace with the proliferation in digital data" (ibid.). Nevertheless, and despite the professed endeavour to be in advance of developments in AI, the MPS appears not to have sufficiently anticipated that the Asake concert of 15th December 2022 would outstrip demand relative to the supply of tickets. Much of this aspect of the overall policing complexity resides with inadequacies in the implementation of successive legislations intended to ban the use by ticket touts of automated software to purchase large volumes of tickets and sell them at hugely inflated prices. In 2018, the Department for Digital, Culture, Media and Sport, published a press release entitled *Ticket bots Ban Comes into Force*. The press release contains a statement from the Digital and the Creative Industries Minister Margot James, in which they admonish the ticket tout secondary ticket sales market in which automated software inflated prices in excess of their market value; and thus, preventing fans from seeing their artists, "at a fair price". The Minister declared in 2018 that "From today I am pleased to say that we have successfully banned the bots. We are giving the power back to consumers". Alas, the triumphant acclaim to have banned the bots has been proven to have been premature, with regard to the extent to which, The Breaching of Limits on Ticket Sales Regulations 2018, has been successful in eradicating the use of computer software programs to enable or facilitate the acquisition of tickets in excess of an imposed limit, with a view to upping financial gain. While it is enshrined in UK law that the breaching of limits on ticket sales is a criminal offence, it is evident from the tragic events at the O2 Academy Brixton on 15th

December 2022 that the digitalised secondary market for concert tickets in conjunction with its inflated ticket sale prices is still insufficiently regulated. Academy Music Group states in its ticketing terms and conditions that: "As an authorised ticket agent, Ticketmaster sells tickets on behalf of the venue, promoter or producer from whom we obtain tickets to sell to you as our 'Event Partner'" (AMG 2023). Without intending to cast aspersions on this official procurement, it is evident from the numerous reports of witnesses caught up in the crowd crush that the secondary market supply chain of tickets had been tainted by nefarious practices. Such that, and according to my analytical review, the circumstances that led to the crowd crush were quite evidently a partial consequence of an automated ticketing market exploitative selling, in excess of the venue's capacity and motivated by profligate gains derived from the price inflated, hyper-advertised concert tickets as part of the commodification of the cultural political discourse of Black communities online; and in so doing breached the community's human right to communicative action. As a further affirmation of my insistence that market distortion in live concert ticket sales is an assault on civil and human rights, on 23rd May 2024 the U.S. Department of Justice released the following notice of pending legal action: "The Justice Department, along with 30 state and district attorneys general, filed a civil antitrust lawsuit against Live Nation Entertainment Inc. and its wholly-owned subsidiary, Ticketmaster LLC (Live Nation-Ticketmaster) for monopolization and other unlawful conduct that thwarts competition in markets across the live entertainment industry". In the UK, on 5th September 2024 the Competition and Markets Authority (CMA 2024) opened an investigation about the dynamic pricing mechanism used by Ticketmaster. Although the CMA clearly intend to provision market-based competition in the live concert music industry, in my opinion the CMA is falling perilously short of an overall investigation into monopoly capitalist activities, third-party automated selling, the use of Artificial Intelligence to inflate demand for live concert music events, and the irregular compliance with consumer protection law.

Colonial Digital Capitalism: Acknowledging concerns raised about the prominence of data analytics to the MPS's future ambitions, it has invested further in improving its service to the public in respect to privacy rights. But its fervour for notoriously privacy depleting and human rights dispossessing market-based data-rich information, technology and digital analytic capabilities presents new and evolving challenges that destabilise MPS's assurance of securing privacy rights. It is a contention of this study that the centrality of data-driven analytics to MPS's operations does indeed produce calculable improvements in policing outcomes; however, it is my contention that this achievement is at a costlier disbursement to the market-based capitalisation of privacy rights. Indeed, a primary contention of this case study is that the centralisation of data sharing, facilitated through digital business operations, is integrating the MPS further into capitalist policing technology markets and the disproportionate commodification of gender racialised data subjects. A consequence of which is an irregularly effectual protection of their right to security in accessing and experiencing public recreational spaces as part of their affirmation of communicative action as a human right.

On 15th September 2023, Lambeth Council issued a *Statement on the O2 Academy Brixton Licensing Sub Committee Decision*. It was announced that the extensive licence review that had commenced soon after the 15th December 2022 crowd crush tragedy that, "Lambeth Council's Licensing Sub-Committee has permitted the O2 Brixton Academy to re-open, but only once it has met 77 extensive and robust new conditions designed to promote public safety, including the safety of both visitors and employees". It was concluded that, "The investigation into whether any criminal offences have been committed is being led by the Met Police, and their work continues. Lambeth Council will do everything we can to support this police investigation so that there are answers and justice for the families of Rebecca Ikumelo and Gabrielle Hutchinson who tragically lost their lives at the Academy in December" (Lambeth Council 2023c). On 13 August 2024 the MPS issued an update in respect to their investigation of the crush incident at the O2 Academy Brixton. The investigation was still active and populated by a team of dedicated detectives. It was stated that, "Over the last 12 months, 100s of hours of CCTV have been meticulously examined, more than 500 witness statements have been taken and over 5,000 pieces of evidence have been seized" (Metropolitan Police Service 2024d). It was further stated that, "We remain focused on establishing exactly what happened that tragic evening, how Rebecca and Gaby came to lose their lives and why a young woman remains in hospital in a very serious condition a year later" (ibid.). It concludes with the heart rendering statement: "No one should ever go to work and not come home". Indeed, as per the thousands of people that went to celebrate the Nigerian artist Asake perform Afrobeat at the O2 Academy Brixton, no one should lose their life in pursuit of the human right of communicative action.

9 CONCLUSION: FEMININE SOUL OF BLACK CRITICAL THEORY 309

REFERENCES

Academy Music Group (2023); *Academy Music Group – Ticketing Terms and Conditions.* Available at: https://www.academymusicgroup.com/o2academy-brixton/ticketing-tcs

Adorno, T., (1941); On Popular Music, *Studies in Philosophy and Social Science,* Vol. 9, pp., 17–48.

Adorno, T., (1997); *Prisms,* Trans, Weber, S and Weber, S., Massachusetts: MIT Press.

BBC (2023); Brixton Academy Crush Victims' Families Still Seek Justice, BBC News. Available at: https://www.bbc.co.uk/news/uk-england-london-65900715

Competition and Markets Authority (CMA) (2024); *Ticketmaster: Consumer Protection Case,* Competition and Markets Authority Cases and Projects, GOV. UK. Available at: https://www.gov.uk/cma-cases/ticketmaster-consumer-protection-case

Department for Culture, Media and Sport, (2018); *Press Release; Ticket Bots Ban comes into Force,* Department for Culture, Media and Sport. Available at: https://www.gov.uk/government/news/ticket-bots-ban-comes-into-force

Du Bois, W. E. B., (1903/1994); *The Souls of Black Folk,* [unabridged text as first published by A.C. McClurg and Co., Chicago in 1903], USA: Dover Publications.

Lambeth Council (2023c); Statement on the O2 Academy Brixton Licensing Sub Committee Decision, 15 September 2023, Lambeth Council. Available at: https://love.lambeth.gov.uk/statement-on-the-o2-academy-brixton-licensing-sub-committee-decision/

Marx, K., (1857/1973); *Grundrisse; Foundations of the Critique of Political Economy,* Trans. Nicolaus, M., London: Penguin Books in Association with New Left Reviews.

Metropolitan Police (2023g); *Families Pay Tribute to Loved Ones Six Months on 319 From Incident at O2 Academy Brixton.* Available at: https://news.met.police.320uk/news/families-pay-tribute-to-loved-ones-six-months-on-from-incident-at-321 o2-academy-brixton-468507

Metropolitan Police (2023h); [Metropolitan Police] Statement of Witness, 14th April 2023. Lambeth Licensing - Licensing Application Documents, 23/00773/PRMREV, Premises Licence (review application) Expired, Brixton Academy 211 Stockwell Road London SW9 9SL. Available at: https://planning.lambeth.gov.uk/online-applications/licencingApplicationDetails.do?activeTab=documents&keyVal=RT9HVVBO0BN00

Metropolitan Police Service (2021a); *Metropolitan Police Service, Business Plan 2021–24.* Metropolitan Police. Available at: Business Plan Met 2024 https://www.met.police.uk/SysSiteAssets/media/downloads/force-content/met/about-us/met-business-plan-2021-24

Metropolitan Police Service (2024d); *UPDATED: Images of Nine People Re Brixton Crush Investigation*, August 13, 2024 16:53 BST, Metropolitan Police. Available at: https://news.met.police.uk/news/images-of-13-people-released-as-part-of-investigation-into-brixton-crush-476903

U.S. Department of Justice (2024); Live Nation-Ticketmaster's Exclusionary Conduct and Dominance Across the Live Concert Ecosystem Harms Fans, Innovation, Artists, and Venues, U.S. Department of Justice. Available at: https://www.justice.gov/opa/pr/justice-department-sues-live-nation-ticketmaster-monopolizing-markets-across-live-concert

References

@ Libertyhq (2023); *Police #FacialRecognition has Indeed been Independently Scrutinised by the Courts which Said Police use Broke Human Rights, Equalities and Data protection Laws.* Liberty. Available at: https://twitter.com/libertyhq

@Asakemusik (2022a); *AsakeLondon; Sunday 11th December.* Available at: https://twitter.com/asakemusik

@asakemusik (2022b); @asakemusik. Dec 17, 2022. Available at: https://twitter.com/asakemusik

@Metropolitan Police Events (2023); *Live Facial Recognition is One of a number of Tactics for the #Coronation Security Operation.* Available at: https://twitter.com/MetPoliceEvents

Academy Music Group (2023); *Academy Music Group – Ticketing Terms and Conditions.* Available at: https://www.academymusicgroup.com/o2academy-brixton/ticketing-tcs

Academy Music Group (2024); Venue Information, O2 Academy Brixton, *Academy Music Group.* Available at: https://www.academymusicgroup.com/companyo2academybrixton/

Academy Music Group, (2022); *We Love Brixton, About Us,* O2 Academy Brixton. Available at: https://www.academymusicgroup.com/o2academybrixton/about-us

ACHPR, ECHR, IACHR (2021); 2020 Joint Law Report, African Court on Human and Peoples' Rights (ACHPR), European Court of Human Rights (ECHR), Inter-American Court of Human Rights (ICHR). Available at: https://echr.coe.int/Documents/Joint_Report_2020_AfCHPR_ECHR_IACHR_ENG.pdf

© The Author(s), under exclusive license to Springer Nature Switzerland AG 2024
P. Odih, *Black British Postcolonial Feminist Ways of Seeing Human Rights*, https://doi.org/10.1007/978-3-031-71877-9

312 REFERENCES

Abiodun, R. (1989). Woman in Yoruba Religious Images. *African Languages and Cultures*, 2(1), 1–18. http://www.jstor.org/stable/1771702

Adejumobi, S. A. (2003); Affirmative Action and the Politics of Social Reform in a Global Context. *The Black Scholar*, 33(3/4), 32–36. http://www.jstor.org/stable/41069042

Adimora, M., (2021); 5 Ingenious Forgotten Female Pioneers of Afrobeat. You Should Know, British Vogue. Available at: https://www.vogue.co.uk/arts-and-lifestyle/gallery/forgotten-women-afrobeat

Adorno, T., (1941); On Popular Music, *Studies in Philosophy and Social Science*, Vol. 9, pp., 17–48

Adorno, T., (2001); *The Culture Industry*, London and New York: Routledge.

Adorno, T., (1997); *Prisms*, Trans, Weber, S and Weber, S., Massachusetts: MIT Press.

Adorno, T., and Horkheimer, M., (1944/1997); *Dialectic of Enlightenment*, London: Verso

African Union (2022); *Statement of the African Union on the Reported Ill Treatment of Africans Trying to Leave Ukraine*, African Union, Addis Ababa, Ethiopia. Available at: https://au.int/sites/default/files/pressreleases/41534-pr-english.pdf

Ajiola, F. O., (2019); Fela Anikulapo Kuti, Afrobeat Genre and Socio-political Activism in Nigeria, *ASUU Journal of Social Sciences, a Journal of Research and development*, Vol., 6, Nos. 1 & 2, January & December, 2019; pp., 165–183.

Althusser, L., (1971a); *Lenin and Philosophy and Other Essays*, Trans., Brewster, B., New York and London: Monthly Review Press.

Althusser, L., (1971b/2014); *On the Reproduction of Capitalism; Ideology and Ideological State Apparatuses*, Trans., from French, Goshgarian, M.G., London, New York: Verso.

Álvarez, M., (2022); Monumentality and Anticolonial Resistance: Feminist Graffiti in Mexico, Public Art Dialogue, 12:2, 178–194, https://doi.org/10.1080/21502552.2022.2112349

Amnesty International (1985); *Nigeria: The Case of Fela Anikulapo Kuti*, Amnesty International, January 1, 1985, Index Number: AFR 44/002/1985. Available at: https://www.amnesty.org/en/documents/afr44/002/1985/en/

Amnesty International (2010); *Fela Kuti, PoC, Nigeria*, Amnesty International. Available at: http://static.amnesty.org/ai50/fela_kuti_en.pdf

Amnesty International (2018); *Toxic Twitter – A Toxic Place for Women*, Amnesty International. Available at: https://www.amnesty.org/en/latest/research/2018/03/online-violence-against-women-chapter-1-1/

Amnesty International (2020); UK: Online Abuse Against Black Women MPs 'Chilling', Amnesty International. Available at: https://www.amnesty.org.uk/press-releases/uk-online-abuse-against-black-women-mps-chilling

REFERENCES   313

Amrute, S., (2016); *Encoding Race, Encoding Class: Indian IT Workers in Berlin*, Durham: Duke University Press.

Anikulapo-Kuti, F. (1989). "Animal can't dash me human rights." Interview with Jane Bryce, *Index on Censorship*, 18(9), 12–13. https://doi.org/10.1080/03064228908534717

Ashcroft, B., (2001); *Post-Colonial Transformation of Colonial*, London: Routledge.

Axon (2021); Axon Enterprise Media Press Kit. Updated January 2021. Available at: https://prismic-io.s3.amazonaws.com/axon-2/93dca185-9d0b-4b87-b1a3-3bdb887dff57_MediaPressKit_AxonEnterprise_2021+%281%29.pdf

Back, L., (1996); New Ethnicities and Urban Culture; Social Identity and Racism in the Lives of Young People, London: Routledge.

Bailey, D., and Hall, S., (1992); *Critical Decade: Black British Photography in the 80s*, Birmingham: Ten.8.

Baker, C., (2020) What female pop-folk celebrity in south-east Europe tells post-socialist feminist media studies about global formations of race, Feminist Media Studies, 20:3, 341–360, https://doi.org/10.1080/14680777.2019.1599035

Barber, L. (1983) "Fela Kuti: The Republic Of Kuti". *Melody Maker*. Fela Kuti. Retrieved February 4, 2024, from http://www.rocksbackpages.com/Library/Article/fela-kuti-the-republic-of-kuti

Barlow, J., and Smith, G., (2019) What The Health (WTH)?: Theorising Southern Black Feminisms in the US South, Agenda, 33:3, 19–33, DOI: https://doi.org/10.1080/10130950.2019.1668725

Barthes, R., (1972/2000); *Mythologies*, London: Vintage Books.

Baudrillard, J., (1994); *Simulacra and Simulation*, Ann Arbor, Michigan: University of Michigan Press.

BBC (2013); *Gabriel Gbadamosi on Fela Kuti*, BBC Great Lives. Available at: https://www.bbc.co.uk/programmes/b0383yt5

BBC (2020); *Creative Diversity Report, 2020*, Vol. 1, BBC. Available at: http://downloads.bbc.co.uk/aboutthebbc/reports/reports/creative-diversity-report-2020.pdf

BBC (2021); *BBC Pulls Out of Stonewall Diversity Scheme*, British Broadcast Corporation 10th November 2021. Available at: https://www.bbc.co.uk/news/entertainment-arts-59232736

BBC (2021a); *Diversity and Inclusion Plan, 2021–2023*, BBC. Available at: https://www.bbc.com/diversity/documents/bbc-diversity-and-inclusion-plan20-23.pdf

BBC (2023a); Brixton Academy Crush Victims' Families Still Seek Justice, BBC News. Available at: https://www.bbc.co.uk/news/uk-england-london-65900715

BBC (2023b); *Catastrophe at the Academy*, File on 4, BBC Radio 4. Available at: https://www.bbc.co.uk/programmes/m001h49y

314 REFERENCES

Bell, M., (2016); Fela Kuti Mento Sandra Izsadore Still Trying to Change the World Through Song, Calgary Herald, August 09, 2016. Available at: https://calgaryherald.com/entertainment/music/fela-kuti-mentor-sandra-izsadore-still-trying-to-change-the-world-through-song

Besseny, A., (2020); Lost in spotify: folksonomy and wayfinding functions in spotify's interface and companion apps, Popular Communication,18:1, 1–17, DOI: https://doi.org/10.1080/15405702.2019.1701674

Bijl, P., (2017) Human Rights and Anticolonial Nationalism in Sjahrir's *Indonesian Contemplations*, Law & Literature, 29:2, 247–268, https://doi.org/10.1080/1535685X.2016.1268769

Bourdieu, P., (1990); The Logic of Practice, Trans., Nice, R., Stanford, California:Stanford University Press.

Brettschneider, M., Burgess, S., and Keating, C., (2017); *LGBTQ Politics a Critical Reader*, New York: New York University Press.

Brixton BID (2021a); *A Bond Across the Pond. A First of its Kind Twinning Joins Two Important Business Improvement Districts (BID) and Forges a Bond Across the Pond in Two Radical Communities of Colour.* Brixton BID. Available at: https://brixtonbid.co.uk/content/uploads/2021/06/BID-Twinning-Brixton-Harlem.pdf

Brixton BID (2021b); *Walk and Talk Initiative, Safer Day and Night.* Available at: https://brixtonbid.co.uk/walk-and-talk-initiative/

Brixton BID (2023a); *About Brixton BIDs.* Available at: https://brixtonbid.co.uk/about/

Brixton BID (2023b); *Brixton Monthly Report – December 2022, Brixton Business Improvement District.* Available at: https://brixtonbid.co.uk/content/uploads/2023/02/LPR_Brixton-BID_-Levy-Payer-Report-Dec-2022_2022_11_v1.pdf

Brixton BID (2023c); *Save the O2 Academy Brixton.* Available at: https://brixtonbid.co.uk/save-the-o2-academy-brixton/

Brixton BID (2024); *Women's Night Safety Summit; Safe Day and Night,* 01/09/24. Available at: https://brixtonbid.co.uk/womens-night-safety-summit/

Bryce, J. (2022). 'Animal can't dash me human rights'. *Index on Censorship, 51*(1), 76–78. https://doi.org/10.1177/03064220221084534

BTG Legal (2023); The 'ChatGPT Effect' – Parsing Privacy and AI Regulation in India. BTG Legal. Available at: https://www.lexology.com/library/detail.aspx?g=93515d89-508a-43a8-ae56-91c785d9cc87

Byfield, J., (2003); Taxation, Women and the Colonial State, Egba Women's Tax Revolt, Meridians: Feminism, Race, Transnationalism, 2003, vol.,3, no., 2, pp. 250–77.

Byfield, J., (2012); Gender, Justice, and the Environment: Connecting the Dots, *African Studies Review*, April 2012, vol., 55, No., 1 (April 2012), pp., 1–12.

Byfield, J., (2015); "From Ladies to Women: Funmilayo Ransome-Kuti and Women's Political Activism in post-WW II Nigeria" in Mia Bay, Farah Griffin,

Martha Jones, Barbara Savage (eds.) *Toward an Intellectual History of Black Women*, University of North Carolina Press, 2015.

Byfield, J., (2016); "In Her Own Words: Funmilayo Ransome-Kuti and the Autobiography of an Archive" *Palimpsest: A Journal on Women, Gender and the Black International* Vol. 5, No. 2., pp., 108–127.

Byfield, J., (2021); *The Great Upheaval: Women and Nation in Postwar Nigeria*, Ohio University Press, 2021.

Cachalia, F., (2018); Democratic constitutionalism in the time of the postcolony: beyond triumph and betrayal, South African Journal on Human Rights, 34:3, 375–397, https://doi.org/10.1080/02587203.2018.1543838

Caprotti, F., Chang, I-Chun & Joss, S. (2022). Beyond the smart city: a typology of platform urbanism. Urban Transformations. 4. https://doi.org/10.1186/s42854-022-00033-9

Carbado, D., (2009); Black Rights, Gay Rights, Civil Rights, in Fineman, A., Jackson, J., and Romero, A., (eds.), *Feminist and Queer Legal Theory: Intimate Encounters, Uncomfortable Conversations*, Farnham: Ashgate, pp., 223–243, pp., 439–441.

Casalini, G., (2021); Trans Ecologies of Resistance in Digital (after)Lives: **micha cárdenas'** *Sin Sol/No Sun*, *Media-N*, *The Journal of the New Media Caucus*, Fall 2021, volume 17, Issue 2, Pages 8-26.

Cashmore, E., (1997); *The Black Culture Industry*, London: Routledge.

Castledine, J. (2008); "In a Solid Bond of Unity": Anticolonial Feminism in the Cold War Era. *Journal of Women's History* 20(4), 57–81. https://doi.org/10.1353/jowh.0.0053

Castells, M., (2010); *The Rise of the Network Society*, Second Edition, Sussex: Wiley-Blackwell.

Change.org (2023a); *Save Brixton Academy, S.B. Started this Petition to Lambeth Council.* Change.org. Available at: https://www.change.org/p/save-brixton-academy-savebrixtonacademy

Change.org (2023b); *Save Brixton Academy from Permanent Closure, Ben White Started this Petition*, Change.org. Available at: https://www.change.org/p/save-brixton-academy-from-permanent-closure

Change.org (2023c); *Business Model*, Change.org. Available at: https://www.change.org/about/business-model

Chi, H., (2011) Interactive Digital Advertising vs. Virtual Brand Community, Journal of Interactive Advertising, 12:1, 44–61, DOI: https://doi.org/10.1080/15252019.2011.10722190

Chimenti, P., (2021) Visualizing (Im)Mobility In Post-Reversion Okinawa: A Comparative Study Of NDU's *Asia Is One* (1973) And Chinen Seishin's *The Human Pavilion* (1976), *Journal of Japanese and Korean Cinema*, 13:2, 118–137, DOI: https://doi.org/10.1080/17564905.2021.1978828

Clark, M., (2020); DRAG THEM: A Brief Etymology of So-Called "Cancel culture", *Communication and the Public*, Vol.5(3–4), pp., 88–92.

316 REFERENCES

Cobo-Piñero, R., (2020) Afrobeat Journeys: Tracing the Musical Archive in Sefi Atta's *A Bit of Difference*, Journal of Intercultural Studies, 41:4, 442–456, DOI: https://doi.org/10.1080/07256868.2020.1779200

Coddington, K., (2017) Voice Under Scrutiny: Feminist Methods, Anticolonial Responses, and New Methodological Tools, The Professional Geographer, 69:2, 314–320, https://doi.org/10.1080/00330124.2016.1208512

Colonial Office (1947–1948); Note on Taxation of Women in Eastern Provinces, Colonial Office: Nigeria Original Correspondence. National Council of Nigeria and the Cameroons: Activities of Mrs Ransome-Kuti. The National Archives, Kew – Colonial office, Commonwealth and Foreign and Commonwealth Offices, 1947–1948, Reference: CO 583/293/1, National Archives, Kew, Richmond, TW9 4DU. Date of Visit: Tuesday 23rd April 2024; Booking Reference: RR147-950-06156K.

Competition and Markets Authority (CMA) (2020); *Online Platforms and Digital Advertising, Market Study Final Report*, 1 July 2020. Available at: https://assets.publishing.service.gov.uk/media/5fa557668fa8f5788db46efc/Final_report_Digital_ALT_TEXT.pdf

Competition and Markets Authority (CMA) (2021a); *Algorithms: How They Can Reduce Competition and Harm Consumers*, Competition and Markets Authority, Published 19 January, Gov.UK. Available at: https://www.gov.uk/government/publications/algorithms-how-they-can-reduce-competition-and-harm-consumers/algorithms-how-they-can-reduce-competition-and-harm-consumers

Competition and Markets Authority (CMA) (2021b); *Secondary Ticketing Websites*. Available at: https://www.gov.uk/cma-cases/secondary-ticketing-websites#full-publication-update-history

Competition and Markets Authority (CMA) (2024); *Ticketmaster: Consumer Protection Case*, Competition and Markets Authority Cases and Projects, GOV.UK. Available at: https://www.gov.uk/cma-cases/ticketmaster-consumer-protection-case

Cottingham, M., & Rose, A., (2023) Tweeting Jokes, Tweeting Hope: Humor Practices during the 2014 Ebola Outbreak, Health Communication, 38:9, 1954–1963, DOI: https://doi.org/10.1080/10410236.2022.2045059

Crenshaw, K. (1988). Race, Reform, and Retrenchment: Transformation and Legitimation in Antidiscrimination Law. *Harvard Law Review*, *101*(7), 1331–1387. https://doi.org/10.2307/1341398

Crenshaw, K. (1991). Mapping the Margins: Intersectionality, Identity Politics, and Violence against Women of Color. *Stanford Law Review*, *43*(6), 1241–1299. https://doi.org/10.2307/1229039

Cushing, T., (2023); Taser/Axon Separating Defense Lawyers From Body Camera Footage With License Agreements, Tech Dirt. Available at: https://www.techdirt.com/2017/05/08/taser-axon-separating-defense-lawyers-body-camera-footage-with-license-agreements/

Dabiri, E., (2020); Don't Touch my Hair, London: Penguin.

Dadzie, S., (2020); *A Kick in the Belly, Women, Slavery and Resistance*, London and New York: Verso.

Davis, A., (2003); *Are Prisons Obsolete?* New York: Seven Stories Press.

Davis, A., (1971a) Reflections on the Black Woman's Role in the Community of Slaves, The Black Scholar, 3:4, 2–15, DOI: https://doi.org/10.1080/00064246.1971.11431201

Davis, A., (1971b); *If They Come in the Morning, Voices of Resistance*, New York: The New American Library, Inc.

Davis, A., (1971/2016a); *If they Come in the Morning, Voices of Resistance*, London/New York: Verso.

Davis, A., (1971/2016b); Political Prisoners, Prisons and Black Liberation, in (eds.) *If They Come in the Morning, Voices of Resistance*, London: Verso.

Davis, A., (1971c) Reflections on the Black Woman's Role in the Community of Slaves, The Black Scholar, 3:4, 2–15, DOI: https://doi.org/10.1080/00064246.1971.11431201

Davis, A., (1983); *Women Race and Class*, New York: Vintage books; A Division of Random House.

Davis, A., (2014) Deepening the Debate over Mass Incarceration, Socialism and Democracy, 28:3, 15–23, DOI: https://doi.org/10.1080/08854300.2014.963945

Davis, A., (2016c); *Freedom Is a Constant Struggle; Ferguson, Palestine, and the Foundations of a Movement*, Chicago: Haymarket Books.

Davis, A., (2022); Foreword, in Ferdinand, M., *Decolonial Ecology: Thinking from the Caribbean World*, Cambridge: Polity.

Davis, A., (2024); Angela Y. Davis. *Women, Race, & Class.* Vol First Vintage books edition. Vintage; 1983. Accessed May 17, 2024. https://search-ebscohost-com.gold.idm.oclc.org/login.aspx?direct=true&db=nlebk&AN=738888&site=ehost-live

Davis, A., and Aptheker, B., (1971/2016); Preface, in (eds.) *If They Come in the Morning, Voices of Resistance*, London: Verso.

Davis, A., Magee, R., Soledad Brothers and Other Political Prisoners (1971/2016); *If They Come in the Morning; Voices of Resistance*, Forward by Bond, J., London/New York: Verso.

Dean, J., (2005); Communicative Capitalism: Circulation and the Foreclosure of Politics, *Cultural Politics*, Volume 1, Issue, 1, pp. 51–74.

Debord, G., (1967/2014); *Society of the Spectacle*, Trans. Knabb, K., Berkeley: Bureau of Public Secrets.

Debord, G., (1988/1990); *Comments on the Society of the Spectacle*, Trans. Imrie, M., London: Verso.

Denzin, N., (1970/2017); *The Research Act: A Theoretical Introduction to Sociological Methods* (1st ed.), Oxon/New York: Routledge.

318 REFERENCES

Denzin, N., (1970); *Research Act. A Theoretical Introduction to Sociological Methods*, New Brunswick and London: Aldine Transaction.

Department for Culture, Media and Sport (2023); *Cultural Recovery Fund Data Report*. Available at: https://www.gov.uk/government/publications/evaluation-and-data-report-for-the-culture-recovery-fund/cultural-recovery-fund-data-report

Department for Digital, Culture, Media and Sport, (2018); *Press Release; Ticket Bots Ban comes into Force*, Department for Digital, Culture, Media and Sport. Available at: https://www.gov.uk/government/news/ticket-bots-ban-comes-into-force

DHSC (2021a); *Chief Medical Officer Urges Public to Get Boosted Now*, Department of Health and Social Care and The RT Hon Sajid Javid MP. Available at: https://www.gov.uk/government/news/chief-medical-officer-urges-public-to-get-boosted-now

DHSC 2021b); *UK Marks One Year Since Approving COVID-19 Vaccine with Boost Day*, Department of Health and Social Care and Maggie Throup MP. Available at https://www.gov.uk/government/news/uk-marks-one-year-since-approving-covid-19-vaccine-with-boost-day

DHSC (2021c); All Adults in England Offered COVID-19 Booster Vaccine, Department of Health and Social Care, Maggie Throup MP and The Rt Hon Sajid. Available at: https://www.gov.uk/government/news/all-adults-in-england-offered-covid-19-booster-vaccine

Diganta Das and J. J. Zhang (2021a) Pandemic in a smart city: Singapore's COVID-19 management through technology & society, Urban Geography, 42:3, 408–416, DOI: https://doi.org/10.1080/02723638.2020.1807168

Du Bois, W. E. B., (1903/1994); *The Souls of Black Folk*, [unabridged text as first published by A.C. McClurg and Co., Chicago in 1903], USA: Dover Publications.

Eggar Forrester Creative (2020); *How Facial Recognition Technology Can be Used in Underwriting*, Eggar Forrester Creative. Available at: https://eggarforresterinsurance.com/creative/blog/facial-recognition-technology-underwriting/

Ellington, T., (2015); Social networking sites: a support system for African-American women wearing natural hair, International Journal of Fashion Design, Technology and Education, 8:1, 21–29, DOI: https://doi.org/10.1080/17543266.2014.974689

Emard, K., & Nelson, L. (2021). Geographies of global lifestyle migration: Towards an anticolonial approach. *Progress in Human Geography*, *45*(5), 1040–1060. https://doi.org/10.1177/0309132520957723

Engelmann, S. (2022); Pollution is Colonialism; Feminist Queer Anticolonial Propositions for Hacking the Anthropocene: Archive and Feminist Queer. *The AAG Review of Books*, *10*(4), 33–35. https://doi.org/10.1080/2325548X.2022.2114761

Eppley, K., (2019) Close reading: What is reading for?, *Curriculum Inquiry*, 49:3, 338–355, DOI: https://doi.org/10.1080/03626784.2019.1631701

Equality and Human Rights Commission (2022); *Preventing Hair Discrimination*, Equality and Human Rights Commission. Available at: https://www.equality-humanrights.com/guidance/public-sector-equality-duty/preventing-hair-discrimination-schools

Ermarth, E. D. (1995). Ph(r)ase Time: Chaos Theory and Postmodern Reports on Knowledge. *Time & Society*, 4(1), 91–110. https://doi.org/10.1177/0961463X95004001005

EtymologyOnline.com (2024); Colony. Available at: https://www.etymonline.com/search?q=colony

Evening Standard (2022); *Asake 'Devastated' After Woman Dies in Crowd Crush Outside*, Evening Standard 17 December 2022. Available at: https://www.standard.co.uk/culture/music/o2-academy-brixton-metropolitan-police-sadiq-khan-asake-london-b1047945.html

Fagg, W. B., (1950). A Bronze Figure in Ife Style at Benin. *Man*, 50, 69–70. https://doi.org/10.2307/2794524

Fagg, W. B., (1963); *Nigerian Images; The Splendour of African Sculpture*, London and New York: Frederick A. Praeger.

Fagg, W. B., (1966); *African Tribal Sculptures*, London: Methuen.

Fagg, W. B., (1967) The Art of Central Africa; Tribal Masks and Sculptures, London: Collins in Association with UNESCO.

Fagg, W. B., (1970); *African Sculpture*, Washington, D.C.: H. K. Press.

Fagg, W. B., (1972); *The Living Arts of Nigeria*, London: Macmillan.

Fela! (2010); Fela! the Musical, National Theatre Archive, National Theatre, London.

Felakuti.com (2023/2024); Story. Available at: https://felakuti.com/gb/story/1938

Felakuti.com (2024); Story:1986. Available at: https://felakuti.com/gb/story/1986

Ferdinand, M., (2022); *Decolonial Ecology: Thinking from the Caribbean World*, Cambridge: Polity.

Fielder, H. (1986) "Fela Kuti: Brixton Academy, London". *Sounds*. Fela Kuti. Retrieved February 3, 2024, from http://www.rocksbackpages.com/Library/Article/fela-kuti-brixton-academy-london-2

Fight For the Future (2022); *Ticketmaster*. Available at: https://futurism.com/the-byte/musicians-ticketmaster-facial-recognition-concerts

Fight for the Future (2023); *Ban Facial recognition at Live Shows*, Fight for the Future. Available at: https://www.banfacialrecognition.com/festivals/

Florini, S., (2014); Tweets, Tweeps and Signifyin': Communication and Cultural Performance on "Black Twitter", *Television and New Media*, Vol. 15(3), pp., 223–237.

320 REFERENCES

Foucault, M., (1980); 'Questions on Geography', in (ed.) Gordon, C., *Power/Knowledge Selected Interviews and other Writings 1972–1977*, New York: Pantheon Books.

Foucault, M., (1986); *Of Other Spaces*, Foucault, M., and Miskowiec, J., *Diacritics*, Vol.16, No. 1 (Spring, 1986), pp. 22–27.

Foucault, M., (1991); *Discipline and Punish; The Birth of the Prison*. trans., Sheridan, A., London: Penguin Books.

Frisina, A., and Hawthorne, C., (2018); Italians with veils and Afros: gender, beauty, and the everyday anti-racism of the daughters of immigrants in Italy, Journal of Ethnic and Migration Studies, 44:5, 718–735, DOI: https://doi.org/10.1080/1369183X.2017.1359510

G4S (2024); Who We Are. Available at: https://www.g4s.com/careers

Gilroy, P., (2007); *Black Britain: A Photographic History*, London: Saqi.

Goffman, E. (1989). ON FIELDWORK. *Journal of Contemporary Ethnography*, *18*(2), 123–132. https://doi.org/10.1177/089124189018002001

Goldberg, S., (2016); *Sexuality and Equality Law*, Oxon: Routledge.

Goldman, R. (1983). "We Make Weekends": Leisure and the Commodity Form. *Social Text*, *8*, 84–103. https://doi.org/10.2307/466324

Gov.UK (2014); *Business Improvement Districts; Information and Guidance on Business Improvement Districts*. Department for Levelling Up, Housing and Communities and Ministry of Housing, Community and Local Government. Available at: https://www.gov.uk/guidance/business-improvement-districts

Gov.UK (2015); *Business Improvement Districts: Guidance and Best Practice*, Ministry of Housing, Communities and Local Government. Available at: https://www.gov.uk/government/publications/business-improvement-districts-guidance-and-best-practice

Gov.UK (2020); *Funding Available Through the Culture Recovery Fund*, Department for culture, Media and Sport and Department for Digital, Culture Media and Sport, Gov.UK. Available at: https://www.gov.uk/guidance/funding-available-through-the-culture-recovery-fund

Gov.UK (2021); *Government-backed Insurance Scheme to Give Boost to Events Industry*, News Story, HM Treasury and Department for Digital, Culture, Media and Sport, published 5 August 2021. Available at: https://www.gov.uk/government/news/government-backed-insurance-scheme-to-give-boost-to-events-industry

Gov.UK (2023); Culture Recovery Fund. Available at: https://www.gov.uk/government/groups/culture-recovery-board

Graham, R., & Smith, 'Shawn. (2016). The Content of Our #Characters: Black Twitter as Counterpublic. *Sociology of Race and Ethnicity*, *2*(4), 433–449. https://doi.org/10.1177/2332649216639067

Grosfoguel, R., (2004); Race and Ethnicity or Racialized Ethnicities? Identities within Global Coloniality, Ethnicities, Vol. 4., Issue, 3., September, pp. 315–336.

Gurr, B., and Naples, N., (2013); Sex and Gender, in (eds) Brunsma, D., Smith, K., and Gran, B., (2013); The Handbook of Sociology and Human Rights, London: Paradigm Publishers Boulder.

Gutiérrez, A., (2022); Situating Representation as a Form of Erasure #OscarsSoWhite, Black Twitter, and Latinx Twitter, Television and New Media, Vol., 23 91) pp., 100–118.

Hagen, S., and de Zeeuw, D., (2023); Based and Confused: Tracing the Political Connotations of a Memetic Phrase Across the Web, *Big Data and Society*, January–June, pp., 1–16.

Hall, S., (1972); *Advertising and its Ideology*, Book Review: The Imagery of Power; a Critique of Advertising by Fried Inglis, The Guardian (London, Greater London, England), Thursday, July 20th, 1972. Available at: https://theguardian.newspapers.com/image/259859352

Hall, S., (2016); *Cultural Studies 1983*, Durham and London: Duke University Press.

Hamelink, C. (2023); *Communication and Human Rights; Towards Communicative Justice*, Cambridge: Polity Press.

Harlow, S., and Benbrook, A., (2019) How #Blacklivesmatter: exploring the role of hip-hop celebrities in constructing racial identity on Black Twitter, Information, Communication & Society, 22:3, 352–368, https://doi.org/10.1080/1369118X.2017.1386705

Harvey, D., (1989); *The Condition of Postmodernity; An Enquiry Into the Origins of Cultural Change*, Oxford: Basil Blackwell.

Hawkins, D., (2003); "When you search a #Hashtag, it Feels Like You're Searching for Death:" Black Twitter and communication About Police Brutality within the Black Community, *Social Media and Society*, April–June pp., 1–12.

Hawthorne, C., (2021); Making Italy: Afro-Italian entrepreneurs and the racial boundaries of citizenship, Social & Cultural Geography, 22:5, 704–724, DOI: https://doi.org/10.1080/14649365.2019.1597151

HDI (2020); *Facial Recognition in Insurance*, HDI, 16 December 2020. Available at: https://www.hdi.global/en-za/infocenter/insights/2020/facial-recognition/

Helm, J., (1967); *Essays on the Verbal and Visual Arts;* Proceedings of the 1966 Annual Spring Meeting of the American Ethnological Society, American Ethnological Society, Seattle and London: University of Washington Press.

Hill, M., (2018); "Thank You, Black Twitter": State violence, Digital Counterpublics, and Pedagogies of Resistance, *Urban Education*, Vol.53(2) pp., 286–302.

Hinchman, K. A., and Moore, W. D., (2013); Close Reading: A Cautionary Interpretation. *Journal of Adolescent and Adult Literacy* 56 (6): 441–450. DOI: https://doi.org/10.1002/JAAL.163

Home Affairs Committee (2020); *The Work of the Commissioner of the Metropolitan Police Service*, Home Affairs Committee, House of Commons. Available at:

https://www.met.police.uk/SysSiteAssets/media/downloads/force-content/met/about-us/stride/macpherson-hasc-transcript%2D%2D-met-commissioner-july-2020.pdf

Hootsuite (2021); *What is social Media Analytics? Everything You Need to Know.* Available at: https://blog.hootsuite.com/what-is-social-media-analytics/

House of Commons Library (2022); *Ticket Sales,* (ed. Conway, l., House of Commons Library. Available at: https://researchbriefings.files.parliament.uk/documents/SN04715/SN04715.pdf

Huff, R., Kline, M., Peterson, D., (2015); *Health Promotion in Multicultural Populations; A Handbook for Practitioners and Students,* London: Sage.

Information Commissioner's Office (2017); *Data Controller: Royal Free London NHS Foundation Trust,* Information Commissioner's Office. Available at: https://ico.org.uk/media/action-weve-taken/undertakings/2014352/royal-free-undertaking-03072017.pdf

Isiani, M., Obi-Ani, N., Obi-Ani, P., Chidume, C., and Okoye-Ugwu, S., (2021) Interrogating the International Monetary Fund (IMF) Policies in Nigeria, 1986–2018, Cogent Arts & Humanities, 8:1, DOI: https://doi.org/10.1080/23311983.2021.1932283

Izsadore, S., (2019); *Fela and Me,* with Oyekunle, S., Nigeria: Kraft Books Limited.

Jefferson, B., (2020); *Digitize and Punish,* Minneapolis: University of Minnesota Press.

Johnson-Odim, C., (2009); 'For their Freedoms': The Anti-imperialist and International Feminist Activity of Funmilayo Ransome-Kuti of Nigeria, *Women's Studies International Forum,* 32, pp., 51–59.

Johnson-Odim, C., and Mba, N., (1997); *For Women and the Nation, Funmilayo Ransome-Kuti of Nigeria,* Urbana and Chicago: University of Illinois Press.

Jones, K., (2023); AI Governance and Human Rights, Resetting the Relationship, International law Programme, January 2023, Chatham House. Available at: https://www.chathamhouse.org/2023/01/ai-governance-and-human-rights

Kecmanovic, D., (2002); *Ethnic Times; Exploring Ethnonationalism in the Former Yugoslavia,* London: Praeger.

Kjus, Y., (2016); Musical exploration via streaming services: The Norwegian experience, Popular Communication, 14:3, 127–136, DOI: https://doi.org/10.1080/15405702.2016.1193183

Klassen, S., and Fiesler, C., (2022); "This Isn't Your Data, Friend": Black Twitter as a Case Study on Research Ethics for Public Data, *Social Media and Society,* October-December, 2022, pp., 1–11.

Klymenko, L., (2020); Choosing Mazepa Over Lenin: The Transformation of Monuments and Political Order in Post-Maidan Ukraine, *Europe-Asia Studies,* 72:5, 815–836, DOI: https://doi.org/10.1080/09668136.2020.1751081

Kniahynycky, R., (2023); Artificial Intelligence: Terms Marketers Need to Know, X Business. Available at: https://business.twitter.com/en/blog/artificial-intelligence-terms-marketers-need-to-know.html

Kristoffer, R., and Burkhanov, A., (2018); Constituting the Kazakhstani Nation: Rhetorical Transformation of National Belonging, *Nationalism and Ethnic Politics*, 24:4, 433–455, DOI: https://doi.org/10.1080/13537113.2018.1522758

Kuti, F., (1977); Colo-mentality, in *Sorrow, Tears and Blood*.

Kuti, F., (1979); Konkome interview, *Konkombe The Nigerian Pop Music Scene*, Shanachie Records. Available at: https://youtu.be/rDe-0mW6o04?si=a4y7lsGXdWHUlsuX

Kuti, F., (1978/2011); *Fela Kuti, Konkombe Interview*. Available at: https://youtu.be/4waYY1HZ318?si=tGh7GXL6Jg1Nt7Q6

Lambeth Council (2022a); @lambeth_.council – Dec 16, 2022. Available at: https://twitter.com/lambeth_council/status/1603758564018880512

Lambeth Council (2022c); O2 Academy Brixton, 211 Stockwell Road London SW9 9SL (Brixton North). Meeting of Expedited Review, Licensing Sub-Committee, Thursday 22 December 2022 10:00am (Item 3a). Available at: https://moderngov.lambeth.gov.uk/mgAi.aspx?ID=57242

Lambeth Council (2022d); Agenda Item, O2 Academy Brixton, 211 Stockwell Road London SW9 9SL (Brixton North). Meeting of Expedited Review, Licensing Sub-Committee, Thursday 22 December 2022 10:00am (Item 3a). Minutes. Available at: https://moderngov.lambeth.gov.uk/mgAi.aspx?ID=57242

Lambeth Council (2022e); *Licensing Sub-Committee, Thursday 22 December 2022*, 10:00am, Microsoft Teams. Available at: https://moderngov.lambeth.gov.uk/documents/g16232/Agenda%20frontsheet%20Thursday%2022-Dec-2022%2010.00%20Licensing%20Sub-Committee.pdf?T=0

Lambeth Council (2023a); *Lambeth Health and Safety Review into O2 Academy Brixton, Lambeth Council*, News and Announcements. Available at: https://love.lambeth.gov.uk/lambeth-health-and-safety-review/

Lambeth Council (2023b); *Licensing – Licensing Application Documents, Lambeth Council*. Available at: https://planning.lambeth.gov.uk/online-applications/licencingApplicationDetails.do?activeTab=documents&keyVal=RT9HVVBO0BN00

Lambeth.gov.uk (2022a); *Statement: Brixton Academy O2 Incident and Review*. Lambeth News; News from Lambeth Council. Available at: https://love.lambeth.gov.uk/statement-brixton-academy-o2-incident-and-review/

Lambeth.gov.uk (2022b); Licensing Sub-Committee; Thursday 22 December 2022; Annex A, Protective Marking, Metropolitan Police, Total Policing; *Form for Applying for a Summary Licence Review Application for the Review of a Premises Licence Under Section 53A of the Licensing Act 2003*.

Lambeth.gov.uk (2022c); *Licensing Sub-Committee, Thursday 22 December 2022 at 10.00am*, Lambeth Council.

Lambeth.gov.uk (2022d); *Licensing Sub-Committee, Thursday 22 December 2022, 10:00am, Venue: Microsoft Teams*. Available at: https://moderngov.lambeth.

gov.uk/documents/g16232/Agenda%20frontsheet%20Thursday%2022-Dec-2022%2010.00%20Licensing%20Sub-Committee.pdf?T=0

Lambeth.gov.uk (2022e); *Agenda. Expedited Review, Licensing Sub-Committee – Thursday 22 December 2022 10:00am.* Available at: https://moderngov.lambeth.gov.uk/ieListDocuments.aspx?CId=116&MId=16232

Lambeth.gov.uk (2022f); *Annex A Summary Review Application.* Available at: https://moderngov.lambeth.gov.uk/ieListDocuments.aspx?CId=116&MId=16232

Lambeth.gov.uk (2022g); *Licensing Sub-Committee 22 December 2022; Item No:3a. Report title: Licensing Act 2003: Section 53A Expedited Review – Interim Steps Hearing – O2 Academy Brixton, 211 Stockwell Road London SW9 9SL.* Available at: https://moderngov.lambeth.gov.uk/documents/s142574/O2%20Academy%20Brixton%20211%20Stockwell%20Road%20London%20SW9%209SL.pdf

Langley, M., (2010) PEACE PROFILE: Fela Kuti, An "African Man Original", Peace Review, 22:2, 199–204, DOI: https://doi.org/10.1080/10402651003751511

Lee, H., and Cho, C., (2020); Digital advertising: present and future prospects, *International Journal of Advertising,* 39:3, 332–341, DOI: https://doi.org/10.1080/02650487.2019.1642015

Legislation.Gov.UK (2003); *Licensing Act 2003, 2003.* Available at: https://www.legislation.gov.uk/ukpga/2003/17/contents

Liberty 2022 (2022); *Facial Recognition / What is Police Facial Recognition and How Do We Stop It?* Liberty. Available at: https://www.libertyhumanrights.org.uk/issue/what-is-police-facial-recognition-and-how-do-we-stop-it/

Liu, J., Davidson, E., Bhopal, R., White, M., Johnson, M., Netto, G., Deverill, M., and Sheikh, A., (2012); Adapting Health Promotion Interventions to Meet the Needs of Ethnic Minority groups: Mixed-methods Evidence Synthesis, *Health Technology Assessment,* Vol., 16, Issue, 44. Available at: https://www.journalslibrary.nihr.ac.uk/hta/hta16440/#/abstract

Loads, D., (2013) Collaborative close reading of teaching texts: one way of helping academics to make sense of their practice, Teaching in Higher Education, 18:8, 950–957, DOI: https://doi.org/10.1080/13562517.2013.810844

Lockett, M., (2010a) Close Reading: A Synergistic Approach to the (Post)Modern Divide, *Changing English,* 17:4, 399–409, DOI: https://doi.org/10.1080/1358684X.2010.528874

London Assembly (2023); More Needed to Keep Londoners Safe on Nights Out, London Assembly, London Assembly Press Release. Available at: https://www.london.gov.uk/who-we-are/what-london-assembly-does/london-assembly-press-releases/more-needed-keep-londoners-safe-nights-out

REFERENCES 325

London Assembly (2024); Women's Night Safety Charter, London Assembly. Available at https://www.london.gov.uk/programmes-strategies/arts-and-culture/24-hour-london/womens-night-safety-charter

London.gov.uk (2017a); *Mayor Outlines Ambition to Make London World's Leading 'Smart City'*, London Assembly. Available at: https://www.london.gov.uk/press-releases/mayoral/mayor-reveals-his-smart-city-ambition-for-london

London.gov.uk (2017b); *Mayor Outlines Ambition to Make London World's Leading 'Smart City'*, London Assembly. Available at: https://www.london.gov.uk/press-releases/mayoral/mayor-reveals-his-smart-city-ambition-for-london

London.gov.uk (2018); Londoners to Help the Capital Become the World's Leading Smart City, London Assembly.

London.gov.uk (2020); Sharing Cities (H2020) – Programme Marketing Material, Mayor of London, London Assembly. Available at: https://www.london.gov.uk/decisions/add2454-sharing-cities-h2020-programme-marketing-material?ac-123579=123572

London.gov.uk (2021a); Digital Transformation Four Regions Project. Mayor of London, London Assembly. Available at: https://www.london.gov.uk/decisions/dd2547-digital-transformation-4-regions-project?ac-129647=129641

London.gov.uk (2021b); MD2805 High Streets Data Service and Partnership – Pilot Programme, Mayor of London, London Assembly. Available at: https://www.london.gov.uk/decisions/md2805-high-streets-data-service-and-partnership-pilot-programme

London.gov.uk (2022a); *Building a Safer London; Police and Crime Plan for London 2022-25*, London Assembly. Available at: https://www.london.gov.uk/publications/building-safer-london

London.gov.uk (2022b); Implementation of policy SI 6 of London Plan. Mayor of London, London Assembly. Available at: https://www.london.gov.uk/decisions/add2581-implementation-policy-si-6-london-plan?ac-134429=134422

London.gov.uk (2023); *Mission 3: World-class Connectivity and Smarter Streets*, London Assembly. Available at: https://www.london.gov.uk/programmes-strategies/business-and-economy/supporting-londons-sectors/smart-london/mission-3-world-class-connectivity-and-smarter-streets

Lugones, M., (2010); Toward a Decolonial Feminism, *Hypatia* 25, no. 4(2010): 742–59. http://www.jstor.org/stable/40928654.

Maedza, P. (2019). *Sarafina!*: The children's revolution from Soweto to Broadway. *South African Theatre Journal*, 32(3), 235–256. https://doi.org/10.1080/10137548.2018.1544503

326 REFERENCES

Magatti, M., (2012); Contemporary Sociological Theory and Techno-Nihilist Capitalism, World Futures, 68:4–5, 296–313, DOI: https://doi.org/10.1080/02604027.2012.679530

Magatti, M., (2012c) Contemporary Sociological Theory and Techno-Nihilist Capitalism, World Futures, 68:4–5.

Marcuse, H., (1941/1982); 'Some Social Implications of Modern Technology', in Arato, A., and Gebhardt, E., (eds) *The Essential Frankfurt School Reader*, New York: Continuum.

Marcuse, H., (1964/2002); *One-Dimensional Man, Studies in the Ideology of Advanced industrial Society*, London and New York: Routledge.

Marx, K., (1857/1973); *Grundrisse; Foundations of the Critique of Political Economy*, Trans. Nicolaus, M., London: Penguin Books in Association with New Left Reviews.

Marx, K., (1887/1982); *Capital A Critique of Political Economy*, Volume One, Introduction by Mandel, E., and Trans., Fowkes, B., Middlesex: Penguin Books in Association with New Left Review.

Mathiesen, T., (1997); The Viewer Society, Michel Foucault's 'Panopticon' Revisited, *Theoretical Criminology*, Vol. 1(2), pp., 215–234.

Matila, T., (2021) White death: Finnish world war two narrative and alternative heritage work in social media, International Journal of Heritage Studies, 27:6, 617–634, DOI: https://doi.org/10.1080/13527258.2020.1843520

May, C., (2015); Beasts of No Nation, Sleeve Notes, *Beasts of No Nation*, 1989, 2014, Under Exclusive License to Knitting Factory Records INC. laws.felakuti.com

May, C., (2015); *Beasts of No Nation, Jacket Inner Sleeve to Beasts of No Nation* by Fela Anikulapo-Kuti, Knitting Factory Records INC.

Mayor of London (2023); *About Business Improvement Districts*, Mayor of London, London Assembly. Available at: https://www.london.gov.uk/programmes-strategies/business-and-economy/supporting-business/about-business-improvement-districts

McCaw, N., (2011) Close Reading, Writing and Culture, *New Writing*, 8:1, 25–34, DOI: https://doi.org/10.1080/14790726.2010.527349

McConn, M., (2018); Close Reading of Literary Nonfiction: The Three-column Journal, The Clearing House: A Journal of Educational Strategies, Issues and Ideas, 91:2, 66–71, https://doi.org/10.1080/00098655.2017.1386001

Mercer, K., (1994); Black Hair/Style politics, in *Welcome to the Jungle*, London: Routledge.

Met Police (2024); *Top Reported Crimes, Brixton Windrush; Brixton Acre Lane; Myatt's Field, Metropolitan Police.* Available at: https://www.police.uk/pu/your-area/metropolitan-police-service/brixton-acre-lane/?yourlocalpolicingteam=about-us

Met Police (2024a); *Homicide Victims in the MPS, Time Period (2003 to March 2024)*, Homicide Dashboard, Met Police. Available at: https://www.met.police.uk/sd/stats-and-data/met/homicide-dashboard/

Metropolitan Police (2022g); Privacy Notice, Metropolitan Police. Available at: https://www.met.police.uk/hyg/fpnm/privacy/

Metropolitan Police (2023); *Renewed Appeal for Witnesses and Footage of the Brixton Academy Fatal Crush Incident*, Metropolitan Police News. Available at: https://news.met.police.uk/news/renewed-appeal-for-witnesses-and-footage-of-the-brixton-academy-fatal-crush-incident-463706

Metropolitan Police (2023b); *How and When BWV [Body Worn Video] Cameras are Used. Metropolitan Police*, Advice and Information. Available at: https://www.met.police.uk/advice/advice-and-information/bwv/body-worn-video-bwv/how-and-when-bwv-cameras-are-used/

Metropolitan Police (2023h); [Metropolitan Police] Statement of Witness, 14th April 2023. Lambeth Licensing - Licensing Application Documents, 23/00773/PRMREV, Premises Licence (review application) Expired, Brixton Academy 211 Stockwell Road London SW9 9SL. Available at: https://planning.lambeth.gov.uk/online-applications/licencingApplicationDetails.do?activeTab=documents&keyVal=RT9HVVBO0BN00

Metropolitan Police Service (2017); One Met Digital Policing Strategy 2017–2020. Available at: https://www.met.police.uk/SysSiteAssets/media/downloads/force-content/met/about-us/one-met-digital-policing-strategy-2017-2020.pdf

Metropolitan Police Service (2021a); *Met Strategic Digital Enabling Framework 2021-25, Met Tech Direction*. Metropolitan Police. Available at: https://www.met.police.uk/SysSiteAssets/media/downloads/force-content/met/about-us/met-strategic-digital-enabling-framework-2021-2025.pdf

Metropolitan Police Service (2021b); *Metropolitan Police Service, Business Plan 2021–24.* Metropolitan Police. Available at: Business Plan Met 2024 https://www.met.police.uk/SysSiteAssets/media/downloads/force-content/met/about-us/met-business-plan-2021-24

Metropolitan Police Service (2022); *Four People Critical Following Incident in Brixton*, Metropolitan Police, News – 16 December 2022 [04:57 GMT]. Available at: Four_people_critical_following_incident_in_Brixton.pdf

Metropolitan Police Service (2022a); UPDATE: Statement from Chief Superintendent Colin Wingrove on O2 Brixton Academy Incident, Metropolitan Police, News - 16 December 2022 [16:46hrs GMT]). Available at: A -UPDATE__Statement_from_Chief_Superintendent_Colin_Wingrove_on_O2_Brixton_Academy_incident.pdf

Metropolitan Police Service (2022b); *Man Injured in O2 Brixton Academy Incident Dies in Hospital*, Update, December 20, 2022 11:15 GMT, Metropolitan Police. Available at: Man_injured_in_O2_Brixton_Academy_incident_dies_in_hospital.pdf

328 REFERENCES

Metropolitan Police Service (2022c); Definitions of Terms of 'Drill Rap Music' Banned/Removed Online, 01 May 2022, Freedom of information request reference no: 01.FOI.22.023585, Metropolitan Police Service. Available at: https://www.met.police.uk/foi-ai/metropolitan-police/d/april-2022/definitions-of-terms-of-drill-rap-music-bannedremoved-online/

Metropolitan Police Service (2023a); *Renewed Appeal for Witnesses and Footage of the Brixton Academy Fatal Crush Incident*, Metropolitan Police News. Available at:

Metropolitan Police Service (2023c); *About the Camera*. Metropolitan Police, Advice and Information. Available at: https://www.met.police.uk/advice/advice-and-information/bwv/body-worn-video-bwv/about-the-camera/

Metropolitan Police Service (2023d); *Privacy and BWV*. Metropolitan Police Advice and Information. Available at: https://www.met.police.uk/advice/advice-and-information/bwv/body-worn-video-bwv/privacy-and-bwv/

Metropolitan Police Service (2023e); *Facial Recognition Technology*, Metropolitan Police. Available at: https://www.met.police.uk/advice/advice-and-information/fr/facial-recognition-technology/

Metropolitan Police Service (2023f); Statement on Release of Research into Facial Recognition Technology, New Scotland Yard. Available at: https://news.met.police.uk/news/statement-on-release-of-research-into-facial-recognition-technology-464791

Metropolitan Police Service (2023g); *The Coronation of His Majesty the King and Her Majesty the Queen Consort*, Deputy Assistant Commissioner Ade Adelekan, Metropolitan Police. Available at: https://news.met.police.uk/news/the-coronation-of-his-majesty-the-king-and-her-majesty-the-queen-consort-466199

Metropolitan Police Service (2023h); *Families Pay Tribute to Loved Ones Six Months on From Incident at O2 Academy Brixton*. Available at: https://news.met.police.uk/news/families-pay-tribute-to-loved-ones-six-months-on-from-incident-at-o2-academy-brixton-468507

Metropolitan Police Service (2023i); Homicides/Murder Data from June 2022 to June 2023 – Att 1, Freedom of information request reference no: 01.FOI.23.031100, Metropolitan Police Service. Available at: https://www.met.police.uk/foi-ai/metropolitan-police/disclosure-2023/august-2023/homicides-murder-data-june2022-june2023/

Metropolitan Police Service (2023j); Referrals and Removals of Drill/Rap music Videos From YouTube, Since September 2020, Freedom of information request reference no: 01.FOI.23.027950, 04 June 2023, Metropolitan Police Service. Available at: https://www.met.police.uk/foi-ai/metropolitan-police/disclosure-2023/june-2023/referrals-removals-drill-rap-music-videos-youtube-september2020/

Metropolitan Police Service (2024); *Top Reported Crimes, Brixton Windrush; Brixton Acre Lane; Myatt's Field, Metropolitan Police*. Available at: https://www.police.uk/pu/your-area/metropolitan-police-service/brixton-acre-lane/?yourlocalpolicingteam=about-us

Metropolitan Police Service (2024b); Removal of Drill Music Video Resulting in Closing Accounts from April 2019 to March 2023. Freedom of information request reference no: 01.FOI.24.036452, Metropolitan Police Service. Available at: https://www.met.police.uk/foi-ai/metropolitan-police/disclosure-2024/april-2024/removal-drill-music-video-resulting-closing-accounts-april2019-march2023/

Metropolitan Police Service (2024c); *Number of Drill music videos, rap and its sub-genre music, Afrobeat, and other Black music referred to other music platforms for removal/ and number of removals granted April 2019 to March 2024 (broken down by year)*, Freedom of Information Request Reference No: 01/FOI/24/039803/U, Metropolitan Police Service (MPS) response 12/09/2024.

Metropolitan Police Service (2024d); *UPDATED: Images of Nine People Re Brixton Crush Investigation*, August 13, 2024 16:53 BST, Metropolitan Police. Available at: https://news.met.police.uk/news/images-of-13-people-released-as-part-of-investigation-into-brixton-crush-476903

Metropolitan Police Service (2024e); "I want to know how the police decide what Afrobeat music songs and videos should be banned/removed from online streaming services", 19/10/2024, Your ref: FOI-20105-24-0100-000; Our ref: 01/FOI/24/039772/E

Metropolitan Police Service (2024f); The Metropolitan Police Service Facial Recognition Technology: Understanding Accuracy and Demographic Differences, Metropolitan Police. Available at: https://www.met.police.uk/SysSiteAssets/media/downloads/force-content/met/advice/lfr/new/understanding-accuracy-and-demographic-differences-v3.pdf

Mirror (2022); *Horror at O2 Academy Brixton as Victim Trampled in Crush 'Thought She Was Dead'*, Mirror. Available at: https://www.mirror.co.uk/news/uk-news/horror-o2-academy-brixton-victim-28747444

Mirza, H., (1997); *Black British Feminism*, London and New York: Routledge.

Moeckli, D., (2016); *Exclusion from Public Space; A Comparative Constitutional Analysis*, Cambridge: Cambridge University Press.

Molefe, M., and Ngcongo, M., (2021) "You Don't Mess With Black Twitter!": An Ubuntu Approach to Understanding "Militant" Twitter Discourse, Communicatio, 47:3, 26–49, DOI: https://doi.org/10.1080/0250016 7.2021.2001553

MOPAC (2022); A Better Police Services for London, MOPAC London Surveys, FY 21-22 (Fourth Quarter) results, Mayor of London Office for Policing and

330 REFERENCES

Crime. Available at: https://airdrive-secure.s3-eu-west-1.amazonaws.com/london/dataset/mopac-surveys/2023

MOPAC (2023a); *Public Voice, Quarter 4 2022-23*, Mayor of London Office for Policing and Crime (MOPAC) Evidence and Insight. Available at: https://airdrive-secure.s3-eu-west-1.amazonaws.com/london/dataset/mopac-surveys

Moore, S. S. (2020). Between the state and the yard: gender and political space in Haiti. *Gender, Place & Culture*, 28(9), 1306–1326. https://doi.org/10.1080/0966369X.2020.1846500

Morris, J., and Powers, D., (2015) Control, curation and musical experience in streaming music services, Creative Industries Journal, 8:2, 106–122, DOI: https://doi.org/10.1080/17510694.2015.1090222

Mpofu, S., (2019) Jesus Comes to South Africa: Black Twitter as Citizen Journalism in South African Politics, African Journalism Studies, 40:1, 67–90, https://doi.org/10.1080/23743670.2019.1610782

Muir, R., (2018); The Beat Goes On. September 2018 – Vogue Retro Article. Available at: https://www.duffyarchive.com/september-2018-vogue-retro-article/

Murphy (British), P. (1981) "Juju, Afrobeat and Highlife". *The Face*. Fela Kuti, Sonny Okosun, Sir Victor Uwaifo. Retrieved February 2, 2024, from http://www.rocksbackpages.com/Library/Article/juju-afrobeat-and-highlife

Museum X., (2021); *Our Story*. Available at: https://www.themuseumx.com/our-story

Myrick, J., Willoughby, J., and Clark, M., (2022); Racial Differences in Response to Chadwick Boseman's Colorectal Cancer Death: Media Use as a Coping Tool for Parasocial Grief, OMEGA – Journal of Death and Dying, pp., 1–20.

National Physical Laboratory (2023a); *Facial Recognition Technology in Law Enforcement Equitability Study*, Final Report, Mansfield, T., Middlesex: National Physical Laboratory. Available at: https://science.police.uk/site/assets/files/3396/frt-equitability-study_mar2023.pdf

National Physical Laboratory, (2023b); *Facial Recognition Technology in law Enforcement Equitability Study*. National Physical Laboratory. Available at: https://science.police.uk/site/assets/files/3396/frt-equitability-study_mar2023.pdf

National Theatre Archive (2010); *Digital Research Pack for Fela!*, National Theatre Archive, London: National Theatre.

Naylor, P., (1973); *Black Images; The Art of West Africa*, Garden City, N.Y.: Doubleday.

Night Time Industries Association (2023); *The Prodigy, Muse, Skunk Anansie, NME, Mixmag join 20,000 Music Fans in Campaign to Save Brixton Academy*, Night Time Industries Association (NTIA), 15th May 2023. Available at: https://www.ntia.co.uk/over-10000-representations-sent-to-lambeth-council-to-save-brixton-academy-says-ntia-sos-brixton-bid/?_ga=2.84646748. 457519409.1684503913-

Nkrumah, K., (1965); *Neo-Colonialism the Last Stage of Imperialism*, London: Thomas Nelson and Sons, Ltd.

Noble, S., (2018); *Algorithms of Oppression: how Search Engines Reinforce Racism*, New York: New York University Press.

Nojan, S., (2021); Racialized Hauntings: Examining Afghan Americans' Hyper(In) Visibility Amidst Anti-Muslim Ethnoracism, *Ethnic And Racial Studies*, DOI: https://doi.org/10.1080/01419870.2021.1931391

O'Dair, M and Fry, A., (2020); Beyond the black box in music streaming: the impact of recommendation systems upon artists, Popular Communication, 18:1, 65–77, DOI: https://doi.org/10.1080/15405702.2019.1627548

O2 (2023); *Micro Location Insights – Detailed Movement Data From O2*. Available at: https://www.o2.co.uk/documents/456036/1067287/O2_Business_Micro_Location_Insights_0121.055_FINAL.pdf/fe06a775-7d4e-ae23-68ed-050b28d1c419?version=1.0&t=1615800453580

Obiagu, A., (2023); Toward a Decolonized Moral Education for Social Justice in Africa, *Journal of Black Studies*, Vol., 54(3), pp., 236–263.

Obioma, C., (2018); Teeth Marks: a Close Reading of the Translator's Dilemma, *Journal of the African literature Association*, 12:3, 241–249.

Odih, P., (1998); *Gendered Time and Financial Services Consumption*, Ph.D Thesis, Manchester: The University of Manchester.

Odih, P., (2007a); Advertising in Modern and Postmodern Times. Sage. ISBN 9780761941903

Odih, P., (2007b); Gender and Work in Capitalist Economies. Maidenhead, Berkshire: Open University Press. ISBN 9780335216727

Odih, P., (2010); Advertising and Cultural Politics in Global Times. Farnham: Ashgate. ISBN 978-0-7546-7711-6

Odih, P., (2014); *Watersheds in Marxist Ecofeminism*. Newcastle upon Tyne: Cambridge Scholars Publishing. ISBN 978-1-4438-6602-6

Odih, P., (2016b); Adsensory Financialisation. Newcastle upon Tyne: Cambridge Scholars Publishing. ISBN 978-1-4438-9531-6

Odih, P., (2019); *Race and Digital Colonial Capitalism: #FassonStRed GoldBrickLane; Graffiti Ethno-map of Fashion Street's Colonial History*. Spitalfields Life: @thegentleauthor, London. Available at: https://research.gold.ac.uk/id/eprint/27008/

Odih, P., (2019a); Adsensory Urban Ecology (Volume One). Newcastle upon Tyne: Cambridge Scholars Publishing. ISBN 9781527523173

Odih, P., (2019b); Adsensory Urban Ecology (Volume Two). Newcastle upon Tyne: Cambridge Scholars Publishing. ISBN 9781527524682

Office of the High Commissioner for Human Rights (OHCHR), (2022); *Ukraine: Civilian Casualty Update 16 March 2022*, Press Briefing Notes, Office of the High Commissioner for Human Rights, United Nations. Available at: https://

332 REFERENCES

www.ohchr.org/en/press-briefing-notes/2022/03/ukraine-civilian-casualty-update-16-march-2022

Ogunfeyimi, A., (2021) The grammar and rhetoric of African subjectivity: ethics, image, and language, Review of Communication, 21:4, 310–326, https://doi.org/10.1080/15358593.2021.2001842

Ogunyemi, C., (2021) Fela Kuti's Black consciousness: African cosmology and the re-configuration of Blackness in 'colonial mentality', African Identities, 19:4, 487–501, DOI: https://doi.org/10.1080/14725843.2020.1803793

Onanuga, A. O. (2023). Interrogating patriarchy and homophobia in Nigeria's *Zikoko* online magazine. *African Identities*, 1–17. https://doi.org/10.1080/14725843.2023.2227354

Outley, C., Bowen, S., and Pinckney, H., (2021) Laughing While Black: Resistance, Coping and the Use of Humor as a Pandemic Pastime among Blacks, Leisure Sciences, 43:1–2, 305–314, https://doi.org/10.1080/01490400.2020.1774449

Owen, F. (1986) "Fela Kuti: Brixton Academy, London". *Melody Maker*. Fela Kuti. Retrieved February 4, 2024, from http://www.rocksbackpages.com/Library/Article/fela-kuti-brixton-academy-london

Pablo Aguera Reneses & Tanja Bosch (2023) Networked masculinities in South Africa: the #MensConference as a case study, NORMA, 18:2, 106–121, DOI: https://doi.org/10.1080/18902138.2022.2051396

Parkes, S., and Rafaeli, S. J., (2014); *Live at the Brixton Academy; A Riotous Life in the Music Business*, London: Serpent's Tail.

Pearce, D., (2023); Help Save O2 Brixton Academy, Demelza Pearce started this petition to Lambeth Council, Change.org. Available at: https://www.change.org/p/save-brixton-acadamy-from-closure?source_location=topic_page

PEW (2024); Americans' Use of Social Media PEW Research Center. Available at: https://www.pewresearch.org/internet/2024/01/31/americans-social-media-use/

PGIM (2021); Disruption in Service Sector Favours Leaders in Health, Finance and Logistics, PGIM Reports. Available at: https://www.pgim.com/press-release/disruption-service-sector-favors-leaders-health-finance-and-logistics-pgim-reports

Potter, J., (2023); Sadra Izsadore: the Artist and Activist Who Enlightened Fela Kuti, Far Out, Sat 28 October 2023. Available at: https://faroutmagazine.co.uk/sadra-izsadore-artist-enlightened-fela-kuti/

Prasad, P., (2016); Beyond Rights as Recognition: black Twitter and Posthuman Coalitional Possibilities, *Prose Studies*, Vol., 38, No. 1, pp., 50–73.

Prime Minister Office (2020); *Prime Minister's Statement on Coronavirus (COVID-19): 23 March 2020*, Prime Minister's Office, 10 Downing Street and The Rt Hon Boris Johnson MP. Available at: https://www.gov.uk/government/speeches/pm-address-to-the-nation-on-coronavirus-23-march-2020

REFERENCES   **333**

Prime Minister's Office (2021); *Urgent Omicron Appeal: Get Boosted Now*, Prime Minister's Office, 10 Downing Street and The RT Hon Boris Johnson MP. Available at: https://www.gov.uk/government/news/urgent-omicron-appeal-get-boosted-now

Prime Minister's Office (2021a); *Prime Minister's Address to the Nation on Booster Jabs: 12 December 2021*, Prime Minister's Office, 10 Downing Street and The Rt Hon Boris Johnson MP. Available at: https://www.gov.uk/government/speeches/prime-ministers-address-to-the-nation-on-booster-jabs-12-december-2021

Prime Minister's Office (2022); *Prime Minister Boris Johnson Gave a Statement to the House of Commons on Ukraine*, Prime Minister's Office, 10 Downing Street and The Rt Hon Boris Johnson MP, PM statement to the House of Commons on Ukraine/ 24 February 2022 - GOV.pdf

Race Disparity Unit, (2021); *Final Report on Progress to Address COVID-19 Health Inequalities*, Race Disparity Unit, Cabinet Office. Available at: https://assets.publishing.service.gov.uk/government/uploads/system/uploads/attachment_data/file/1038338/2021-12-03_Final_COVID-19_disparities_report___updated_3_Dec.pdf

Radi, T., (2022a); Cultivating Credit: Financialized Urbanization Is Alienation!, Journal of Palestine Studies, 51:1, 4–26, DOI: https://doi.org/10.1080/0377919X.2021.2015995

Radi, T., (2022b); Cultivating Credit: Financialized Urbanization Is Alienation!, Journal of Palestine Studies, 51:1, 4–26, DOI: https://doi.org/10.1080/0377919X.2021.2015995

Radioshrine (2011); *Fela Kuti Speaks*, Fela Radio Shrine, (ed.) Mabinuori Kayode IDOWU aka ID, Radioshrine.Com. Available at: https://youtu.be/Lp_xEwQ2Osc?si=vLvxnXC2_VH9wM0N

Ramírez, M., and Adzich, T., (2023); When monuments fall: anticolonial disruptions and decolonial urban practices (2022) Plenary Commentary, Urban Geography, 44:6, 1084–1092, https://doi.org/10.1080/02723638.2023.2217619

Ramirez, M., & Williams, B., (2022); #Migente: Latinx Twitter's Reaction to the Super Bowl LIV Halftime Performance, Howard Journal of Communications, 33:1, 58–77, https://doi.org/10.1080/10646175.2021.1929581

Ransome-Kuti, F., (1947); "for Women: She Speaks for Nigeria / We Had Equality Till Britain Came", Daily Worker (London, August 18, 1947). Reprinted "We Had Equality till Britain Came", in (ed.) Wayne, T., *Feminist Writings from Ancient Times to the Modern World: A Global Sourcebook and History*, London: Bloomsbury.

Ransome-Kuti, F., (1947–1948); *The Plight of Nigerian Women, Funmilayo Ransome Kuti, (President Abeokuta Women's Union and Member of the Pan-Nigerian Delegation)*, National Council of Nigeria and the Cameroons Activities of Mrs Ransome-Kuti, Nigeria, Colonial Office: Nigeria Original

334 REFERENCES

Correspondence. National Council of Nigeria and the Cameroons: Activities of Mrs Ransome-Kuti. The National Archives, Kew – Colonial office, Commonwealth and Foreign and Commonwealth Offices, 1947–1948, Reference: CO 583/293/1, National Archives, Kew, Richmond, TW9 4DU. Date of Visit: Tuesday 23rd April 2024; Booking Reference: RR147-950-06156K.

Ransome-Kuti, F., (1949/2021); A Talk About Women, in (ed.) Russell, A., *Great Women's Speeches: Empowering voices that Engage and Inspire*, London: White Lion Publishing/The Quarto Group.

Reeves, J., (2016); Automatic for the people: the automation of communicative labor, Communication and Critical/Cultural Studies, 13:2, 150–165, DOI: https://doi.org/10.1080/14791420.2015.1108450

Richardson, A., (2017) Bearing Witness While Black, Digital Journalism, 5:6, 673–698, DOI: https://doi.org/10.1080/21670811.2016.1193818

RichClicks (2023); RichClicks is Ready to Become Your Agency Partner for Twitter Ads Strategy, RichClicks. Available at: https://www.richclicks.co.uk/digital-advertising/twitter-ads

Romero, M., (2013); Race, Class, and Gender, in (eds.) Brunsma, D., Iyall Smith, K., and Gran, B., *The Handbook of Sociology and Human Rights*, London: Paradigm Publishers.

Salawu, O., (2019) Abàmì Èdá: Personhood and Socio-political Commitment in Fela's Music, Muziki, 16:2, 4–21, https://doi.org/10.1080/18125980.2020.1781547

Sanjay, S., (2013); Black Twitter? Racial Hastags, Networks and Contagion, New formations, Number 78, Summer, pp. 46–64

Sealy, M., and Hall, S., (1993); *Vanley Burke: A Retrospective*, Chadwell Heath: Lawrence & Wishart Ltd.

Sharma, S., (2013) Black Twitter? Racial Hastags, Networks and Contagion, *New Formations*, Volume 78, Issue 78., pp., 46–64.

Shetty, S., (2018); *Decolonising Human Rights*, Speech Delivered by Salil Shetty, Secretary General of Amnesty International, at the London School of Economics on 22 May 2018. Amnesty International.

Shi, L., Shi, C., Wu, X., and Ma, L., (2022) Accelerating the development of smart city initiatives amidst the COVID-19 pandemic: the case of health code in China, Journal of Asian Public Policy, 15:2, 266–283, DOI: https://doi.org/10.1080/17516234.2021.1902078

Shifman, L., (2014); *Memes in Digital Culture*, Cambridge, Massachusetts.

Shonekan, S., (2009); Fela's Foundation: Examining the Revolutionary Songs of Funmilayo Ransome-Kuti and the Abeokuta Market Women's Movement in 1940s Western Nigeria, *Black Music Research Journal*, Spring, Vol.29., No.1., pp., 127–144.

Sims, J., Pirtle, W., and Johnson-Arnold, I., (2020); Doing hair, doing race: the influence of hairstyle on racial perception across the US, Ethnic and Racial

Studies, 43:12, 2099–2119, DOI: https://doi.org/10.1080/01419870.2019.1700296

Skinner-Thompson, S., (2021); *Privacy at the Margins*, Cambridge: Cambridge University Press.

Söderström, O., (2021) The three modes of existence of the pandemic smart city, Urban Geography, 42:3, 399–407, DOI: https://doi.org/10.1080/02723638.2020.1807167

Sonn, J., and Lee, J., (2020) The smart city as time-space cartographer in COVID-19 control: the South Korean strategy and democratic control of surveillance technology, Eurasian Geography and Economics, 61:4–5, 482–492, DOI: https://doi.org/10.1080/15387216.2020.1768423

Soyinka, W., (1983); *Aké The Years of Childhood*, New York: Aventura/Random House.

Stevens, L., and Maurantonio, N., (2018) Black Twitter Asks Rachel: Racial Identity Theft in "Post-Racial" America, Howard Journal of Communications, 29:2, 179–195, DOI: https://doi.org/10.1080/10646175.2017.1354789

Statista (2024); Worldwide Internet User Demographics, (ed) Petrosyan, A., World Digital Population 2024, *Statista*. Available at: https://www.statista.com/statistics/617136/digital-population-worldwide/

Strauss, A., and Corbin, J., (1990); *Basics of Qualitative Research; Grounded Theory Procedures and Techniques*, London: Sage.

Sprengel, D., (2020); *Feminist and Critical Race Approaches to Analyzing the Emerging Role of 'Culture' in Music Streaming Services*, Welcome to the International Association for the Study of popular music UK and Ireland Branch, Posted: January 9th 2020. Panel Proposal for the Society for Ethnomusicology Annual Meeting, Ottawa, Canada October 22–25, 2020. Available at: https://www.iaspm.org.uk/feminist-and-critical-race-approaches-to-analyzing-the-emerging-role-of-culture-in-music-streaming-services/

Stonewall (2021); *Stonewall Statement on BBC Leaving the Diversity Champions Programme*. Stonewall 10th November 2021. Available at: https://www.stonewall.org.uk/about-us/news/stonewall-statement-bbc-leaving-diversity-champions-programme

Summer Harlow & Anna Benbrook (2019) How #Blacklivesmatter: exploring the role of hip-hop celebrities in constructing racial identity on Black Twitter, Information, Communication & Society, 22:3, 352-368, DOI: https://doi.org/10.1080/1369118X.2017.1386705

Swiss Re (2016a); *A New Longitudinal Source of Health Data and Facial Analytics*, Swiss Re. Available at: https://www.swissre.com/institute/research/topics-and-risk-dialogues/health-and-longevity/A-new-longitudinal-source-of-health-data-and-facial-analytics.html

Swiss Re (2016b); *Health Monitoring: Making Sense of Sensors – Event Summary*. Available at: https://www.swissre.com/institute/research/topics-and-risk-

336 REFERENCES

dialogues/digital-business-model-and-cyber-risk/health-monitoring-summary-video.html

Tarlo, E., (2016); Entanglement; The Secret Lives of Hair, London: Bloomsbury.

Tate, S. A. (2009); Black Beauty: Aesthetics, Stylization, Politics, Farnham: Ashgate Publishing.

Tendayi Sithole (2012a) Fela Kuti and the oppositional lyrical power, Muziki, 9:1, 1–12, DOI: https://doi.org/10.1080/18125980.2012.737101

The Welcome People (2023); *An Innovative Approach to Street Management*, The Welcome People. Available at: https://www.thewelcomepeople.com

Ticketmaster Business (2018); *Live Nation and Ticketmaster Unveil Plans for Facial Recognition Technology*, Ticketmaster Business. Available at: https://business.ticketmaster.com.au/business-solutions/live-nation-and-ticketmaster-unveil-plans-facial-recognition-technology/

Ticketmaster (2024); Our Story. Available at: https://business.ticketmaster.co.uk/why-ticketmaster/our-story/

TuneCore (2024); *What is Music Publishing?* Available at: https://www.tunecore.co.uk/music-publishing-administration

Twitter (2023a); *The Twitter Ads Auction*, Ads Help Center, Twitter. Available at: https://business.twitter.com/en/help/troubleshooting/bidding-and-auctions-faqs.html

Twitter (2023b); *How Twitter Ads Work, Twitter Ads Help Center*, Twitter. Available at: https://business.twitter.com/en/help/troubleshooting/how-twitter-ads-work.html

Twitter (2023c); *Twitter Ads Pricing*, Twitter Ads Help Center. Available at: https://business.twitter.com/en/help/overview/ads-pricing.html

Udis-Kessler, A., (2021); *Queer Inclusion in the United Methodist Church*, New York, London: Routledge.

United Kingdom National Health Service (2021/2022); *Booster Dose of the Coronavirus (COVID-19) Vaccine*, National Health Service (NHS). Coronavirus (COVID-19) Vaccination. Available at: https://www.nhs.uk/conditions/coronavirus-covid-19/coronavirus-vaccination/coronavirus-booster-vaccine/

United Nations (1948); Universal Declaration of Human Rights, United Nations. Available at: https://www.ohchr.org/en/human-rights/universal-declaration/translations/english

United Nations High Commissioner for Refugees (UNHCR) (2022); *Operational Data Portal Ukraine Refugee Situation, Refugees Fleeing Ukraine (since 24 February 2022) 3,489,644*, Last Updated 20 March 2022, UNHCR. Available at: https://data2.unhcr.org/en/situations/ukraine

United Nations High Commissioner for Refugees (UNHCR) (2022a); *Refugees Fleeing Ukraine (since 24 February 2022) 4,019,287*, Last Updated 29 March 2022, UNHCR. Available at: https://data2.unhcr.org/en/situations/ukraine

REFERENCES   337

United Nations Human Rights (2022); Ukraine: Civilian Casualty Update 16 March 2022, United Nations Human Rights Office of the High Commission, *United Nations*, 16 March 2022. Available at: https://www.ohchr.org/en/press-briefing-notes/2022/03/ukraine-civilian-casualty-update-16-march-2022

U.S. Department of Justice (2024); Live Nation-Ticketmaster's Exclusionary Conduct and Dominance Across the Live Concert Ecosystem Harms Fans, Innovation, Artists, and Venues, U.S. Department of Justice. Available at: https://www.justice.gov/opa/pr/justice-department-sues-live-nation-ticketmaster-monopolizing-markets-across-live-concert

Van Binsbergen, W., (2005); 'An incomprehensible miracle' – Central African clerical intellectualism versus African historic religion: A close reading of Valentin Mudimbe's *Tales of Faith, Journal of African Cultural Studies*, 17:1, 11–65, DOI: https://doi.org/10.1080/0090988052000344638

Van Kerkhove, M., (2022); Update on Omicron by Dr @mvankerhove from @ WHO's Q and A. Available at: https://twitter.com/mvankerkhove/status/1481008746558115847

Vasudevan, P., Ramírez, M., Mendoza, Y., and Daigle, M., (2023); Storytelling Earth and Body, Annals of the American Association of Geographers, 113:7, 1728–1744, https://doi.org/10.1080/24694452.2022.2139658

Vergès, F., (2021); *A Decolonial Feminism*, Trans. Bohrer, A., London: Pluto Press.

Vogue, (2018); *The Beat Goes On*, Muir, R., September 2018 – Vogue Retro Article. Available at: https://www.duffyarchive.com/september-2018-vogue-retro-article/

Voice Online (2021); *Nigerian artists pile pressure on UK over looted Benin Bronzes*, (ed.) Fieary, S., 23rd September 2021. Available at: https://www.voice-online.co.uk/news/2021/09/23/nigerian-artists-pile-pressure-on-uk-over-looted-benin-bronzes/

Wacquant, L., (1993); From Ruling Class to Field of Power: An Interview with Pierre Bourdieu on La Noblesse d'État, Theory, Culture & Society 1993 10:3, 19–44

Wagner, J., (2006) Visible materials, visualised theory and images of social research, *Visual Studies*, 21:01, 55–69, DOI: https://doi.org/10.1080/14725860600613238

Walcott, R., (2015); Genres of Human: Multiculturalism, Cosmo- politics, and the Caribbean Basin, in (ed.) McKittrick, K., *Sylvia Wynter On Being Human As Praxis*, London: Duke University Press.

Westminster City Council (2021a); *Ambitious Plans will Reinvent the Nation's High Street and boost London's Recovery*, Westminster City Council. Available at: https://www.westminster.gov.uk/news/ambitious-plans-will-reinvent-nations-high-street-and-boost-londons-recovery

338 REFERENCES

Westminster City Council (2021b); *Marble Arch Business Improvement District Successful Ballot*, Westminster City Council. Available at: https://www.westminster.gov.uk/news/marble-arch-business-improvement-district-successful-ballot

Westminster City Council (2021c); Tickets for Marble Arch Mound Available Now, Westminster City Council. Available at: https://www.westminster.gov.uk/news/get-set-summit-marble-arch-mound-summer

Williams, A., and Gonlin, V., (2017); I got all my sisters with me (on Black Twitter): second screening of *How to Get Away with Murder* as a discourse on Black Womanhood, Information, Communication & Society, 20:7, 984–1004, DOI: https://doi.org/10.1080/1369118X.2017.1303077

Williams, S., (2020) The Black Digital Syllabus Movement: The Fusion of Academia, Activism and Arts, Howard Journal of Communications, 31:5, 493–508, DOI: https://doi.org/10.1080/10646175.2020.1743393

Williams, B., Collier, J., Wadley, B., Stokes, T., and Coghill, K., (2022) "Should I Straighten My Hair?": Narratives of Black College Women with Natural Hair, Journal of Women and Gender in Higher Education,15:2, 134–156, DOI: https://doi.org/10.1080/26379112.2022.2067861

Windmill Software (2023); *People Counting: Eight Technologies to Measure Footfall*. Windmill Software. Available at: https://www.windmill.co.uk/footfall-technology.html

Women and Equalities Committee (2021); *Reform of the Gender Recognition Act, Third Report of Session 2021-22*, House of Commons Committee Report, UK Parliament. Available at: https://publications.parliament.uk/pa/cm5802/cmselect/cmwomeq/977/report.html#heading-9

World Health Organization [WHO]., (2023); *WHO Coronavirus (COVID-19) Dashboard*, Overview, World Health Organization. Available at: https://covid19.who.int

X Business Outlook (2023); Digital Advertising – Search Results. X Business Outlook. Available at: https://business.twitter.com/en/search.html?limit=10&offset=0&q=Digital%20advertising%20&searchPath=%2Fcontent%2Fbusiness-twitter%2Fen&sort=relevance

York, J., (2021); *Silicon Values: The Future of Free Speech, Under Surveillance Capitalism*, Verso: London.

Zambakari, C. D. (2020). Interrogating Liberal Theories of Rights: An Analysis of Rights in the African Context. *Interventions*, 22(7), 860–878. https://doi.org/10.1080/1369801X.2020.1753550

Zuboff, S., (2019); *The Age of Surveillance Capitalism; The Fight for a Human Future at the New Frontier of Power*, New York: PublicAffairs, Hachette Book Group.

Zurich (2017); Our Customers: at the Center of Everything We Do, Zurich. Available at: https://www.zurich.com

Index

A

Abeokuta, Ogun State Nigeria, 67–69, 76–78, 80, 82, 115, 256, 260
Abeokuta province, 78, 82
Abeokuta Women's Union (AWU), 76, 78–80, 85, 155
1946, 76
Abiodun, Rowland, 111, 112
Absolutist nationalist liberation ideology, 66
Academy Brixton London, 2, 19
Academy Music Group (AMG), viii, 47, 49, 50, 54, 274, 275, 279, 280, 304, 307
Accumulation of user-generated advertising, 128
Activist praxis, 19
Actors and networks of advertising surveillance, 17–18
Actuality
  international market capitalist competition, 141
  interoperability social media, 141

Adejumobi, Saheed, 62, 83
Adelekan, Commander Ade, 14, 45, 210
Adequate levels of literacy
  medical provision, 77
  sanitation, 77
Adorno, Theodor, 90–93, 97, 98, 100, 300, 301
Ads and Trend Takeover, 126
Adsensory inscriptive technologies, 18
Advancing post-independence, 33, 251
Advertisement, 92, 126, 143, 145, 273, 285
  maximising advertiser's performance, 145
Advertising
  ideology, 7–9
  inscriptive technologies, 18, 100, 123, 137, 190
  and marketers, 127
  technologies, 18, 100, 123, 137, 142, 144, 190, 275

© The Author(s), under exclusive license to Springer Nature Switzerland AG 2024
P. Odih, *Black British Postcolonial Feminist Ways of Seeing Human Rights*, https://doi.org/10.1007/978-3-031-71877-9

340 INDEX

Advertising visual culture
  amplified face-value, 147
  Asake concert, 16, 25, 47, 147,
    208, 306
  automated computer programme,
    146, 147
  Black music 147
  Black Twitter, 147
  concert tickets, 147
  harvested secondary market
    ticketing, 147
  heightened consumer demand, 147
  heightened visual techniques, 147
  hyper-sensationalised, 147
  O2 Academy Brixton, 15th
    December 2022, 147
  simulacra market-based ticket
    sale, 147
Aesthetic atmosphere, 112
Aesthetic gentrification, 5, 25, 159
African American
    choreographer, 89, 90
African and European commercialised
    imitation, 108
African, Caribbean diaspora, 129, 209
African colonies, 62
African cultural identity, 70
African diaspora, 3, 22, 23, 99
African ethnic-cultural value, 137
African feminist musicology
  development of Afrobeat, 155
  give voice, 155
  interpolation, 155
  Izsadore, Sandra (Musician), 155
African highlife, jazz, funk and
    traditional Yoruba music, 83
African music, 22, 43, 155
African racial heritage, 4
African sculptures, 102, 105, 110
African slaves, musicology
  connotating uncontrolled
    sexuality, 163
  European White male, 163

  mastery bodily sensation, 163
  rife animalistic denotations, 163
  Western ideal of conquering
    civilisation, 163
African spirituality, 74
African Yoruba musicality, 40
Afrobeat culture industry 1980s
  African highlife band, 154
  Brian Duffy's photograph of the
    Koola Lobitos band, 154
  colonial lineage, 155
  feature piece *The Beat Goes On*, 154
  photographer Brian Duffy, 154
  racial heritage ethnic cultural
    identity, 154
  Vogue October 1961, 154
  Vogue publishes a retrospective, 154
Afrobeat feminist Sandra Izsadore, 25,
    34, 153–163, 165, 168,
    170–172, 178
Afrobeat human and civil rights, 67,
    71, 83, 87
  Beasts of No Nation, 215–218, 220,
    244, 251, 255, 256
  decolonial praxis 173, 217
  post-colonial era, 217, 218
Afrobeat linguistic repertoire
  composed in narrative format, 161
  conversation with colonialism, 161
  enhanced prominence of Pidgin
    English, 161
  nonlexical syllables, 161
  Yoruba chanting recitation, 161
Afrobeat(s)
  aficionados, 88
  bands, 95
  music community, 3
  music creative, 99, 101, 103, 108,
    112, 113
  musician, 109, 110, 112
  Nigerian musician, 109, 127, 256
  pioneered, 94
Agro-petrol economy, 34, 253

INDEX 341

AI-assisted decision-making
operates, 143
AI digitality, 127
Ake: Years of Childhood, 80, 115
Alake of Abeokuta, 80
Algorithm advertisement
bid, 143
monetised competition, 143
target audience, 143
Algorithm capitalism, 33, 277
Twitter's auction, 143
Algorithmically-based pricing
cumulatively over time, 145
disproportionately affect older
consumers, 145
increases in prices, 145
techniques, 145
Algorithmic deciphering conscious and
unconscious needs, 91
Algorithmic profile,
personalisation, 110
Althusser, Ideological State Apparatus
body of Ideological State, 234
Classical Marxist conjecture, 234
culture industry, 233, 234, 241, 247
function of ideology, 234
interview of Fela Anikulapo-
Kuti, 234
Repressive State, 232–234, 242
state, 234
State Apparatus on the other, 234
subconscious human identity, 234
superstructure, 234, 241
theorise subjectivity, 234
Althusser, interpellation
agency of the individual, 243
becoming its subject, 239, 243
cultural-economy of British colonial
mentality, 243
limitations, 32, 244
potentiality of resistance, 242, 243
Amnesty International 1985
Decolonising Human Rights, 174

Shetty, Salil, 174, 175
Anglo-Nigerian, 42, 109, 160
Annihilate this space with time, 6
Annihilation of space by time, 6
Anthem-like choruses, 42
Anthropo-zoomorphic mask, 108
Anti-British, 81
Anticolonial, 98, 245, 249
digital cultures, 98–114
feminism, 19, 20, 33, 34, 61–64,
67–98, 100, 103, 113, 115
movements, 65, 157, 168
Anticolonial feminist
feminist praxis, 66, 85, 114, 116
formulation of absolutes, 86
politics, 63
Anti-essentialism, 13
Anti-racist activism, 136
Anti-racist critique, 137
Apparatus of the state, 18
Application for the Review of a
Premises Licence, 53
Appreciation of scale, 125
Appropriation of the Feminine
Antecedents, 98–114
April 24th 1986: granted freedom, 40
Ap Security, 50
Ap Security whistleblower, 50
Architecture of Twitter, 136, 137, 140
Archive Studio of the National Theatre
London, 92
Arena *Teacher Don't Teach Me
Nonsense*
backstage interview, 156
depiction, independence from
colonial rule, 156
documentary filmed 1984, 156
Glastonbury music festival, 156
Pan-Africanist movement, 156
performance Fela Anikulapo-
Kuti, 156
Armatrading, Joan, 41
Art Deco, viii, 278

342 INDEX

Artificial Intelligence (AI), 100, 126, 127, 143, 144, 202, 306, 307
Arts Council of Great Britain, 104
Asake Nigerian Afrobeat, 19
Ashcroft, Bill, 32, 218, 219, 244, 246–248, 250–252, 258, 262–264, 266–268
  acclaimed restitution, 218
  anticolonialist intransigence, 32, 244
  appreciation cultures, 244
  attributes diversity, 268
  autonomous agency, 32, 244
  bring order, 218
  civilization, 218
  colonial discourse, 32, 244, 246, 247, 252, 263, 264, 266
  colonialist delineation, 32, 244
  colonial occupation, 218
  colonial subject, 32, 244, 252
  colonised nations, 218
  critically interpellation, 32, 244
  discursive tools, 32, 245, 246
  embattlement Others, 32, 244
  by European nations, 218
  formulation absolutes, 32, 244
  hegemony of the dominant culture, 32, 244, 246
  imperial nation, 218
  impervious hegemony, 32, 244
  infrastructural capacities, 218
  interpolation, 33, 221, 225, 247, 258, 262, 264, 266, 268
  interview, Prof Emerita Jane Bryce, 32, 34, 245, 258
  porous hegemony, 32, 244
  postcolonialism, 32, 219, 244
  post-colonial supposition, 32, 244
  Post-colonial Transformation, 32, 217, 225, 244
  potentiality of transformation, 32, 244
  self-determination, 32, 245, 246, 252

silenced, 32, 244
silencing resistance, 32, 244
subaltern discursive speak, 32, 244, 246
voice of colonized heard, 32, 244
Assemblage of surveillance, 17
Astonishing spectacular broadcasting, 19
Astoria, viii
Authentic
  anticolonial activism, 90
  depiction artist's political conviction, 90
  mother, Funmilayo Ransome-Kuti, 89, 90
  praxis, 90
  vernacular, radical, 134
Authenticity, 135, 276
Automated communicative labour
  automated psychotherapy, 144
  capitalist profitability, 144
  contingency, 144
  human communicativity, 144
  motivation momentum, 144
  speaking human subject, 144
  unpredictability, 144
Automated disruptors
  algorithmic discourse generator, 144
  automatically, generated journalist news text, 144
  automation of oral and written discourse, 144
  field of Artificial Intelligence (AI), 144
  issue of automation, 144
  transformation into advertising, 144
  transformation of digital communication, 144
Automation
  advertising, 142–144
  Artificial Intelligence (AI), 144
  automation of oral and written discourse, 144

INDEX 343

Automation communicative justice, 34
  digital generated music, 90, 107
Autonomous independent
  thinking, 97
Axes of ethnicity, 20, 60
  gender dimensions, 20, 64

B

Babangida, General Ibrahim, 33, 253,
  259, 260, 262
Baez, Joan, 41
Bailey, Shaun, 52
Bayo Dosunmu (Lambeth Council's
  Chief Executive), 52
BBC File on Four
  Documentary, 46–53
BBC newscast its File on 4
  documentary, 19
BBC Radio 4–File on 4 documentary,
  46, 48, 49, 293, 296
BBC reporters, 47, 51
BBC spectacular monopoly, 48
Beasts of No Nation
  capitalistic culture industry, 216
  decolonialism, 216, 220
  engendered post-colonial
    intervention, 216
  feminist post-colonial, 216
  human rights in Nigeria, 216, 220
  Index on Censorship in 1989, 216,
    247, 258, 259, 264, 267
  neocolonial public/private,
    216, 220
  post-colonial album, 216
  praxis of Fela Anikulapo-Kuti,
    216, 220
  rooting in anticolonial, 216, 220
  The Vinyl©1989, 216, 217
Benin City craftsmen, 105
Benjamin, Walter, 97
The Best Of Fela, 90

Biometric surveillance
  biased and discriminatory, 197
  the Black music industry, 91,
    176, 197
  Dame Cressida Dick, 196
  disproportionately inaccurate on
    black, Asian female faces, 197
  facial recognition, 196–202, 204
  frontline policing decision-
    making, 197
  live facial recognition
    (LFR), 196–204
  Metropolitan Police Service (MPS),
    29, 198, 201
  policing of live music events, 197
  technology algorithms, 190
Biopolitics of marketised, 18
Black African human right, 43
Black body, 4, 18, 129, 130, 132, 133
Black British, viii, ix, 1–34, 41, 43, 86,
  98, 159, 182, 204, 209, 224
Black British Biafra diaspora, 14
Black British born, 5, 159
Black British feminism
  Black British born, 5, 159
  cultural form, 5, 159
  embodied capital, 159
  first-generation daughter, 5, 25, 159
  14th June 2017, Grenfell Tower
    London fire tragedy, 5, 159
  Nigerian Biafra diaspora, 5, 25, 159
  urban ecology, 5, 25, 159
Black British feminist identity
  behaviour of the colonized, 164
  colonial dichotomy, 163, 164
  colonial, gender system, 163
  European White female, 163
  grotesquely sexual and sinful, 164
  homebound, 163
  human Other, 163
  non-gendered, 164
  personalities/souls, 164

344 INDEX

Black British feminist identity (*cont.*)
promiscuous trope, 164
reproduced race and capital, 163
sexual purity, passivity, 163
subjugated, delimited of rights, 163
White, European, bourgeoisie
man, 163
Black British LGBT, 41
Black British London, ix, 25
Black British urban
communities, viii, 4
Black British youths, 4
Black communities, 18, 133, 135,
136, 139, 168, 307
Black consciousness, 20, 33, 171, 251,
260, 302
Black cultural and racialised sexual
identities, 133
Black cultural identity, 131, 136, 137
Black culture industry, 89, 142, 171
Black experiences of embodiment, 133
Black female, 24, 25, 29, 79, 154,
162–166, 182, 199, 204,
205, 208
Black female matriarch
brutal force of circumstances, 166
enslaved subject, 166
praxis resistance, 4, 5, 25, 103, 159
promoting the consciousness, 166
reproductive labour, 166
resistance, 166
resistance space, homestead, 166
reveal spaces, 166
Black female security
business community, 182
local authorities, 182
local music, 182
policing regulators, 182
racialised heterotopic, 182
urban space music venue, 182
Black female slave
domestic work, 166

labour of females, 166
members immediate family, 166
ministering needs, 166
slave community, 166
Black feminist anticolonial
framework, 148
Black journalists within the
mainstream, 134
Black Lives Matter (BLM)
cultivating black identity, 140
hashtag, 140
hip hop celebrities, 140
practices of advertising, 140
racial identity using, 140
Black London born, 4
Black masculinity, matriarchy
ancestral beliefs, 162
grieving son, 162
in Kalakuta Republic to Dodan
Barracks, 162
mental trauma, mother's coffin, 162
Yoruba culture, 162
Black music cultural reproduction
cultural form, 296
distinguished capital, 296
the field of online petitions, 296
gain prominence, 296
live music venue, 182, 276, 288,
290, 296
longue durée reproduction of
capital, 296
networked connections, 296
online platform change.org, 296
saving the O2 Academy
Brixton, 296
social capital, 296
willingness to collaborate, 296
Black music cultures, viii, ix, 16, 18,
26, 29–33, 51, 55, 147, 159,
176, 202, 271–296, 301,
304, 306
Black music cultures of Afrobeat(s), ix

INDEX   345

Black music entertainment, ix, 15
Black music events, 49, 51
Black music industry
  activist, 155
  Black musician manager, 155
  Black Panther civil rights
    movement, 155
  caricaturing prose, 155
  encountering Izsadore culture
    industry, Kuti's political
    identity, 155
  familiar stylised, 155
  heavily affiliated, 155
  vogue piece, 155
Black nationalism
  anti-Western dominance, 23
  changing his name from Ransome
    to Aníkúlápó, 155
  colonial history, 155
  principles of Black nationalism, 155
  sonic attacks, 155
Black Panthers, 83, 154, 155,
  165, 217
Black people for land, 161
Black public sphere, 134
Black Twitter, 124, 129–140, 144,
  145, 147, 148
Black Vernacular English, 131
Black women's bodies, 61
Body-land realities, 61
Boseman, Chadwick, 132, 133
Both imaginary and real, 123
Boundaries of political discourse, 138
Brigadier Tunde Idiagbon, Chief of
  Staff, 178
Amnesty International 1985, 178
British, American Black artistic
    vernacular
  human environment, 207
  racialised social injustice, 207
  sacred or forbidden places, 207
  state of crisis, 207
  type of space, 207

British Broadcasting Corporation
  (BBC), 19, 46–53, 71, 73, 79,
  156, 291, 292, 294, 304
British colonial
  Africa, 23, 65, 170
  colonialists, 69, 166, 250
  colonial rule, 23, 77, 83, 85, 88, 98,
    104, 159, 238
  colonial rule in Africa, 65
  colonial system, 63, 74, 76, 78
  system of taxation, 78
British colonial era
  indigenous cultural identity, 113
  suppression, 113
British Colonial Offices, 82
British cultural and ethnic diversity, 48
Britishness, 1, 9, 14
British of Benin City in 1897, 104
British Settled Migrants, 43
British settled Nigerian diaspora, 43
British treatment
  hands of Civil Servants of the
    country, 85
Brixton Academy, viii, 42, 43, 50, 51,
  53, 128, 140, 208, 221, 224,
  272, 273, 275–278, 287, 290,
  292, 294
Brixton Astoria, viii
Brixton community
  accolade of "Top signed on Change.
    org," 274
  campaign, 208
  Change.Org platform, 273, 274
  safe gigs over the years have
    shown, 274
  sign-values of competitive
    capitalising metrics, 274
  tragic incident, 274
Brixton critical incident, 15, 45–53,
  55, 203, 291, 305
Broadway Run, Fela!, 89
Buhari, Muhammadu (Major
  General), 40, 259

346 INDEX

Business Improvement District (BID)
BID levy, are given a vote on the
BID proposal–the ballot, 183
BID proposal, 183
businesses that pay business rates,
within the business district, 183
cooperation, 183
establishing distinct routes, 183
local authority for evaluation and if
endorsed agreement to manage
the ballot, 183
predicated on it achieving a simple
majority in the balloted vote,
the proposed bid is
established, 183
Business model of X, 125, 127
Butler, Judith, 10
Byfield, Judith, 80, 82, 86, 87

C
Capitalist commercial interests
Black Codes, Jim Crow, 169
codified race-based terror, 169
codified racism, 169
legalized convict labor, 169
old slave codes, 169
permeate legal rationalities, 169
private lives of Black workers, 169
prohibited social intercourse, 169
white employers degree of
control, 169
Capitalist commodification, 97
Capitalist consumer economies, 8
Capitalistic abundance, 139
Capitalistic communicative justice
advertisement monetised, 143
advertisement space bidding, 143
advertising competition, 143
target audience, 143
targeting, sensing same interest, 143
Twitter auction algorithm, 143
Capitalistic culture industry, 103, 216

Capitalistic digital media, ix
Capitalistic investment, 5, 25, 159
Capitalistic mode of production, 138
Capitalist production, 5, 46, 47, 93,
100, 231–233, 241, 242
Capitalist profitability
automated communicative, 144
contingency, 144
expense speaking human
subject, 144
motivation momentum, 144
psychotherapy human
communicativity, 144
unpredictability, 144
Capitalist regime of accumulation, 16
Capitalist technologies, 139, 196
Capital Vol.1, Marx, 6
Case of Fela Anikulapo-Kuti, 40, 41,
233, 234, 242, 246, 247, 262
Case study, ix, 3, 9–11, 14–18, 34,
43–44, 46, 51, 123, 146, 148,
199, 202–204, 211, 216, 305, 308
Catalysts to innovative expression, 93
Centrality of Blackness to the culture
industry's colonial capitalism, 99
Change.org
branded petition, 273
business model, 273
connected to supporters, 273
create petitions, 273
financing, 273
free at the point of use, 273
free of charge, 273
online petition service, 273
ordinary people, 273
petition starters, 273
promotion of their petition, 273
requires financial investment, 273
Chimera of individuality, 90
Circulating online in time/space
compressed, 122
Circulation time, 6
Citizenship, 9, 85, 87, 134, 175, 192

City Hall, 52
City of Lagos, 5, 159
Classical sculpture, 105
Clickbait journalism, 48
Click through
  boosted posts, 273
  change.org petition, 273
  Facebook, 273
  petitions civic advertisements, 273
  promoted petitions, 273
  sponsored tweets, 273
Close reading, 5, 8–14, 94, 96,
  115, 156
Club Premises Certificate under the
  Licensing Act 2003, 53
Colonial binary
  approximations, 20, 64
  of culture and society, 20, 64
Colonial capitalist exploitation, 7
Colonial commemoration, 61
Colonial digital capitalism, ix, 4, 5, 18,
  23, 24, 31, 121–148, 182,
  196, 307
Colonial discrimination, 5, 25, 159
Colonial exploitation
  colonial administrations, 81, 173
  colonial situations, 173
  cultural, political and economic
    oppression, 173
  dominant racial/ethnic groups, 173
  expropriation and domination, 173
  institutional structures, 173
  processes of administration of
    colonisation, 173
  racialized ethnic groups, 173
Colonialism
  colonised female as matriarch, 165
  enslaved community parallels, 165
  illegitimate occupier, 165
  matriarchate at times, 165
  matriarchy, 165
  spaces for resistance, 165
  spaces of collaboration, 165

Colonial logics, 20, 61, 64
Colonial masters, 99
Colonial mentality, 40, 67, 71, 73,
  153–179, 215, 243, 263
Colonial municipality, 63
Colonial Office, 80, 83
Colonial Office statement, 83
Colonial oppression, 19
Colonial system, 6, 20, 63, 64, 74,
  76, 78, 164
Colonial systems of knowledge, 20, 64
Colonisation, 4, 127, 163, 172–174,
  176, 218, 225, 247
Colonised, ix, 4, 20, 32, 43, 61,
  63–66, 69, 74, 86, 91, 115, 122,
  129, 163, 164, 188–190, 218,
  219, 244, 246, 247, 258, 264
Colonised through expropriation, 129
Colonising features of digital
  communication, 24, 123
*Comments on the Society of the
  Spectacle*, 16, 272
Commercial digital spaces, 130
Commercialisation security
  Angela Davis, 177
  carceral system, 177
  disabuse Black people, 177
  disenfranchise, 177
  human and civil rights, 177
  private employers, 177
  private prison company–G4s, 177
  private security Africa, 177
  profiteering criminal justice
    system, 177
  systems of repression, 177
Commercialised Black music
  cultures, 16
Commercially contradictory
  programmatic metrics
  advertisement automation, 144
  auction operating model, 143
  Twitter's free speech policy, 143
Commercial mass-media, 47

348 INDEX

Commodification
  communicative action
  automated communicative
    labour, 144
  automated psychotherapy, 144
  capital to eliminate
    unpredictability, 144
  human rights digital labour, 144
  profitability, 144
  speaking human subject, 144
Commodification of anticolonial
  feminism, 103
Commodification processes, 116
Commodity capitalism, 83, 91, 100,
  129, 144
Commodity fetishism of online
  communication technology, 138
Commodity-form, 3, 46, 90, 91, 96,
  177, 217
Communication and human
  rights, 3, 248
Communication and transportation, 6
Communication as ceaseless circular
  transmission, 138
Communication feminism, 23
Communication ISA
  Althusser, 232–234
  distinction, 232
  Ideological State Apparatuses, 232
  material relations, 232
  materiality, 232
  observationally, 232
  operational, 232
  private *vs.* public sphere, 232
  public domain, 232
  realm of ideality, 232
Communication networks of the
  audience, 145
Communicative action, viii, 7, 20, 25,
  33, 98, 103, 113, 116, 122, 124,
  130, 136, 148, 156, 159–161,
  221, 237, 261

as a human right, 3, 7, 19, 23,
  34, 55, 176, 262, 303,
  307, 308
of Yoruba tribal art, 111
Communicative action technology
  advertiser's auction bid, 143
  platform, 143
  promotional display, 143
  quality of the advertisement, 143
  secure space/time, 143
  Twitter's Ads auction API, 143
Communicative capitalism, 23, 24,
  122–125, 127, 129, 144
Communicative Capitalism:
  Circulation and the Foreclosure of
  Politics, 24, 123
Communicative discourse and
  activism, 24
Communicative human rights, 5,
  67, 121–148
Communicative justice, 33, 34, 55
Communicative message, 23
Computer programme harvested
  Black music, 147
  heightened consumer demand, 147
  O2 Academy Brixton, 147
  secondary market ticketing, 147
Conceptualises the fetishisation
  advertising, 139
  capitalism operates, 139
  interchangeable objects, 139
  nuanced and complex, 139
  its message and the subject, 139
  politics into technology, 139
  transform the medium, 139
Conceptualising fetishisation of politics
  complex ways capitalism, 139
  generalise, 139
  interchangeable objects, 139
  medium its message, 139
  subject into advertising, 139
  technology, 139

INDEX 349

Concerns relevant to feminist
economics of sub-Saharan Africa
collusion social structural, historical
patriarchal processes, 254
colonial feminist perspective, 254
colonial power, 254
distinctly exacerbating gender
inequity, 254
field of feminist human rights, 254
gendered processes of neocolonial
progression, 254
gender inequality, 254
International Monetary Fund
(IMF), 254
militarisation of the political
enforcement, 254
post-colonial praxis, 254
restrained Nigeria's fiscal
policy, 254
World Bank imposed debt
restructuring programmes, 254
Condensation
reformulated simplistically
liberalism, 139
technological solutions, 139
Conditions of intensification of
mediated
communications, 132–133
Conjunction with the internationally
renowned feminist musicians, 41
Consciousness-raising lectures, 96
Conspiracy of Hope concert tour, 41
Consumer citizen, 275
Consumer Rights Act 2015, 147
Contemporary anticolonial praxis, 103
Contemporary iconography of
Afrobeat, 88–98
Converging data-stream, 138
Copyright law, a colonial logic, 20, 64
Cornucopia of merchandise including
CD compilations, 90
Cosmological worldview, 102

Council licensing sub-
committee, 44, 308
Countering rationalities: safe spaces for
females in crisis
heterotopia, 205–209
Counterpropositions in public
space, 20, 64
Counterpublics, 124, 129,
130, 136–138
Counterpublic sphere, 135
Covid-19 pandemic, 129, 133,
190, 207
Craft channels of communication, 110
Criminal Justice and Public Order Act
1994, 147
Crisis heterotopia
bridge connecting both
communities, 207
exchanging ideas, 207
status of the Brixton (London, UK)
and Harlem (US), 207
Twinned Districts, 207
twinning exchange of e-commerce
products and services, 207
Critical disidentification, 129
Critical humanism, 137
Critical incident 15th December
2022, 45–53
Critical incident scene, 14, 45
Critical intellectuality, 73
Critical judgement, 7, 8
Critical pedagogy, 73–75, 136
Critical theory, 4–7, 20, 23, 84, 90,
91, 107, 114, 116, 226–231,
241, 268, 299–308
Crowd capacity, 146, 279
Crowd crush, ix, 19, 44, 51, 148, 182,
208, 209, 211, 304, 307, 308
*Crush Victim's Family Call For
Answers*, 46
Cultivate counterpublics, 136
Cultural anthropology, 101

350 INDEX

Cultural heterogeneity, 136
Culturally creative products, 90
Cultural political campaigns, 7
Cultural political impact of networked
communications, 129
Cultural political relevance of
Funmilayo Ransome-Kuti, 99
Cultural representations, 2
Cultural Studies 1983, 7
Culture and society taxation, 64
Culture industry, 4, 83, 84, 89–94,
97–101, 103, 116, 142, 171,
172, 216, 225, 226, 229, 230,
233, 234, 241, 242, 246–248,
258, 259, 264, 267, 268,
302, 304

D
The Daily Worker, 79
Data-driven advertising
of advertising space, 144
automation of the programmatic
buying, 144
context, 144
data-based real-time bidding
(RTB), 144
Data-driven approach, 126
Data-stream of communication, 132
Davis, Angela, 28, 41, 157, 161, 163,
165–171, 176–178
*The Black Woman's Role in the
Community of Slaves*, 165
Freedom Is a Constant Struggle, 171
Sandra Izsadore, 165, 168, 170, 178
struggle against racism, 171
Davis, Miles, 41
Dawning of Afrobeat, 91
Dean, Jodi, 23, 24, 122–125, 127,
138, 139, 141
communicative action, 24, 122,
123, 127, 139, 141
detached from the specificity, 124

technological application, 124
Debord, Guy, 16–18, 46–49, 147,
272, 275–277, 282, 292–296
absolute spectacular
surveillance, 272
contradiction, 272
control comes *vs.* value, 272
cultural significance, 272
impracticalities of processing, 272
La Société Du Spectacle, 16
liberal democratic, 272
licence suspension, 272
online petitions opposing, 272
online petition strategy, 272
private companies surveillance, 272
private hegemony of meaning, 272
proliferating surveillance
technologies, 272
resistance strategies, 272
Save Brixton Academy, 272
spectacle, 16, 46
Debut on Broadway, 88
Decaying aura, 97
Decca West Africa limited, 84
Decolonial diaspora studies, 4,
9, 10, 13
Decolonial Ecology
Angela Davis, 157
assaults on the environment, 157
human expressions, 157
Malcom Ferdinand, 157
National Alliance Against
Racism, 157
Political Repression, 157
racial capitalism, 157
racism and the environment, 157
state violence, 157
Decolonial feminism, 25, 26, 153–179
Decolonial feminists struggle
Euro-centric epistemology, 161
recognition of knowledge, 161
Western-patriarchal economic
ideology, 161

INDEX 351

Decolonial Harlem BIDs
    artistic cultural political
        initiative, 206
    audio testimonials, 206
    Brixton BID, 206
    local community, 206
De-colonising colonial mentality
    anticolonial feminism, 171
    decolonial feminist praxis, 171
    decolonial feminists, 171
    decolonialism, 171
    de-thinking, 171, 172
    interviewing Sandra Izsadore, 171
    mainstream feminism, 171
    Olufunmilayo Ransome-Kuti, 171
Decrease in surplus labour time, 6
Deep unconscious mistrust, 97
Dehumanization of Black bodies, 130
Depoliticising, 139
Dialectic of Enlightenment, 97
Digital advertising, 124–130, 140,
    143–145, 147
Digital advertising disruptions, 124
Digital advertising is
    meritoriously, 128
Digital banking disruptors, 146
Digital biometric surveillance racism
    biometric facial scanning, 198
    data collection, 197
    discrimination, 29
    facial recognition, 197–198
    feminist human rights
        perspective, 198
    MPS and South Wales Police, 197
    National Physical
        Laboratory, 197–198
    Retrospective Facial
        Recognition, 198
    test evaluation of facial
        recognition, 197–198
    True-Positive Identification Rate
        (TPIR), 198

Digital capitalism
    exploitation of Black Music, 147
    promotional culture is
        disconcerting, 147
Digital communicative justice
    advertising, 144
    algorithmic discourse
        generator, 144
    Artificial Intelligence (AI), 144
    automation of oral discourse, 144
    automation of written
        discourse, 144
    communicative capitalism, 144
    rapidly generated journalist news
        text, 144
    transformation of digital
        communication, 144
Digital community tribe, 114
Digital cultural production, 130
Digital Economy Act (DEA)
    2017, 146
Digital image production, 3, 15
Digital labour communicative action
    advanced capabilities of
        generative, 144
    algorithmic identities capable, 144
    attractive humanity of the
        literary, 144
    automated communicative
        labour, 144
    Black Twitter, 144
    mimicking the rhetorically, 144
    political efficacy of this
        community, 144
Digitally amenable sources of
    data, 135
Digitally informationalised data, 3
Digitally policing, viii, 303–308
Digitally policing human rights, viii
Digital media, ix, 103, 108, 147
Digital music technology are
    sculpting, 110

352 INDEX

Digital policing
  additional security routes
    proffered, 182
  Business Improvement District
    (BID) schemes, 182
  extraordinary risk assessment, 182
  hyper-vigilant digital policing
    surveillance, 182
  insurance premiums, 182
  live music, 182
  venues in urban inner-cities actively
    seek, 182
Digital policing business model
  Business Improvement
    Districts, 182
  business steered partnerships, 182
  local activities and allow, 182
  Local Government, 182
Digital policing strategy, 3, 47, 211
Digital-race assemblage approach, 137
Digital subaltern, 135
Digital Surveillance Heterotopias
  BID, 186–190
Digital technology, 5, 107, 108, 111,
  114, 142, 191, 203
Diminution of women's status, 77
Direct intervention, 19
Directorate of Professional Standards,
  2, 45, 210
Disentangle confected art, 97
Displacement of labour into
  advertising, 144
Displacement of resistance away from
  mainstream politics, 138
Disquieting algorithmic systemic
  analytics to data aggregates, 145
  corroborate profiling, 145
Dissident present, 18
Dissimulated convergence between
  politics and promotional
  culture, 129
Dissimulation of knowledge, 125
Distorted self-consciousness, 23, 98

Documentaries Afrobeat
  brutality of police violence, 164
  Fela! the musical, 23, 90
  File on 4 BBC, 19
Dot.com technology, 125, 141
Du Bois, W.E.B. (1903), 20–23, 98,
  301, 302
Duffy, Brian, 153, 154
  photographed, 153
  Vogue October 1961
    exhibition, 154
Dystopian cynicism about the jazz
  genre, 98

E
East Rutherford, 41
Economic circulation, 6
Egypt 80, 41, 71, 215, 216, 255
The Emperor Jones, 89
Enable real-time global open
  platform, 141
Endeavour to communicate with a
  tribe, 114
Eniola (Akinbo) (Niyola) Soyinka, 80,
  101, 112
Entrepreneurial artefact of commercial
  choice, 122
Environmental desolation
  capital of a cultural form, 158
  critical reflections, 158
  environmental crisis, 158
  habitus, 158
  hazardously extractive oil, 158
  mineral mining, 158
  oil industry in Nigeria, 158
  Sandra Izsadore, 158
Environmentally sustainable, 5, 159
En Vogue Afrobeat
  casting her mesmerising
    persuasion, 155
  cognisant popular media, 155
  intellectually facile stylisation, 155

INDEX 353

interview with Sandra Izsadore, 155
original new direction, 155
sensationalist exotic female
muse, 155
vivacious artist Fela Anikulapo-
Kuti, 155
Ergonomic, 5, 159
Ethico-synoptics, 211
digital surveillance, 210
Ethics of Justice
African-American feminism, 168
Angela Davis, 168
anti-apartheid, 168
decolonial feminist perspective, 168
discriminatory racist policing
practices directed at Black
communities, 168
Fela and Me, 168
global decolonial feminist
movement, 168
Sandra Izsadore, 168
European art, 108, 110, 114
European cultural prestige, 114
European humanism, 62
Europeanness of British coloniality, 64
Evolution of digital accountability
praxis, 134
Exchange control, 40
Exchange value, 5, 6, 122, 124, 125
Execute a responsive strategy, 134
Exploitative extractive communication
technologies, 122
Extant social problems, 134

F
Facebook, Instagram, 24, 109,
141, 273
Face-value trading networks
contextually, 147
exchanged, 147
standardised market value, 147
value, 147

Facile and simplistic cultural display, 97
Fagg, William, 104–111, 114
Fallibility of surveillance
technology, 17
Fantasy of abundance, 122–128, 141
Fantasy of activity, 123
Fantasy of participation, 125, 129–140
Fantasy of wholeness, 123, 141–148
Fastest-growing advertising
medium, 125
Fecundity, 163
Fecundity and hyper-connectivity of
Twitter, 136
Federal High Court, 40
Feigns to be global because its promise
of universal coverage, 141
Fela and Me Sandra Izsadore
environmentalist concerns, 158
oil extraction in Nigeria, 158
tribute to Fela Anikulapo-Kuti, 158
Fela Anikulapo-Kuti, 19, 26, 32–34,
40–43, 61, 67, 68, 70–76, 83,
84, 87, 89, 93, 95, 115, 155,
156, 158–161, 163, 164, 167,
169, 170, 172, 178, 215–218,
220, 221, 226, 227, 229, 231,
233–240, 242, 243, 246–248,
250, 251, 253–256, 258–264,
267, 268
Fela Anikulapo-Kuti conceptual
boundary differentiation, 172
colonial mentality, 71, 164, 172,
215, 243
de-thinking, 172
enduring legacy, 172
Felakuti.com, 41, 42, 88,
154, 238–240
Fela Ransome-Kuti Eurocentric
representation
Brian Duffy, 153
racial identity, 154
vogue, 153
Vogue October 1961 exhibition, 154

354 INDEX

Fela! the musical
  National Theatre, London,
    60, 89, 92
  performances Off Broadway, 96
Female traders, 77
Feminine soul, 3, 299–308
Feminine soul of Afrobeat, 3, 4, 19,
    26, 39–55, 61, 67–88, 159, 160
Feminist antecedents, viii, 4, 7, 19, 20,
    33, 34, 55, 71–76, 83–85,
    87–88, 116
Feminist human rights, ix, 59–116,
    175, 198, 254, 261
Feminist human rights antecedents of
    Afrobeat, 34
Feminist human rights legacy of
    Funmilayo Ransome-Kuti, 88
Feminist musician, 41
Feminist sensibilities, 42
Feminists of colour
  cultural location and racial
    identity, 175
  human rights definitions, 175
  notions of white western
    masculinity, 175
  the specificities of women's
    experience, 175
  universalising, 175
  women's-rights-as-human-
    rights, 175
Feminist theoretical framework, 55
Festival situationism, 20, 64
Fetishisation of politics into
    technology
  interchangeable objects, 139
  medium its message and the subject
    into advertising, 139
  subject into advertising, 139
  ways capitalism operates, 139
File on 4 documentary, 19, 46–53,
    293, 294, 296
Financial Conduct Authority (FCA)

  identify consumers predicting, 145
  opaque pricing techniques, 145
Financialisation, public space
  categories of data, 189
  classification into spending power
    categories, 189
  demographic profile of consumer
    footfall, 189
  digitally colonised consumer, 189
  financial composite, 189
  surveillance, 189–190
First-generation, 5, 14, 25, 159
First-order semiological system, 128
Fiscal policy, 33, 167, 244, 251, 254
Foreign exchange earnings, 34, 253
Forensically digital advertising, 141
Forensic sociological
    investigation, ix, 15
Formulaic interchangeability, 96
Foucault, Michel, 185–187, 190–193,
    195–196, 207, 211
  of other spaces, 185–187
Foucault, in *Of Other Spaces*
  aggregated, 187
  Brixton BID, 187
  calculation of footfall, 187
  conjunction with location
    metrics, 187
  contextually space of
    encampment, 187
  distribution of the space of
    'site,' 187
  epistemology of the space of
    site, 187
  footfall is measured by the number
    of visits, 187
  GDPR compliant data analytics, 187
  presence sensor located, 187
  procedure of measurement, 187
  proximity, 187
Fragmenting images, 46
Frankfurt School, 90, 99, 116, 301

INDEX 355

Fraudulent tickets, 49
Free Fela campaign, 41
Free speech technology
  advertisement automatically, 143
  auction, 143
  auction operating model, 143
  campaign, 143
  commercially contradictory
    programmatic metrics, 143
  Twitter's free speech policy, 143
Frictionless continuity in the culture
  industry, 91
Functionality of African tribal art, 114
Funk, jazz, 83, 154, 155
Funk, jazz and Nigerian elements, 42
Funmilayo Ransome-Kuti Yoruba
  tribe, 104

G
Gaby Hutchinson (venue security
  operative), 19, 44, 303
Gender-based racialisation, 20, 64
Gender discrimination onto Nigeria's
  subjugated cultural identity, 82
Gender discriminatory injustices, 76
Gender discriminatory system of
  taxation, 78
Gendered irregularities of the British
  colonial taxation, 77
Gendered space and security–digital
  surveillance heterotopias
  bid, 189–190
*Gender, Justice and the
  Environment*, 86
Gender racialised colonial
  discrimination, 5, 25, 159
Generational differences, 33, 242,
  251, 256
Generative automated communicative
  labour, 144
Gentleman, 1973 album, 164

Germane to African tribal art, 114
German intellectuals, 90, 301
Ghanian highlife, 154
Giants Stadium, 41
Glastonbury 1984, 73
Glastonbury mid-summer
  Festival, 71, 73
Global economic restructuring of
  African nations, 254
Globally dispersed diaspora, 137
Government documents, 15
Grand historicism, 13
Grenfell Tower London, 5, 25, 159
Grenfell Tower London fire tragedy,
  5, 25, 159
Grier, Pam (civil rights
  campaigner), 41
Grounded theory methodology, in the
  weeks and months prior
  to my, 222
Grundrisse, 5, 301
Gyrating female dancers, 96

H
Habitus, viii, 4, 5, 25, 89, 101, 151,
  159, 160, 268, 281,
  282, 285–290
Habitus identity
  agency, 281
  field of power, 281
  highest form in the field of
    power, 281
  metrics meaningful, 281
  metrics of the petition, 281
  problems immaterial capital
    approximating, 281
  signifying recognition of digital
    labour, 281
  structural homology, 281
Hall, Stuart, 7–9
Hancock, Herbie, 41

356   INDEX

Harlem Brixton community twinned, 206, 207
Hashtags, memes, 130, 132, 135
Health and Safety (Enforcing Authority) Regulations 1998, 52
Health and Safety Review into O2 Academy Brixton, 52
Hegemony of Englishness, 71
Hermetically sealed capitalist production, 93
(Her)story of the Afrobeat of Nigerian, 98
Heterogeneous technological features, 136
Heterotopic space
  Foucault, 195, 196
  humankind, 191
  network of knowledge, 192
  propinquity, 191
  space of site (and also emplacement), 187, 190–193
High-pricing tariff digital banking, 146
Historical basis of Afrobeat, 23, 98
History of the Brixton Academy, 275
Hollywood *rags to riches*, 93
Humanist in the moral sense, 67
Humanitarian, 40, 156
Human-rights-as-political-strategy, 65
Human rights feminism, 68–70, 85–87
Human right to communicative action, 33, 55, 262, 307
Human right to education, 68–76
Human security, 86
Hyde Park, 1
Hypercapitalist, 129, 130
Hyper-connected advertising, 124
Hyper-connectivity of Twitter, 136
Hyper-interconnectedness, 128
Hypermediated networking architecture, 132
Hyper-networked connections, 130
Hyper-sensationalised, heightened by visual techniques associated with Black Twitter, 147

I

Idealized naturalism, 106
Ideology and Ideological State
  agencies production of communication, 232
  apparatuses, 18, 170, 221, 231–243
  non-physical violence, 232
  operation of ideological conditioning, 232
  post-colonial *Index on Censorship Organisation*, 232
  repressive is proving, 232
Ideology of the culture industry, 91, 97
Ife, 103, 105–107, 111, 227
Ife-Benin tradition, 107
Igbo and Yoruba story telling traditions, 97
Igogo festival, 112
Ikumelo, Rebecca, 19, 44, 47, 127, 303, 308
The Imagery of Power: A Critique of Advertising, Hall, 7
Images racist brutality, 135
Immediate suspension of the licence, 44
Imperative of capital accumulation
  Afrobeat, 91
  cultural forms, 91
  profit motivation, 91
Imperialism and colonialism, 62
Imperialist repressive, 66
Individualistic art, 93
Indulgence of art, 114
Industrial civilisation, 8
Industrial production of culture, 91

Informatic-coded digital syntax:
  memetic properties of the Twitter
  platform, 136
Informationalised security, 17
Infostream, 125
Infringements of human rights, 134
Inglis, Fred, 7–9
Inherent illogicality of intent, 164
Instability of capitalistic colonialism
  digital surveillance, 176
  ethico-synoptics, 29, 211
Insurantial evaluation, 55
Insurantial risk, 55
Integrated spectacle, 17
Interchangeable features of
  communicative capitalism, 23–24
Internationally manufactured
  racism, 98
International Monetary Fund (IMF),
  34, 177, 253–256, 260
Interoperability between social
  media, 141
Interporlates, 161
Intersecting disordering, 5, 25, 159
Intersectionality, 27, 28, 55, 61, 63,
  133, 157, 175, 251, 261, 262
Intersectionality of patriarchy, 61
Intersectionality of race, gender and
  sexuality, 55
Intertextuality, 31
Introjection
  agency, 225
  mechanical reactions, 226
  mimesis, 226, 229
  ossified, 226
  resistance, 226
Invasive surveillance, 17
Italian Renaissance style, viii
Izsadore, Sandra, 25, 34, 153–163,
  165, 168, 170–172, 178
  Black Panthers, 154, 155, 165
  civil rights activists, 154, 178
  decolonial feminism, 25, 159

J
Jane Bryce, Emerita (African-
  Caribbean feminist Prof), 32, 34,
  215, 220–224, 226, 227, 229,
  231, 236–238, 240, 242, 243,
  245, 246, 248–251, 254,
  256–261, 265–268
Jay Z, 89, 92
Jazz aficionados 1960s London, 154
Jazz boom, 153
Jazz fashion portfolio, 154
Jazz fashion portfolio assortment
  parades, 154
Jazz into African Yoruba, 40
Jazz temporality, 99
Jewish academics, 90
Johnson-Odim, C., 63, 68, 76, 77,
  79, 85, 87, 88, 115
Jones, Bill T., 89, 90, 93, 94

K
Kalakuta Republic, 87, 89, 160,
  162–165, 167, 257
Kalakuta Republic studio, 40
Knabb, Ken, 16
Knitting Factory Records, 42, 91, 216
Koola Lobitos, 154, 155

L
Labyrinthian algorithmically, 133
Lagos, 5, 40, 41, 83, 84, 88, 89, 93,
  96, 108, 154, 155, 159, 162,
  178, 216, 223, 227, 228, 238,
  260, 262
Lagos, Nigeria ('The Shrine'), 41, 88,
  93, 96, 223, 227, 238–240
Lambeth Council, 44, 52–54, 184,
  186, 208, 272, 275–277,
  296, 308
Lambeth Council's Licensing Sub-
  Committee, 44, 308

358   INDEX

Language and communicative action
  commentary on Nigeria, 160
  critical political, 160
  lyrics from songs, 160
  online interview, 156
  personal experience, 130, 160
  time/space compressed, 122, 156
Language-processing chatbots, 144
Leavis, F.R., 7, 8
Legacy of Afrobeat, 155
Legacy of colonialisation, 4, 98, 218
Legacy of colonialism, 98, 218
Legislative regulation, 10
Lenin Peace Prize, 87
Lewis, Jim, 89, 93
Licencing of Black music
  entertainment, ix
Licencing regulation, 10
Licensing, 12, 51–55, 216,
  240, 275
Licensing Act 2003, 44, 53–55
Licensing Act 2003, Section
  53a, 54, 55
Licensing Authority's Sub-
  Committee, 54
Linear time of risk, 66
Linguistic category, 96
List like Whiskey, Burna Boy, 101
The Living Arts of Nigeria, 108
Locationally isolated Black human
  bodies, 132
London Assembly, 27, 51, 52
London Borough, 51
London Borough of Lambeth, 54
London Fire Brigade, 2, 14, 45, 210
London's Brixton Academy, 42
London's Night Czar, 52
London's River Thames, 5
London's urban ecology, 5, 159
London's vibrant 1960s artistic scene
  and cultivated music
  affiliations, 154

Longue durée, 46, 296
Lyrical composition and
  production, 172
Lyttleton, Oliver, 85

M
Machine learning programmes
  in AI, 126
Mainstream media, 135
Management of surveillance, 17
Marginalised voices, 135
Market-based capitalism, 34, 253
Marx, Karl (1857/1973), 5, 6
Marxist decolonial feminist
  colonisation domination through
    appropriation of land, 173
  primitive accumulation, 173
  subjugation of its human
    population, 173
Marxist ecofeminism, 5, 158
Mass-media technologies, 47
Materialised a contemporary
  form, 116
Materialized through technology
  fetishism, 123
Maternal ancestors, ix, 4, 43
Maternal health care for women, 80
Maternalistic universal appellations, 86
Matriarchal ethics of care, 162
Mayor and London, 51
Mayor and London Boroughs, 51
Mayor of London, 52
Mba, N., 63, 77, 85, 87, 88, 115
Mclean, Jordan, 93
Mechanically reproducible, 96
Media-assisted citizen activism, 135
Media and culture, 170
Medium and the capacity of social
  media, 124
Medium of digital music technology
  human rights, 116

as a means of West African Nigerian diaspora human rights sculpture, 116
Nigerian diaspora, 116
sculpture, 116
West African, 116
Message within dot.com media communication, 24, 123
Metaphor and materiality, 103
Metaphysical forces of the world, 102
Methodologically, 7
Methodology, 10, 219, 220, 266
Metropolitan colonial power, 65
Metropolitan Police, 10, 219, 220, 266
Metropolitan Police Service (MPS), 2, 3, 14, 15, 19, 29–31, 46, 53, 197, 198, 201, 203–205, 305–308
Metropolitan Police's Summary Licence Review, 55
Mirroring of its sign-making, 48
Mitchell, Joni, 41
Mobile-mediated sousveillance, 134
Mobilisation of surveillance, 18
Mobilising native activities, 20, 64
Mode of capitalist accumulation, 122
Modernist perspective, 12
Modes of collectivity, 129
Monique Carboni, 60
Monique Carboni Photographer, 60
Monopolist practices social media making connections, 141
networking opportunities of its users, 141
Moral disruptors, 74
Moral exemplar, 74, 76
Morphing of message into contribution is detrimental to politics, 124
Motherhood provided a strategic basis and preparation for politics, 86

Movement of the people (MOP), 41, 162
Multi-millionaire endowment, 92
Municipal stakeholders, 52
Murtala Muhammed, 40
Musical theatre extravaganza Fela, 91
Music-influenced 3D, 101
Music theatre production, 88, 89

N
Nano-seconds offers, 122
Narration Musicology, 80
Narrative sequencing of my interviewee, 99
Narrative structuring, 95, 96
National Archives, 62, 68, 82, 114
National Council for Maternity and Child Welfare, 79
National Council of Nigeria, 79, 82, 86
National Council of Nigeria and the Cameroons (NCNC), 79, 82, 86
Nationalist ideologies, 63
The National Theatre Live, *Fela!*, 89, 91
National Theatre, London South Bank, 89
Native authority, 63, 69, 79, 83
Native Nigerian culture, 101
Necessarily at market value, 146
Neocolonial, 33, 34, 70, 74, 75, 87, 88, 161, 170, 215, 216, 219–221, 244, 250–267
Neoliberal capitalism, 122
Neoliberal privatisation, 176
Networked communications, 122, 124, 125, 129
Networked communications technologies, 122, 129

360 INDEX

Networked Masculinities in South Africa, 133
New Critical, 12, 13
New Jersey, 41, 217
News, viii, ix, 2, 14, 19, 45, 47, 52, 72, 127, 134, 141, 144, 291, 303, 304
The Niger Basin Tribes, 107
Niger Delta, 104, 110, 158
Nigeria and Africa, 33, 251
Nigeria-based creative, 99
Nigerian Afrobeat, Asake, viii, 32, 44, 124, 128, 182
Nigerian antiquity sculpture, 105
Nigerian art and sculpture, 104
Nigeria native tribal art, 108
Nigerian Biafra diaspora, 5, 25, 159
Nigerian cultural heritage
  childhood stories, 5, 159
  chorus of protestors, 5, 159
  collapsing city dwelling, 5, 159
  diaspora urban ecology, 5, 159
  habitus, 4, 159
  witnessing, 5, 159
Nigerian derivation of Afrobeat, 4
Nigerian diaspora, 5, 11, 43, 108, 116
Nigerian digital-music sculptor, 116
Nigerian economy, 34, 253, 262
Nigerian ethnicity, 103
Nigerian ethnocultural, 96
Nigerian femaleness, 43
Nigerian immigrants, 14
Nigerian post-colonial imagination, 61
Nigerian sculpture antiquity, 104
Nigeria, the Yoruba tribe, 99, 104
Nigerian Union of Teachers, 68
Niger River, 104
Nkrumah, Kwame (1909–1972, Ghana, First Prime Minister), 156, 250–254
Nobel Prize-winning writer, 80
Nominated for a Grammy, 89

O
Obioma, Chigozie, 10, 11
Officers, London Ambulance Service, 2, 14, 45, 210
Oil extractive chemicals, 5
Oliver Theatre
  Fela! the Musical, 89
  sell-out season of 53 performances, 89
Olufela Olusegun Oludotun Ransome-Kuti, 67
Olufunmilayo Ransome-Kuti (1900–1978), 19, 61, 64, 67–88, 171
One Dimensional Man, Marcuse (1964), 225–249
Online petition
  capital of a cultural form, 281, 282, 285, 290, 296
  cultural capital, 285, 287, 289
  distinction, 282, 288
  pseudo-Gemeinschaft of digitally, 295
  technical capital, 285, 287, 288, 290
  technology of spectacular surveillance, 295
Online social media contribution, 141
Online speech, 122
Operating BIDs
  collaborative exchange, 183
  local businesses, 183–186
Oppositional ideologies the disaggregation, 18
Ordered harmonious whole, 102
Original Broadway Cast Recording, 91
O2 Academy Brixton critical incident
  capitalist surveillance, 182
  community in public recreational spaces, 182, 205
  decolonial feminist praxis, 182

INDEX 361

disproportionately Black British female, 182
excitation, 182
fatal crowd crush, 182
15th December 2022, viii, ix, 2, 3, 9, 14, 15, 18, 19, 25, 32, 34, 44–55, 123, 127, 140, 141, 147, 148, 182, 203, 205, 208, 209, 272, 275, 291–293, 303–306, 308
hyper-digital surveillance, 182
matrix of colonial digital capitalism, ix, 18, 182
private Black female subject, 182
public colonial digital, 182
technological surveillance matrix, 182
O2 Academy Brixton's premises licence, 44, 53
O2 Brixton Academy, viii, 2, 9–11, 14, 19, 32, 34, 45–53, 182, 205, 308
O2 telecommunications brand, viii

P

Pan-African, 62, 260
Pan-African goals and Ubuntu and communalism principles, 75
Pan-Africanist, 40, 62, 156, 251
Pan-Africanist ideals, 67
Pan-ethnic, dynamic racial belonging, 137
Pantheon of gods, 102
Paradox, 11
Para-social relationships with celebrities, 133
Patriarchal native traditionalists, 69
Patriarchally structured domestic division of labour, 80
Pedagogy and epistemology of knowledge, 70
Perception of "registering," 138

Personalised pricing harms
aggregates personalised advertising, 145
analytics to data, 145
digital market, 145
online digital markets, 145
Petition makers
identity and structuration of resistance to spectacle, 278–296
subjectivity, 278–296
Petroleum-led manufacturing, 34, 253
Phenomenology of a performativity, 10
Physical conditions of exchange, 6
Physical-optical, 15
Physiognomy of gender, 97
Pidgin English
disenfranchisement of illiteracy, 161
fearful of the political, 160
fearless at inciting the wrath of the military, 160
provocative communicative action, 160
Pinkett Smith, Jada, 92
Platform's digital technoculture, 136
The Plight of Nigerian Women, written in 1947–1948, 68, 81, 86
Political culture, 14, 258
Political dimensionality, 138
Political economy of the sign, 48
Poll tax are forcible demanded of the women, 78
Port Harcourt, 40, 178
Positionality, 2, 9, 12–14, 23, 43, 95, 98, 135, 247, 256, 266, 268
Post-colonial African-Caribbean, 34
Post-colonial encounter, 221, 231
Post-colonial feminism, 5, 32, 33, 251, 256
Post-colonial feminist antecedents, 7, 19, 55

362 INDEX

Post-colonial feminist critical
theory, 4–7
beyond "one dimensional
man," 226–231
Post-colonial feminist
critique, 250–267
decentering neocolonial cultural-
economy, 251–267
Post-colonial feminist rhizome
mapping economic and freedom
of expression human
rights, 254–267
Post-colonial feminist
subjectivity, 231–243
interpellation and ideological state
apparatuses, 231–243
Postcolonial, ix, 1–34, 42, 55, 61,
72–74, 86, 209, 215–268,
271–296, 302, 303
Posthuman coalitions, 129
Postmodernism, 12, 13
Powerful apparatuses of control, 91
Power/knowledge contestations, 137
Praxis of oppositional post-
coloniality, 61
Precolonial amenities, 83
Premises Licence Holder, 53, 54,
274, 304
Preserve cultural heritage, 111
Primeval ancestors of the tribe, 102
Primitive accumulation of
communication, 129
Principal of Abeokuta Grammar
School, 67
Print and broadcast media, 24, 123
Prisoner of Conscious, 41, 178
Fela Anikulapo-Kuti, 41, 178
Professional practice, 16, 135
Programmatic buying, 144, 145
Programmed computer software, 295
Promotional advertising, 16, 25, 128
Propaganda, 47, 81, 133
Propertied urban planning, 6, 25, 159

Pseudo-Gemeinschaft, 3, 4, 138, 194,
196, 295
Pseudo-world, 46
Public data harms, 135
Public space surveillance, 29, 199
Purchasable features of Twitter's
official digital advertising, 143
Purchase of concert tickets
consumer protection, 146
online secondary tickets market, 146
Pursuit of media propaganda, 133

Q
Queens, band and audience, 96

R
Racial identities, 71, 72, 115,
130–132, 136, 140, 154, 175
Racialised Black body, 133
Racialised colonial discrimination,
5, 25, 159
Racialised digital gaze
private people in public
space, 196–204
surveillance heterotopias
BID, 196–204
Racialised gendered
inequitable, 20, 64
Racialized social hierarchies, 64
Racial trauma, 132
Racism, 27, 42, 72, 98, 129–132,
136, 157, 158, 169–171, 178,
179, 207, 209
Racism and power, 130
Racism is not sexualism, 42
Ransome-Kuti, Funmilayo, 34, 69, 70,
74, 76–78, 80–82, 85–90, 99,
103, 104, 114–116, 160, 162,
166, 229, 230
Rapidly colonising and
dehumanising, 144

INDEX 363

Reciprocity of perspective, 124, 156, 222, 288
Record label Decca, 84
Red gold coast, 7
Reflexivity, 8, 221
Refracted (his)tories of the political subject-interpolating feminist post-colonialism, 243–250
Reframed as exhibiting anticolonial concern, 24
Refugee migrants, 301
Regulation of Investigatory Powers Act 2000, 54
Reifying of race-based advantage, 135
Render illegal discrimination based on the racialised characteristics of hair, 113
Requesting a Summary Review, 54
Review of a Premises Licence, 53
Revolutionary, 26, 33, 73, 87, 115, 122, 159, 169, 170, 235, 242, 251, 258, 295
Revolutionary imprint, 33, 251
The Revolutionary Songs of Funmilayo Ransome-Kuti, 87, 115
Rhetorical meaning, 11
Rhizomatic morphology, 110
Rialto Bridge, viii
Right now a system of conditional sale is in vogue, 78
Right to cultural participation, 75
Risk and financialisation, 15
Risk assessment, 47, 49, 55, 182, 202
Romanticism, 97
Royal Warrant holder, Hardy Amies, 154

S
Santana, Carlos, 41
Save Brixton Academy from Permanent Closure, 274
Scripting of subjective thoughts, 138

Sculpting of images of deity and spirits, 101
Sculpture as a medium, 103
Sculpture is communicatively functional, 114
Section 51 "Application for review of premise licence," 53
Section 52 of the Licensing Act 2003, 53
Self-regulating markets, 62
Settled Migrant Communities, viii, 43
Sex-based discrimination in the collection of taxes, 78
Sex-based discrimination in the taxing of women, 82
Shawn "Jay-Z" Carter, 89, 92
Shonekan, Stephanie, 87, 115
Shuffering and Shmiling, 84
'Signifyin' on Twitter allows Black, 132
'Signifyin' performances, 131
Simulacra, 3, 31, 100, 101, 141, 147, 194, 276
Simulacra of market-based ticket sale amplified, 147
   face-value, 147
   face-value of the concert tickets, 147
Simulacrum of the purchasable features of Twitter
   official digital advertising programme, 143
   promoted Accounts, 143
   Twitter Trends and Trending, 143
Situational indexing of memes, 133
Smart City, 189, 190, 303–308
Smart City analytics, ix
Social democratic and civil rights, 122
Social media
   analytics, 194–196, 208
   colonial digital capitalistic social media, 196
   computer-mediated communication, 196

364 INDEX

Social media (*cont.*)
  congruous online, 196
  gender racialised irregularities, 196
  High Street Footfall, 186–189
  live facial recognition, 196
  time compressed inverted
    reality, 196
Social media platform Twitter,
  @asakemusik, 128
Social media platform X, 125, 127
Social reproduction, 80
Society of the Spectacle (Guy
  Debord), 46, 293
Sole Native Authority (SNA), 77, 78
Sony Pictures Entertainment, 92
The Souls of Black Folk, 20, 98, 301
South African government, 10
Southern Nigeria, British Colonial
  Protectorate, 68
Soyinka, Eniola, 80
Soyinka, Wole, 80, 115, 239
Spatial barrier to intercourse, 6
Specialist Crime, 2, 14, 45, 210
Spectacle, 2, 3, 16–18, 33, 46–53, 55,
  84, 122, 147, 271–296
Spectacle of licencing risk, 46–53
Spectacular, ix, 1, 3, 18, 19, 48, 49,
  52, 141, 142, 148, 165, 167,
  272, 276, 277, 291–295
Spectacular cultural
  commodification, ix
Spectacular demonstration, 167
Spectacular digital capitalist
  exploitation, 148
Spectacular information/
  promotion, 148
Spectacular reporting, 52
Spectacular surveillance, 18, 272, 295
Speed of delivery, 131
Spike Lee, 89
Spiritual ceremonies, 102
Spiritual make-up, 97
Spotify for Artists, 110

Squat at Decca West Africa limited
  recording studio, 84
Structural Adjustment Programme
  (SAP), 33, 34, 253, 261
Structural relations of class, gender
  and race, 100
Structuration, 7, 9, 14, 18, 27,
  130, 278–296
Subcultural synecdoches, 133
Summary Licence Review application
  (under section 53a of the
  Licensing Act 2003), 55
Summary Review, 53–55, 280
Supernatural universe, 102
Surging crowds, 44
Surplus labour time, 6
Surveillance/disinformation, 16
Surveillance is an apparatus of the
  state, 18
Surveillance spies, 18
Surveillance technological
  innovation, 17
Surveying Black community
  digital capitalistic surveillance, 182
Suspending the licence, 55
Swinging London of the 1960s, 154
Symbolism, 11, 164, 207, 234
Synergistic approach, 12

T
Teacher Don't Teach Me Nonsense (Fela
  Anikulapo-Kuti), 42, 71–76, 156
Technical and creative processes, 97
Technical rationalities, 91, 97, 190
  commercially contradictory
    programmatic metrics, 143
Technological architecture of
  Twitter, 140
Technological fetish in operation
  foreclosure, 139
  online technology, 139
  technology is manufactured, 139

INDEX **365**

Technological mediation, 130, 136
Technological mediation of anti-racist protests, 130
Technological panoptic dystopia, 17
Technological rationality, 93, 225–227, 295
Technologization of music, 83
Technology and urbanism, 111
Theatre complex at 37th Street and 10th Avenue, 96
Thursday 15th December 2022, 2, 14, 44, 45
Ticket Resales, 146
Ticket Sales Regulations 2018, 146, 306
Time and space compressed condition, 6, 156
Tony-award-winning choreography, 93
Transatlantic, 1, 42, 62, 156, 163, 209, 256, 300
Transnational scope of Twitter, 137
Trending algorithms, 136
Triangulate, 12
Tribal ancestors and gods, 102
Tribal communities, 62, 102
Tribal Masks and Sculptures, 106
True African style, 96
Twinned District, 207
    crisis heterotopia status of the Brixton (London, UK), 207
Twitter advertising digital technology, 142
Twitter auction algorithm will compare the advertisement bid, 143
Twitter programmatic digital advertising suite, 145
Two-ness of a West African identity generations, 98
Typography of anticolonial feminist, 86

U

Unbanked market segment data-stream upon, 146
    pricing tariffs of digital banking, 146
United Nations (UN), 3, 75, 231, 262
United Nations Declaration of Human Rights of 1948, 75, 113
United Nations in its 1948 declaration, 3
Universal God of Creation, 102
University of Ibadan, 99, 115
Urban digital surveillance, 29, 182
    space of emplacement, 186
Urban ecology, 5, 25, 159, 186

V

Valuable currency, 92
Velocity and connectivity messaging, 122
Vergès, Françoise, 25, 159, 161, 172–174
    praxis, dissuaded by nihilistic "empty ideologies" because it, 25, 159
Vernacularisation, 66
Violence against women and girls (VAWAG), 26, 28, 205
Viral weaponizing, 133
Visible data, 15
Visualised theory, 15
Visuality, viii, 14–18, 101
Vogue's glimpse of the 1960s jazz scene, 154
Vulnerability to outbreaks, 132

W

Ways of seeing, 110, 302
Weblinks from Twitter to AI, 126
We Had Equality Till Britain Came, 77

366 INDEX

Well-being of the spectacle, 16
  advertising ingenuity, 16
West African art, 101, 111
West African artistry across the
  diaspora, 111
West African diaspora, viii, ix, 4, 7, 23,
  27, 98, 159, 209, 302
Western capitalism, 13, 174
Western chronology of narrative
  structure, 95
Western colonial bifurcation, 61
Western linear chronological
  schema, 96
Western medium 3D (digital
  media), 103
Western narrative, 94–96
Whereby the respondent's, 281
Whistleblower, 49, 50
Wingrove, Colin (Chief
  Superintendent), 2, 14, 45
Woman in Yoruba Religious Images,
  111, 112
Women paid tax in Abeokuta, 82
Women Race Class (Davis, 1983), 161
Women singers, 43
Workshopping, 133
Worshipped in female cults, 102
www.ntlive.com National Theatre
  Live, 91

Y
Yabis his audience, 96
Yoruba, 40, 42, 67, 68, 83, 91, 97,
  99, 104–108, 111–115, 154,
  160–162, 238
Yoruba art and myth, 107
Yoruba art, hairplaiting, 112
Yoruba cosmological concept, 107
Yoruba cultural heritage, 67
Yoruba divination deity, 112
Yoruba female sculpture art of hair
  anticolonial feminist human
    rights, 113
  plaiting, 113
  relates, 113
Yoruba kingdoms, 105, 106
Yorubaland, 82, 99, 106
Yorubaland around Ogun
  State, 99
Yoruba music, 83, 114
Yoruba music cultivated into protest
  songs, 114
Yoruba mythology of the river goddess
  Oshun, 111
Yoruban rites, 96
Yoruban rites and idiosyncratic
  rituals, 96
The Yoruba term for mother,
  Iya, 115

Printed in the United States
by Baker & Taylor Publisher Services